CHAOS, COMPLEXITY, AND SOCIOLOGY

CHAOS, COMPLEXITY, AND SOCIOLOGY

Myths,
Models,
and
Theories

Raymond A. Eve
Sara Horsfall
Mary E. Lee
Editors

SAGE Publications
International Educational and Professional Publisher
Thousand Oaks   London   New Delhi

For information address:

 SAGE Publications, Inc.
2455 Teller Road
Thousand Oaks, California 91320
E-mail: order@sagepub.com

SAGE Publications Ltd.
6 Bonhill Street
London EC2A 4PU
United Kingdom

SAGE Publications India Pvt. Ltd.
M-32 Market
Greater Kailash I
New Delhi 110 048 India

Printed in the United States of America

Library of Congress Cataloging-in-Publication Data

Chaos, complexity, and sociology: Myths, models, and theories /
    editors, Raymond A. Eve, Sara Horsfall, Mary E. Lee.
        p.   cm.
    Includes bibliographical references and index.
    ISBN 0-7619-0889-7 (acid-free paper). — ISBN 0-7619-0890-0
(pbk.: acid-free paper)
        1. Social sciences—Philosophy. 2. Chaotic behavior in systems.
    3. Complex organizations. I. Eve, Raymond A., 1946- .
    II. Horsfall, Sara. III. Lee, Mary E.
    H61.C4335   1997
    301'.1—dc21   97-4611

This book is printed on acid-free paper.

98 99 00 01 02 03 10 9 8 7 6 5 4 3 2

Acquiring Editor: Peter Labella
Editorial Assistant: Corinne Pierce
Production Editor: Astrid Virding
Production Assistant: Karen Wiley
Designer/Typesetter: Ravi Balasuriya/Rebecca Evans
Cover Designer: Candice Harman
Print Buyer: Anna Chin

Contents

Foreword
Chaos and Social Science

"Postmodern science" sometimes appears to be little more than a way of using concepts such as nonlinearity and chaos to support New Age magical thinking or the animus of political interest groups. Such strategic misinterpretations of legitimate scientific ideas are not new—evolutionary theory was used to support deterministic views of human nature and human history, relativity was used to support moral relativism, and quantum theory was used to support random or aleatory theories of creativity and innovation. But there is a solid core of real intellectual progress in the new science that has emerged in the past two decades; in this essay I shall attempt to summarize that progress in the form of a list of conceptual tools that it has either provided or refined, and point out their special value for the social sciences.

What is the new science to which I refer? Various terms have been associated with it: chaos theory, nonlinearity, self-organization, dissipative systems, irreversibility, complexity, dynamical systems, fractal geometry, catastrophe, bifurcation, emergence, and so on. Particular disciplines tend to adapt the new thinking to their own traditions, and then claim that their version is the pure one and the others are merely metaphorical and unscientific uses of it. For instance, mathematicians tend to treat the field as an extension of limit theory and complex topology, classical physicists as a problem in probability or turbulence, thermodynamicists as an issue in the study of entropy, chemists as a refinement

of theories of catalysis and phase boundaries, biologists as a description of ecological feedback, sociologists as a way of modeling statistical variations in a
population, information scientists as a cybernetic issue, humanists as a confirmation of the subtlety of artistic meaning, and so on. Large divisions are beginning to arise—between those who study "deterministic chaos" and those who
allow an element of the random into the picture; between those who believe it
can be useful only when strictly confined to mathematical descriptions and those
who hold that it marks the one-way bridge from math into physical reality;
between those who see it as something that can take place within the traditional
framework of space as we understand it and those who feel it demands new
definitions of space itself; between those who regard the field as reconcilable
with classical notions of time as a spacelike dimension and those who see it as
confirming the uniqueness and irreversibility of time; between those who see it
as a new piece of content within science and those who regard it as implying
modifications in scientific method; between those who see it as a supplement to
the mechanism of evolution and those who regard evolution itself as a special
case of nonlinear emergence; and between those who see it as a confirmation
of human freedom and responsibility and those who see it as another scientific
reduction of the human to the mechanistic.

I believe that these centrifugal, territorial elements in the new science are
premature; at present we do not yet know enough about where the distinctions
ought to be made to start cutting in a panic for disciplinary purity. We may in
the process miss some valuable connections, by means of which we may jettison
unnecessary concepts (on the order of Priestley's "phlogiston"), unify whole
fields of knowledge, and develop effective new methods of investigation and
technological application. As I will argue here, the power of the new science
may be precisely that it offers intelligible ways of obtaining deterministic systems out of randomness, randomness out of deterministic systems, space out of
mathematical logic, irreversible time out of reversible space, scientific method
out of scientific content, living systems out of nonliving matter, and human
freedom out of biocultural necessity.

What the new science has done, in effect, is to place within our grasp a set
of very powerful intellectual tools—concepts to think with. We can use them
well or badly, but they are free of many of the limitations of our traditional
armory. With them we can dissolve old procrustean oppositions—between the
ordered and the random, for instance—and in the process reinstate useful old
ideas such as freedom. New concepts, such as emergence, become thinkable,
and new methods, such as nonlinear computer modeling, suggest themselves as
legitimate modes of study. I have divided these new conceptual tools into six
categories: a new view of cause and prediction, a richer understanding of feedback and iteration, a revolution in the idea of time, an anthology of new recog-

nizable structures and shapes, the idea of the attractor as a way of dissolving old dualisms, and the technique of modeling.

Unpredictability and the Rehabilitation of "Freedom"

Traditional hard science bases its canons of proof on the successful prediction of the results of controlled experiment or observation in a context of agreement with established fact and mathematical and logical coherence. Much of the universe, given reasonable margins of random variation and a license to describe it in statistical rather than absolute terms, can be well understood in this way. This method, which has proved enormously useful and will continue to do so, is now shown to have limits; the new science shows us what they are and how other methods can take up where the traditional ones leave off.

The possibility of predicting an event relies on two assumptions: that the chain of causes is recoverable and that the universe is fundamentally deterministic in its nature. If the capacity for straightforward prediction is conceived of as comprising the sum total of understanding, what we have learned from the investigation of complex feedback situations is, on the face of it, dispiriting. One discovery is that the initial conditions of a process may be irrecoverable: any chain of reasoning one might try to use to establish them would require the examination of an exponentiating number of possible earlier states, each of which in turn has an exponentiating number of originating conditions, and so on. A second discovery is that since such processes are critically dependent on their initial conditions—what is known as the "butterfly effect"—and a starting point arbitrarily close to the true one could produce quite different results, there is no way of even approximating those conditions using traditional methods of inference. A corollary is that if we are given a set of initial conditions, even with great exactness, the interactions among the elements of such a system will rapidly overwhelm any algorithm for their solution, as when destinations are continually added to the traveling salesman problem in mathematics. Thus it looks as if we may have to abandon the close dependence of proof on prediction.

It might be argued that those parts of the universe that behave in nonlinear ways are still deterministic in theory, though not in practice, in the sense that we are not yet able to establish the chain of determination. In other words, all we need to solve the traveling salesman problem is a big enough and fast enough computer. If this argument held, we would be back on the familiar ground of traditional science, which has always been able to argue consistently that the world is deterministic but that the limits of present human observation prevent us from establishing cause in many cases. But we know now that this inability to establish the chain of causal connection is not just a limitation in practice, solvable for instance by improved instrumentation or measurement, but a limitation in theory: there is not enough time or information-processing power in the universe to complete the necessary calculations. The computer would have to be growing at a rate faster than the speed of light and miniaturizing itself below the threshold of the quantum graininess of space. And if causal determination in such cases is true in theory but theoretically impossible to establish in practice, determinism as a universal proposition begins to approach the condition of a metaphysical assertion, neither provable nor unprovable, of the type that Ludwig Wittgenstein showed to be meaningless.

Thus the first great tool offered by the new science is the concept of the inherently unpredictable situation—a situation unpredictable in itself, not just by virtue of the limits of its observer. We are spared the labor of attempting to predict such situations and thus can devote our efforts to understanding them in different ways, for "unpredictable" does not necessarily mean "unintelligible," or inaccessible to knowledge and understanding. Prediction may in such cases simply not be one of the handles by which a thing can be cognitively picked up, but there may be others. Another way of putting this is to say that *freedom* now recovers its meaning as a word usable by science and philosophy. In a knowably deterministic universe, freedom is either a nonsense word or a word mistaken in its usual definition. The same could even be said for a deterministic universe whose chain of determining causes could never be observed or established—but only if there were an absolute separation between ontology and epistemology, that is, between what a thing is and how it is known. But, as we shall see, the new science confirms the message that has been coming to us from a number of sources already, such as quantum mechanics: that the observer and the observed cannot be detached from each other and that observation—knowing—is an ontological event. If the future of parts of the universe is inherently unknowable, that is an ontological fact about them, giving the attribution to them of causal determination the status of a religious act of faith. What *can* be predicated of them is freedom. And freedom now becomes a rich and useful concept, reciprocally defined by, and suggesting ways to understand, nonlinear complexity.

"Free" traditionally does not by any means imply "disordered" or "random." It was only in the desperation measures of the existentialists, faced with the logical positivist universe of their times, that freedom came to be identified with "gratuitous acts" or motiveless whims. Freedom implies discoverable meaning in an act—indeed, it distinguishes an act from an event. A free act is one that may be unpredictable but that, after it has occurred, is retrodictable in that it "makes sense." Predictable events—and I must reiterate that this argument does not preclude their existence and the great usefulness of studying them—are in certain senses symmetrical with respect to past and future: that is, there is no difference between knowing that they will happen and knowing that they have happened. Free events—acts—are of a different class, asymmetrical with respect to past and future. What can be known about them before they happen is fundamentally different from what can be known about them afterward. What the new science has shown us is simply that there are such acts, that such a class of events exists.

One implication of the traditional meaning of "freedom" for the new science is that it might make sense to look for some analogue or equivalent of choice, intention and purpose in those nonlinear situations where determination becomes impossible, since those qualities are usually present when we correctly describe an act as free. Perhaps it seems odd to ascribe purpose or intention to the formation of a stable vortex in a turbulent flow, a crystallization, a complex chemical catalytic feedback process or even the self-organization of fetal plant cells. But given the fact that the process is ordered, and even ordering, and given that the ascription of deterministic cause to such a system is unscientific metaphysics, what other kind of order can they possess? Certainly what is going on is hugely more primitive than what happens in a choosing human mind, but the implication of the new science is that it may be of the same kind, or at least more like choosing than like the knowably deterministic order we observe in classical mechanics. Or, to turn the argument around one more time, human choosing may be not as mysterious as we have chosen to make it; perhaps it is only the most complex and most articulated member of a class of free, orderly events with many examples throughout the physical world.

Just as the traditional meaning of "free" can be helpful when we cast around for an orderliness to replace predictability when it fails us in the new science, so the new science can be useful in fleshing out the inner workings of "freedom" in the traditional sense. For instance, the essential element in the unpredictable processes we are now investigating is *feedback,* especially repeated feedback or iteration, so that the multiple folding of the system on itself will have the scope and time to exhibit its emergent properties and new forms of organization. Our human freedom, and the freedom that we commonsensically (and rightly, in my view) ascribe to other higher animals, feels subjectively simple, immediate, and handy. What the new science suggests is that this experience of our own and others' freedom as unified and uncomplicated may be (beneficially) misleading: it is a consequence of the user-friendliness such a complex operation must possess if it is to be at all useful to an animal designed to survive. As with many other very sophisticated neural operations, such as the calculation of trajectories, the formulation of grammar, and the interpretation of camouflaged and partly occluded shapes, an elegant hierarchy of subroutines and servo-mechanisms presents the results and controls to us in a clear and comprehensible form, not bothering us with details. Our experience of our freedom, then, is the generalized shape of a fantastically complex feedback system by whose inner workings we are for the most part mercifully untroubled. It is only the anguish of a momentous decision or the genius of a great play or novel that reveals to us, at moments, the iterative richness and difficulty of the process.

But here, too, certain philosophical difficulties are dispelled by the identification of nonlinear unpredictability with the traditional meaning of freedom. Freedom felt so simple and homogeneous a thing to us that we could not but ascribe to it an uncomposite, unique, indescribable, and irreducible essence, and thus we were persuaded to construct systems of metaphysics to house it and position it within the world: hence centuries of mind-body problems, and tortured issues of reference and ethical philosophy. But if the apparent simplicity of freedom is the "operating system" of a highly complex, but common, phenomenon of turbulent self-organizing feedback, many of the old problems simply go away.

The implications for social science are far-reaching: essentially we will not be unscientific in replacing, where appropriate, a "predictable cause" model of explanation with a "free choice" one, but to explain an event in terms of free choice no longer means to throw up one's hands and go no further with research but instead to turn one's research efforts to the history and semantics of the complex personal and social feedbacks that underlie it.

Feedback as Norm

The second major conceptual tool that is offered to the social scientist by the new paradigm is the notion of the *primacy* of nonlinear historical process. Obviously, feedback is no new discovery—scientists and engineers have been wrestling with it practically for thousands of years, and conceptually for at least two hundred. But if we examine, for instance, a speed ball governor on a nineteenth-century steam pump, or an explanation of price instability in a Victorian treatise on trade and currency, or the detailed examples in an Enlightenment essay on political economy, we will see that the turbulence that must be explained or dealt with is always set within two types of givens. The first is given materials with fixed properties (but certain wayward and disorderly propensities attributable to impurity of substance). The second is given abstract laws, obtainable by reason and observation, but preexisting the situation and providing for it a rigid framework within which variation becomes intelligible and explicable. Indeed, "intelligible" and "explicable" are implicitly (and thus circularly) defined in terms of such a model.

One of the great changes that has occurred in the foundations of our thinking is that it is now becoming thinkable to place the properties of the material and the abstract laws of science *second,* as emergent properties of the turbulent feedback itself, which now assumes a primary role. In addition, the randomizing and disorderly propensities of materials, and their impurities, cease to be discounted as a mere "margin of error" but are revealed as another level of turbulence and feedback, at a smaller scale, interacting with the larger-scale instabilities that originally caught the attention of the systematizer. Indeed, impurities can now be controlled and put to use, as in the precise doping of semiconductors or the new emphasis on mixed-use zoning in city residential planning.

Increasingly, the nonlinear iteration of dynamical processes is seen as the originating condition of scientific laws, rather than the reverse. The four forces of physics, and even the value of the constants that govern them such as the gravitational constant, the electron volt constant, the speed of light, and Planck's constant, are now seen as having, so to speak, crystallized out of the unruly melt of the Big Bang together with certain quite arbitrary "choices" such as the collapse into a matter rather than antimatter universe, or later on the handedness of the organic chemistry of life. The interactive process of physics in the early universe preceded the emergence of the laws of physics. Likewise, the structure and behavior of a living organism may be strongly influenced, in lawlike fashion, by the required functions it must perform in an ecological niche: but those structures and behaviors can only be those inheritable, with variation and selection over the available time, from its ancestral genus, and furthermore, the ecological niche is only the resultant of many parallel genetic histories, each a nonlinear gene-pool turbulence in itself. Thus functional ecological efficiency loses its priority in biological reasoning and, though still operative, becomes secondary to the historical experience of the species. In human affairs, it is beginning to look as if history and tradition are far more powerful determinants of how a society is organized than the economic and political "forces" that nineteenth-century social theory reduced to social laws. It is somewhat bizarre and anachronistic that such thinkers as Michel Foucault, who assert the primacy of paradigms of power and knowledge, much as nineteenth-century thinkers extolled hydraulic theories of the psyche and society, should have obtained their curious vogue. Perhaps their popularity is a symptom of the exhausting labor of intellectual transformation and the desire for relaxation and comforting certainties, however paranoid. But as the evidence mounts for the infinite miscibility and superimposability of cultures and weltanschauungs, for the continuous emergence of new frames and values for the assessment of social experience, for the victory of creative renewal over established power, the idea of the primacy of history, even individual acts and decisions, gains ground in the social sciences.

Related to this change is another, concerning the robustness of complex systems. It used to be thought that the more complex a system was, the more elements it contained, the more intricately they were connected, and the greater the interdependence of all, the more fragile such a system would be, the more subject to disruption and catastrophic collapse. We were warned again and again of the dangers of a nuclear chain reaction that would consume the planet, of the collapse of the entire "fragile" ecosystem because of the removal of a few vital but unseen key species, of the danger of a single word or gesture to a growing child, whose psyche might be scarred for life, and of the unraveling of the "fragile" fabric of society by some disaster or mistaken social policy. Simple systems seemed more stable and predictable—stable *because* predictable. But the good news (or the bad news!) seems to have been that complex and interdependent systems can be amazingly robust and enduring. With feedback can come redundancy and the proliferation of unintended backup systems. The *strange attractor* of a complex system can be massively damaged and insulted, but come back with renewed force. This is not to say that all complex nonlinear systems are stable—there are some that are balanced on a hair, and exquisitely controllable as a result, such as the energy networks we use to run our appliances, the seeds of domesticated plants, and the human body. Rather, the point is that stability has nothing to do with the relative simplicity or complexity of a system. There can be unstable simple systems and stable complex ones.

Furthermore, stability does not even need negative as opposed to positive feedback systems to maintain itself. That is, a homeostatic process such as a thermostatically controlled temperature environment, with feedbacks designed to return the system to a given status, is not inherently more stable than a system whose positive feedback is continuously producing new behaviors and structures. In an unchanging universe, the first type of system, with negative feedback, would obviously be more stable. But in a universe like ours, a positive feedback system, with unpredictable new properties being produced all the time, may well have a better chance of running just to stay in place, and anticipating outside dangers that might put a stop to its entire history. James Lovelock, the great ecologist and Gaia hypothesist, surprised and disappointed the environmental preservation community by pooh-poohing the dangers of technology to the planetary ecosystem. We might be able to wipe ourselves out, he said, but the web of life on this planet was so robust that it would go on merrily without us. By implication, it might also go on merrily with us, continuously overbalancing and correcting itself as we do when we walk on two legs. We need not fear for positive feedback systems, for all their unpredictability; their unpredictability may be a survival advantage. We do need to understand such systems, however, and to preserve our own cultural reserves of unpredictable positive feedback so as to be able to respond appropriately to those that surround us.

Likewise, in the area of social policy, the attempt to change established nonlinear systems by the use of socioeconomic laws is turning out to be disappointing. After the principled application of a trillion dollars, the "cycle of poverty" remains untouched in the country's urban areas; indeed, it has gained strength. We may have been trying to push a string. The new nonlinear science would suggest that the answer, if there is one, may lie in a totally unexpected direction—in the emergence, perhaps, of some artistic or religious or cultural attractor that will suddenly form the basis of a new kind of market of exchange and a new dimension of interdependence. Since the application of money, which is stored and abstracted negative obligation, has proven to exacerbate the problem, or at least to leave it untouched, perhaps the problem has something to do with the direction of the flow of obligation, or a difference between the perception of its flow and its actual flow, or with an attempt to constrain its flow in one direction or another when it should find its own way, or in a misinterpretation of the meaning of money, or with the use of obligation—money—as a tool in the first place.

Time

Perhaps the most fundamental change that has been brought by the new science is the recognition that time will not go away. To explain: the hidden agenda of much of science and philosophy has been to eliminate the conceptual problems of change, especially innovation, by reducing time to the status of an illusion, a spacelike dimension, a logical impossibility, a construction of our nervous systems, a cultural convention, or a semantic problem. Mathematicians have tended simply to ignore time. Physicists have sought to establish situations in the realms of the extremely small, the extremely closed, the extremely cold, the extremely hot, and the extremely brief, where time does not seem to have a preferred direction and can be treated, as it is in a traditional Cartesian graph of speed, in the Minkowski diagram, and in the Feynman diagrams of reversible particle interactions, as a kind of space. Other scientific and scholarly disciplines have sought to mitigate the one-way nature of time by finding events completely and adequately contained in their causal antecedents, thus reducing time to the status of logical entailment. Cultural critics have tried to relativize time out of existence, by asserting—usually without sound anthropological evidence—that other cultures do not share the West's obsession with "linear" time and possess instead an eternal or cyclic view of temporality.

But the new science has shown conclusively that time is irreducible, irreversible, and asymmetrical. Unlike as in space, one can only go in one direction in time: one can go from London to Paris, or from Paris to London, but one can only go from 1988 to 1998, not from 1998 to 1988. And this distinction continues to apply all the way down to the quantum level of reality. The moment there is enough of anything for nonlinear feedback relationships to emerge, these relationships begin to exhibit emergent statistical properties that are at least subject to the increase of thermodynamic entropy over time. The effect on each other of two individual fundamental particles may indeed be timeless, in the sense that it could without changing the picture be run backward in time (with appropriate reversals of charge and parity), but the universe ceased to be composed exclusively of such temporally pure interactions at some tiny fraction of a second into the Big Bang. Mathematically, the logical necessity of time can be expressed by the statement that in plotting the outcomes of any sufficiently complex and nonlinear statistical situation, there are not enough spaces even in Hilbert space, which is the space of all possible connectivities, to do so (personal communication with Ilya Prigogine). Such situations do in fact have outcomes: therefore, time must exist as "wherever" it is that such outcomes are worked out.

The gift of time as an irreducible reality may be a rather unwelcome one to the social sciences. But it has certain advantages as well. One is that the study of history is significant. That is, the details of historical events are not the mere epiphenomena of socioeconomic laws that, once understood, would eliminate the need for detailed research (except as an occasional check on the correctness with which the social scientist applies the laws). Instead, historical events in all their idiosyncrasy are themselves the irreducible meat of what is going on; each one in itself consists of a partly lawlike and partly valid interpretation of all other historical facts. This is not to say that history is just "one damned thing after another" or that intelligible relations among events cannot be accurately discerned after the fact, or even that public policy is rationally impossible. There are indeed vocabularies—some of them quite ancient and traditional—that deal rather well with the kind of complex, cladistic, statistical, self-adjusting, and self-referential realities of history. They include the languages of classical political philosophy, the implicit value system in all storytelling, the practical craft languages of the performing arts, and the religious terminology of moral choice, damnation, and redemption—or karma, dharma, and *moksha*. Historical events can be well understood in terms of who was in the right, what sacrifice the king failed to make, why justice was served in this case and not the other, how after such a beginning and such a middle, an ending of such a kind was required; even how bad luck necessarily dogged such and such a leader, because of his hubris, or how such a people neglected its ancestors and fell into decay. We will take a look at appropriate language for complex emergent properties when we examine the idea of the strange attractor.

Another advantage in conceding the reality of time is that social scientists need no longer take on questions by their very nature insoluble, and they can thus concentrate their efforts on projects with some hope of success. One way of putting this is that social scientists are now justified in taking on what used to be called the tragic vision. The corollary of the fact that the universe is in very real senses free is that its members may choose very definitely to do one thing and not another and that nothing will stop them. Character becomes fate, not despite the fact that character is alterable by training and habit, but because of it. Some predicaments may not have solutions. Some disasters may not be avoidable. Public policy can gradually change our habits, but cannot deflect the impulse to do what our habits suggest; thus such a view would imply a greater emphasis by government, and by its social science advisers, on the cultivation of virtue in the population, and a somewhat lesser priority on the immediate fixing of problems.

Not that this is a pessimistic view. The tragic vision is the only realistic form of true optimism, and the only sound basis for hope and progress. The anguish of tragedy can only come from gigantic loss and waste. Such loss and waste can only come about if there is something supremely valuable and dear to be lost and wasted; a worthless and trivial world cannot contain anything whose loss and waste would be worth mourning. The world must then be meaningful, or at least productive of meaning. But if the world can supply, create, or grow objects or persons with such supreme value that their loss is tragic, then the world can do it again; tragedy is at base a triumphant assertion of our universe's power to generate, freshly every generation, springtimes and children, hostages whose loss would be the cause of infinite suffering. Tragedy affirms something even darker, even more splendid, more terrible: the ability of at least some human beings to adequately suffer, to give the accurate emotional response to such loss. This ability is godlike; may we be protected from having to exercise it! But if one's preparedness to act and to suffer is robust enough, there is an exhilaration in this view of life.

A New Anthology of Recognizable Shapes

One of the most important components of a scientific vocabulary is an anthology of shapes whose observed presence carries with it testable implications and the suggestion of a series of research questions. Ancient Babylonians and Egyptians possessed a group of right triangles with integer sides, which were the foundation of their sciences and technologies of surveying, architecture, and hydraulics. The Greeks expanded that anthology of triangles by means of the Pythagoras theorem, and added a rich collection of other shapes: the regular solids, cones and cylinders, some complex curves, parallelograms, and so on. As graph axes, conic sections, sine curves, distributional bell curves, catenaries, Fourier functions, toruses, multidimensional topologies, vectors, tensors, scalars, and so on were added, the power and range of science and technology increased. Whenever one of these shapes showed up in the real world, or even in some isomorphic diagram of the real world, the investigator would know that certain quantitative operations were probably taking place there, operations already well understood by mathematicians, with implications about the inner process that was generating the outward form.

We have just experienced a huge increase in our anthology of forms, indeed the discovery of a whole new class of forms, equivalent in importance to the great expansion that took place when calculus was devised. These new forms range from the "cusp catastrophes" of René Thom through the cornucopia of fractals discovered by Benoit Mandelbrot, to the strange attractors of Lorenz, Hénon, Feigenbaum, and others. They are, in Mandelbrot's words, "grainy, hydralike, in between, pimply, pocky, ramified, sea-weedy, strange, tangled, tortuous, wiggly, wispy, wrinkled"—and, one might add, often beautiful. Such patterns have a number of characteristic features, some or all of which may be present. They include irregularity, discontinuity, and a tendency toward fragmentation (though always with an underlying and intangible orderedness to the eye); self-similarity (the repetition of forms exactly or approximately at different scales); scaling symmetries in general, including similar ratios, detail frequencies, and rhythms of recurrence; an infinite depth of detail within a bounded domain; a three-dimensional look, as if one were peering into a universe of strange objects of various sizes at different distances; and for each type of form, a characteristic "style," like the style of an artist, ranging from the flying scuds and gullwings of the logistical set and the pinwheels and paisleys of the Mandelbrot set, to the rich weave of the Lorenz attractor and the foams and bubbles of the Newton square root algorithm. But even far less elegant shapes, like the boom-and-bust curves of ecological crisis and the "random walk" of the Dow Jones average, can now, to the practiced eye, mean much more than a confusing and unintelligible disorder.

Until now we had indeed seen such shapes in nature, including that part of nature called human society, and artists had celebrated their beauty for millennia without realizing their deep connections with each other and the principles of their construction. Just so, neolithic artists probably enjoyed, without knowing why, the parabolic curves of animal muscle, the cones and cylinders approximated by hill and tree, and the satisfying stability of triangles and circles. But now, whenever we see fractal scaling in clouds, turbulences, electrical discharge patterns, stock market fluctuations, animal populations, star cluster orbits, the aperiodicity of a dripping faucet, the beating of a human heart, the developmental process of a plant fetus, the reverberation of a thought in the brain, and so on, we know that we are probably dealing with a certain type of iterative process in a highly communicative system, and we can begin to ask the right questions about it. Furthermore, if we suspect that some such process is at work, we can begin to refine our data, for instance by mapping it onto a phase space or vector space, until we find—or significantly, do not find—the kind of shape that is its signature. In the social sciences such techniques have already been put to use in the study of crime statistics, voting patterns, and so forth; the potential is enormous.

Strange Attractors and Nondualism

The Platonic distinction between the world of the ideal forms and the world of perceptible physical process has proven hard to get rid of. Aristotle, as a biologist, could see embodied in living organisms the intentionlike and purposelike and apparently rational structures that served their functions, and was thus inclined toward an unplatonic monism. But he was still pushed into dualisms of his own, between the natural and the artificial, and between the material and efficient causes, on one hand, and the final and formal causes, on the other. (Indeed, we may even speculate that his four causes were an attempt to paper over the Platonic dualism of ideal and actual.) He was so pushed because there existed nothing in Greek physics or mathematics that could account for the growth of functional structure out of mere inert matter, or for generativeness in the realms of lines and numbers. Greek mathematics abhorred surds, the irrational numbers and lengths that cropped up when one tried to relate the side of a triangle to its hypotenuse, or the circumference of a circle to its radius, and sought ways—Pythagoras' theorem was the most brilliant—to renormalize or eliminate such indefinite quantities. In themselves they seemed infinite regresses, mental traps, circular arguments, reductions to absurdity—unintelligible by definition, cacophonies in the harmony of the cosmos. Yet it is precisely the irrational numbers, the nonrecurring decimals, that are the first dim sign of physical generativeness, the threshold of a world in which physical objects might understandably display emergent properties resembling sensitivity, function, and even purpose.

But without a full embrace of such quantities, Western thought was doomed to return again and again to dualism. Meanwhile it devised more and more ingenious ways of giving an integer-based logic a grip on the irrationals, such as the infinitesimal calculus, Fourier analysis, and limit theory. The sign, though, that such measures still left a margin of the ungraspable was that the dualisms persisted: Aquinas' soul and body; Descartes' mind and matter; the epistemology and ontology of the Enlightenment; the Kantian *Naturwissenschaft-Geisteswissenschaft* split of the nineteenth century; the intentional-extensional, sign-referent distinctions of the linguistic philosophers; and the deconstructionists' guilty denial—and thus, in their own terms, the acknowledgment—of the nontextual, their dualism of text and (denied) nature, the second term *sous rature*.

The birth of chaos and complexity theory marks the end of a major class of dualisms. One way of putting this is that we are no longer afraid of nonrecurring decimals. This is partly because, as lazy animals, we now have computers that can do the tedious iterative computations for us, to any desired accuracy, and thus the issue changes from one of the calculable versus the incalculable to one of the appropriate degree of acuity for a given problem. In another sense, as the scope of science widened from situations chosen for their absolute predictability to one that takes in more and more complex and open systems, we have had our noses rubbed in the fact that it is the most normal thing in the world for emergent properties to be confected out of complex brews of feedback in ordinary collections of physical stuff. The issue is not how higher, more active realities emerge out of lower, more passive ones, but how to stop this happening when we do not wish it so. The art of the elegant closed experiment now stands revealed as a way of trying to make sure matter in bunches does *not* show its proto-spiritual bent for creativity.

The strange attractor, that is, the fractal form embedded in any nonlinear feedback process, is the graphic and undeniable evidence of the life and freedom embodied in physical reality. To see these objects is to see something for the first time in history. We had indeed seen their results in ordinary space, but had taken their beauty for granted as part of the necessary optimism of a living being. Now we see them in their own phase space, their beauty even richer for their abstractedness. It is as if for the first time we were able to stare unimpeded at an ideal form, not through a glass darkly, but face to face. And this ideal form is not detached from matter, in another world, a blueprint for its fumbling and messy copy here below, but very precisely *in* and defined by the process that it shapes and governs.

Thus a number of very old problems are on the verge of going away. How does a word "mean"? Precisely, perhaps, as a physical process "means" its strange attractor. How can a new species arise? As the new strange attractor of the nonlinear interactions of the proteins produced by the newly mutated fetal genes. How does a thought have a nonlocal existence in a brain? How can a higher primate have a self? Precisely as a self-organizing turbulence has an attractor. Even the most difficult issues of all, involving values, may be accessible in the new terms. How can a historical action be right or wrong? Questions of this kind cannot and should not be avoided; the atrocities of our century—the Holocaust, the Gulag—were permitted by the historicist assumption that right and wrong were locally relative, and that no larger, deeper, prior, or higher principle could be justified. We need some basis on which facts on the ground can be critiqued—yet that does not require revelation-based metaphysical commitments. For it is no solution to return to the sometimes mutually exclusive moral authorities of religion, which are almost as capable of horrifying violence as the historicist ideologies were. But if we treat religious moralities as various attempts to approximate values that are culturally universal, and if those values can be redescribed as the strange attractors of vast generative processes involving the whole species, and perhaps planetary life itself, we may begin to have at our disposal an instrument of moral judgment on history that is both real and at the same time superior to local anomalies and disruptions, as attractors are. Perhaps the fact-value distinction, which leaves us with two mutually incommensurable but equally indispensable descriptions of the world, with no theoretical means of translation between them, can be assimilated to the much more manageable distinction between physical processes and the attractors that govern them.

Modeling

More practical than these speculations, yet as far-reaching in its consequences for the social sciences, is the new method that has been both forced on us and recommended to us by the study of nonlinear complexity. The four tools of classical science are observation, logical/mathematical analysis, hypothesis, and experiment. To these we can now add a fifth: modeling, or, more precisely, nonlinear dynamic modeling. In a sense modeling has always been a part of science. One cannot observe without relying on the default model of the world wired into our sensorium and sensory cortex; in a sense any logical/mathematical analysis of data is a sort of passive model, based on a particular type of math such as statistics or topology; a hypothesis is a static model in the scientist's mind, and the questions a given experiment is designed to presuppose a model of a desired answer. But such models have until now been fixed and inflexible, and based as they are on a linear conception of cause and consequence, they are confirmed or deconfirmed in an all-or-nothing way. In any case they have no theoretical justification in the logic of scientific method. They are, as it were, like the remnants of traditional crafts or empirical common sense or natural history or imaginative intuition in a procedure that should not need them.

But now we have not only the technology—the computer, capable of endless, fast, accurate iterations of operations involving many mutually dependent elements—but also some of the theoretical machinery of fractal math and chaos science that are needed to transform modeling from a necessary nuisance into a fully fledged part of science. Instead of creating a hypothesis, testing it on the experimental and observational facts until a counterexample shows its flaw, and then trying another, we can now create an accurate facsimile of reality by successive tweakings of the variables and the connections among them, run the model in a computer as long as we like, check that its behavior continues to resemble that of the reality, and then read off what those parameters are. This procedure reverses the top-down, theory-to-phenomena approach of classical science, and thus can provide an admirable complement to it.

We have been forced into the use of dynamic nonlinear models partly by the fact that the phenomena that remained to be explained by science were the ones whose etiology was too complex to have been dealt with by earlier methods— and some of them, such as weather, ocean currents, metabolism, ecological succession, genetic evolution, and so on, had practical importance that offered big payoffs for small increments in comprehension. It also turned out that such processes were precisely the way the universe actually generated its systems and structures in the first place: established processes tend to act in a lawlike, linear way, while emerging realities, "at the edge of chaos," tend to have some positive feedback generator behind them. To handle the complications of such situations, we turned to computers, with their formidable iterative powers, and found ourselves—somewhat to our surprise—not just describing the universe but creating possible universes and then selecting the one closest to the actuality. But the experience of creating universes, however limited in scope, put at the disposal of even fairly ordinary thinkers the sort of imaginative extrapolation formerly available only to genius.

In a sense the most powerful proof that one understands something is surely that one can build one that works. And if it is objected that we cannot really know what is going on at each step of the process, this itself may be an insight about the real nature of the universe—the universe does not know either, so to speak, until it has done it, and it can forget what it did quite soon in a sufficiently complex process. In many fields we do not need computers to put the same new insight to work. We can find out about neolithic culture by making flint knives, about ancient Greek music and astronomy by reconstructing their musical instruments and astrolabes, about quaggas and aurochses by breeding their lines back out of interbred domestic stock, about genes by building one and turning it on, about the social structure of a remote tribe by mounting ethnodramatic performances of their weddings and funerals, and about the Civil War by reenacting Shiloh and the Wilderness. We can know by doing, and systematize the long-standing informal "black market" by which art and technology supply information to science.

* * *

As is already becoming clear, social science stands in the long run to be one of the major beneficiaries of the new science. Social science, dealing as it must with the complex two-way interactions of many complex organisms, themselves feedback systems of almost unimaginable depth and complication, has until now been forced to use logical and mathematical instruments originally designed to deal with hugely simpler systems. The mathematical science of statistics, now the most sophisticated and the most widely used tool of social science, is most appropriate to thermodynamics and probabilistic distributions, where it really comes into its own. The picture it gives of social systems, however, is severely limited—with the result that the forte of social science has been to confirm or deconfirm commonsense hypotheses already current for thousands of years among thinking people rather than to generate truly new ideas, perspectives, and knowledge. This is not a criticism of social science—already the field has proven its enormous value to the human race, despite the conceptual handicaps under which it has labored.

But the essays in this book are the first fruits of an approach that is as appropriate to social science as calculus is to the study of motion, or as non-Euclidean geometry was to relativistic physics. Now we must learn to use this new, powerful instrument.

FREDERICK TURNER
University of Texas, Dallas

Preface

This book is about the place in sociology, as well as in the other social sciences, of the revolutionary ideas often referred to as chaos theory. Chaos theory has already established a legitimate place for itself in a number of the physical sciences, such as geology and fluid dynamics. There appears to be hope that it can also provide powerful new tools and conceptualizations for the social sciences. It is, however, widely recognized that application to the social sciences will prove difficult because of the complex nature of the phenomena of interest, and because of our frequent inability to impose rigorous controlled conditions for the conduct of many studies. Nonetheless, this book will show that chaos theory is already being successfully applied in a number of areas of sociology and that it will eventually prove vitally important in many other areas of our discipline.

What *Is* Chaos Theory?

Nearly all of us have been taught to believe that if we have enough data on hand that is valid and reliable, if our methods of analysis are correct, and if our use of statistics is without fault, that there should be a definite mathematical solution to any given problem. What makes chaos theory both troublesome to many, but also so powerful in certain applications, is that the theory shows with mathematical precision that for many relatively simple problems (let alone complicated ones) there is no sure way of finding a single and definite answer–no matter how well we have proceeded. For many phenomena that involve feedback, chaos theory shows that this uncertainty of prediction is inevitable. By the use of the term feedback here, we simply mean to refer to situations where a future state of a system depends on an earlier state of the same system. Another way of saying the same thing is in terms of mathematics. If the variable we wish to explain appears on one side of the equal mark in an equation (let's call it X_1), and also the value of one or more of the explanatory variables on the other side of the equal mark is a function of X_1 at some earlier point in time, feedback has occurred. Admittedly, even this definition seems complicated. However, in reality, it is easily apprehended that there are very few problems in the social sciences where the value of one or more of the so-called explanatory variables has not been influenced at some point in time by that which we wish to explain. Take voting behavior as an example. Certainly we can predict that the more wealthy people are the more likely they are to vote Republican. However, can we be sure that some of their wealth has not resulted from networking with other wealthy people because they were already Republicans? Many similar examples are easy to think up.

Sensitivity of Initial Conditions

One thing that chaos theory shows us is that for many simple mathematical relationships, the outcome of the operation of the explanatory variables is exquisitely sensitive to very small differences in the initial conditions under which the analysis was begun. This is the so-called "Butterfly Effect." Allegorically, the Butterfly Effect asks whether it is true that under some conditions if a butterfly beats its wings in Hong Kong today, is it not possible that this may change the weather in Miami three days later? While the allegorical example would be an extreme case, it is easy to see how sensitivity to initial conditions might be fairly common in the social sciences.

The Problem of Identifying Chaotic Systems in Advance

The real anxiety raised by chaos theory for many of us stems from the fact that it is nearly impossible at this point in time to say ahead of time just *which* dynamic systems will result in chaos, and which will not. Only some proportion of systems that involve feedback exhibit the characteristics that are the signatures of chaos. Two equations (or sets of simultaneous equations) that involve feedback terms can look remarkably alike and still one may yield a chaotic

solution while it's near twin does not. Because of this, one disturbing implication of chaos theory is that a substantial number of the empirical analyses presented in the top social science journals where the authors have purposively or
inadvertently left out the feedback effects are likely to be exercises in pseudo-
science. In other words, if the feedback terms had *been* allowed to operate in a
manner consistent with the real world, the results of attempts to mathematically
solve such path models would sometimes have been not a specific solution but
instead, the creation of a "strange attractor."

A strange attractor is a complex mathematical figure containing infinitely
repeating detail in both its fine and gross structure (a number of them are depicted throughout this book). What each of the millions of dots that compose
a strange attractor actually represents is a single solution to an iterative equation
involving feedback (when chaos is present).

When one sees a strange attractor, it is easy to see why some have said that
"chaos" was a poor choice of words to describe the systems that interest us here.
It is true that some problems are chaotic in the sense that one cannot say *where*
the next dot will appear in the complex pattern representing the strange attractor. However, it is equally true, and easy to see, that there is a great deal of
systematic patterning in the attractor. Any dot representing a single iteration of
our chaotic equation will fall *somewhere* within the pattern formed by the attractor. (For this reason, some prefer to speak of "deterministic chaos," others
of "complexity theory"). Nonetheless, since it is impossible to say where the
next solution will appear, only that it will be somewhere within the pattern
formed by the attractor, it is clear that no single, determinant mathematical
solution can be expected in many cases. How many published empirical articles
would suffer this fate if the feedback terms were included? Unfortunately, there
is no sure way to know. The safest answer is a sizable number would be affected.

Some Other Concepts Related to Chaos Theory

Chaos theory would be interesting enough if it merely gave us an explanation
for why often our computations seem unstable, or even outright wrong, when
everything seems to be in order. It gives us, however, a host of other interesting
new ideas for the social sciences. The complex pattern of a strange attractor is
produced by the repetitive iteration of very simple rules. Often the total system
resulting from the operation of simple equations with feedback terms included
begins to manifest *emergent properties* that could never have been predicted
ahead of time by looking only at the original very simple rules for interaction
among concepts. Could this be telling us, for example, that social structure is
actually composed of emergent properties that very simple rules for individual

interactions create in ways that we have but dimly understood? If so, it follows that changes in very simple rules about how we interact with one another socially, politically, or economically might result in a completely different social structure after a few million cycles of interaction. We can only hint here at this phenomena, but the full implications are well explained in several of the chapters within.

Self-organizing systems also seem closely wed to chaotic dynamics. Let sand drip from a tube upon a table for a few hours and what do you see? At first glance, you will see a sand pile. Look closer and longer however, and you will see avalanches of sand grains from time to time. It may be surprising, but predicting the path of a single grain of sand in such an avalanche would defy our most powerful computer because the avalanche is a chaotic system (it involves so many interaction effects as grains of sand bump each other, the path of a single grain becomes infinitely complex to compute–like lining up the colors on a Rubik's Cube). However, the sand pile itself stays the same shape! It does so because it is a self-organizing system. Could this example be similar to the operation of society? In other words, in spite of millions of chaotic events, including even births and deaths, that afflict individuals within society, the social structure itself continues largely unchanged?

Like all theory, chaos theory is a symbolic representation of the world, a symbol system created by human minds to describe the world as closely as possible while leaving out fine detail so as not to overwhelm one with minute detail. Chaos, however, is not a static theory, but a dynamic one that captures movement and change, and as such, represents a powerful ally to more traditional theories of social phenomena. It presents powerful and exciting new ways of representing a host of highly dynamic phenomena and systems. However, at the same time, it cautions us that the world may not be as easy to predict as scientists have here-to-fore told us it would be.

A Plethora of Myths

This book will also try to separate fact from fiction regarding the nature and operation of chaos theory. Perhaps because to date the math remains difficult to master, or perhaps because so many of the aspects of the operation of chaos theory are dramatic and often counter-intuitive, it is today the case that many misconceptions, myths, and outright misrepresentations have grown up around the subject of chaos theory. We will try throughout this volume to make it clear what chaos theory really is, how it really operates (and doesn't), and to lay to rest some of the more common misunderstandings about its operation and its implications for sociological theory.

A History of the Project

This book had its beginnings in a discussion following three sessions on Non-linear Sociology at the Southwest Sociological Association Meeting in Dallas in 1995. Texas sociologists were the primary presenters of the papers given at that session. The lively discussion moved from room to room as the sessions changed rooms. One result of these discussions was that the editors established an Internet discussion group (entitled N-Linear) with its host site at Texas A&M University. A surprising number of energetic debates quickly emerged on the Internet discussion group, many of the participants from far corners of the world. Using that Internet discussion group and other Internet pathways, a call for papers was announced on the Internet, and that brought abstracts from an amazing number of points on the globe. One year later, some of the papers that were to eventually be published were presented at the Southwest Sociological Association Meeting in Houston in 1996. Several other papers were presented at American Sociological Association later in 1996. Reviewers for potential papers had meantime been recruited from around the world, again largely by Internet communication. The book you hold in your hands represents the reviewers' opinions of the best selections in the world available in the social sciences as of this date.

Many thanks to the kind organizers of the Southwest Sociological Association and the American Sociological Association who allowed us to use their meetings as a launching pad for our project. Thanks, too, to the reviewers who took the time to read through the various papers. Thanks also go to Texas A&M University for the computer resources that supported the Internet discussion group. And many thanks as well to Sage Publications and particularly to one of their editors, Peter Labella, for having the foresight and support and commitment to the social sciences necessary to bring this volume to the hands of the readers.

In closing, let us note together that chaos theory presents us with a rare and exciting opportunity. Probably not since victory was seized in the bloody and hard-won battle to displace the Earth from the center of the physical solar system (and even the universe) has a set of ideas and the accompanying mathematics been so likely to change the nature of how we see everything in the cosmos, and every individual in the cosmos. Application of the ideas within this book, such as chaos, complexity, self-organization, criticality, and emergence may well send science in general, and social science in particular, on a wild amusement park ride of the mind in the next few decades. We hope you'll come along for the ride. It promises to be a bit scary, but it should also be hugely exciting and rewarding.

THE EDITORS

Emerging New Directions: Myths and Theories

1

The Myth of
Postmodern Science

Bob Price

A common misconception about theories of chaos and complexity is that they are in some sense "postmodern science." But the constellation of ideas that falls under the general heading of "postmodern" is typically not positivistic, not empirical—not what we generally conceive as scientific lines of inquiry. Meanwhile, theories of chaos and complexity (hereafter abbreviated "complexity"), while recognizing the need for a modification of the reductionist classical model of science, remain grounded within the "scientific" tradition.

To show comprehensively the differences in origins, outlooks, and projects of the complexity paradigm, on the one hand, and postmodernism on the other, would require more than a book chapter. Moreover, we should be apprehensive about speaking of one complexity, since a range of views falls under that heading. We should be even more cautious about speaking of one postmodernism, as the views of postmodern theorists diverge markedly. Nonetheless, complexity theorists do share a set of common themes and interests, and so do the postmodernists. Contrasting these two families of ideas will show why postmodern science is a contradiction in terms.

The best way to proceed in this case is to consider the postmodern critique specifically as it applies to the question of knowledge and the classical science model itself. The writings of Michel Foucault are eminently well suited to this task. Much of Foucault's critique is representative of the concerns of post-modernists in general. Moreover, his views on physical and human science and the question of subjectivity have been particularly influential within postmodern intellectual circles. So while detail is forfeited by focusing on the ideas of a single postmodernist, the increase in clarity gained from specific comparisons between the complexity paradigm and Foucault makes this a good trade. Demonstrating the incompatibility of ideas in the complexity paradigm and those of such a central figure from the postmodernist camp should help to disabuse readers of the notion that theories of chaos and complexity are in any sense postmodern projects.

The complexity view is, in its most general articulation, that modern socio-logy (and all science) is in need of modification. By correcting inadequacies in our scientific paradigm, we may appropriately and fruitfully continue to do "science." Foucault, on the other hand, and typically postmodern in this regard, sees modern science as being in need of problematization. His goal is to show the fundamental, irreparable shortcomings and contingencies in the concept of human science. Complexity offers covering laws; Foucault abhors totalizations. Both views emerge from different historical contexts and domain assumptions.

Different Contexts

Complexity theorists draw from a classical science view that has survived nu-merous reformulations. The dramatic paradigmatic shift resulting from the ad-vent of quantum mechanics is an illustrative example. Physics was able to ac-commodate the apparent contradictions of quantum mechanics (particles popping into and out of existence, supersymmetry, the uncertainty principle), in spite of their counterintuitiveness. Why then, complexity theorists ask, should social science be so resistant to the concept of social nonpredictability, a basic insight of complexity theory, when it is intuitively appealing and empiri-cally supported? Like quantum theory, complexity is a reconstruction rather than a deconstruction of the classical science model.

Foucault's context is, of course, quite different. His consideration of the hu-man sciences draws on Bachelard's philosophy of science and Canguilhem's history of science (Gutting 1989). More generally, Foucault writes from a post-modern, poststructural, constructivist vantage. Foucault takes from postmod-ernism the concepts of fragmentation and multiplicity, the linguistically created subject, and the challenge to causality. As a poststructuralist, Foucault attacks structuralism's "scientific pretensions"—the quests for foundation, truth, objec-tivity, certainty, and systems. Where Kant endeavored to determine a priori, necessary conditions governing reason, Foucault seeks to show what *appears* to be such to reveal their contingency and historical origin (Gutting 1989). Moreover, Foucault criticizes the structuralist view of an unchanging human nature. However, Foucault did borrow from the structuralists the emphasis on language and the de-emphasis of the subject (Best and Kellner 1991). Some theorists interpret Foucault as reacting primarily against Marxism (Poster 1989). On balance, however, Foucault's arguments appear aimed mostly at structural and empirical assumptions.

A Terribly Brief Overview of Foucault

Foucault, like postmodernists and poststructuralists generally, stresses the "arbitrary and conventional nature of everything social—language, culture, practice, subjectivity, and society itself" (Best and Kellner 1991:20). His "archaeological" approach is concerned with identifying relations of knowledge that make particular concepts possible in the first place. In other words, Foucault seeks to discover the conditions of emergence of the questions we ask (Foucault 1970). That is, Foucault is interested in the idea that in the current era, thought is not about the natural world, but about the conditions that make thought possible (Cooper 1981).

Archaeology is undertaken to uncover the discursive rules that constitute bodies of knowledge. Because of their linguistically derived nature, Foucault takes issue with the practice of considering objects of knowledge "real." Instead, he wants to "dispense with 'things.' To 'depresentify' them . . . to substitute for the enigmatic treasure of 'things' anterior to discourse, the regular formation of objects that emerge only in discourse. To define those objects without reference to the ground, the foundation of things, but by relating them to the body of rules that enables them to form as objects of a discourse and thus constitute the conditions of their historical appearance" (Foucault 1972:48).

The rules governing discourse are neither universal nor grounded in structures of the mind. Rather, they are historically contingent and situationally specific. Archaeology seeks to specify the rules governing a given knowledge. This set of rules is called the historical a priori. The historical a priori "is not a condition of validity for judgments, but a condition of reality for statements" (Foucault 1972:127). To sum up, the historical a priori is constituted of the rules of all knowledge, perception, and truth. "They are 'the fundamental codes of a culture' which construct the 'episteme,' or configuration of knowledge, that determine the empirical orders and social practices of a particular historical era" (Best and Kellner 1991:41). Archaeology can in this sense be thought of as the study of epistemes (Cooper 1981).

An episteme is an organization of relations that allows a discourse to make sense. Foucault describes the episteme as "something like a world-view, a slice of history common to all branches of knowledge, which imposes on each one the same norms and postulates, a general stage of reason, a certain structure of thought that the men of a particular period cannot escape—a great body of legislation written once and for all by some anonymous hand. By episteme, we mean, in fact, the total set of relations that unite, at a given period, the discursive practices that give rise to epistemological figures, sciences, and possibly formalized systems" (1972:191).

Discursive formations, then, are knowledges that result from linguistic practices, as opposed to phenomena of the nondiscursive realm. These are connected, and "archaeology also reveals relations between discursive formations and non-discursive domains (institutions, political events, economic practices and processes)" (Foucault 1972:162). Moreover, objects of knowledge may have both discursive and nondiscursive conditions of existence (Cousins and Hussain 1984).

By now it should be quite clear that Foucault shares the postmodern penchant for seeing the social world as more or less linguistically constructed. This contrasts markedly with the more conventional goal of most complexity theorists: making sense of a world that exists objectively, regardless of our language games. Compare Foucault's postmodern characterization to that of Niklas Luhmann, a student of complexity. Luhmann does not deny the importance of language. On the contrary, in his view social systems are generated by people interacting through symbols. But the resulting systems are not taken to be so contingent as in the postmodern rendering. Instead, social systems are autopoietic systems, capable of self-reproduction, and this implies at least a bit of autonomy for the system from the people who live in it (Luhmann 1990a).

One or Two Disciplines?

Both complexity theorists and Foucault are interested in the history and philosophy of scientific pursuit. Both are in some sense trying to transcend the extant classical science model. But because of their differing views of the relationship between human science and physical science, and because of their different ontologies in general, they propose radically different responses.

A fundamental question in this respect is whether sociology is "science." Complexity theorists answer in the affirmative. For all the ambiguities of social reality, sociology is still an empirical endeavor. In fact, some advocates of the complexity paradigm claim that it puts social science on an equal footing with the "hard" sciences; both address phenomena that are inherently unpredictable beyond a certain point, regardless of the rigor of the method used. That is, some would argue that complexity reveals that all of science (not just social science) should abandon the pretense of determinism beyond the realm of some very simple systems. Thus, sociology is part of one larger undertaking, "science." And Luhmann (1982) maintains that "truth" is the communicative medium of science, just as money is the communicative medium of the economy. No self-respecting postmodernist would brook that claim for an instant.

For his part, Foucault's emphasis on discursive considerations is typical of postmodernists. He sees the human sciences as knowledges rather than sciences proper—they yield bodies of knowledge, but do not meet the formal criteria for "science." This is a result of the place of the human sciences in the modern episteme—half way between opinion and rigorous science (Foucault 1970). Foucault implies different discursive systems for the "hard" sciences and the human sciences. Thus, Marx and Freud, for example, are "founders of discursivity" whose works remain important guideposts in contemporary debate. This is not the case in biology or physics, where the original texts are fully digested and surpassed by the works that follow them (Rabinow 1984).

Complexity theorists suggest that "science" is not the problem, but that classical science is. Social science has internalized the hypothetico-deductive Newtonianism of the classical science model (Wallerstein 1992). This classical orientation was developed during the Enlightenment, at a time when the universe was viewed as reasonably static. It should not surprise us, therefore, to observe that classical science emphasizes stability and nomothetic laws. Complexity theorists argue that the classical paradigm has taken us as far as it can. Classical science is unable to describe the world "as it is." Objectivity becomes a more subtle concept as we come to recognize the complexity of social systems and the irreversibility of dynamics. Where Foucault would say that the entire concept of science is flawed and incorrigible, Prigogine and Stengers, advocating the complexity paradigm, write: "Classical science, the mythical science of a simple, passive world, belongs to the past, killed not by philosophical criticism or empiricist resignation but by the internal development of science itself" (1984:55). In Luhmann's terms, science has the capacity for reflexivity; it can use the tool of truth to specify procedures to get at the truth (Turner 1991b).

Objective or Subjective Reality

Foucault takes a common postmodernist tact in declining to consider a realm "beyond" the objects of discourse, such as things known by experience or objects of an essence. This results from his contention that we cannot establish an

epistemology for determining what is real or imaginary, because such an epistemology would itself be a discourse with conditions of existence (Foucault 1970).

Objects are created through discursive practices, and therefore present problems for the question of history and historical objects, as well as for the question
of reality itself. Foucault's analyses are historical, but they are case studies more
than histories. Thus, they should be evaluated in terms of their intelligibility
rather than their exhaustiveness. Foucault cannot demonstrate by gathering
"all" of the data, but he can explain by showing the conditions of existence and
emergence. Similarly, Foucault shows "beginnings"—configurations of elements—rather than the absolute origins out of which phenomena develop. In
this way, he tries to avoid the teleology of historical theories (Cousins and
Hussain 1984).

According to Foucault, power plays a critical role in the construction of reality. Knowledge and power are inseparably intertwined. (Consider, for example, prisons as one object of discursive practices.) Even history is a construct.
Cousins and Hussain summarize: "The point is that the conventional distinction
between forms of reality, and between reality and fiction, rests on an ontology,
which is itself a discourse. Its distinctions and categories are therefore no less an
artifact than the objects to which it is applied" (1984:260-261). For Foucault,
then, knowledge is not neutral. Instead, power and knowledge in the modern
era have created domination.

Contrast this typically postmodern characterization to that of most complexity theorists. The latter accept that there is a reality "out there," although their
paradigm recognizes that complex interactions can obscure that reality. Luhmann (1982) has spent considerable effort exploring the mechanisms social
systems develop to hold their complexity to a manageable level. Ideologies, for
instance, are a form of conceptual simplification, prescribing certain notions
and proscribing others. And some ideologies may indeed work at cross-purposes
to science's goal of discerning truth. But this is a long way from the characteristic
postmodernist stance that all knowledge is necessarily ideological and political.
That is, complexity theorists do not see the situation as hopeless; science is not
incorrigible.

To reiterate, complexity theorists generally believe in an objectively extant
world, but they also believe that an unreformed science—one employing classical assumptions and categories—cannot see that world clearly. Prigogine and
Stengers speak to this issue: "Nature is cross-examined through experimentation, as if in a court of law, in the name of a priori principles. Nature's answers
are recorded with the utmost accuracy, but the relevance of those answers are
recorded in terms of the very idealizations that guided the experiment" (1984:42).

Consequently, classical science produces a filtered vision of reality. "There
are striking examples of facts that have been ignored because the cultural cli-

mate was not ready to incorporate them into a consistent scheme. . . . Meteorites were thrown out of the Vienna museum because there was no place for them in the description of the solar system" (Prigogine and Stengers 1984:307).

In sum, while complexity theorists are quick to agree that the conventional, linear scientific models and metaphors we have been using have provided a limited picture of reality, they do not normally agree with the postmodern position that reality per se is subjective and contingent.

Global Properties and Totalizing Claims

One of the basic insights of complexity theory is that dynamic systems tend to evolve in the direction of increased complexity over time. This is not to say that all systems move toward infinite complexity, only that they rarely simplify. The question of why this is so remains less clear. Stochastic drift is certainly at work in evolution, but only as a proposer of changes. Such drift brings nothing to the explanation of why complex changes work better. A "phylogenetic ratcheting" of some type seems to be in effect—it is easier to evolve more stuff than less. Organisms and systems do not usually evolve themselves into nothingness; typically, they add new features on. "The universe is indefinitely intricate. A more highly differentiated and integrated organism is a more powerful sensor and computer. Hence elaboration yields more information without limit" (Benzon and Hays 1990:39). Greater information pays off with a more effective search, more efficient extraction of energy and matter, and more flexible responses to vicissitudes. Drawing on these insights, Luhmann builds on the functionalist view of evolutionary change. He borrows from Spencer, Durkheim, and Parsons the definition of evolution as "the process of increasing differentiation of a system in relation to its environment" (Turner 1991b:102). Luhmann then argues that the mechanism for selection of one social alternative over another is "communicative success." Some types of communication are more flexible than others and allow for better adjustment to environmental realities (Luhmann 1982).

Having accepted the notion of increasing complexity, we can interpret it in different ways. For example, Rasch holds that complexity can be understood either as merely emerging out of simplicity or as generated from simplicity in the process of observation. Both responses are represented in social theory. "I take Jurgen Habermas' formulation of a reconstructive science of universal pragmatics to be a preoccupation with the former, reductionist view of complexity, while Niklas Luhmann's elaboration of a systems theory approach hinges on the notion of contingency that comes with observation and therefore represents the latter, in my view, more complex and adequate approach to the study of complexity" (Rasch 1991:70).

Regardless of the fact that complexity theory does not necessarily see evolution toward increased complexity as "progress," one can assume that Foucault would protest. He resists such grand schemes and the "inhibiting effect of global, totalitarian theories" (Foucault 1980:81). Complexity meets Foucault's definition of a totalizing scheme. In its place, Foucault calls for the recognition that "knowledge is perspectival, requiring multiple viewpoints to interpret a heterogeneous reality" (Foucault, quoted in Best and Kellner 1991:35). What complexity theorists perceive as a legitimate articulation of objectively extant general principles, Foucault would probably dismiss as teleological "myths."

The concept of holism is relevant in this context. Not surprisingly, complexity theory and Foucault arrive at different opinions of holism. Sociology has seen a variety of systems theories. General systems theory, for example, focuses on the totality rather than its constituent parts. Thus, it adheres to holism in the conventional sense of the word. Complexity theory views this type of holism as just as problematic as the reductionism it nominally opposes—the conventional systems theory holism is reduction to the whole. Holism typically overlooks the interactions and the organization, whereas complexity pays attention to them. Thus, Luhmann states,

> Autopoietic systems, then, are not only self-organizing systems, they not only produce and eventually change their own structures; their self-reference applies to the production of other components as well. This is the decisive conceptual innovation. It adds a turbocharger to the already powerful engine of self-referential machines. Even elements, that is, last components (individuals) that are, at least for the system itself, undecomposable, are produced by the system itself. Thus, everything that is used as a unit by the system is produced as a unit by the system itself. This applies to elements, processes, boundaries, and other structures and, last but not least, to the unity of the system itself. Autopoietic systems, then, are sovereign with respect to the constitution of identities and differences. (1990a:3)

Meanwhile, Foucault not only does not want to move toward any kind of holism, he seeks to break up currently operating "totalizing histories" and their unities "and then see whether they can be legitimately reaffirmed; or whether other groupings should be made" (Foucault 1972:26). (In all fairness, this does resonate with Luhmann's [1990b] idea of "de-ontologization," although Luhmann does not go so far in the direction of denying reality.) Archaeology diversifies rather than unifies, and it allows the historian to discover multiplicity in discourses (Best and Kellner 1991). "Discourse . . . is so complex a reality that we not only can, but should, approach it at different levels with different methods" (Foucault 1970:xiv).

Complexity theorists respond with the assertion that it is possible to identify global properties. To take just one example, consider self-organization: "People trying to satisfy their mutual needs unconsciously organize themselves into an economy through myriad individual acts of buying and selling; it happens without anyone being in charge or consciously planning it. . . . Atoms search for a minimum energy by forming chemical bonds with each other, thereby organizing themselves into structures known as molecules. In every case, groups of agents seeking mutual accommodation and self-consistency somehow manage to transcend themselves, acquiring collective properties such as life, thought, and purpose that they might never have possessed individually" (Waldrop 1992:11).

Foucault does not build general conceptions of society; he does not accept a deus ex machina or even "principles" of human societies (Cousins and Hussain 1984). Consequently, complexity and Foucault talk past each other insofar as complexity is global and Foucault is particular (except that Foucault's philosophy is applied globally!).

Rupture

Complexity theory's view of rupture and discontinuity revolves around the concept of the phase transition or bifurcation point. Bifurcations are the branching of social phenomena seen during chaotic episodes. Systems that are going along in a more or less stable, deterministic way can suddenly be pushed into a state of chaotic dynamics, and at such times dramatic changes are possible. By extrapolating the mathematical consequences of bifurcation cascades to the social realm (which may or may not be appropriate), Young goes so far as to say that after three bifurcations, most systems "will have exploded into far-from-stable nonlinearity" (1991:327). So it may be that if income differences, for example, become two, then four, then eight, then sixteen times greater between rich and poor, chaos, in the form of nonnormative behavior, is much more likely.

Similarly, Artigiani suggests that revolutions occur when societies are pushed to bifurcation points, whereupon they leap to new stabilities. One consequence: the new order is more complex and requires the exploitation of more energy from the surrounding environment (Artigiani 1987).

Bifurcation points suggest a new role for social forecasting; the behavior of nonlinear systems cannot be predicted, but the onset of chaos may be open to anticipation. Thus, we cannot predict precise situations, but we can forecast the time of structural breakdown. Hansson summarizes these points: "Small-scale chaos can destroy parts, but depending on the parameters this will either stabilize the situation or drive it to a new state. If we can find such bifurcation points based on parameters this could lead to an ability to estimate the effort needed to produce a change at a given time" (1991:56).

Foucault's concept of rupture is quite different. He speaks of discontinuity in the postmodern sense, although his view of social rupture is not so extreme as that of some of his postmodern colleagues (Best and Kellner 1991). Postmodernists are united by their conviction that we are entering a fundamentally new age—a time so different that it can no longer be considered part of the modern era. It is a postmodern era, with different rules and modes of thought than were typical of modernity.

Transitions from one era to the next are a major object of Foucault's thought. When such a rupture occurs, as when society moved from the renaissance to the classical era, "things are no longer described, expressed, characterized, classified, and known in the same way" (Foucault 1970:217). Of the emerging postmodern episteme Foucault writes, "Something new is about to begin, something that we glimpse only as a thin light low on the horizon" (1970:384).

Foucault prefers to explore such discontinuities rather than the continuities historians consider (and to some extent fabricate) (Gutting 1989). Cooper observes that both *The Order of Things* and *The Archaeology of Knowledge* seek "to analyze discontinuities, to establish differences . . . to give rise to a radically disjunctive temporality" (1981:43).

The important point here is that we should not confound theories of chaos and complexity with postmodernist critiques just because both camps are using words like "discontinuity." They are not talking about the same things.

Summary and Conclusion

Both Foucault and the theorists of complexity question the current approach to social science. Specifically, both take issue with the linear classical science model on which conventional sociology is founded. However, their critiques of this model—and its assumptions about prediction, cause and effect, and objective truth—come from different starting points. Consequently, they are led to different interpretations of the problems and to different solutions.

Considering themselves part of the scientific community, complexity theorists seek to broaden the scope of empirical inquiry. They portray complexity as the "new view of science." In the same way that the Frankfurt school said, "Yes, there is empirical knowledge, but there is hermeneutic and critical knowledge as well," adherents to the complexity paradigm say, "Yes, there are linear, predictable phenomena in social systems, but there are also many more nonlinear processes." Complexity theorists argue that scientific inquiry can be conducted more profitably if processes such as emergence, phase transition, and dissipation are incorporated into its framework.

Foucault's critique—doubly significant for our purposes because it is by and large representative of the general postmodern critique in these particulars—originates from outside the "scientific" community. Foucault does not even situate himself within the modern episteme, claiming that to analyze the nature of knowledge as he does, one must adopt a postmodern vantage. Rather than suggesting ways to correct shortcomings of our mode of inquiry, he dedicates most of his energies to demonstrating that our view of "Man" and society have no objective reality. Thus, the usual objects of inquiry warrant less attention than the question of what historical conditions led to our current episteme and the knowledges it proffers.

We have seen that where the complexity school conceives sociology as part of the larger concern of "science," postmodernists challenge the very notion of science. Foucault maintains that "human science" and "science" are two separate entities, the former composed essentially of discursively formed opinion (but only marginally less "objective" than the latter). Such fundamental differences account for the divergence of views on a host of related issues.

While postmodernists emphasize the need to avoid totalizing theories and all-encompassing explanations, the complexity theorists hold that there are universal principles that work in all dynamic systems. Theorists of complexity assert that local rules produce global properties, that systems move in the direction of increased variation and complexity, and that there is an "edge of chaos" that strikes a balance between stagnation and anarchy. Meanwhile, Foucault denies even the "reality" of the subject.

Progress for Foucault is an illusion—yet another totalizing concept growing out of the modern conditions of knowledge. Societies and their members do move from one arrangement to the next over time, but there is no direction to the journey. The paradigm of complexity, for its part, does not necessarily see increasing complexity as progress. However, most complexity theorists posit a logic, an evolution of sorts, as societies move in the direction of greater complexity with time.

The postmodern vision of discontinuity hinges on the movement from one age to the next—the modern giving way to the postmodern. Foucault studies the transition from one episteme to the next. Ruptures occur as the historical a priori changes, giving rise to new discursive formations. On the other hand, complexity theorists discuss discontinuity in terms of transitions as social systems move through bifurcation points. As societies reach the critical stage that pushes them toward the realm of chaotic dynamics, new paths open up for them. Traveling down a given path results in new stability at a more complex level (usually). A sociology using the first image of discontinuity is very different from one using the second.

Even fundamental views of human agency are tempered by the basic premises both parties bring to the debate. Although Foucault sees power as dispersed and available to individuals as a tool for resistance, his overriding image is of individuals having to react to the discursive formations they encounter in society. Power and knowledge are two aspects of the same process, and all views and information are therefore a result of the "will to knowledge." Although the possibility exists of breaking free from the totalizations of the modern era, most people live their lives bound to the contingent formations created within the modern episteme.

Complexity offers a more optimistic view of agency. Although stable systems have general, deterministic properties, the nonlinearities in all societies leave room for autonomy. Cause and effect are not tied in such a way that the individual has no room for self-determination—or room to affect the larger society, for that matter. Subjectivity is not a creation of language, as many postmodernists would argue, but is an objectively real, emergent property of biological and social life.

None of these are idle distinctions; the very questions sociologists ask will change with the adoption of one perspective or the other. Furthermore, the various disagreements outlined in this chapter are largely incompatible—we cannot have it both ways. Sociologists cannot sensibly be postmodernists and complexity theorists, because postmodernists and theorists of chaos and complexity are undertaking entirely different projects. Postmodernists want to deconstruct science; complexity theorists want to reconstruct it.

2

From Enlightenment to Chaos

Toward Nonmodern Social Theory

Mary E. Lee

Sociology in Society

> Sociology can only describe society in society. . . . It is a science of the social
> system and a social system of science. To make matters even more complex, as a
> science and, as a social system, sociology is also an internal observer of whatever
> system it participates in.
>
> (Luhmann 1994:132-133)

What will society look like in the age that succeeds the modern age? This is a
question much asked as we near the beginning of a new millennium. For social
scientists, this is as much a question about the future of our discipline as a
question about society itself. What will social science look like in the new era?
As Luhmann suggests, questions about change as it moves society beyond the

modern era are also questions about the content and conduct of social science, as well as science generally.

In sociology, the term "modernity" typically describes a pattern of cumulative change that has led society to and through "industrialization" (cf. Featherstone 1988, 1989). Scientific inquiry and a concomitant standardization in modes of production are seen as forming the very foundation of society's "modernization project." But the promise of modernity—amelioration of the human condition—seems unfulfilled. Many now herald the arrival of a "postmodern" age during which the vestiges of modernity will at last wither away. Much is heard, in both the "physical" and the "social" sciences, about a coming era that will be characterized by the reign of "chaos"—the mathematical theory of chaos, that is. Found in widely ranging application, theories of mathematical chaos are used in developing models of such seemingly disparate processes as fluid dynamics, heart rates, population growth, and economic transactions (Jantsch 1981; Coveney and Highfield 1990). Some believe the concept is so powerful and robust that it will become the basis of an often conjectured, unifying "theory of everything" (cf. Horgan 1995; Barrow 1991).

In the next few pages, I begin an examination of the theoretical usefulness to the sociological enterprise of chaos and related concepts. In keeping with a central proposition of chaos theory—that the present state of affairs can only be understood in terms of the past—my examination begins with a brief history of sociological time.

Modernity and Postmodernity

> Postmodernism is a disappointed form of modernism. It shares with its enemy all its features but hope.
>
> (Latour 1991:17)

The sociological definition of modernity is rooted in Western society's widespread adoption of the concept of social progress as arising from advances in human knowledge and reason. Social science was born at a time when science was not so easily divided between the "natural" and the "social." Men of science (and they were almost invariably white, European men) were curious about and conducted systematic inquiry into all aspects of the world in which they lived, generally without specialization. The new system of reasoning that emanated from Europe in the early Age of Enlightenment was considered as inherently progressive. It was thought capable of ever producing newer and better knowledge. Eighteenth-century thinkers strove to establish a "science of morals" as their mission: betterment of humankind and humankind's plight in this world through reason. Human reason was thought to constitute progress: history progresses because human rationality progresses. The idea of "active" human progress guided by reason became a kind of new evolutionary law that then drove modernization. In the modern era, the view that reason and rationality are synonymous with quantifying, calculating, and computing came to dominate both Western culture and social theory (cf. Becker 1967).

Recently, speculation about the age that will succeed the modern age has gathered under the banner of "postmodern." As a transformation in culture, postmodernity is most often posed as a deep societal questioning of both the means and ends of science and, ultimately, the modernization project. Postmodern culture seems rooted in a belief that, for most in the world, the promise of modernization—alleviation of individual suffering through the universal application of human reason—seems unfulfilled. Postmodern culture is portrayed as ephemeral, fragmented, and disordered; transient relationships and values seem demanded by postmodern extremes of individualism (cf. Habermas 1975; Bell 1976; Baudrillard 1983; Harvey 1989).

Correspondingly, postmodernity as a transformation in the content and conduct of social science is seen as dawning recognition that the "local" has more value to social theory than does the "universal" (e.g., Seidman 1994). For postmodernists, "universal" or "general" social theory, as typified by Parsonian general action theory, is too rational, too quantifying, too calculating—in short, too modern. General social theory, goes the argument, has been no more successful in explicating human behavior than has been the culture of universal reason in ameliorating the human condition. This "failure" of general social theory must mean that, at best, the questions asked by such theory are absurd. At worst, the very idea of such theory is bogus, an instrument of universal domination wielded by white males in Western societies to tyrannize and subjugate others. At any rate, the conclusion of postmodern social theorists seems to be that even if general theory were desirable—and they believe it isn't—the problems encountered in devising general theory are insurmountable. Only localized narratives of the myriad quandaries of everyday life as experienced firsthand are truly explanatory of the human condition and, thus, only local theory is possible.

Moving beyond Modernity

> Modern life has taught us that both nature and humankind are more complicated than the dialectical notions of the nineteenth century supposed.
>
> (Raskin 1987:29)

The implication of the "postmodern" label attached to such theoretical positions, similar to the one outlined above, is that society and social theory are now in for something completely different. But are we? Both the social and theoretical questions about the relationship between individuals and society seem familiar. My preceding account portrays modernity as springing directly from the Age of Enlightenment to underscore the concept of "rational progress" that fueled the sociological definition of modernity. Postmodernity, therefore, is seen by many as a burgeoning social movement that will take society (and social theory) beyond modernism; it is seen as a new challenge to the old ideal of human progress through universal reason. But challenges to "Enlightenment rationalism" are certainly not new. "Rationalism" has long spurred debates and countermovements, not the least of which was romanticism. Multiple dimensions of an antithesis to rationalism are evident in the art, drama, and literature as well as the social, political, and epistemological thought of the romantic movement, wherein exaltation of the individual appeared as a common theme.

While Enlightenment thinkers wished to guide human society toward a consensual community based on knowledge gained through universally applied rules of reason, romanticists championed knowledge of the world gained through unfettered human experience. Thus, a modern paradox was born of the friction between Enlightenment and romantic ideals: a tension arose between the "transient and fleeting" and the "eternal and immutable" (cf. Baudelaire 1965) while humankind attempted to realize, as phrased by Kant, "maximum individuality" within "maximum community" (cf. Becker 1968). Much of the sociological work on modern society seems to underscore the tension of everyday life in a culture based on the "received" ideas forming this modern paradox, including the writings of Durkheim, Weber, Marx, and Simmel. Given this long history of contrapositioned social ideals, it is not difficult to see recent social and cultural events, described as postmodern by some, as being only a heightening of those modern tensions. Perhaps, as Bell (1976), Harvey (1989), and others describe, the modern tension between the "transient" and the "immutable," the "individual" and the "community," has been heightened by current methods of transportation and communication, which generate a technological compression of space and time.

The Age of Modernity—including recent events in late modernity that are currently labeled as postmodern—has been an era defined by the unfolding of this received modern paradox. Paradoxes are unfolded by creating distinctions out of an underlying unity that presents us with a dilemma. Such distinctions can produce useful results, helping to untangle concepts and refine thoughts. However, there is a point at which the unfolding of distinctions ceases to be useful; then, a return to questions about the underlying unity of the paradox can be productive (cf. Luhmann 1994). Such a return may be necessary, now, to move social theory beyond modernity.

Does a shift in social-theoretical emphasis to the local and individual justify a conclusion that we have moved beyond the precepts and concepts of modernity? Looking back at the past century, we find that this question has been asked repeatedly by social scientists: should more theoretical attention be given to the "individual" or the "social"? Furthermore, the task of explicating some theoretical connection between the individual and the social has for many years been called for by social theorists such as Anthony Giddens, Randall Collins, Jonathan Turner, James Coleman, Karin Knorr-Cetina, and others who seek "micro-macro linkages." However, to move beyond modernity, social theorists are finding that we must seek something rather more complicated than a simple bridge between the opposed sides of a twofold dialectic.

Toward Nonmodern Social Theory

> First, give up the postmodernism debate, not because it is wrong, but because it is right. Second, study the present, not to prove a point, but to think the reality of the world as it is. Third, reread the classics, not to return to origins, but to recognize that the world-We of the 19th century was the false face of modernity's divided and multiplied natures.
>
> (Lemert 1994:151)

In saying that postmodernism is "right," Lemert is not suggesting that contemporary Western culture will resolve the modern paradox by abandoning the idea of social consensus in favor of unbridled individualism. Nor is he suggesting that Western social theory will resolve the modern paradox by abandoning general theory for localized narratives. Quite the contrary, recent reemphasis of the individual in both culture and in social theory has restored a balance to the sociological unfolding of the modern paradox. Earlier in this century, in both culture and social theory, the unfolding of modernity seemed to be proceeding only along the lines of deterministic, overarching, and overwhelming "iron cages" of calculating reason, committing local events and individuals to the status of "cogs in a wheel." Recent, postmodern reemphasis of the individual is important in reminding us that the "local" is as multifarious in its attributes as it is essential in shaping the "global."

But does it follow that social science must therefore abandon "general" or "macro" theory? Interestingly enough, the closer we look at the interaction of individual components in either the universe or in social organization, the more difficulty we have in describing these interactions and their results only in linear, local, and deterministic terms. The recent theoretical and applied focus on individuals situated in local contexts brings us to the point of recognizing that "unfolding the modern paradox" is no longer useful as the primary occupation of social theory.

The modern paradox has not been resolved by abandoning reflection on the individual, but neither can it be resolved by abandoning reflection on society.

Society is the product of individual actions, actions that are enabled or constrained by society. Human individuals both affect and are affected by their "environment." These relationships are so obvious that we take them as given in the course of everyday life. However, obviousness does not mean that these relationships are simple or easy to model and explain. We cannot understand the nature of society by looking only at patterns of microinteraction, but neither will we understand it simply by solving detailed macroscopic equations. We must be able to understand how the social evolves or emerges from the local, and in turn alters the local. This in itself is not a new notion to social theorists, as variants of this principle have been seen in numerous explanations of the physical and social world at differing times throughout all of history. Today, however, we have new tools to help in building our understanding of that world—tools that were not available to Durkheim, Weber, Simmel, Marx, or even Sorokin or Parsons.

Nobel physicist Heinz Pagel (1988) wrote that just as the first microscopes revealed new frontiers of knowledge in the seventeenth century, the present frontiers of knowledge are being revealed through the "macroscope" of today's computers. Contemporary computing power allows us to approach micro-macro linkages from a "bottom-up" perspective, actually modeling the processes by which global structure arises from local interaction. To borrow an idea from Latour (1991), these new approaches are "nonmodern," meaning that they are not based in an unfolding of the modern paradox into dichotomies of local versus global, individual versus social, or even, as we shall see, order versus disorder or human versus "nonhuman." In this sense, the current localized narrative approach to explanation known as "postmodern" is still distinctly "modern"; that is, it is still based in the dichotomies of the modern paradox.

Complexity, Self-Organization, and Chaos

Complexity is a key concept in nonmodern approaches to modeling change processes in many fields of inquiry. Complexity is not a property just of the number of component parts or even the direction of their relationships, but of the variety of their interactions and thus the possibility to align into many different configurations. No matter how large the number of components, if there is no potential for components to interact, align, and organize into specific configurations of relationships, there is no complexity. Even if components are organized, but within such completely confining arrangements that no further possibilities for variety in interaction are left open, there is no complexity. Complexity, therefore, has to do with the interrelatedness and interdependence of components as well as their freedom to interact, align, and organize into related configurations. The more components and the more ways in which components can possibly interact, align, and organize, the higher the complexity. Current work has many approaches to defining and measuring that complexity; to name a few: physical, computational, algorithmic, information-based, logical (cf. Pagel 1988; Horgan 1995). However, one measure seems to have correspondence among various usages of the term complexity: the probability that any specific configuration of relationships between individual components will obtain.[1]

Another key concept in nonmodern models of change is that of self-organization. Components, their relationships, and change in these relationships over time are, by definition, self-organizing if no "external" factors are needed to model the change in component relationships over time. In conventional, modern, "grand" theories of change, external conditions have provided the parameters for component behavior. Such "mechanistic" models have described change among components that have invariant parameters in a set of specified conditions. The elements of these modern models have been abstract units with invariant properties: properties and parameters are invariant; properties are always independent of parameters.

However, in nonmodern models of complex self-organization, parameters are determined not by externalities but by other components in the model. Such models describe cumulative change in components and their relationships over time, models wherein properties are not always independent of parameters and the component relationships themselves are subject to continuous change. This means that descriptions using linear chains of finite equations are of limited usefulness in modeling complex change processes (cf. Kampis and Csanyi 1990). The difficulty in designing descriptions of such complex dynamics is one with which sociologists are very familiar.

While models based in the concept of self-organization do not use externalities to describe change in component relationships, components can be thought of as being "organized" into levels of complexity. They form hierarchies of "successively more encompassing sets" similar to a set of Chinese boxes (Grobstein 1973:31). Such levels are "nearly decomposable" (Simon 1973; Pattee 1973; Nicolis 1986) in that most of the change within a level can be explained by describing change in relationships between components at that level. But note that levels are only nearly decomposable: the whole cannot be explained in the absence of any of its parts. This, however, is not the same as saying that the whole is merely a summation of its parts. Indeed, global properties emerge that are not reducible to the sum of local properties.

Complexity and self-organization are probably more important theoretical concepts than is that of chaos itself. They are the underlying precepts on which nonmodern models of society can be built—models in which the theory of mathematical chaos may or may not be useful to describe certain social dynamics. If helpful at all, the theory of mathematical chaos may be helpful in exploring specific operations of social change that are complex, self-organizing, and adaptive by offering new methods to describe change over time in relationships between components and between levels of component relationships. In the case of so-called deterministic chaos, sets of deterministic, time-differential equations in a model of change processes yield apparently indeterministic, unpredictable results. The mathematical equations used are nonlinear, meaning that the dependent variable changes at rates that are not simply first-order powers of change in the independent variable. Furthermore, those coefficients are not dependent exclusively on value change in the independent variable but also on change in the "boundary conditions" or parameters of the model. When model parameters are dynamic, these dynamics "map" from initial conditions to properties at later points in time. This results in what "chaologists" call "extreme sensitivity to initial conditions." The behavior of the model becomes so complicated that given a specific set of initial conditions, future properties cannot be predicted even though the model consists of sets of equations that are each, independently, deterministic or solvable. The extent to which model behavior becomes unpredictable is the extent to which the model is "chaotic" (Crutchfield 1994).

This does not mean that model behavior is completely random, as patterns of behavior can be discerned. Typically, when researchers say that such patterns are chaotic, they are not saying that there is no order at all to the behavior; they are saying that the patterns are those of an "odd balance" between order and disorder that has been described as resting on the "edge of order and chaos" (Waldrop 1992). Such models reveal no one point of equilibrium between order and disorder, since there are many. Two-dimensional projections reveal a tree pattern that represents the history of state changes. Successive iterations of state descriptions, when modeled in n-dimensional "phase space," may exhibit "basins of attraction," sometimes called "strange attractors," that represent the system's bounded "preference" for an organization of microstates into a specific range of macrostates. Such strange attractors represent a state range that is somewhere between complete order and complete disorder, a place where seemingly some of the most interesting things in the universe take place (cf. Coveney and Highfield 1991).

Complex, Self-Organized Adaptation

In fact, it seems that the evolution of complex systems can best be described as a self-organizing series of nonlinear differentiating processes wherein variation within one level of complexity iteratively produces variation in other levels over time (cf. Freese 1988). Operationally hierarchic (Chinese box) models of self-organization can be used to describe how microscopic or local interactions give rise to complex macroscopic structures in which the relationships of interacting microcomponents continually combine, recombine, and change as a result of their own interactions. Hierarchical levels are determined by the number, location, symmetry, and degree of operational interdependence among components that maintain flexibly bounded but ordered relationships among themselves. In such self-organized levels of operation, change is "adaptive"; that is, relationships between components at one level change in response to changes taking place in other levels. Interactive component relationships create hierarchical levels of complexity. Protracted over time, component interactions "feedforward" to produce the macroscopic configuration of components that is discernible at any given point; "feedbacks" describe the continual accretion of effects from previous interactions, which may in turn alter lower-level interactions and higher-level configurations at the next point in time. Feed-forwards and feedbacks are essential descriptive features in models of hierarchical self-organization.

According to both self-organization theory (e.g., Prigogine and Stengers 1984) and experimental simulations (e.g., Kaneko 1991), although the occurrence of events that produce hierarchical, macroscopic organization is probabilistic, the feedback effects may be deterministic. Thus, macroscopic conditions can enable or constrain local behavior even though, sometimes, the effects are inherently destabilizing. Feedbacks produce a range of probabilities for "conditions of action" at local levels, which in turn lead to events that coalesce into new macroscopic assemblies of operational dependency with new possibilities for producing deterministic feedback effects, whether those effects are stabilizing (order producing, aggregating) or destabilizing (disaggregating, symmetry breaking). Seemingly random microscopic behavior can obscure elements of deterministic macroscopic feedbacks. Conversely, macroscopic facades that appear to be stable can conceal underlying probabilistic behavior at local levels.

Such approaches to modeling social change are distinctly nonmodern precisely because they can be employed without resorting to the modern dichotomies of local and global, individual and social, or, if chaotic, between order and disorder.

A Conceptual Outline of Complex, Self-Organized Adaptation

Think of three hierarchic levels of components with complex relationships (L1, L2, and L3), as shown in Figure 2.1.

Since each level is nearly decomposable, the relationships of components within each level can change without affecting the other levels. In fact, change within L1 effects change in L2 only if relationships in L2 are asymmetrically dependent on the ongoing operation of L1 such that the state of L1 acts as a "bounding" condition for L2, and change within L1 passes the threshold at which those bounding conditions are altered. When change in L1 reaches that threshold, relationships within L2 will change. Think of change over time in L1

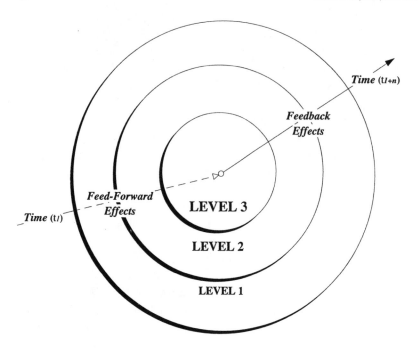

Figure 2.1. Hierarchical levels of self-organization.

that effects change in L2 and change in L2 that effects change in L3 as "feed-forward" effects. L3, on the other hand, affects L2 and L2 affects L1 only though "feedback" effects. These feedback effects can be such that the operation of L1 and its feed-forward effects to L2 are stabilized. These are sometimes known as "negative" feedbacks. However, changes in L2 may be such that the feedback effect to L1 eventually changes relationships in L2, which may in turn change the feedforward effect of L1 to L2 and then L2 to L3 as well as feedbacks from L3 to L2 and L2 to L1. While none of the components of the L1-L2-L3 model are "external," the levels can be nearly decomposable. That is, most change in L2 can probably be described as resulting from change taking place in the relationships of components within L2, without describing changes taking place in L1 or L3. However, the complexity of L2 cannot be truly modeled or appreciated without a description of its coevolution with L1 and L3.

Human Interaction and Complex, Self-Organized Adaptation

To add some concrete elements to the example, think of groups of humans interacting. Most of the change in a human relationship group (L1) can be explained by describing change that takes place in the relationships between members of that group. In other words, much change in the group is the effect of local interactions. The continued existence of another group, L2, may be asymmetrically dependent on the continued existence of the group L1. That is, the continuing existence of L2 is dependent on the existence of L1 even though the existence of L1 is not dependent on the continuing existence of L2 (just as, for example, the continuing existence of families is not dependent on the continuing existence of family counseling organizations but family counseling organizations would cease to exist without families). In such cases of asymmetrical dependency, the relationships within L1 act as a set of "bounding conditions" for L2. Changes in relationships within L1 may reach the threshold at which the bounding conditions for L2 change, since those conditions are derived from the state of relationships within group L1. Because of the asymmetrical dependency, group L2 affects group L1 only through feedbacks. However, effects from change in group L2, precipitated by change in group L1, may change the bounding conditions for the next higher-level group, L3. To provide a somewhat oversimplified illustration, consumers (L1) support certain retail establishments (L2), which may in turn support manufacturing firms (L3). Consumers can be born, mature, get married, divorced, move away, and even die (change in L1) without effecting change in L2. However, the characteristics of L1 act as a bounding condition for L2 and, if change in the consumer population (L1) reaches a certain threshold—a "baby bust," for example—change in retail establishments (L2) takes place. With the arrival of the baby bust generation, perhaps fewer child-oriented goods are demanded and relationships within and among the retail firms will change as employees are laid off or hired elsewhere, lines of products are no longer ordered, and so on. A possible feedback effect to L1 may be that as employees are laid off, they decide to have fewer children, later in life. A subsequent feed-forward effect would be a further drop in the demand for child-oriented goods. Change in retail firms (L2) could reach a threshold such that retail orders for child products are significantly reduced, and relationships within the manufacturing firm level (L3) are affected. Suppose many of these manufacturing firms (L3) go bankrupt. Feedback effects might include that retail firms specializing in those goods are forced to close entirely (feedback effect of L3 to L2), and consumers decide that an adequate selection of children's goods can be found only through mail-order catalogs (feedback effect to L1). This is sometimes called a positive feedback, one that continually reinforces change. In this case, the feedback continually reinforces a disaggregating change and retail firms could conceivably be displaced in the dependency hierarchy by manufacturers' direct catalog sales (which might or might not be a stable arrangement). However, positive feedbacks can also continually reinforce aggregation, as Arthur (1990) has shown in the case of Beta versus VHS in the videotape market.

Human Society and Complex, Self-Organized Adaptation

In addition to the "individual" versus "social" paradox, Bruno Latour (1991) has suggested another paradox unfolded during modernity—another in which modern distinctions are no longer producing useful results. This distinction is the one drawn between humans and the various nonhuman elements of the universe that human culture has relegated to "the environment." Here, also, is an underlying unity that presents a paradox: humans are factors in the "environment" of nonhumans just as nonhumans are factors in the human "environment." Latour maintains that the unfolding of the human/nonhuman distinction began when the task of inquiry into the universe in which we (human and nonhuman) exist was divvied up in a modern pact between "natural scientists" and "political philosophers." For Latour, to move beyond the modern, we must rescind this pact and return to the question: "What is the collective made of? What ties us [human and nonhuman] all together?" (Latour 1991:11).

To illustrate Latour's point, let me give a further example of hierarchical, adaptive self-organization—one built on a foundation provided by Freese (1988). "Human society" is capable of being described primarily in terms of the relationships between humans and changes in those relationships over time. But, as noted, humans are affected by nonhumans, just as nonhumans are affected by humans. Think of humans and their relationships as constituting Level 2 (L2). Now, think of two broad classes of nonhumans (and all the relationships within each class) as forming two other levels in a hierarchic, asymmetric, operational dependency structure. One class of nonhumans (and the relationships within that class) constitutes Level 1 (L1): those that are the most strictly nonhuman and on which humans depend for their existence, for example, weather, flora, and fauna. The second class of nonhumans (and the relationships within that class) constitutes Level 3 (L3), consisting of the products of humans/nonhuman interaction, such that the level depends on and affects humans and their relationships. This class would include human artifacts such as tools, art, houses, and machines. Much change in society, especially the short-term change that is localized within the level "society," can be explained by describing only changes in relationships between humans. However, recall the asymmetrical dependencies. To exist, humans depend on the interactions of nonhuman flora, fauna, weather, and so on. The existence of human artifacts depends on interaction of humans and nonhumans. In other words, social change cannot be truly explained without describing the coevolution of all levels (Lee 1994).

As outlined earlier, the behavior of components at each level is engendered or limited not only by interactions within that level but also by change that affects the parameters provided by higher and lower levels, since the states of levels above and below act as bounding conditions for behavior at the level "human society." Due to asymmetrical dependencies, change taking place in differing levels has correlative correspondence when certain thresholds of change are reached—the effects "propagate" over time to other levels. Chaotic dynamics can occur in bounded continuous flows or successions of discrete states in which nonlinear parameters provided by neighboring levels give rise to exponential divergence at the level we are interested in. In the above example, available raw materials (water, earth, plant life, atmosphere, etc.) represent bounding conditions for human social arrangements. These parameters are themselves related such that a change in one, beyond a certain threshold, could lead to a nonlinear effect on the others.

Some relationships between components and levels are such that changes produce aggregation and order; at the same time, other changes can produce disaggregation and disorder (cf. Kaneko 1991). In effect, the L1-L2-L3 system is in a continual state of flux between change processes that produce order and those that produce disorder. For example, at the level of society, human "technology" can effectively speed up the rate at which relationships between components are changing, producing disaggregation and disorder. However, human ideologies that allocate the rights to and benefits of technology tend to stabilize and sustain, over time, certain types of relationships, effectively reducing operational dimensionality, producing aggregation and order (Lee 1994).

Conclusion

Let's return to Latour's (1991) question: what ties all of us—human and nonhuman—together? The task of describing the interaction of individual human and nonhumans in a society and a universe that alters and is altered by each is an enormous undertaking and might indeed be called "grand theory." But nonmodern grand theory will not depend solely on descriptions of coupled, uncoupled, or loosely coupled macroscopic orders; its models will include terms that describe local interactions. However, as we have seen, while local levels may be "nearly decomposable," they do not constitute closed systems. Local interactions are seldom thoroughly insulated from macroscopic feedback, no matter how loosely coupled. And, even if completely "uncoupled" from other social structures, human society is still bounded by other complex interactions. For example, even if the most insular "local culture" were able to continue an isolated existence in today's world, change in that local society could not be fully explained without describing its coevolutionary change with local nonhuman flora, fauna, and artifacts.

This undertaking of describing the coevolution of human and nonhuman individuals and the macroscopic orders that both facilitate and constrain local relationships will require that we make use of all available languages in our descriptions. Note the difficulty I have had in describing, in the vocabulary and syntax of natural language, the concepts of complex self-organization. The formal vocabulary and syntax of mathematics yield much more precise descriptions. But, as postmodernists remind us, while mathematical equations may be more precise, they may not fully capture the contingencies and possibilities extant at local levels.

For example, why does narrative explanation offer the best description of the interpersonal signaling and interpreting that takes place as humans interact in microcontexts? Is it perhaps because mathematics is not a very good language to use in describing the ideas, values, and ideologies that are transmitted during interpersonal interchange? It would not only be difficult but probably of questionable import to encode numerous local instances of interpersonal signaling and interpreting into continuous or even uniform discrete data points (cf. Freese 1988). Thus, we will likely never demonstrate patterns of "chaos" in interpersonal signaling and interpreting, though this does not mean that they do not exist. Complexity theory (e.g., Baier and Klein 1991; Morrison 1990) tells us that local levels are where "chance" and "opportunity" are most likely to make an appearance, operating in a stochastic fashion. Furthermore, self-organization theory tells us that "threshold" effects of these local-level events produce change in its bounding conditions for higher-order levels and are important to understanding change at those levels. Additionally, the effects of higher-order feedbacks should be observable at the local level, with implications to subsequent feed-forward effects. Should feedback effects be deterministic rather than probabilistic, as theory suggests, this has importance to many areas of social science—studies of policy issues, for example. Since we cannot ignore local events in explicating social dynamics, local events must be explained using the languages best suited to describe them.

Why do sociometric studies seem to offer such good descriptions of social communication? Is it because such studies can ignore the meaning content of signals, concentrating, instead, on the coherence of the signal and the connectors between interacting components? Why is it that, to date, only historical-comparative studies seem to capture the "big picture" of change in macroscopic social organization? Is it because we lack theories to identify essential relationships that need to be tracked at that level as well as the protocols necessary to gather standardized, consistent data about the essential components of those relationships?

Advantageously (but not coincidentally), the underlying principles of theories of complex, self-organized adaptation lead to a conclusion that a variety of languages and methods are actually necessary if we wish to produce an ongoing description of differing relationships that behave quite differently at differing levels. In other words, detailed descriptions must use differing languages and methods of analysis to be consistent with the differences in operational behavior at these levels. As one moves up the operational hierarchy, mathematical chaos theory might yield valuable descriptions of social dynamics. Lack of adequate data is always a problem in modeling social process, but a better understanding of complexity and the applicability of mathematical chaos theory to social dynamics is helpful to determining the types of data that may need to be generated. In the meantime, more fully developed nonmodern, theoretical models of society as complex, self-organizing, and adaptive can afford a more consistent interpretation of data that are gathered through widely divergent existing methods and of the descriptions given in differing methodological languages.

Have we learned the lessons of modernity and postmodernity? Can we leave behind the unfolding of the modern paradox and move toward nonmodern social theory? In developing such theory, can we make use of both narrative prose and mathematics to describe a world in which individual human and nonhuman interaction events cumulate through linear and nonlinear, local and global, probabilistic and deterministic processes? Will we come to recognize "the false face of modernity's divided and multiplied natures," becoming able to "think the reality of the world as it is" and better "describe society in society"? If we answer yes to such questions, we can begin movement toward a "nonmodern era" in social theory—one that has neither absolutism nor nihilism as its most likely outcome.

Note

1. This can be calculated using a generalizable formula for entropy, such as the Kolmogorov-Sinai equation used by Nicolis (1986) and Kaneko (1991), and can be expressed as transitional probabilities in a tree diagram and, further, as Markov and semi-Markov chains (Nicolis 1986:42-45) or a coupled map lattice (Kaneko 1991) that models the distribution of states. There is much discussion about the appropriateness of entropy as a measurement in "thermodynamic" versus "informational" systems. However, if one does not claim an invariant systemwide property of thermodynamic conservation (although this property may hold at certain levels), one can accept a more generalizable interpretation of entropy as a measure of the probability of obtaining x macrostate given n microstates. More in-depth discussion of this argument can be found in Bailey (1990b); Dyke (1992); and Weber, Depew, and Smith (1988).

3

The Persistence
of "Emergence"

Kevin Mihata

When things get together, there then arises
something that was not there before, and that
character is something that cannot be stated in terms
of the elements which go to make up the combination.
It remains to be seen in what sense we can now
` *characterize that which has so emerged.*
(Mead 1938:641)

Arthur E. Murphy opens G. H. Mead's *The Philosophy of the Present* (1932) by reminding readers that the concepts "process" and "emergence" have been persistent themes in social thought. We have long known that the world is not nearly the simplistic place we often make it out to be in our theories. Quite the contrary, it is intrinsically dynamic and multidimensional—and concepts like emergence are a way of conceptualizing this complexity. Mead and his contemporaries—for whom, according to Murphy, emergence was a

AUTHOR'S NOTE: I gratefully acknowledge the constructive comments and helpful discussion of Mary Lee, Gary Hamilton, Howard Stine, Art Nishimura, and two anonymous reviewers.

catchword—were neither the first nor the last to address this complexity. These and other attempts to integrate complexity into sociological theory parallel recent consideration of emergence in the natural and physical sciences. While the application of concepts from the "new sciences" of chaos and complexity to sociology is by no means simple, this new research can lend insight into some long-standing questions in sociological theory.

Emergence: Old and New

Conceptualizations of Emergence

The concept of emergence is most often used today to refer to the process by which patterns or global-level structures arise from interactive local-level processes. This "structure" or "pattern" cannot be understood or predicted from the behavior or properties of the component units alone. This is not a new idea. Mead, for example, notes that water, when broken down into oxygen and hydrogen, loses the character of the combination of the two: one cannot quench thirst or put out a fire with oxygen and hydrogen. In the doctrine of emergence, the combination of elements with one another brings with it something that was not there before (Mead 1932:641).

Contemporary complexity theorists focus on how global structure arises not just from local interaction but from interaction based on relatively simple rules. A flock of birds exhibits a uniform behavior usually associated with central coordination. This collective behavior results from individual birds free to "act" but following simple "flocking" rules (e.g., stay close to surrounding birds but not too close). Yet the rules do not, in themselves, predict flock behavior; the exact form of the structure, the flock, is neither entirely random nor predictable.[1] In this sense, complexity theory addresses emergence as a problem of scale, its "subject" consisting of a single layer of component units, their interaction routines, and their patterns of behavior (cf. Cohen and Stewart 1994; Cowan, Pines, and Meltzer 1994; Casti 1994).

Nagel (1979:374) notes that early theorists were also interested in "emergent evolution," emphasizing the emergence of novel structures or properties; qualities, structures, and modes of behavior may appear "the like of which has never been previously manifested elsewhere."[2] Contemporary complexity theory (and the overlapping but separate theories of chaos and self-organization) reflects this interest in its focus on complex adaptive systems. Complex adaptation is characterized not only by a high degree of interaction among component parts but also by the way that the particular nature of this interaction—the way that the system is organized—generates outcomes not linearly related to initial conditions. Whereas linear organization is generally predictable in its conse-quences, emergence is characterized by a nonlinear mode of organization that can generate nonobvious or surprising consequences (Bechtel and Richardson 1992:266). Thus, emergence concerns not only relationships among parts of a "whole" but also the possibility of new levels emerging over "evolutionary" time and the nonlinear relationships between qualities or properties at different levels. Complex systems are not only nonlinear but also adaptive.

"Historical Facets" of Emergence

In a review of the "historical facets" of emergence, Stephan (1992) distin-guishes several variations of emergence, including emergence as nonadditivity, novelty, nonpredictability, and nondeducibility. Nonadditivity is largely implicit in the others, so I briefly discuss the remaining three below.

Novelty

Emergence implies the appearance of something new, but defining "new" remains problematic. Crutchfield (1994) argues that there is always some ad hoc quality to the recognition of new "patterns" or "organization" in a sys-tem. While such patterns may merit consideration in their own right, the onto-logical validity of a perceived novelty remains unclear. Because patterns must be "recognized" by the observer, any observed structure or patterns may be an artifact of the research question; other patterns may go unnoticed for the same reason. As a system changes over time, new structure may or may not be "new" or novel in the evolutionary sense. For example, new patterns of income distri-bution arising over time in a capitalist society, while substantively significant to social scientists, do not necessarily indicate evolution of the intrinsic properties of capitalism. Or perhaps they do—that is an empirical question. Pattern for-mation alone does not necessarily indicate evolution.

How, then, can we understand qualitative change in the intrinsic properties of the system over time? According to Crutchfield (1994:518-519), this requires a somewhat "deeper" notion of emergence. "Intrinsic emergence" directs atten-tion to the evolutionary effects of emergence on the system itself. In a complex adaptive system, patterns of intrinsic emergence "take on their 'newness' with respect to other structures in the underlying system"—hence the emphasis on complex adaptive systems. While pattern change may be a universal property of a system, intrinsic emergence refers to novel properties that emerge and sub-sequently influence future evolution into an entirely new "type" of system (though neither the type nor the dynamics are predictable). In short, "the system itself capitalizes on patterns that appear."

Thus, as Nagel (1979:378) puts it, "Perhaps the most intriguing suggestion in the doctrine of emergent evolution is that the 'laws of nature' may themselves change, and that novel patterns of dependence between events are manifested during different cosmic epochs." Emergent structure is not only an outcome but may also influence future events, making possible the evolution of qualitatively different kinds of systems. This can occur both through the influence of emergent phenomena on the parts, such as the effect of culture on individuals, and through the emergence of entirely new dynamics within the system.[3] The evolution of human culture, for instance, makes possible new technologies (in the broadest sense), creating in turn new dynamics within human culture.

Nonpredictability and Nondeducibility

The behavior of complex systems is often unpredictable in the straightforward sense that we cannot anticipate the future state of a system given knowledge of initial conditions. This may occur because the system is chaotic (i.e., characterized by deterministic chaos), for example, in weather forecasting. While a hurricane demonstrates emergent features (and in this way may be relevant to complexity theory), hurricane behavior and prediction are more accurately the subject of chaos theory.[4] Short-term prediction may be possible—for example, we can easily predict the weather minutes ahead, but not months ahead—perhaps even in human systems (cf. Saperstein 1995 and later in this volume).

Although chaos and complexity theories overlap, the problem of prediction that derives directly from emergence is somewhat different. In the case of emergence, while it is often said that properties of higher levels of organization "are not predictable from properties found at 'lower levels' " (Nagel 1979:367), this kind of prediction is better described as logical deduction. Deducibility refers to the ability to logically deduce laws or rules describing macroproperties of a system from laws or rules that produce the properties of its microparts (Stephan 1992). Emergent properties at one level cannot be deduced from properties of parts at lower levels.

Darley invokes a similar image of emergence from a "computational" viewpoint, defining emergent phenomena as those for which "the amount of computation necessary for prediction from an optimal set of rules . . . can never improve upon the amount of computation necessary to simulate the system directly from our knowledge of the rules of its interactions" (1994:412). Here lack of prediction derives from the absence of an algorithmic "shortcut" or set of equations to which the system can be reduced (i.e., a set of rules from which behavior can be deduced). There is no shorthand representation of the system; simulation trials constitute the optimal computational solution to prediction.

Nonpredictability and nondeducibility are inherent properties of some systems—not simply a function of randomness or error in conceptualization or measurement.

The Paradox of Emergence

The Persistence of Emergence in Social Theory

Mead was by no means the first or only theorist to address problems of complexity and emergence. While emergence may no longer enjoy its former status as a catchword among social theorists, the concept perseveres in sociological theories ranging from symbolic interactionism to rational choice to social cognition.[5] Unfortunately, the problem with complexity is that it is—well, complex. It is difficult to conceptualize, much less operationalize, emergent phenomena. Thus, as intuitive and even obvious as the idea of emergence may be, it has not advanced much beyond rhetoric, metaphor, or disclaimer. If anything, the effect has been to trivialize emergence as either too obvious or trite to be theoretically useful, or too complicated to be practically useful.

Yet is there really a choice? The alternative—reductionism, wherein the universe can be reduced to an understanding of its smallest parts—ultimately renders social science insignificant if not illegitimate, as all disciplines can eventually be reduced to physics. If human behavior exhibits qualitatively unique properties that cannot be reduced to biology, much less to physics (e.g., consciousness), then emergence is intrinsic to any internally consistent epistemological and ontological framework for the study of human behavior. There can be no purely reductionist sociology, save one based on a transcendental explanation of consciousness, independent of physical reality. It is precisely emergence that justifies the study of the individual sui generis rather than as a mere collection of organs (or cells or atoms).[6]

An emergent phenomenon is therefore at once a whole but made up of parts; intuitively simple yet infinitely complex; universal in the process by which it comes into being (emergence) but specific in its particular instance. In our attempt to understand it, we are left with "the paradox of the rules giving a succinct, complete description of the system, whilst still revealing almost nothing about it" (Darley 1994:414).

The Search for New Answers

No technical (or empirical) solution, however sophisticated, can solve an underlying paradox; that is a theoretical question. Yet advances in computing power and new methods of computer simulation have enabled significant advance in our understanding of emergence. It is worth considering how the method most commonly employed to model emergence, computer simulation, might benefit sociological research.

Computer Simulation

Computer simulation has proven essential to research in complexity theory because only computers can "solve" the multiple interactions or iterations in models of complex systems. Most simulation of complex systems attempts to describe through experimentation (rather than "predict") general properties of such systems.[7] Such an approach is epitomized by research in "artificial life" (see Langton [1989, 1995] and Brooks and Maes [1994] for a variety of examples). This research, sometimes including simulated social systems (e.g., economics or game theory), has typically modeled interacting individual "agents," often adaptive and autonomous to some extent (Maes 1995).

Simulation does not replicate the empirical world, but it is more than merely hypothetical. If the rules of the system are unknown (i.e., the hypothesized rules do not correspond to the laws of "reality"), the simulation will diverge from reality. To the extent that the rules are universal, however (and the implementation of those rules correct), so too must the outcome be universal. In some cases, when our knowledge of the rules is relatively good (e.g., weather forecasting), simulation may constitute a practical empirical approximation (i.e., simple prediction) at a given level of precision (a few days) for a given research question (What's the weather going to be like?). Although the same cannot be said for prediction of social systems, simulation can help clarify how such systems work.

Simulation in Sociology

There have been several recent applications of computer simulation to sociological research (e.g., Hanneman, Collins, and Mordt 1995; Hanneman 1987, 1995),[8] and simulation also has a more established history in other disciplines (e.g., game theory, economics, evolutionary ecology) where established assumptions of rationality can be used as system rules.[9] Again, rather than prediction, simulation is employed to study the emergent implications of a set of rules, or to illuminate general properties of systems. For example, computer simulation of rice farming practices in Bali has shown not only the emergence of structure over time consistent with traditional practices but also that such structure is more efficient than modern (i.e., Green Revolution) practices (Lansing and Kremer 1995).

Simulation by no means obviates other techniques, least of all basic empirical research. Much remains unknown about social systems at virtually every level. In many cases, we simply may not know enough to produce a useful simulation even for heuristic purposes. But computer simulation makes possible new kinds of knowledge about complex systems—and possibly, new explanations for emergents that we have been able, to this point, only to intuit.

Conclusions

The Paradox Reconsidered

Emergence is not an isolated or esoteric problem. Consider, for example, that as fundamental as culture is to social science, there is surprisingly little consensus on its definition and even less on how it works. Yet from the perspective of emergence, the long-standing difficulty of defining, measuring, and linking culture to behavior should not be surprising. No emergent phenomenon can be defined along a single dimension or set of dimensions (e.g., culture as beliefs or values); such an approximation sacrifices its emergent character. No emergent phenomenon can be "measured" or otherwise operationalized at (reduced to) lower levels. Perhaps most critically, no emergent phenomenon is causally linked in any simple way to its individual parts—that is, after all, the nature of emergence.

Instead, what we describe most often as culture is an emergent pattern existing on a separate level of organization and abstraction from the individuals, organizations, beliefs, practices, or cultural objects that constitute it. Culture emerges from the simultaneous interaction of subunits creating meaning (individuals, organizations, etc.). At the same time, it also emerges in each individual, through socialization, experience, and interaction. Thus, culture is emergent not only within each level of analysis but also across multiple levels. It is facile to look for a simple causal relationship between abstract emergent culture and the empirical behavior of individuals—and equally facile to deny the existence of culture, or other emergent phenomena, on such grounds. Ironically, the paradox of emergence comes in part from reductionism itself: the application of reductionist questions to phenomena that cannot be explained by reductionism, creating questions that are inherently unanswerable.

New Answers, New Questions

Combining the relativity of "structure" across scale with emergent evolution produces a model that is dynamic, process oriented, and evolutionary (thus contingent and "unpredictable"). But emergentism is neither "pseudo-science" nor "anti-science" and—notably—does not preclude the utility of reductionist (or holistic) approaches. Instead, it reflects a "middle position" that "allows for systems in which the parts do make distinctive contributions, but in which the way the parts are put together . . . leads to unexpected behaviors of the system as a whole" (Bechtel and Richardson 1992:266).

The problem with reductionism is that it simply cannot explain everything. The assumption has always been that our lack of understanding of complexity derives from inadequate or incomplete theories—that our epistemology and ontology were correct, but our theories were wrong. In retrospect, that assumption is little more than a leap of faith. The question of emergence has persisted not because it is a useful metaphor, but because it is an empirical reality.

We can, as do Cohen and Stewart (1994:442), freely admit that we do not know exactly what a science of emergence would look like. Yet this does not obviate the need for such a project. As they emphasize, "We must put the dynamics back" into theories, focusing on the emergent "features." What is needed is "a theory of features, an understanding of how the geographies of spaces of the possible conspire to create new patterns and combined dynamics."[10] This returns full circle to the concept of emergent evolution and the "process" prototypes found in Mead and other early sociological theories: a qualitative approach to understanding complexity emphasizing dynamic process. Mathematics, computer science, and physics thus confirm the intuition long-held by philosophers and social theorists.

Notes

1. This is an often-cited example and was one of the first simulations of complex behavior. See Reynolds (1987).

2. The emergence of novelty over time links theories of complexity and self-organization. Self-organization refers to the process by which microlevel units "self-organize" into macrolevel structures, that is, without external "cause." Thus, self-organization produces emergent structure. It is particularly important to fields such as evolutionary biology (e.g., Kauffman 1993), where the question of origins is of primary importance.

3. The process by which a global-level, emergent phenomenon affects its constituent parts has been called "downward causation" and is the subject of debate among philosophers of science. That debate is outside the scope of this chapter, although it is worth noting that most sociologists would accept some degree of influence of the macro on the microlevel, whether it be strictly "causal" or less strongly, "constraining." It suffices here to note that the evolution of the system over time may make possible new kinds of interrelationships and hence, new causal relationships, at both the global and local levels. See Beckermann, Flohr, and Kim (1992) for further discussion.

4. In mathematically deterministic chaos, a set of nonlinear equations has indeterministic results although each equation is deterministically solvable given specific initial conditions. Since no measurement can be infinitely precise, over repeated iterations, results can approach effective randomness due to the nonlinearity of effects.

5. See, for example, Lal (1995) for an overview of symbolic interactionism, Turner et al. (1994) on social categorization, West and Zimmerman (1987) and West and Fenstermaker (1995) on gender as "an emergent property of social situations," and Coleman (1986, 1990) and Blau (1964) for a diverse range of examples.

6. Emergence is more accurately a middle ground between reductionism and holism (cf. Bechtel and Richardson 1992).

7. Darley notes that a "true emergent phenomenon is one for which the optimal means of prediction is simulation" (1994:412). If emergent phenomena are irreducible, there can be no predictive shortcut, even with ideal knowledge of initial conditions. So although not predictive in the simple sense, simulation is at least as accurate as any reductionist approximation.

8. For some recent sociological applications of simulation deriving from game theory, see also three articles in *American Sociological Review*, vol. 61, no. 2 (1996). Others are found in Langton (1989). See also a special issue on computer simulation and sociological theory in *Sociological Perspectives*, vol. 38, no. 4 (1995), edited by Robert Hanneman.

9. The microlevel rules need not be rational, of course. In fact, sociological theory offers many alternative sets of rules: rewards, motivations, social roles, schemas, situations, identities, or positions in the social structure. The particular rules are independent of simulation per se.

10. Cohen and Stewart extend their discussion to "complicity," the occurrence of the same emergent feature arising in different systems (i.e., systems with different rules). This shifts emphasis from the "internal" rules governing parts of the whole to meta-level rules outside the whole influencing how it is formed by those parts. Indeed, complexity theory covers only a limited part of emergence; "complicity isn't even in the picture" (1994:442). A full discussion of complicity, and the implications therein, remains unfortunately beyond the scope of this chapter.

4

Chaos and Complexity
Necessary Myths

Kurt W. Back

In this chapter, chaos and complexity theory in sociology are discussed as part of a series of new ideas and techniques that appear in the social sciences and are greeted with varying degrees of enthusiasm and dismay. This series can be traced back to gestalt and field theory, continuing through sociometry, information theory, game theory, catastrophe theory, and fuzzy sets to the current impact of chaos and complexity theories. I shall treat these events as phenomena that are objects for sociological analysis. From this point of view they appear as myths in the sense in which anthropological theorists have used the term, which is not pejorative, but as an essential element in the cohesion and endurance of a culture, in this case Western science. This analysis can help in understanding the nature of social science and of its development.

The Nature of Myths in Science

Social groupings are held together by some implicitly accepted principles and rules that are not always stated in so many words, but provide nonetheless standards of ideas and action for members of the group. These standards, norms, social representations (Farr and Moscovici 1984), noumenal rules (Laslett 1989), or, in the context of science, paradigms (Kuhn 1962) form the basis for the cohesion of the society and are necessary for its smooth functioning. However, these representations do not conform completely to common experience; they are schemata, abstractions, simplifications. There is a world beyond the norms of society, and the pictures given by the social representations clash with personal experience. Functioning societies must have mechanisms to deal with this discrepancy.

Myths are one way of dealing with this tension. Myths or their equivalents occur in virtually all associations; they seem to be a condition of societal persistence. While there are many conflicting opinions about the origins and transformations of particular myths, there are some common traits of all myths about which we find widespread agreement. Myths are stories current in a society; they are widely accepted although they are not taken as literal truth (Lévi-Strauss 1958). They are elaborations of historical events, natural phenomena, common human experiences, or traditional behavior that form the heritage of a society. Their popularity rests on their function of making troubling inconsistencies acceptable by these stories about the origin of features of societies, or by a larger scheme in which the inconsistencies vanish, or by reference to the future where all the vexing problems will be solved. In this way they can validate norms, actions, and social arrangements that are inconsistent, but must be reconciled to introduce order into the worldview of the members of these communities. In the development of these myths, new solutions are introduced and judged in the society. They resonate with personal experience and have salutary effects on the society; this can explain their long persistence. Myths are seen neither as truth nor as pure inventions. They are pleasant hypotheses; they could and should be true.

The community of science can be seen as a special culture. The norms of this culture were developed during the scientific revolution, superseding the medieval culture that had based its authority on revelation and tradition and the myths thus propagated. Science based its authority on experiment and observation, but it needed something to counteract extreme raw empiricism. I argue that this nonempirical component is the role of mathematics as the ultimate source of authority. The analysis and presentation of facts derived from observation uses mathematical techniques as far as possible. Statements become acceptable only when they are couched in mathematical language and give results in numbers and formulas. New areas of knowledge are recognized when they can present their claims in mathematical form.

However, mathematics is not just a convenient way of representation. It may represent an ultimate reality, as has been claimed since Plato. Rom Harré (1965), among others, has claimed that science has taken the Platonic path of judging truth by abstract forms, not Aristotle's of classifying empirical data. Current philosophers of science see in mathematics a world in itself; Karl Popper (Popper and Eccles 1977) calls it world 3, not observable by perception, but not subjective either. The French philosopher Michel Serres (1993) calls geometry the one kind of absolute truth that cannot be deconstructed. Thus, mathematics forms an authority for scientists, a myth of perfection.

The mainstream development of mathematics from the seventeenth century on was influenced heavily by the needs of the rising sciences led by the model introduced by Isaac Newton; adherence to his rules and the mathematics based on them became the cachet of acceptable science. The fundamental rule of procedure is to analyze first, synthesize later (the analytic-synthetic model); the standard mathematics relies on arithmetic, algebra, and real and complex analysis, exploring more and more deeply the riddle of continuity of the number system.

The mathematical formulation can be stated as follows: any situation can be expressed through numbers and the number system can be represented by a continuous line that is infinitely divisible. Changes can be expressed by a functional relationship between these numbers. Thus, if we know all the numbers and their functional relations, we can derive any sequence of numbers (the dependent variables) from sequences of other numbers (the independent variables). The procedures of science based on this mathematical perspective assume that we can assign numbers to any state of affairs, that ever-increasing accuracy in measurement is possible and will lead to better theories, and that we can handle the requisite number of variables. Any state of affairs that cannot be handled in this way must either be transformed into a manageable form or is outside the purview of science.

The resulting picture shows a world of regular changes, functioning like a mechanical machine, giving intellectual support to the rise of technology and industry. Correspondingly, this ideal type of science was attacked because it justifies machine civilization in its ideological and social consequences. Opponents suggested an array of alternatives, from abandonment of cold reason for intuition to piecemeal alterations of the basic model (Cunningham and Jardine 1990; Harrington 1996; Back 1997, 1998).

Social Science and Mathematics: Statistics as the Norm

The implications of this so-called Newtonian model became more problematic as it was applied to the new biological, psychological, and social sciences, such as physiology, experimental psychology, and political economy, where the assumptions of this paradigm are less justified. The data in these sciences are difficult to isolate because of their complex interrelations; this throws grave doubts on the validity of isolated, simplified, crucial experiments as well as the abstraction of functional laws from observation (as had been possible, for instance, in the study of planetary motions); the units, such as cells, individuals, and groups, are not infinitely divisible, preventing the use of the elegance of the calculus.

Social scientists sought rescue in probabilistic models and developed the science of statistics (Krüger, Daston, and Heidelberger 1990; Stigler 1986). Probability, originally describing the bases of reasonable judgment, became an aspect of the laws of nature; the normal distribution around a mean that occurred in so many conditions was seen as part of the living and social world (hence the name of this distribution). Biological and social laws could then be divided into these laws themselves, corresponding to the laws of the physical sciences and the distributional aspects subject to the laws of statistics (Daston 1990). Moreover, experimental data included measurement and observation errors subject to the same probability laws, and the same model applies to the work of all sciences.

The techniques of statistics tend to obliterate the distinction between continuity and discontinuous units: data smoothing and estimation of simple curves through least error methods produce simple continuous data from essentially discrete data. The theory of sampling shows that the observed data can be seen as points in a continuous universe. Social scientists developed impressive mathematical techniques to investigate and apply the nature of the probabilistic component of their data, sometimes to the neglect of their substantive meaning. Counting, probability theory, and statistics produced remarkable insights and understanding and guided social science to respectability.

The Mathematical Myths

The picture presented by conventional mathematical and statistical methods clashes with immediate experience of the physical and social world. This clash with commonsense experience is more vivid in the human sciences because they reflexively include the scientist, at least in part. Subjective aspects intrude themselves even into abstract discussion, and this discrepancy becomes a threat to the status of science but particularly to the human and social sciences. This threat encouraged some rebels in these sciences to abandon the scientific paradigm altogether and to advocate a more humanistic approach (Coser 1975).

The main discrepancies between model and experience in the sciences are the following:

1. Simple elementary particles and traits are transformed into the complex structures and experiences of the experienced world. We experience the existence of complex wholes, but can distinguish the parts. In particular, we are aware of ourselves as individuals, but we also experience the groups to which we belong; we can call this the paradox of accumulation.

2. The model incorporates simple, smooth relationships; experience shows the world as consisting of irregular, jagged boundaries, and many instances of discontinuity. In fact, sudden changes in individual lives as well as history are exactly the important events that we want to study; this is the paradox of discontinuity.

3. The units and concepts are not as clear in actual experiences as are needed for the traditional scientific model. In fact, scientific theory demands precise definition and elimination of any connotative meaning. This, again, is an artificial, though necessary, abstraction from common experience; this is a problem of misplaced accuracy.

A culture will defend itself against such threats to its basic principles by several means; creating myths is one of these. Myths try to alleviate the strains, explaining them as necessary or temporary inconveniences. New mathematical techniques fulfill such a function for the culture of science by giving partial remedies to obvious defects and also by promising a rosy future. In this future, a new mathematics can fit the requirements of social sciences as well as any utopian myth. However, none of these myths has been able to fulfill revolutionary promises; they seem to have given partial relief, "saving the phenomena" (Duhem [1908] 1969). This fate demonstrates the strength of the traditional model that involves the use of standard statistics consonant with a physical model.

A schematic representation of the fate of these new techniques can be sketched as follows:

1. The identification of a new mathematical procedure;
2. The application of this procedure of unresolved questions in social science;
3. A skeptical reception in the established science with claims of faddism and similar reactions;
4. The formation of a following for this mathematics;

5. The claim for a new science resolving many previous problems;
6. The diffusion into popular —nonscientific culture";
7. Reaction and disillusionment;
8. The adaptation of the technique to the established model.

The techniques that have been thus proposed deal with one or more of the troubling paradoxes. We may discern a progress in this sequence and see chaos and complexity theory as the latest member of this sequence, incorporating many of the features of the earlier experiences.

An Early Myth: Holism and Pseudo-Mathematics

The holistic approach in experimental psychology in the early parts of the century was a comprehensive attempt at a new myth, challenging mainly the paradox of accumulation. However, it suffered from its mainly rhetorical use of mathematical terms. I shall treat it in some detail, because it shows the aspirations and dangers of such an ambitious approach (Harrington 1996).

One of the first applications of the Newtonian model in the human sciences was the development of experimental psychology. Psychologists tried to distinguish themselves from the philosophers in whose departments they were based through use of the experimental method (Ash 1995). The separation could be advocated because of the physiological base; factors could be isolated in laboratories and outcomes observed, similar to the work of the physicist. The model then became a relation of simple inputs to outputs of the organism, or "stimulus-response" psychology. This model had all the advantages and disadvantages of its analytic-synthetic origin; the trust that simple relations could be added to produce more complex systems was misplaced. Reflex arcs could not be added up to whole organisms and individuals could not be added to produce social units. The immediate result was that research was restricted to topics that are compatible with the physical model; in essence this is cognition, the representation of the physical world.

This narrow view became hard to maintain; here we find a revolt in the beginning of the twentieth century claims of gestalt psychology. Gestalt psychology attacks the search for the smallest components as the basis of theory. The smallest units, such as atoms or sensations, are not the objects of experience or the world we live in. Thus, at least in human sciences, meaningful forms must be the object of study to lead to an autonomous science of psychology. These forms would not yield to a purely arithmetical analysis: their tendency to lead to good form would follow aesthetic criteria. However, here the original gestalt psychologists stopped. They did not search for appropriate techniques of analysis and rested content to expand a traditional model by adding the myth of the gestalt (Köhler 1920).

Field Theory

Offsprings of gestalt psychology went beyond the restrictions. Kurt Lewin made one early attempt to create the mathematics that could function as a utopian myth in social science. This attempt is significant because although it faced several of the problems of the mechanical model, it led to a definite tradition, that of field theory.

Lewin tried to expand this scientific approach to new aspects of human action and also to interpersonal units. For this purpose, he introduced new mathematical terminology and called his approach topological psychology and field theory (Lewin 1936, 1951; Back 1998). Both are appealing terms: topological refers to spatial relations, such as inclusion and exclusion, structure, and direction, and can be used to describe meaningful action; field theory emphasizes the whole situation over its parts and does not recognize independent units as such—thus, it addresses the importance of discontinuity. In addition, Lewin leaned toward mathematical terminology, adopting a few ideas and diagrams from geometry (Back 1992). He also favored formulas over verbal explanation, using the cachet of mathematics without its rules of procedure. Thus, his most popular formula, $B = f(P,E)$, says that behavior is a function of the person and the environment, without specifying how any of these are to be measured or what the functional relationship could be. Even more, the formula is supposed to say that P and E are interdependent and have joint effects, contrary to what it really does indicate. Like any utopian myth, field theory postpones the technical problems of mathematics for future solutions and stresses the appeal of its intuitive insights.

Field theory held out the promise of a revolution, but did not disturb the ruling mode of thought in psychology. Rather, it adapted its techniques to the dominant arithmetical analysis; especially after its migration to the United States, the statistical analysis of experiments superseded the phenomenological study of each case (Back 1992; Zukier 1989). This compromise led to the opening of new topics for experiments, for instance, studies of emotions, intentions, and interpersonal relations. The long life course of this theory cannot be explained purely on its empirical success; it presented a language that could become a myth of a promised scientific revolution. Carl-Friedrich Graumann (1992) shows that references to the main terms of Lewin's theory have declined to practically zero in psychological literature, while Lewin's own status as prominent founder of the science has rather increased. This is appropriate for a myth and its founder. It also legitimates the introduction of new myths of this kind.

New Maths and New Myths

Information Theory

Verbal communication has many functions—such as transmission of information and production of solidarity, distinction, influence, or self-expression—and is sufficiently ambiguous to serve as a myth for a new science. But communication was not restricted in its importance to social science; it was also an important problem in electrical engineering. Here the accuracy and efficiency of transmission of information, regardless of content, became a problem with the expansion of electronics. Claude Shannon (Shannon and Weaver 1949) separated these aspects of communication and developed a mathematical theory of communication that could measure purely the transmission of symbols; it became immediately very valuable for engineering problems, the construction of networks, and the assessment of different transmission systems.

Information theory looked like the first mathematical technique designed specifically for studying human interaction. The analogy with language in the interpersonal sense was apparent and even the operations of codings and decoding, of combating noise and efficient use of redundancy, made immediate sense. The restriction to purely technical transmission problems seemed to be an obstacle, but in exchange the presence of exact formulas for information, redundancy, noise, and channel efficiency gave a hope for scientific advancement in the traditional path of the natural sciences. While holism approached the particular problems of social science without a systematic use of mathematics, information theory introduced definite mathematical concepts and procedure, but left open the further applications.

However, this use of the theory followed quickly. In the monograph that announced this theory, William Weaver (Shannon and Weaver 1949) contrasted two sets of mathematical concepts—one mechanical and the other aesthetic— and assigned entropy and information to the latter category. This indicates a hope that one would here find a scientific way to represent social and humanistic topics. These general ideas spread into many realms of thought, such as art and literature (Moles 1966) and grand social theory (Bailey 1990a), but it did not humanize social research, as Shannon had hoped.

Sociometry

The challenge of representing the aggregation of individuals into larger wholes remained. A purely geometric theory tried to help here: this was sociometry, which developed into network theory. The history of this theory alternates between topical and mathematical interests. The formal description of interpersonal networks owes its origin to Jacob Moreno (1934), who wanted to expand individual psychotherapy into group therapy and in the course of this endeavor invented sociometry. He graphed attraction and aversion between people as directional links and so made appealing diagrams of group structure. He rarely went beyond pure inspection of these sociograms, essentially a subjective procedure. He claimed to have found a new paradigm for the study of the person and human relations, but the claims did not penetrate beyond a tightly knit group of followers. He was one of the few scientists who consciously tried to create a myth, as indicated by the titles of his books, *Who Shall Survive?* (1934) and *The Words of the Father* (1941).

More mathematically oriented workers in this field invented different procedures to summarize the characteristics of different configurations. The most successful system of analyzing sociograms was through the use of matrix algebra; its introduction relates to the use of topology. In fact, sociometry uses one aspect of topology, namely, the connection of two points. The appealing graphical representation of sociometry and topological psychology becomes more abstract but algebraically more useful through its analogy to matrix algebra (Festinger 1949; Luce and Perry 1949). Different graphs can be compared and types of graphs determined through exactly defined manipulations, contributing to a mathematics of discrete units. Again the new paradigm became a mathematical technique, designed to deal with topics of interest to the social and behavioral scientist but stopping at the description of these networks. In current usage the term "sociometry" is seldom found, while "network analysis" is more popular; this is an indication of how Moreno's messianic claim to founding a new science of interpersonal aggregates is now abandoned.

Game Theory

The development of network analysis proves the limits of this purely structural approach. Even the introduction of "networking" into common language, as a way of working with others without any particular affect, shows a lack of dynamics. The mathematics of dynamic relations started with the invention of game theory by von Neumann and Morgenstern (1947). They introduced intentions of individuals, not merely as nondescript points in a social relation but as rationally motivated actors. In the model of game theory, the individuals—players—want to maximize their gains or at least to minimize losses. Thus, it becomes a good model for studying how people should act if they are perfectly rational and have complete knowledge, and if we can measure the probabilities of success and the values of expected outcomes (Weintraub 1992). Thus, game theory does not represent actual behavior but a standard against which we can measure actual events.

Game theory made an additional step in leaving behind the traditional model. It introduced a way of mastering discrete dependent variables, namely, choices, and thus demonstrating rules for dealing with broad categories of behavior, the same way in which human decisions are made. Although the theory only shows how people would act if they were rational, it gave the hope that here was a step in adapting mathematics to actual human behavior.

The techniques that I have discussed up to now start from simple models of units of individual behavior and progress toward realistic, but complicated, interpersonal situations. More recently, scientists have introduced mathematical techniques that start closer to the concerns of social scientists and derive their concepts from their needs.

Catastrophe Theory

The first theory deals with a condition that is often neglected by standard scientific procedures, namely, the rare but significant occurrence of abrupt changes (Back 1992). Catastrophe theory attacks directly the paradigm of continuity and infinite divisibility, concentrating instead on discontinuity, the regions that are exceptional in the general theory of mathematical analysis. These points are especially important in dealing with human events; history deals with revolutions and decisive wars, sociology stresses social change over social stability, action is distinguished by irrevocable choice (Poston and Stewart 1978). Catastrophe theory develops a model to demonstrate the conditions under which these rare situations occur, classifying them into a small number of basic types depending on the independent (control) variables.

We can note distinctive properties in this theory: it does not pretend to give exact measurements or lead to exact predictions and it is strictly qualitative, classifying certain shapes according to topological properties (Thom 1975; Zeeman 1977). This work transcends the conventional model of change by showing that different regions can have distinctive properties and that concentration on these properties can give valuable insights without numerical analysis. The theory specifies conditions under which small changes in independent variables can have immense effects. Here it takes a new look at the concerns of gestalt psychology and especially Lewinian field theory in the light of modern mathematics (Back 1992; Thom 1983:87).

The introduction of catastrophe theory excited popular imagination and was disseminated in the general press. Exaggerated hopes were quickly deflated in attacks from two directions: one could argue that it lacked mathematical foundations and also that its statements about abrupt change just confirmed general knowledge (Sussman and Zahler 1978). While the theory flourished in some physical fields, such as geology, it has become more of a curiosity in the social sciences. It has been applied to diverse special conditions, such as war policy (Isnard and Zeeman 1976), revolutions (Zeeman 1979), dynamics of curriculum change (Thompson 1979), prediction and control of prison riots (Zeeman et al. 1976), and changes in settlement patterns (Renfrew and Poston 1979), but has not been accepted as a possible alternative to mainstream model, or even as a supplement.

Fuzzy Sets

However, catastrophe theory justified mathematical use of qualitative distinctions, undermining traditional statistical procedures. Another new theory, fuzzy set theory, introduces the everyday use of language into a rigorous system. It starts with the proposition that membership in a set is not an all-or-none proposition but a question of degree (Kaufmann 1975). This degree of membership is not strictly an arithmetic property; one can use qualifiers like "quite," "a little," or "very," although it is often denoted by numbers. One can compare two individuals by more or less membership in a set, but not by the size of the difference. Even with this rough differentiation, one can develop a new kind of logic and algebra that effectively describes actual decision processes or linguistic meaning (Zadeh 1975).

If one takes this technique seriously, it revolutionizes the use of mathematics in social science, but one has to think differently and admit limits of refinement and accuracy to deal quite realistically with the actual situation (McNeill and Freiberger 1993; Kosko 1993). Strictly speaking, the use of even simple statistical measures, such as the mean, is eliminated; the results avoid spurious accuracy, but stay in natural units, just as actual human thought processes do. They are reached by a strict procedure within these limits.

Fuzzy logic has shown itself to be valuable in technical and engineering applications. In many of them, such as thermostats, television, and photography, its invocation has a powerful appeal in advertising. As a technique in social science, however, it seems too radical a deviation from the traditional (Newtonian) model of science. In applications here, social analysts have pulled back from abandoning the use of arithmetic and analysis of real variables. They have fallen back on more powerful numerical procedures, giving up realism for computational elegance (Woodbury and Manton 1982). The paradoxes of accuracy and continuity in human sciences have yet to be faced.

Complexity and Chaos

Chaos theory and its associated ideas seem to incorporate the ideas that are the residues of previous attempts at holistic theory (Coveney and Highfield

1995), selecting and integrating the main features of the other techniques. It starts with the immediate experience of a chaotic-looking world and of the complex structures that constitute it. It also follows the general human desire to find some order in it, if any exists (and perhaps to impose some, if none exists). There are limits in understanding this world beyond which analysis cannot go. Chaos theory accepts this predicament, but does not assume that this order will be simple in the sense of the formulas and curves of our mathematics; it strives toward a language that can mirror the world as we experience it and even some of our reactions to it, such as aesthetic pleasure. Some of the chapters in this book describe the techniques.

Complexity theory also shows a way to deal with the aggregation problem. The most important innovation here is recognition of complexity as a primary variable. The question is not how different particles form a whole system; they start that way. The task of science then becomes to describe this complex system and its changes, both empirically and mathematically. The behavior of a chaotic mathematical function is just as surprising and unpredictable as the behavior of one organism. The task of the social scientist becomes that of finding a rapprochement between description of appropriate observations and of mathematical functions. Thus, the analytic functions of traditional mathematics have been supplemented by fractal functions that mirror the actual world with its irregularities and even the imagined world of the artist (Mandelbrot 1983). This may be the aim toward which diverse myths of mathematics have been pointing.

I shall not try to predict the future course of this theory; we are in the course of its development and have reached the stage at which technical terms, such as strange attractors and fractals, have come into the common language. We should not be surprised if it follows the course of the other methods. But in this context, it looks like a step in the progression of social science, integrating the ideas of its predecessors in a new synthesis.

Conclusion

If we so desire, we can see this as a progressive accumulation of new insights that create a new mathematics appropriate for the human and social sciences. The various attempts that I have sketched here show a common dissatisfaction with the traditional statistical model and a creative succession of scientists who have challenged that model, while working within the general paradigm of a science that uses the language of mathematics for its ideal expression. The diverse new methods they have created serve as myths to overcome the gulf between the model and human experience. Chaos and complexity theory may be a step in this progression or perhaps be close to its culmination.

We must face the possibility that this task is not feasible, that mathematics is not sufficient to encompass the human and social world, and that this paradigm of science is not adequate to this task. We may then have to turn to other aspects of imagination and creativity, perhaps those that are embedded in art and literature, to create a new and adequate paradigm. The current myths in science may help us in creating this paradigm; chaos and complexity theories may turn out to be major steps in this direction.

5

Nonlinear Dynamics and the Micro-Macro Bridge

Thomas S. Smith

One of the long-standing theoretical issues in sociology is the problem of how to bridge levels of analysis—to move from accounts of the behavior of individuals to explanations of the properties of groups and social systems. Coleman (1964) first formulated this problem for social theory as an issue of theoretical reductionism, using an analogy based on what had occurred a century earlier in the field of thermodynamics. Studying the interactions of large numbers of gas molecules, scientists then working in the area of statistical mechanics had been able to synthesize Boyle's Law—a universal conditional statement characterizing the aggregate behavior of an entire system of gas molecules. If sociologists had a suitable theory of individual behavior, Coleman reasoned, they would one day be able to make equivalent theoretical advances—to produce a theory of social life in which they, too, could move across comparable levels of analysis, deducing or otherwise synthesizing the properties of groups from knowledge of the behavior of individuals. The issues involved in addressing this problem are still with us and remain at the heart of the so-called micro-macro problem in social theory.

What bothered Coleman about the social theory of the time—the 1950s and 1960s—was its implausible but convenient postulation of principles of action at the level of groups and social institutions. His favorite whipping boy was functionalism's notion that groups and institutions "behaved" so as to maintain themselves. The dangers implicit in such claims included a kind of anthropomorphism wedded to reification, a compound fallacy of which one of its chief perpetrators at the time, Talcott Parsons, was fully aware—the fallacy, as Parsons himself had put it in the 1930s, of misplaced concreteness (1937). To Coleman, what seemed to be the fallacy here was the attribution of principles of action to group-level "units of analysis." In his view, groups didn't act, individuals did, a conclusion that led him to become a vocal advocate of so-called methodological individualism, a position that never interfered with his ongoing efforts to build a suitable bridge from the analysis of individual behavior to the analysis of groups, networks, and larger social systems.

Coleman's vision for sociology subscribed to the dominant reductionistic research strategy at work elsewhere in science in the 1950s. Had he succeeded in his own bridging project, sociologists would not thereafter have found it necessary to postulate principles of action at the level of social systems, as had been the case with functionalist theories (Parsons 1951). With still further bridging, neither would they have been obliged to treat other analytically separate levels of analysis, such as cultural systems, as if they too could be characterized by still further distinct principles of action, as in the approach to cultural analysis glimpsed but never realized in the programmatic essays of Clifford Geertz (1973).

The micro-macro problem, as first formulated in Coleman's early work, provides a useful subject for introducing a number of ideas used in the essays in the volume. In particular, I propose to consider how a "solution" to part of the micro-macro problem can be derived from recent theoretical and computational work in sociology, work that closely resembles but grew up independently of research in other fields that have been centered on the study of complex adaptive systems. To many sociologists unfamiliar with this work, the study of complex systems will seem far removed from their own ongoing research, since this new area of inquiry has been dominated by cognitive scientists studying artificial life and neural networks, physicists and mathematicians modeling hitherto intractable problems such as fluid turbulence and deterministic chaos, meteorologists interested in atmospheric dynamics, cosmologists reasoning about the evolution of the universe, chemists concerned with complicated chemical reactions such as those able to account for the appearance of life, and biologists concerned with morphogenesis or with population change and evolutionary dynamics. This is an extremely heterogeneous collection of subjects. Yet the reason these diverse phenomena get grouped together as part of the new study of "complexity" suggests why knowing something about them has become pertinent to the problems of social theory.

The deep theoretical affinity of these subjects arises from the fact that understanding all of them hinges on modeling interactions—how, that is, the parts or components of systems combine, organize, and interact. Formal models of such interaction, as scientists in these areas have discovered, have a generality that transcends substantive differences separating the observed phenomena themselves. Thus, for example, studying molecular interactions in a spin glass has proved to be important in understanding the growth of neural networks. Similarly, studying linked cross-catalytic and autocatalytic reactions in chemical systems has provided formal tools for modeling the evolution of cooperative behavior in iterated Prisoner's Dilemma games. In all of these subjects, interaction is the key. For this reason, formal approaches to interaction such as those provided by game theory or population biology have become favorite tools not only of economists and other social scientists but also of researchers trying to model how diverse entities interact, from competing species in an ecosystem to species of molecules in a chemical soup.

Scientists working in these diverse areas have learned from one another. Many do not now object to being grouped together because all have benefited from revolutionary advances in the past few decades in the power of computing. All formal approaches to studying how the parts of systems interact have increasingly made use of computational strategies that would have been beyond the capacity of existing technology only a few years ago. So profound have been the changes ensuing from the increasing use of powerful computers as tools of scientific and theoretical research that the look of scientific philosophy has itself begun to change.

For most scientists, the paradigm of scientific genius up to the present time has been the solitary researcher whose sojourn with a question led to solving deep problems while working alone. Usually this has meant profound simplifications of nature—cutting up observed systems into naturally occurring parts and studying each separately, often using mathematics not requiring great computational power, typically involving linear approximations of relationships known to be nonlinear, and of necessity ignoring any more complicated interactions arising among parts or between systems. For much of the history of science, indeed, many of the real problems of understanding complex natural systems have either been ignored because they were thought to be intractable, or they have been pushed aside by reductionistic philosophies in which it was assumed that phenomena as yet not understood in simple terms merely mapped current ignorance. This is now changing, thanks mostly to the power of computing to render previously intractable problems open to investigation using computational techniques. Science has not thereby been rendered nonexperimental and phenomenological, but scientific realists now find it easier and easier to profit theoretically by looking toward computational research.

For sociologists, the meaning of this profound change in other areas of study ought to be clear: because social interaction itself has long been regarded as the foundation for social life more generally, new computational resources provide means of gaining unprecedented access to interaction's dynamics. Moreover, the same techniques have begun to make it clear that many deep philosophical issues in social research are in reality questions not only of epistemology but also of ontology. Among the most central of these questions are those concerning emergentism and reductionism, whose current analyses bear directly on the micro-macro problem. Indeed, as I will try to make clear, analyzing emergence opens up many of the problems presently giving direction to research on complex adaptive systems.

Emergentism

Complexity is the keyword. A complex adaptive system is a system in which interactions give rise dynamically to emergent phenomena that are resilient in the face of perturbations. An example would be fluid convection—the bulk torroidal movement shown by fluid molecules when heat imparted to the system of which they are part creates a (known) temperature difference between the top and bottom layers of the fluid. What defines such an emergent phenomenon is that it cannot be understood merely as an aggregative product of the entities or parts of the system but arises through their organization. Interaction often yields such structures, forms that cannot be understood through simple linear decompositions of a system into its interacting parts. The problem of studying these complex interactions has become the focus of research on complex systems—systems in which interactions among parts are marked by nonlinear dynamics.

But how ought one to decide what the appropriate interacting parts of a system are—the correct units of analysis? Implicit in Coleman's reasoning about social systems, for example, was what he took to be a self-evident assumption—namely, that individual persons were the building blocks of social life: there were social systems, and then there were the entities composing social systems, individuals. Assumptions such as this about levels of analysis and units of analysis bear directly on theory development, as philosophers of science in the past several decades have made abundantly clear. Unsurprisingly, a conclusion of their work is that research programs in a science depend on how scientists decide such basic questions—what is the system in question, what are the entities composing it, and how do the entities combine and organize to produce the system itself?

Reductive explanations of the kind that enabled statistical mechanics to synthesize Boyle's Law can arise only from first recognizing discontinuities in nature, natural breaks between levels of organization—between, in this case, the level of gas molecules and the level of the system of gases. Once levels are recognized, the task then becomes either modeling the connection between levels or figuring out bridging laws able to connect statements about regularities observed at different levels.[1]

Merely specifying levels of nature entails the recognition that parts or entities at a lower level somehow combine to produce the upper level. Especially where the properties of the parts are unlike the properties of the whole, this can be a difficult job. Without a traditional, "top-down," deductive theory of such systems, often the scientist must try only to model how the parts interact, hoping that his or her model will then show "bottom up" how the properties of the system emerge. This has been a strategy in the study of nonlinear phenomena.

Parts can produce wholes in endless ways. In the simplest cases, parts interact by cumulating—adding themselves one by one into an aggregate or a mass, like a sandpile. In nature, however, the least interesting sandpiles are those that in fact seem to be understandable as simple linear combinations of grains of sand. Even in such seemingly simple cases, we often find strange behavior that cannot be explained by models assuming only linear aggregation. As we drop grain after grain of sand onto the pile, for example, the pile gets higher and higher. Eventually, we reach a critical point after which additional particles are likely to produce periodic avalanches—cascades of sand down the side of the pile, decreasing the angle of the sides. Avalanches are not linear phenomena but catastrophes—profound discontinuities in the aggregate behavior of the pile. When avalanches occur, the simple additive model fails, and we need to consider more complex models of the behavior of the whole. (On avalanches as examples of "self-organized criticality," see Bak, Chen, and Creutz [1989] and Bak and Chen [1991].)

Failures to understand the properties of a whole in terms of the properties of its parts opens the possibility that reductionistic explanations of the kind Coleman admired will never be developed to explain such systems. This becomes increasingly likely in proportion to the degree to which the parts of a system do not combine additively—in proportion, that is, to what can be described as the degree of complexity present in the interactions and combinations of the parts. Catastrophes are extreme examples of nonlinear phenomena, but there are endless other examples throughout nature. And, indeed, what scientists in many fields have been learning in the past several decades is that such nonlinearities are intrinsic to nature's coherence—the source not only of periodic quakes, slides, turbulences, and instabilities but of order, pattern, attraction, coherence, and beauty as well.

If you want to understand nature, as Whitehead once remarked, seek simplicity but then distrust it. Nature is the more remarkable not for being additive but for being otherwise.

Anti-Antireductionism

Reaching such a conclusion should not lead to disparagements of reductionism, which as a research strategy continues to make sense when the properties of systems can in fact be understood in terms of the properties of their parts. As Wimsatt (forthcoming) has persuasively argued, working scientists ought to strive to be both reductionists and emergentists. If one takes Wimsatt's position, it is still fairly easy to see that few natural systems actually lend themselves to being fully understood reductionistically.

For example, almost nothing about social systems is suitable to being understood as an aggregative product of lower-level entities. This does not mean that forces arising at lower levels do not cause changes in individual behavior or lead to structural features of social systems. In fact, there are obvious conditions under which properties of individual behavior, social interaction, and social organization can be seen to depend on psychological and on biological activity. But even if some properties of social systems had mechanistic explanations in terms of the known behavior and interaction of parts at lower levels of analysis, it would not necessarily follow that those phenomena were not in some sense emergent. Social systems are not in any way like sandpiles, despite the fact that some features of individual and social behavior are mechanistically understandable in terms of the properties of and interactions among lower-level entities.

Nonlinear Dynamics in Social Systems

Among the most interesting implications of recent neurobiological research, for example, is the notion that attachment behavior is biologically innate. Distress signals from infants cause mothers to attach themselves to their babies, and such attachment causes the release of calming opioid peptides in the limbic structures of the brains of both mothers and infants. Attachment thus serves a biological function—arousal-modulation. A baby's distress signals—its cries and its fussing—communicate and spread its arousal into those able to perceive them, triggering innate attachment behavior.

What we see in the behavior of babies and their mothers are innate physiologically implanted forces, matters that remain active in all human beings apart from their age, sex, or biological relationship. Starting from the observation that interaction is what provides the pathway for attachment, one can thus derive several interesting consequences: (1) Under conditions of increasing arousal and distress, interaction comes under the control of this innate mechanism; (2) deeply implanted patterns in social interaction thus have their origins in biological activity; and (3) as arousal and distress spill into social interaction, interaction acquires properties that could only arise through nonlinear dynamics.

One of the first implications of these observations is that methodological individualists may have it all wrong. When it comes to specifying the basic unit of analysis appropriate to understanding the strongest forces working to create social systems, for example, nature itself speaks unequivocally. All we have to do is look at the first system of social interaction of which any human being is a part—infant-caregiver interaction. The forces at work between babies and their mothers are what everyone starts with, and they remain with us throughout life. First and perhaps foremost, the work of the innate brain-behavior connections active in attachment—the stimulation of endogenous opioids through attachment behavior—means that the same unevadable physiological forces we can observe in heroin addicts are present in everyone, though usually in less extreme degrees. Second, it means that the basic "unit of analysis" that evolution itself has built into the human condition is the incorrigible coupling of individual persons into caregiving dyads. By virtue of the fact that the innate pathway to endogenously produced opioids drives people to recapitulate caregiving—to configure themselves in social arrangements of attachment—the deepest template for all social life, and hence the basic unit of analysis appropriate to understanding the deepest forces at work in organizing social life, is dyadic interaction. Third, the proximate biological function of social interaction is arousal-modulation.

Consider what all this means from the point of view of the present chapter's concern with emergence and complex adaptive systems. The individualist perspective on social life tries to understand how a theory of the individual person can produce something we would recognize as a social system. The unit of analysis is the person. But the argument presented here says that you don't need a theory of the person to understand social life's deepest organizational form, the dyad. Dyadic dynamics arise through an innate physiological system that operates interpersonally. Biologically speaking, dyads are easier to explain than individuals—they are built into the physiological functioning of the species. Indeed, a theory of the dyad would therefore appear to be logically prior to a theory of the individual.

Whatever its specific content, such a theory would ultimately tell us that the strong forces we sometimes see at work in interaction can displace and override other forces at work in social life. The theory certainly would not claim that there are never other forces at work in interaction—indeed, it is other forces, such as those arising through culture and cognitive activity, that loosen and damp the biological dependence of the person on attachment. More in line with the way things work is that anxiety and arousal seem simply to parameterize biologically driven organization at the heart of social life. As anxiety and arousal pass beyond certain thresholds at which individual persons acting alone are no longer able to modulate them (as is always true in the case of babies), they spill into interaction, pushing it into nonlinear conditions. As this occurs, we can no longer understand social life using simple models that aggregate individuals, because it is under these conditions that social life begins to develop emergent properties—properties that arise when proximate physiological forces operating in dyadic couplings begin to produce dynamically sustained patterns and stable arrangements.

When this happens, biological forces are driving interaction. Ultimately, as this reasoning tells us, there would be no recognizable social life at all without such physiological pressures behind interaction. Plain and simple, social life is biologically constrained, a conclusion that implies that social systems themselves need to be understood as phenomena emergent from biological activity.

Curiously, individual behavior under conditions not controlled by arousal does not require this same conclusion, and a theory of the individual apart from biology would then have warrant to explain behavior. Such reasoning might seem to provide support for one of the claims sometimes present in social theory—namely, that the development of nonbiological structures like "self" enables persons to "transcend" their biological nature. It does not follow from such reasoning, however, that social life itself can be understood apart from biology. Indeed, as the present viewpoint suggests, social systems themselves are biologically driven emergent phenomena—systems whose deepest structuration arises in the service of a biological function.

Complexity

Wimsatt (forthcoming) has shown that a number of conditions must be fulfilled before we are entitled to conclude that a system is aggregative. In proportion as these conditions are not present, we find increasing nonreducibility in the system's properties. Such a conclusion would then alert us to the need to understand the properties of the system as emergent and to focus accordingly on understanding how they come into being through interaction. Viewed otherwise, such a conclusion would direct us to modeling such a system's natural complexity.

For a system to be aggregative in Wimsatt's sense, it must exhibit the following characteristics:

1. Inter-substitutability and re-arrangeability of parts
2. Size-scaling: qualitative similarity with addition or subtraction in the number of parts

3. Invariance under decomposition and reaggregation of parts
4. Minimal interactions among parts: a linearity condition in interaction (no co-operative or inhibitory interactions among parts)

Viewed as a whole, no social system can be described by these criteria. Indeed, if the argument made earlier is correct, it is in the nature of the emergence of social systems that interactions among persons acquire increasingly nonlinear properties. At best, there are small interaction neighborhoods in which the forces present among persons are so weak that interaction itself might be approximated in some linear way—a condition, following Wimsatt (forthcoming), we might call neighborhood aggregativity. Employees working side by side in a bureaucratic office might provide an example, under conditions where their interaction is minimized. But as soon as we look beyond the office to the larger organization in which they are employed, we find conditions violating the aggregativity rules. Indeed, as soon as some perturbation passed through the office itself and the employees interacted in other than minimal ways, they would become a nonaggregative system. For similar reasons, no family is nonaggregative, no emotional relationship is nonaggregative, no markets are nonaggregative, and no real organization is nonaggregative.

Wimsatt's stringent aggregativity conditions point to places where organization invariably entails emergence. Interestingly, his conditions can be understood as elaborations and extensions of the analysis originally provided in Herbert Simon's (1969) essays on the architecture of complex systems, particularly in Simon's important work on decomposable systems (Ando, Fisher, and Simon 1963).

Chaos, Self-Organization, and Globally Coupled Systems

Wimsatt's reasoning about nonaggregativity—that it is mainly produced by nonlinearity in the interaction process describing a system—is supported by research on "globally coupled chaotic systems," where investigators have now isolated several phases (coherent, ordered, partially ordered, and turbulent) through which systems move with increases in the degree of nonlinearity in the interactions of their components (Kaneko 1994). The ordered and partially ordered phases of these systems are associated with the appearance of well-known and carefully studied emergent phenomena—self-sustaining and self-organizing properties, such as fluid convection, that can be taken as models for emergence more generally.

What is ordinarily called chaos, as such studies show, has very little to do with random, stochastic fluctuations, but is the product of a deterministic process. Any bifurcation diagram showing an indefinitely extended branching process illustrates how this is possible: the apparently chaotic behavior we see associated with a "strange attractor," for example, merely represents how a system under the control of such an attractor can jump around among the virtually infinite number of deterministic branches shown in such a diagram. Some strange attractors have extremely complex fractal organization and give rise to erratic behavior that is impossible to tell apart from genuine random, stochastic chaos.

Interestingly, a process that produces deterministic chaos can also produce order. So long as the temperature differential between the top layer and the bottom layer of a heated fluid stays within a known range, for example, we can induce fluid convection, the torroidal molecular movement mentioned earlier. Heated to a higher level and pushed still further away from equilibrium, however, we can cause the fluid to pass through yet another phase transition and to boil—to display turbulent, chaotic behavior.

Convection is an example of "self-organization," spatial and temporal organization that appears when the system is pushed away from thermodynamic equilibrium into a nonequilibrium region described as "far from equilibrium." Many systems including social systems develop distinctive patterns of self-organized behavior in equivalent far-from-equilibrium conditions. In turn, many of these can be understood as "dissipative structures." All dissipative structures, such as fluid convection, depend on a metabolism, a means of building organization and pattern out of an energy source. So long as the energy is relatively constant, the metabolism sustains the pattern.

Interaction has such a dissipative metabolism, though it is more complex than convection. Interaction scavenges distress signals and hence is driven by anxiety and arousal. Without anxiety behind it, interaction is left unfueled and eventually stops. The basic anxiety scavenged by interaction is what arises in relation to the production of endogenous opioids and is not unlike the kind of anxiety one observes in a substance abuser deprived of his or her fix. As attachment yields opioids whose effects begin to decay, the brain produces physiological signals—discomfort that appears in the form of distress signals. These signals, communicated to others, then innately bring about further attachment and further opioid release. The whole system works as a dissipative structure, because interaction is being fueled by the dissipation products of the brain systems controlled through attachment. If there is no anxiety or distress, there is no interaction; if there is no heat, there is no convection current.

The Micro-Macro Problem: Some Conclusions

This chapter began with the suggestion that parts of the micro-macro problem now seem tractable when considered in relation to computational studies of the kind common in research on complex systems. What I mean by this claim is that emergent patterns within social systems that cannot be "deduced" top-down through traditional forms of deductive reasoning (or that are at least extremely difficult to deduce from existing theories) can nonetheless be computed—that is, they can be shown to emerge bottom up on the basis of simulations of social interaction.

This is not to claim that one can compute everything there is about social systems—one can't. But many of the patterns that appear in social interaction, and hence many of the structural features of social systems that arise only through social interaction, can be so computed. For example, an appropriate formal model of interaction as a coupled system translates into nonlinear mathematics of the kind used in computational work in other fields. Research summarized later in this book (Smith and Stevens 1995a, 1995b, 1996, forthcoming) shows results of simulations using these models. What these simulations show is that regular features of dyadic interaction can be computed. When the same model is generalized to simulate networks, many of the regular features of social networks can also be computed. That is, we can see these patterns and forms of organization emerge as stable solutions to the appropriate system of equations. This work has been extended in many directions, and it promises to render other structural features of organizations and networks likewise susceptible to understanding on a bottom-up basis.

Simulating large numbers of actors coupled together in a system of social interaction entails specifying local rules governing their interactions, and then using computational techniques similar to those employed to model neural networks. But even the first steps taken toward modeling social interaction's complex dynamics along these lines have produced emergent macroscopic structures. A fair fraction of the micro-macro problem in social theory thus appears to reduce to the study of how global effects arise from local dynamics in systems of interaction. This was James Coleman's intuition in the 1960s. His own simulation projects were biased by the common reductionistic research strategy of the time and framed in terms of the dominant logical positivist model of theory reduction, but they were governed by the correct intuition.

It is not clear what the limits of this research strategy ultimately will prove to be. Yet many matters that only a decade ago were thought to be analytically and computationally intractable have yielded to simulation in recent years, and many more are within reach as the power of computing increases still further. What is certain is that all social research can benefit enormously from the computational strategies even now widely used elsewhere. No subject is more likely than sociology to profit from modeling interaction's complexity. As this research grows in the years to come, concepts such as those discussed in this book are likely to become central to the way we make sense of the social world.

Note

1. Sometimes naturally occurring discontinuities in real-world settings are not at all clear to a working scientist, or they are disputed on the basis of religious and philosophical claims. (Cartesian dualism, for example, entailed recognizing essential differences of kind between material and mental phenomena, and left only the former open to scientific understanding.) Yet when recognition of natural discontinuities does lead to separating levels of analysis, the scientific project begins of understanding how the levels are related.

6

Nonlinear Dynamics, Complexity, and Public Policy
Use, Misuse, and Applicability

Euel Elliott
L. Douglas Kiel

Practitioners of public policy as well as their social scientist cousins who prowl the halls of academia are always on the lookout for new tools and technologies for both understanding what effect public policy can have on defined social phenomena and the nature and extent of the outcomes that can be achieved. The need to develop a better understanding of policy processes has become especially acute given the increased complexity and interrelatedness of issues. This understanding, coupled with the recognition that evolution is about the evolution of complexity itself (Prigogine and Stengers 1984), reinforces the need for public policy to respond to issues of and develop solutions for the challenges of increasing social complexity.

New theoretical perspectives have traditionally been the purview of those in the universities. Theoretical frameworks as diverse as systems theory, cybernetics, rational choice theory, and others have been adapted to meet the needs of both theory and practice in the realm of public policy (Etzioni 1985). Some of these approaches, such as cybernetics and systems theory, have been borrowed from mathematics and the natural sciences, and they have experienced varying degrees of success.

This chapter explores the relevance of the emerging sciences of complexity, and the attendant study of nonlinear dynamics and chaos, to social phenomena that are the objects of public policy. These new sciences originating in fields ranging from biochemistry to meteorology to computer science have appeal to the policy sciences because the sciences of complexity are inherently interdisciplinary (Lewin 1992; Waldrop 1992). One need not be a lifelong student of the policy sciences to understand that the social phenomena that generate policy problems are rarely so simply constructed as to fall only within the purview of one of the traditional social sciences of sociology, economics, or political science. Scholars have already espoused the potential of these new sciences to aid in the solution of a range of policy problems (see Dobuzinskis 1992; Kiel 1992; Gregerson and Sailer 1994; Angelides and Caiden 1994). The current state of the applications of these emergent sciences to public policy problems, however, demands an assessment of the possible uses and applications of these new sciences, but also an identification of their possible misuse. This chapter thus examines the use, applicability, and in some cases, potential misuses that chaos theory, nonlinear dynamics, and the more expansive area of the sciences of complexity may play in the development of possible solutions and policy responses to social problems.

While nonlinear dynamics offers new tools and concepts for gaining a greater understanding of social phenomena and policy problems (Dobuzinskis 1992; Kiel 1992), it also suggests limitations on the ability of policy analysts and policymakers to change the dynamics of social phenomena. This chapter discusses both the potential for improved understanding and the practical limitations that the complex dynamics of social phenomena impose on policymakers and analysts.

Complexity, Nonlinear Dynamics, and Chaos Defined

Prior to exploring the relevance of chaos and complexity to public policy, it is first necessary to present some initial definitions. The fact that the sciences of complexity are still evolving hinders the development of a generally agreed on definition of even the term "complexity." In fact, some students of complexity even argue against a unified definition in fear that succinct definition may inhibit further insight into exactly what entails complexity (Mayer-Kress 1994b).

Gell-Mann (1994) shows that complexity can be a function of the number of interactions between elements in a system. From this perspective, a system with few variables but multiple pathways of interaction would be more complex than a system with many variables but only one-way, sequential interaction. Nicolis and Prigogine (1989), for example, prefer measures of complexity based on system "behavior" rather than on any description of system interactions.

Computer scientists focus on two definitions of complexity. Algorithmic complexity concerns the length of the message (computer program) necessary to describe a system. Computational complexity, a measure of the length of the description of a system, concerns the amount of time (central processing unit time) necessary to compute the description of the system. Both of these definitions are, however, subjective since the length of the message (program size) and the speed of processing are contingent on who writes the message and the relative speed of the central processing unit.

What is generally agreed among students of complexity is that "complex" systems exhibit nonlinear behavior (Lewin 1992; Waldrop 1992; Coveney and Highfield 1995). Nonlinear behavior is often referred to as positive feedback in which internal or external changes to a system produce amplifying effects. In short, nonlinear behavior means that small changes in system variables can have disproportionate outcomes. Prigogine and Allen (1982:7) emphasize the nonlinear nature of social systems with these remarks, "Nonlinearities clearly abound in social phenomena, where a yawn, a desire for an automobile with fins, or a lifestyle can spread contagiously throughout a population." Jay W. Forrester (1987:104) reinforces this point when he notes, "We live in a highly nonlinear world." Furthermore, it is important to recognize that it is the interactions in the social realm that produce the nonlinearities that make the social realm a world of surprises (Brown 1995:140).

The study of nonlinear behavior in nonlinear systems has developed into a field of study labeled nonlinear dynamics. Scientists from a variety of fields are attempting to understand systems that reveal change (dynamics) that is disproportionate and often surprising. Over the past decade, nonlinear dynamics has developed into an interdisciplinary field that crosses the social and policy sciences (Brock, Hsieh, and LeBaron 1991; Kiel 1992; Elliott and Kiel 1996).

The study of nonlinear behavior, such as social systems, has also spawned an interest in one of the temporal behaviors nonlinear systems can generate, chaos. While nonlinear systems can over time exhibit stable behaviors or equilibria and periodic behavior such as sinusoidal waves, chaos has received the greatest attention of the behavioral regimes of nonlinear systems. Chaotic behavior is time series behavior evidenced by data points that appear random, and devoid of pattern, yet show an underlying order. This underlying order is generally shown via the graphical method of mapping lagged data points on a Cartesian plane. It is these mappings that define the attractor or order in a chaotic time series.

Chaos has received considerable attention because the seemingly random spread of data in a chaotic time series can be generated by simple deterministic algebraic equations. This means that simple dynamics can over time generate extremely complex time series behavior. This point emphasizes the connection between nonlinear dynamics, chaos, and complexity. While chaos represents complex time series behavior, it is also evident that such temporal complexity can be created by both simple and complex dynamics. We thus see that we live in a world in which both simplicity and complexity can generate increased complexity.

Chaotic behavior is also identified by the fact that data points remain within stable parameters. Data points may bounce around considerably but do not exit upper or lower bounds. During unstable periods, such as chaos, nonlinear systems are susceptible to internal or external shocks that may drive the system to new regimes of temporal behavior. This phenomenon, known as "sensitivity to initial conditions" or in the popular press as the "butterfly effect," exemplifies those instances where a small change (the flapping of a butterfly's wings) may generate disproportionate change (a tornado). Perhaps what is most interesting about systems operating in chaotic regimes is that exacting long-term prediction is impossible. Short-term prediction, however, does appear to be possible in the highly nonlinear regime of chaos (Gordon 1991).

We can now see that the study of complex social systems is confounded by the potential for nonlinear behavior and chaos. Since complex social systems are composed of multiple interactions and pathways between relevant variables, many of which are dynamic, nonlinear behavior is thus highly likely. In fact, some social scientists expect that most social phenomena are nonlinear (Brown 1995). This does not mean that these social phenomena are in constant chaos but rather that they have the potential for positive feedback and chaotic interludes.

Prediction, Control, and Public Policy

Since the time of the Enlightenment and the Newtonian revolution in physics, we in the West have developed a very specific view of the relationship between science and society. Presumably, through a scientific and, as our counterparts in the physical (particularly physics and mathematics) science fields suggest, a "deep" understanding of some phenomenon, we will attain the ability to develop predictive models of the way some phenomenon or class of phenomena will behave. In turn, by virtue of this knowledge and understanding, we can gain control over nature: that is, we can, given some set of tools, manipulate, within some set of parameters, the outcome in a manner that is consistent with some definition of the public interest.

The birth of "scientific public administration" in the 1920s was based on the assumption that a rationalized public service, structured and administered in a routinized manner, would yield certain predictable outcomes (Denhardt 1993). At about the same time, Keynesian economic theory emerged in the midst of the Depression era, and was premised on the belief that macroeconomic control via public policy was possible and desirable. Perhaps buoyed by success in World War II, the Marshall Plan, and other notable successes such as unlocking the secrets of the atom, there was a new and exalted view of the social sciences and the role of social scientists in the postwar order.

It is perhaps no accident that the work of the soon-to-become famous psychologist B. F. Skinner, whose research into operant control was popularized in *Walden Two,* or Aldous Huxley's *Brave New World,* originated in the 1930s. The possibility of achieving enormous gains for humankind, which was assumed to be almost infinitely malleable, beckoned on the horizon. As government in the twentieth century began to take on more and more responsibilities and functions, moving from the classical nineteenth-century liberal role of the "night watchman" state to the activist government of the present day, assumptions of social science knowledge leading to predictive outcomes have proliferated.

Nonlinear dynamics and the related sciences of complexity lead us to question the extent to which we may be capable of both prediction and control in social and policy systems (Casti 1990). We do not suggest that it is impossible, but that an awareness of the constraints, and even the desirability, of the control facet of normal science is called into question.

On the other hand, nonlinear dynamics and complexity studies may add to our knowledge of social dynamics. Nonlinear dynamics and complexity teach us that social evolution is produced by both deterministic historical factors and chance events that may push social phenomena to new regimes of behavior. By better understanding the confluence of chance and determinism in social system evolution, we may better learn when and how to direct policy responses.

Uses of Nonlinear Dynamics and Complexity Relevant to Public Policy

Scholars have produced a substantial body of literature explicating models that draw from nonlinear dynamics and complexity studies. The decision to use these emerging analytical tools for public policy studies requires a consideration of when it is best to use these methods. If, as we understand, most of the social realm is nonlinear and subject to complex interactions, then one is tempted to assume that nonlinear dynamics and complexity studies are appropriate for all social science and policy studies. This approach, though, would neglect the reality of what has been learned from traditional statistical studies of the social realm. Clearly, the behavioral revolution has contributed greatly to what we know about the effect of public policies and what is known about potential policy interventions.

The determination to use these new methods for policy studies can, however, be specified. These methods should be used when the analyst is aware of changing relationships between variables that are likely to generate nonlinearities or when a study involves a highly multivariate phenomenon in which multiple interactions also present the potential for nonlinear behavior.

Perhaps the most rigorous application of the methods of nonlinear dynamics to date, in the area of policy studies, are Courtney Brown's (1994, 1995) analyses of U.S. environmental policy. Methodologically, Brown uses nonlinear regression analysis. This is not to be confused with the rather simple polynomial expressions used for curvilinear regression. Brown's nonlinear least squares analysis incorporates data about individual variables, global system variables, and longitudinal data. Brown's analysis of environmental policy includes longitudinal data concerning environmental degradation, economic activity, political structure, citizen attitudes, and electoral outcomes. His research shows how political and policy choices in the United States can produce environmental damage across the globe. Most significantly, Brown's research can inform policymakers how their choices have effects far beyond even their own national borders.

Another application of nonlinear dynamics to the policy arena is Alvin Saperstein's (1996b) examination of the nonlinearities in international arms races. Saperstein has developed a series of models incorporating nonlinear interactions that show how the quid pro quo of arms escalation between enemies results in heightened tensions and the likelihood of war. The value of both Brown's and Saperstein's work is that these efforts show how the tools of nonlinear dynamics can be used to inform both national and international policy.

One of the more interesting bodies of work using the tools of complexity is Peter Allen's (1982) modeling of urban growth. Urban growth is obviously a highly complex phenomenon including a multiplicity of variables with dynamic relationships. Allen has developed a modeling approach that interjects random variables as his models evolve in time. Allen has initiated an approach to modeling that no longer searches for the one correct answer, but instead presents multiple possible outcomes that change with each iteration of the model. Allen presents a world of multiple choices and possibilities for policymakers.

An area in which nonlinear dynamics and complexity studies have been integrated in policy studies is in the field of public health. It has long been recognized that epidemics in human populations follow a logistic growth curve. In a 1989 study, Stanley used mathematical models integrating random elements to forecast the spread of AIDS in the United States. One of the unexpected results of Stanley's research was her forecast that the AIDS epidemic would soon show high rates of contagion in the teenage population. This group was originally seen as a low-risk group for AIDS. Stanley's results were verified later by Selik, Chu, and Buehler (1993), who first noted the rapid spread of AIDS among teenage women. Stanley's research shows how nonlinear methods can generate the surprises and unexpected results typical of nonlinear systems behavior. Most important, this work shows that it may be possible to anticipate unexpected outcomes with the proper analytical tools. While the gap between knowledge and action always seems to persist, such analysis may serve to better prepare policymakers for the multiple possibilities that social phenomena produce.

Misuse of Nonlinear Dynamics and Complexity in the Social Realm

Recognizing that we live in a highly nonlinear world does not mean that nonlinear dynamics and complexity studies are necessary for all policy studies. In cases where we have statistical confidence that interactions between variables are highly stable over time, traditional statistical tools are quite valuable. Many social phenomena exhibit predictable and stable properties that may have substantial payoffs for policy analysts and policymakers.

One example of such a stable phenomenon in the United States is the well-known relationship between educational attainment and income level. This relationship has already served to inform a large pool of U.S. public policies. For example, policies that encourage students to stay in school or that offer mentoring to "at risk" students are tied to the recognition that increased educational attainment at the individual level also leads to increases in national income. Similarly, at the systemic level improving education and income levels in developing countries almost invariably yields lower birthrates, which in turn may positively influence a society's per capita income or other measures of national well-being.

Other areas of national domestic policy are also well understood without the tools of nonlinear dynamics and complexity. In the budgetary arena in the United States, it is not difficult to make simple extrapolations about the ultimate fate of the Medicare or social security trust funds, if nothing is done to alleviate the budgetary pressures on these programs. While the budgetary situations for each of these programs may show occasional instability, it is possible to make statistically confident statements about budgetary prospects with sufficient precision to direct the actions of policymakers.

We can thus see that both traditional statistical or linear analysis and nonlinear dynamics and complexity analyses should be complementary rather than exclusionary. We simply do not need to throw out what we know actually works in the social and policy sciences. What nonlinear dynamics and complexity studies do contribute is an enhanced means for understanding systems with multiple interactions that often overwhelm traditional social science and policy science techniques.

Our review of the literature applying nonlinear dynamics and complexity studies to public policy does not reveal identifiable misuse of these tools. Thus, we emphasize the point that new tools and approaches often lead to a headlong migration toward these new methods without consideration of what is both lost and gained. Careful assessment as to what is already known about a particular policy area and its dynamics and interactions should serve as the guide for the decision to use or not to use these new approaches.

Applicability of Nonlinear Dynamics and Complexity to Policy Problems

Public Policy Problems and Positive Feedback

Economists, more than other social scientists, have made considerable headway in understanding nonlinear dynamics and complexity in economic systems (Anderson, Arrow, and Pines 1988; Barnett, Geweke, and Shell 1989). Economists have begun to realize that the amplification of positive feedback in economic systems requires a rethinking of economic theory. As Arthur (1990) notes, conventional economic theory, as well as systems theorists, has assumed the prevalence of negative feedback in social and organizational systems. In economics, negative feedback takes the form of diminishing returns, a concept elevated to the status of an economic law of nature.

Arthur contends that the assumption of negative feedback, and hence diminishing returns, does not adequately reflect reality. A more accurate picture of reality would allow for the fact that those stabilizing forces do not operate. If that is the case, then there is no single equilibrium point for the economy, but a multitude of potential equilibrium points.

The implications for macroeconomic policy making are substantial. Efforts to plan and predict over a medium to long run may be futile. Economic projections diverge drastically from actual outcomes. The intrusion of unexpected chance factors, when interacting with already complex dynamics in a social system, can lead to outcomes at odds with the expected rationality of market economics. To use Arthur's example, BetaMax failed not because of its inherent inferiority but because of small chance factors early in development that tilted the playing field toward VHS (Arthur 1990). Others (Mirowski 1989; Rosser 1991) have explained the dilemma that complex nonlinear systems are for the orthodox assumptions of economists and their ability to forecast macro-economic trends (also see Berry and Kim 1996).

Public Policy and Controlling Chaos

An interesting body of literature from the physical sciences has appeared founded on attempting to control the erratic and apparently random behavior of chaotic time series. This literature may have considerable relevance to policy analysts and policymakers. While it is necessary to understand that chaotic inter-ludes may not be especially common in social systems, nonlinear systems can produce other types of surprising and sometimes explosive behavior (Kiel 1992). It may be, then, that knowledge of the means of controlling erratic time series behavior may provide knowledge about altering the dynamics of known nonlinear social phenomena.

While we recognize that chaos may have functional value in natural systems, it is not the case that the rhetoric of chaos is always readily translated from natural to human systems dynamics. We simply do not know if genuine mathe-matical chaos is or would be functional in an area of social systems behavior. What if, for example, it was discovered that national crime statistics revealed high-dimensional mathematical chaos? Few intellectuals of any ideological bent would be happy with such knowledge and public policy actors would scurry to impose their unconscious Newtonian control weltanschauungs on the "prob-lem." People of action prefer a level of predictability in systems that chaos only minimally provides. Such predictability minimizes risks.

Let us reorient our thinking for a minute and assume that chaotic behavior in social systems is dysfunctional. If this were true, what resources would be available to inhibit chaos? Natural scientists have discovered three methods for controlling chaos under experimental conditions (Ott, Grebogi, and Yorke 1990; Ditto and Pecaro 1993). The approaches identified by natural scientists to control chaos include altering or minimizing system parameters, interjecting small perturbations to smooth dynamics, and altering the orbit of a system by cybernetic assessment and feedback. All of these methods have their analogs in public policy; the question for policy analysts and policymakers is whether—given the above—the implementation of such control mechanisms is either de-sirable or possible.

Imagine using the first chaos control technique to reduce the parameters of criminal behavior as evidenced in crime statistics. Policy analysts might start by identifying the historical average behavior of these statistics. A second step would likely include setting parameters for the goal of reduced crime by defining a limit of acceptable variation based on historical data. Successful public policies toward crime would then be policies that keep crime data within the chosen parameters.

This perspective toward improving a social "problem" is akin to total quality management efforts in industry founded on reducing variation in outputs. In short, the quality of the relevant public policy is measured by the amount of variation in the system to be affected. The obvious problem with such a policy approach is that it provides no information as to how to reduce the variation in the system. Neither liberal assumptions of rehabilitation nor conservative notions of punishment seem to have any real effect on crime in the United States. If crime is largely a result of demographic bubbles of high proportions of individuals in the 15- to 25-year-old age range, public policy interventions may be of little value. The politics of contemporary democratic polities are largely antagonistic to limitations on procreative activities. Policy analysts and policymakers may thus know a social phenomenon is "chaotic," but may at best simply be able to watch the fascinating time series that are generated.

The second method for controlling chaos entails the definition of and implementation of small perturbations in chaotic systems in an effort to alter or smooth its dynamics. The fundamental problem here epitomizes the issue of the demands of modesty in light of our knowledge of complex social phenomena. What small trigger might alter the wild dynamics of our chaotic crime data? The hope here is that some minimal effort might be employed that generates positive feedback, infiltrates an entire system, and leads to positive change. For example, Peat (1991) has suggested that in a complex world such "gentle action" should be the guide for public policy. Such gentle action could, of course, also be used as a means to generate negative (adjusting) feedback to alter the temporal dynamics of a social phenomenon.

The reliance on small perturbations (gentle action) to change chaotic phenomena also belies the fact that chaotic systems may show considerable resilience. Small perturbations may have nonlinear explosive effects, but this outcome is not preordained. In fact, complex systems damp most perturbations. Prigogine's work (Prigogine and Stengers 1984) revealed that systems far from equilibrium were most likely to respond to small fluctuations, break up, and eventuate in new levels of order and complexity. Without proper definition and confirmation of what entails far-from-equilibrium conditions in the social realm, efforts at the identification and use of nonlinear public policy butterflies are likely to be of little value.

The third method for controlling chaos involves a cybernetic approach to information retrieval and response in an effort to change system dynamics. In the realm of public policy, this approach would require that social phenomena of concern be tracked continuously for evidence that a time series, as evidence of the phenomena, was becoming chaotic or erratic. This approach raises issues about both the ability of governmental apparatuses to carry out such a task and perhaps an even larger issue of whether this kind of governmental response is even desirable.

Using our model of crime statistics, it is possible to imagine a scenario in which law enforcement was organized such that crime statistics would be monitored on a daily basis. Even if such a national endeavor could be conducted successfully in a federal political system, the reality is that crime would likely be increasing in some geographic regions and decreasing in others. Would we then be willing and able to reallocate local and national resources? The practical political constraints under such circumstances are truly daunting.

Perhaps even more important, do people committed to democratic governance want a government in which the government itself and other forces of social control can respond with immediacy to social problems? Of course, a distinction must be made here between responding to an urgent immediate crisis such as a natural disaster versus dealing with longer-term, more complex, social problems. The multiple inputs of democratic policy processes and the structural inhibitions to efficient decision making ensure that democratic governance is somewhat cumbersome. Most political scientists would agree that this cumbersome approach has value by ensuring proper debate and processing through legislative procedure. Efficient government that can readily inhibit social system dynamics may also serve to limit positive fluctuations of unknown but salubrious value.

Public Policy and the Tools of Complexity

At least two of the intellectual resources emanating from the study of complexity may help policy scientists better understand and cope with the complexities of social phenomena. These new tools are modeling and game theoretical approaches that attempt to capture the multiple interactions extant in complex systems while also incorporating the multiple outcomes and behaviors that result from complex system behavior.

As noted previously, Allen's (1982) models of urban growth provide a new means for model development. While Allen's efforts rely on the basics of model construction including variable identification and the definition of mathematical relationships, he also incorporates elements of chance. Allen's models generate randomly selected values that may alter model outcomes from model iteration to iteration. Thus, Allen has introduced the element of chance into the known deterministic elements of urban growth. What is most important about Allen's approach is that the policy analyst's devotion to clear answers is replaced with the recognition that multiple possible outcomes typify the evolution of social phenomena. Allen (1982:110) characterizes his modeling efforts in this manner: "It moves away from the idea of building very precise descriptive models of the momentary state of a particular system towards that of exploring how interacting elements of such a system may 'fold' in time, and give rise to various possible 'types' corresponding to the branches of an evolutionary tree." While Allen's models epitomize the limits of prediction in complex systems, they do confirm that multiple strategies are necessary for policy systems to cope with the potential outcomes of complex social phenomena. Allen's work also reveals that these models may help policy analysts to anticipate the variety of outcomes that may accrue from any specific policy intervention.

An increasingly cited game theoretical application, of value to policy studies, and emerging from the literature of complexity studies, is Stuart Kauffman's (1993) creation of $N-K$ games. Kauffman's work concerns the evolutionary fitness of biological systems. These gaming efforts rely on a rather simple construct that defines N as the number of parts in the system and K as the number of interactions between the parts in the system. Kauffman's research shows that at critical levels both excessive N (parts) and K (interactions) can diminish adaptive fitness. These findings have interesting implication for understanding the phenomena that we define as policy problems and the set of potential solutions to these policy problems.

Using Kauffman's game in assessing policy problems could serve as a means to determine when a problem is likely to reach a critical state at which time governmental action would be necessary. For example, it might be that defined problems such as "poverty" might have an effect on the overall adaptive capacity of a region or an entire social system. The challenge for the policy analyst, though, is to define the elements of both N and K that constitute poverty and its linkages with the larger socio-politico-economic milieu. This new game theory could quite simply inform us as to when levels of social complexity are genuinely deleterious.

Public Policy, Complexity, and the Problem of Marginal Returns

All of the above approaches for controlling chaos work well under laboratory conditions. Scientists in these settings can control relevant variables and examine results in real time. This reality, however, reinforces the fact that the relative complexity of the social realm continues to differentiate the sciences. This differentiation and the seemingly limited opportunities for experimental success in the policy sciences confirms that beyond the challenge of the complex time series behavior of nonlinear social systems is the deeper problem of system complexity.

The sciences of complexity have correctly emphasized evolutionary processes as the evolution of complexity itself. This understanding also confirms that the best adaptive match for complexity is greater complexity. The societal complexity that serves to enhance evolutionary fitness, however, also serves to limit the prospects for successful public policy that alters systems dynamics.

In an incisive and underappreciated work, Tainter (1988) examined the decline of several historical cultures considered highly complex for their epochs. Tainter's major conclusion as to why these societies declined was that their internal complexity damped the effect of their most robust policy efforts. The available set of solutions to such complex societies, although quite extensive, are limited in their effects. In short, what leads to systemic decline is the problem of marginal returns. As societies become more complex, even the most arduous efforts to change social dynamics provide only minimal benefit.

In contemporary industrialized societies, we can begin to see that it is the problem of complexity rather than the problem of or prospect of chaotic time series that presents the fundamental challenge for public policy. While one might argue that it was "simple" historical dynamics that generated modern complexity, it is doubtful that simple solutions will greatly alter system dynamics and individual behavior. One primary challenge for policy scientists is to provide means of analyses that minimize the tendency of policy actors to resort to simple solutions in a complex world.

The challenge for public policy studies and policy analyses newly cognizant of chaos, nonlinearity, and complexity is to develop models that provide better means for identifying the amount and kinds of resources necessary to alter dysfunctional dynamics while ensuring that potentially positive dynamics are not destroyed. Attempting to take these kinds of analyses beyond the pale of ideology will be a critical challenge. A first start is to limit our reliance on naive economic equilibrium-seeking models that only serve to simplify and mechanize societal dynamics (Giarini 1985).

A more complete understanding of complexity in the policy sciences may also lead to a more reasoned understanding of both the limits and possibilities and resource demands for changing social system dynamics. Modeling approaches that provide a sense of the costs (in time, money, and energy) and the kinds of policy efforts best suited to particular social "problems" would be a great step forward. Such an approach would provide a means for determining whether society was prepared to tackle particular problems given the cost/benefit ratio. This approach would necessarily be superior to current "blind" atheoretical and unempirical efforts to change social and individual dynamics. While imposing such rationality into public policy debate may not limit misguided efforts and political posturing, it may provide a middle ground for reasoned assessments of what can be changed and at what costs to society. We may find that some of our greatest hopes for social change may be dashed. On the other hand, we may find that more strategic and targeted attacks on social problems may require fewer resources than previously expected.

Conclusion

The modesty that must accrue from attempting to change behavior in complex social systems does not mean that public policy interventions should not be employed. In those cases where a stable and predictable response is known, related policy is eminently sensible. In areas such as tax expenditures where consumers and corporations do behave as Newtonian machines in response to interest rates or tax abatements, public policy is quite effective in altering behavior. The fundamental problem of both conservative and liberal social policy in the face of complex nonlinear dynamics is that both make assumptions of simplicity that fail to match the deep and multiple interactions that create complex phenomena. Both approaches seem to deny that at best, marginal returns from public policy in complex nonlinear systems will accrue. The further possibility that simple rules may generate complex behavior does not mean that simple policy can alter complex behavior.

We demonstrate in this chapter the utility of nonlinear dynamics and the sciences of complexity and the insights they provide in furthering our understanding of public policy processes and policy analysis. We argue that nonlinear systems are highly likely among social phenomena and that this recognition calls for a healthy questioning of our ability to predict particular outcomes as well as querying whether—even given such predictive ability—such control is always desirable. Nonlinear dynamics within organizations and social institutions allow for the possibility of learning and growth that would otherwise produce rigidities that severely inhibit the ability to respond to the environment.

Because the elements of change, time, and variation are characteristic of many nonlinear dynamical systems (see Kiel and Elliott 1992), a more modest approach to both theory and practice is called for. Sweeping theory and generalizations should be replaced by more modest efforts to develop heuristic approaches or "rules of thumb," both for understanding and practical policy intervention. What is called for, in our view, can be seen as a paradox. While our current historical era is seen as a period of great transformation, the challenges of complexity and the limits of our public policy tools may limit us to a world of only incremental change and marginal returns on even our best public policy investments.

If nonlinear dynamics and its attendant lessons tell us anything, then, it is that we must be exceedingly cautious about what we can hope to accomplish in understanding public policy and furthering public policy goals. Unless, of course, one wishes to conduct social experiments for the sake of experimentation. The lessons of nonlinear dynamics do not work well for those who believe that, through the manipulation of relevant politics and economic and social inputs, desirable social outcomes are realistically attainable. Of course, we would point out that such social engineering efforts encompass different visions of both the Left and Right, from the social control efforts of the Soviets to construct a New Soviet Man to the belief of the Social Darwinists toward the end of the past century that, through preventing certain ameliorative actions (whether on the part of government or private actors is essentially immaterial), we, as a society, could achieve a substantial evolutionary improvement in both the individual and society through "the survival of the fittest."

Nonlinear dynamics and complexity theory suggest not that any and all policy prescriptions should be avoided because they will always be doomed to failure. It is not a recipe for doing nothing. But we should be cognizant of the fact that social phenomena are enormously complex in their history and evolution and that we need to be modest in terms of our claims for predicting particular outcomes, and even in creating policies that affect the most "significant" variable in a dynamic system.

7

Self-Organization of the Economy
A System-Theoretical Reconsideration of Georg Simmel's *Philosophy of Money*

Helmut Michael Staubmann

Applied social research aside, virtually all theoretical models within sociology can be interpreted, to a greater or lesser extent, using concepts of contemporary systems theory such as nonlinearity, complexity, emergence, and autopoiesis. However, none of these theories approximates contemporary systems theory more closely, both in substance and formulations, than the sociology of Georg Simmel. In the mid-1980s, Niklas Luhmann began to apply his previously elaborated general theory of social systems to economics. If one compares the work of Luhmann and others who appeared in his wake (see Baecker 1993; Hutter 1994) with *The Philosophy of Money* (1990), a work that predates

AUTHOR'S NOTE: This study was supported by the Austrian Program for Advanced Research and Technology (APART) of the Austrian Academy of Science.

them by nearly a century, one can conclude that Simmel had anticipated important elements of the theory of self-organization of the economy. This implies the
anticipation of concepts of a nonlinear sociology in a more general sense, which
will be demonstrated by the example of an advanced understanding of causality
and complexity.

Simmel's "Radical-Constructivist" Perspective on Monetary Values

The fact that Simmel called his opus magnum *Philosophy of Money* and not
Sociology of Money, a title rather more indicative of its actual contents, may
well stem primarily from the heavy emphasis that he places in his work on the
discussion of methodological preconditions of a sociology of money. The universal formula (*Weltformel*), as Simmel called it, which proceeds parallel to a
formula of economic value, would today be considered a radical-constructivist-
perspective (see also Kaern 1990).[1] For Simmel, the two formulas are parallel
because "any object, whether physical or mental, exists for us only in so far it is
produced by the soul in its living process, or, more precisely, in so far it is a function of the soul" (1989:208, cf. 1990:174).[2] But just how is the world of mental
and physical objects produced by the soul? The answer consequently leads to
the concept of autopoietic self-organization.

Regarded within the scope of the history of ideas, however, the key to understanding the soul's production of mental and physical objects lies in the work
of Immanuel Kant, an important figure in Simmel's philosophical orientation.
Heinrich Rickert attempted to characterize the core of Kantian philosophy as
follows: "Kant sought and found objectivity in subjectivity" (1921:1). To this
we must add that objectivity is not dissolved into subjectivity, but rather is interpreted as something distinctly identifiable. In contrast to what appears at first
glance to be an analogous postmodern position, the objective concept of reality
and the validity of intersubjective concepts of value are not unfounded because
they were constructed and thus relative. Rather, subjectivity and relativity are a
necessary part of both objective reality and concepts of value. In terms of truth
and in terms of value, it seems to be paradoxical that they are valid, not despite
the fact that they are constructions but precisely because of it.

Simmel introduced this Kantian approach to modern social science. In his
first major work, the two-volume *Einleitung in die Moralwissenschaft* (Introduction to Moral Science), Simmel established it as his central concern: "The monu-
mental doctrine of Kant which, whether accepted or rejected, underlies all modern philosophy—that our knowledge is only the knowledge of images and does
not penetrate beyond to the thing itself—this doctrine has not yet born fruit

within the realm of practical application. Not only is the knowledge of things a mere act of imagination, but rather the having of them as well, the very possession has its entire sense only in the internal circumstances which it evokes or represents. Possession is a psychological phenomenon, a perceptual mode linked to a particular imagined reality" (1991:392). A few years later, in the process of working out his *Philosophy of Money*, Simmel worked to develop this concept into a comprehensive analysis of the modern money economy.

Simmel begins with the assumption that in every case, an action can only be carried out within a description of the outside world—the reality—and a conception of the significance for goals—the values. In accordance with modern radical constructivism, neither reality nor value can be understood apart from the culture in which they are both found; thus, they cannot be taken as given facts, independent of psychological and social processes. However, the separation of subject and object, conditioned by evolution and emerging from a state of indifferentiability, objectifies both dimensions. The origin of objects, the point at which experience encounters resistance, is precisely the same origin of values: the object of desire pits itself against the will. Thus, there arises the awareness of the independence of ideas from the process of having been imagined, just as economic values can likewise be conceived as, so to speak, subject-independent, although, in both cases, they are distinctions that are internal to the system itself. Simmel expressed it more concisely: "Just as the world of being is my representation, so the world of value is my demand" (1990:69). In the process of differentiation, several things arise simultaneously—objects, values, and the Ego of human actors—each claiming independence, so that they can only be understood as correlative concepts. Values cannot be subsumed by the Ego of an individual human agent or by the physical objects to which they relate.

In his *Philosophy of Money*, Simmel defines the human being as an "objective animal" (1990:291)—capable of creating his or her own reality. He then explores this concept in the economy. Objectification of economic values is a two-stage process. The first step away from the pure subjective enjoyment of physical objects is accomplished through distancing required by the difficulty of their acquisition or production.

The second, more important, step is accomplished once there is an exchange; especially, when money is introduced. Two processes of value creation thus become intertwined: one value must be deployed to ascertain a second one, which makes it seem as though objects mutually determine each other's values. It is through exchange that value first becomes intersubjective, or better, suprasubjective. Through this process of exchange, things express their value through each other, so that the assignment of a value takes place beyond the realm of subjective wants. The emergence of objectivity and the simultaneous unity of the object is produced through the reciprocal interaction of the elements. Like other forms of measurement, monetary values have a completely relative character because it is not qualities that are being compared, but rather differences in the relationship of quanta. In this case, it is sufficient "that the *proportions* of the measuring substances are reflected in those being measured in order to be completely determined, without there necessarily existing any kind of essential equality between the two substances. Thus, two *things* which are qualitatively different cannot be equated, but two *proportions* between two each qualitatively different things can be equated" (Simmel 1989:141, cf. 1990:132-133). The relationship, then, is a pure construction, independent of the values or qualities of the things measured.

In regard to money, we can conclude that not only does money as a measure of economic values not need a substance value of its own, but such a substance value would actually be detrimental to its function as money. Money is a scale, and as a measuring instrument, it is substantial only to the extent that it exists. Expressed in cybernetic terminology, it is low in energy and high in control qualities. The shift from substance value to functional value itself takes place through a relational process. Money refers to the relationship of a quantity of goods to a quantity of money. The price is a proportionate share of the total money quantum that corresponds to the goods' proportionate share of the total goods quantum.

Money thus assumes a place among the contents of culture that, according to Simmel, consists of those constructions "each of which is subordinate to an autonomous ideal" (1990:447). Just as "the slogan l'art pour l'art characterizes perfectly the self-sufficiency of the purely artistic tendency" (Simmel 1990:447), one could speak of money for money's sake in the realm of economic affairs or, as Luhmann expresses it, of payment for payment.

"Double Contingency," "Emergence," and "Opening through Closure" in Monetary Operations

Further elaboration of a self-organization theory of the economy is based on this fundamental insight, namely, that specific forms of reciprocal interactions produce emergent orders. The concept of reciprocal interaction alone, however, is too general for a theory of self-organization. The task, then, is to find those forms not produced from simply adding cause and effect, but from a self-referential cycle whereby new, emergent elements are created precisely as a result of this cycle. This brings us to the concept of double contingency.

For Niklas Luhmann, double contingency is the beginning of social emergence. Luhmann found this idea in the work of Talcott Parsons, who regarded double contingency as a component of every form of interaction and communication. The concept of contingency has two dimensions, which are linked to each another. On the one hand, it means dependency. This leads to the understanding of a double dependency in social interactions. This dependency becomes problematic only when each participant is unclear as to how the other is acting. On the other hand, contingency means uncertainty. The uncertainty inherent in interaction and communication constitutes for Parsons a complementary interest in the development of a common system of symbols, which reduces uncertainty. A relatively stable mutual orientation and ordered interaction can then take place. In contrast to Parsons's structuralist interpretation, Luhmann relates the problem to elementary processes of social systems, namely, to communications. According to Luhmann, communications as emergent social elements can be specified in the case of the economic subsystem of society as payments.

It is important here to keep in mind that double contingency is not simply a matter of a doubling or a summation of two simple contingent situations. Rather, as Simmel states in economic terms, this is the "linked two-foldedness of the fact [in the English edition (1990:83): "connected *double event*"; italics added] that a subject now has something which it previously did not have and, correspondingly, no longer has something which it previously had" (1989:62). Thus, even the most elementary economic event, namely, that of monetary exchange, cannot be traced back to the two sides of the transaction (as conceptualized in rational choice theory).

An implication for sociology is that institutions such as language, customs, law, and religion cannot have come to exist from summation of individual acts but rather, in every case, can be thought of only as interindividual (supraindividual) constructions, each with its own interindividual history. In terms of monetary exchange, for example, we assume that this did not grow out of individual acts of exchange but rather emerged from supraindividual forms, such as donations or gifts, since "exchange is a sociological formation sui generis, an original form and function of interindividual life" (Simmel 1989:89, cf. 1990:100).

The origin of an *emergent* construction sui generis with qualitatively new characteristics implies that the emergent institution cannot be traced back to the environment from which it emerged, nor can it be explained in terms of that environment. In social life, psychological and biological factors exemplify this. Therefore, it is impossible for a phenomenon of life "to develop it out of combined elements of a lower order, the physical and chemical as the mechanistic theory of life suggests" (Simmel 1922:133).

The description of monetary exchange as an emergent quality implies a characteristic that is expressed by the term "operational closure" in the theory of self-organization. Operational closure means a decoupling of the emergent system from the environment, which simultaneously is a precondition for the opening on the emergent system level. And so all of the system's processes are mutually dependent: closure, distancing, synthesizing its own unity, determining its own law and by doing so creating a border and thus the ability to open up by self-controlled communication and interaction with the environment.[3]

It is in this sense that, expressed in Simmel's terminology, the modern money economy overcomes the "solipsistic economy" (meaning the natural economy; cf. 1989:73, 1990:90[4]), in which value serves solely (simple contingency) as a measure of effort. Accordingly, Simmel argued against the view that need or pleasure, scarcity or utility constitutes the basis of economic values. Exchange requires no individual conception of value; rather, "all that is needed is accomplished in the act of exchange itself" (Simmel 1990:90). It is only through the objectivity toward one's own desires that finally develops in the act of exchange that it is possible for a value to exist. As a consequence, needs appear to be determined by objects. Solipsistic needs are thereby depleted of power. The solipsistic economy is thus overcome by exchange and the renunciation that is implicit in it. Explicitly formulated by Simmel in an analogy to Kant's epistemology whereby the conditions of experience are likewise the conditions of the objects of experience, Simmel states that the possibility of the economy is likewise the possibility of the objects of the economy.

The "Autopoiesis" of the Economy

In contemporary systems theory, this situation of self-organization on a self-referential basis is called autopoiesis. The concept of autopoiesis was formulated by Humberto R. Maturana and Francisco J. Varela (1980), whose definition of autopoietic systems as a special class of systems reads like a generalization of some passages from The Philosophy of Money: An autopoietic system is "organized (defined as a unity) as a network of processes of production (transformation and destruction) of components that produces the components which: (i) through their interactions and transformations continuously regenerate and realize the network of processes (relations) that produced them; and (ii) constitute it . . . as a concrete unity in space in which they (the components) exist by specifying the topological domain of its realization as such a network" (Maturana and Varela 1980:78-79).[5] It is precisely this formulation that, according to Simmel's theory of money, holds true for the economy. Autopoiesis is the production and reproduction of elements that bring forth their own elementary emergence in this process: "The unity of the elements, though, is nothing extraneous to the elements themselves; rather, it is the form of coexistence persisting in and only displayed by themselves" (Simmel 1989:104, cf. 1990:108). It is this thought that Simmel regards as the philosophical significance of money, namely, that it "is the most visible and clearest reality of a formula of general being, according to which things find their meaning in relation to each other, and the mutuality of the relationships in which they are involved constitutes what and how they are" (1989:104, cf. 1990:128-129).

Analogous to Luhmann's idea of payment as the basal economic operation, the emergent elementary event, value is constituted according to Simmel through giving and taking under conditions of a monetary economy. "What could possibly motivate us to endow objects, beyond the naive subjective enjoyment that they afford, with the particular significance that we call value? It cannot be due simply to their scarcity. For if scarcity existed simply as a fact . . . we would take it as a natural and, in the absence of differences, perhaps quite unconscious determination of the external cosmos. . . . The source [of values] is, that for these things, something must be paid. . . . Thus, without price . . . there is no value" (Simmel 1989:78, cf. 1990:93).

In this process of elementary self-referential reproduction of the economy through payment, money plays a role that was first identified by Talcott Parsons (see Parsons and Smelser 1956) and reformulated by Niklas Luhmann (see 1976, 1995) as a symbolically generalized medium of communication and interaction. Money, then, is nothing but a special case of an entire "family" of media. This conception of money as a medium of self-organization of economic exchange can already be found, however, in the work of Georg Simmel. Likewise it was Simmel who formulated what can be recognized as groundbreaking analogies to media such as power, truth, influence, trust, and law. To cite just one of many possible examples: "The 'accumulation of capital' as a means of power is merely a particular instance of a very general norm that is valid in many other non-economic spheres of power" (1989:522-523, cf. 1990:382). Simmel grouped these types of media together under the heading of "secondary symbolism" (1990:151) to distinguish them from symbols of "naive mental states." Just as the inadequacy of natural exchange in kind was solved by means of money, the violent pursuit of interests is replaced by power as a generalized symbolic medium in the realm of politics. This symbolization turns representatives of collective power into symbols, or "condensed potential form" (Simmel 1990:149)—allowing them to accomplish their ends. Money can thus be grouped together with power as a form of potential.

Nonlinearity of Exchange

A point that has been repeatedly emphasized (and criticized) in Parsons's media theory is the non-zero-sum characteristic of communication and interaction based on media. This thought plays an essential role in Simmel's philosophy of money. For Simmel, the significance of exchange lies in the fact that the sum of the values is greater afterward than it was before the exchange occurred. This has economic implications: value is created not only through production but also through exchange. In terms of systems theory, this is the point at which economic activity becomes nonlinear as a result of social and cultural evolution. If robbery is characterized as a zero-sum transaction with respect to the economic values in question, then the exchange transaction based on what Simmel called the "peace treaty" develops a surplus value, in the same manner as such a value comes to exist in every cultural form of communication and interaction.

Simmel develops his argument from the fact that natural payments in kind are replaced by monetary payments, which is advantageous for parties on both sides of an exchange. The exchange by no means presupposes an equality of value. The parties to an exchange agree only when each receives more than he or she gives, and this holds true on both sides of the bargain. These may appear to a nonparticipant observer to equalize each other, but from the perspective within the exchange, equivalents do not change hands. A commonsense interpretation would assume the existence of a finite quantum of goods for the satisfaction of needs, and these are distributed according to ownership. A transfer that favors one party takes place at the cost of the other, so that the exchange economy is understood as a process of shifting back and forth of values that arise from "production." In terms of culture, however, it can be seen that, for example, the provider of a piece of (valuable) information as a rule suffers no loss from the transfer. "Such is the civilizing influence of culture that more and more contents of life become objectified in supra-individual forms: books, art, ideal concepts such as fatherland, general culture, the manifestation of life in conceptual and aesthetic images, the knowledge of a thousand interesting and significant things—all of this may be enjoyed without any one depriving any other" (Simmel 1990:291). Simmel labels this change of ownership in the interest and to the advantage of both parties as the functional progress of culture. In its inception, this assumes equal power and voluntary participation on both sides of the exchange.

The nonlinearity of Simmel's system of reasoning is further expressed in the breakdown of linear dichotomies: nearness and distance, subjectivity and objectivity, individual and societal, and so on are seen not as mutually exclusive opposites but rather as a relationship of mutual improvement; that is, the development of one side of a dichotomy is a precondition of the development of the other side.

This points to fundamentally different theory options than found in the conceptions of linear models. The difference can be clearly seen, for example, in Simmel's views on the dichotomy of things as they are and things as they should be (reality and morality), a matter central to methodological discussions in the social sciences. For Simmel, the actuality of life does not stand in opposition to an ideal-normative world; rather, these two different worlds each comprise the totality of life, existing as a dualism within the individual. They do not thereby oppose one another; rather, their interrelationship is one of mutual benefit and/or hindrance. They can by no means be conceived of as existing in a zero-sum relationship (see Simmel 1994:150ff.).

Relativity of Causality

The core concept in Simmel's sociology has already been described as that of "reciprocity" or "reciprocal interactions" by which emergent orders are constituted. The German expression *Wechselwirkung* used by Simmel includes a reference to causality that could well be translated as "reciprocal effect" or "reciprocal causation." Applied to the understanding of exchange it "is not the addition of two processes of giving and receiving but rather a new, third one which emerges while each of the two processes is, absolutely simultaneously, the cause and effect of the other" (Simmel 1989:73-74, cf. 1990:90). The simultaneity of processes in reciprocal interactions in Simmel's sense relativizes the use of causal methods but at the same time keeps causality as a necessary assumption of scientific research. This is true for the elementary reproduction of social systems and even more so for complex social structures.

In *Philosophy of Money,* Simmel addresses the problem of causality in connection with the relationship of money to complex sequences of purposes of human action. Whether one regards the contents of reality from the perspective of its causes or its consequences marks for Simmel the great diametrical opposition of intellectual history. This leads to the difference between causal and teleological thought. A drive as a psychological trigger for a mode of behavior ends with the triggered behavior and, in this sense, produces it in a causal way. The behavior is more or less pushed forward from behind. This is contrasted to an action that is effected by a given goal, where the intention more or less pulls it forth. The goal does not end in the action, but rather in the success of the action.

In the causal case, there exists neither a qualitative equality nor one of content between the driving force and the result. The teleological case, though, is quite different. Indeed, here as well, a cause in the sense of an indeterminate psychological drive must be present, because conceptual contents are "powerless" or "lacking in energy" and require real energy to attain effectiveness. Furthermore, the drive ends with the implementation of the action, such that the entire procedure remains subjective. Teleological action, however, requires a sort of control of success, which becomes the foundation of the interaction between subject and object. Goal-oriented or purposeful action is thus held together through the unity of consciousness. It effects a differentiation of the Ego from the object-world and constitutes a conscious interweaving of subjective energies with objective existence. "The conflict over the competence in the area of our actions between causality and teleology settles itself in this way: given that success, according to its content, is present in the form of psychological effectiveness before cloaking itself in the form of objective visibility, the stringency of the causal connections is not interrupted in the least. For them, contents are only relevant once they have become energies and, to this extent, cause and success are absolutely separated, while, on the other hand, the identity of the ideal contents has absolutely nothing to do with real causes" (Simmel 1989:255, cf. 1990:205).

The significance of these views becomes clear when one contrasts the foundation of Simmel's sociology with that of Max Weber, who by definition established the causal explanation as the task of a sociology conceived as a science of action. In accordance therewith, Parsons criticized Simmel's sociology: "And above all he does not anywhere attempt to work out what *causal explanation* of the acts in a given class means, how the motives are to be thought of as 'producing' acts" (1994:64).[6] Although Simmel's conception of sociology as a science of social forms that constitute themselves in reciprocations or interactions implies that the stringency of the causal connections are not interrupted in the least, in anticipation of concepts in chaos theory they are the basis of highly complex phenomena that are hardly predictable.

Reduction and Production of Complexity in Modernity and the Evolution of a Monetary Economy

"Symmetry stands at the beginning of all aesthetic motivations." Thus, Georg Simmel began his considerations on the subject of sociological aesthetics (cf. 1992). What he wanted to express with this formulation with respect to the field of aesthetics is a cultural tendency that is reflected in economic affairs just as it is in other areas of life, namely, a specific characteristic of the form of the management of complexity in traditional societies and in their phase of transition to modernity. In traditional societies, indeterminate complexity is made determinate by means of periodic regularity that finds its symbolic expression in the form of symmetry. The induction of meaning in a state of chaos that takes place in this way then begins itself to assume higher forms of complexity to thereby free itself from the forced constriction of that symmetry. Thus, (post-)modern complexity takes the form of asymmetry, which despite, or rather, precisely as a result of, the breakdown of symmetry and its limitations has an increased ability to create order.

What symmetry is in the spatial dimension, rhythm is in the dimension of time. Both are, so to speak, different forms of one and the same fundamental motive, a developmental path that can also be found in money and finance. It displays certain rhythmic characteristics as a type of intermediate stage: out of the chaotic randomness in which its initial appearance must have vacillated, it then succeeds to a stage that is marked by at least a certain principle and a meaningful form, until, at a still further stage gains a continuity in its self-presentation through which it is able to adjust itself to all practical and personal necessities, free from the constraints of a "rhythmic, though in a higher sense nevertheless random, schema" (Simmel 1989:686, cf. 1990:491-492).

This form of development of money is not a simple schema that could be applied in all cases; it is, however, a general pattern found in the development of culture and in a way of life that is conditioned by this schema. If the purpose for dividing a series of activities into rhythmically repeated periods is to conserve strength by means of habituation and periods of rest, then the cultural purpose of symmetry is found in the production of meaning, in a specific form of sociocultural semantics. When applied to society, this means that the whole of society can be organized into a centralized hierarchy, with the capacity to be ruled from a central point. The organization of military forces into regiments (*centuriae*) as well as the tendency of dictators to implement symmetrical constructions of society that includes their preference to the respective symbolism are illustrations of such a semantics.

If this stage, characterized by an ordered way of life, indeed constitutes a form of progress compared to previous phases, it nevertheless soon collides with its limits. Symmetric-rhythmic schemata have the character of an attempt of subjective assimilation that is not in accordance with the complexity of the object-world. Analogous to what Simmel labels as the functional progress of culture in the economy, the development of more advanced capacities of dealing with the world of objects leads to a breakdown of the schemata, a direct consequence of which is the enabling of a higher form of internal control. The higher form of asymmetry has become the predominant pattern of sociocultural semantics, the style of life going parallel to our modern money economy. This idea, recursively applied to social science and its methodology, includes that mechanistic and linear reasoning has finally come to its limits. However, it does not at all mean the end of theory as such but rather, that we are at its beginning.

Notes

1. Simmel's epistemology can be characterized as "radical-constructivist" in the sense that from his point of view, objects (reality) and their values are a pure construction. But Simmel's position can be contrasted to the positions that conclude from this fact that every claim to objectivity is untenable, that is, only a matter of power as maintained by a series of thinkers throughout

history—from the ancient Greek sophists to the "left-Hegelians" like Max Stirner (see Simmel 1995:382) and, in recent times, by postmodernists. Simmel reverses the argument, providing what is actually a Kantian solution: objectivity is a construction but it is objectivity that is constructed. In other words, "objectivity" *is* a construction, but that does not imply its "deconstruction" as subjectivity. On the contrary, constructedness is a precondition of objectivity. "Constructed objectivity"—although growing out of subjectivity—is to be thus differentiated from "pure subjectivity." This is a core idea of Simmel's theory of culture whether in regard to the values of art, of the economy, of religion, or of science.

2. All Simmel quotes are my own translation. The standard English edition of *The Philosophy of Money*, translated by Tom Bottomore and David Frisby, contains a highly selective interpretation. This quote, for example, they translate as follows: "that any object . . . exists for us only in so far as it is conceived by the active process of the mind." In the two sentences before this one, Simmel argues explicitly against the materialistic theory of money in favor of a transcendental theory derived from transcendental philosophy. Any materialistically oriented epistemologist might concur with the way Bottomore and Frisby interpret Simmel in the given quote. It does not necessarily imply, in our terminology, a radical-constructivist point of view.

3. Seemingly far away from economics, Simmel developed in this sense a theory of the framing of paintings. The frame contributes to the unity of a painting by providing a border that closes it up against a background making it thereby accessible (see Simmel 1922:46ff.).

4. Bottomore and Frisby use the term "self-sufficient economy." This turns the meaning upside down. The modern money economy is self-sufficient in the exact sense of the term as used by Simmel. This understanding is demonstrated in the quote above, that is, that culturally developed forms (as in the case of modern art and l'art pour l'art) tend to become self-sufficient. We interpret this here as autopoietic in contrast to nondifferentiated precultural or protocultural forms. Early art forms are not self-sufficient: they imply religious, economic, and other components, and the same is true of the early economy. By overcoming a solipsistic stage, these forms then become self-sufficient. We refer to this phenomenon with the system-theoretical expression: "opening through closure."

5. Maturana and Varela (1980) developed the concept of autopoiesis exclusively for the analysis of biological systems or "living systems" and argued explicitly against application in sociology by Luhmann. However, the definition of autopoiesis is a generalization, which makes it possible to respecify it to other scientific areas. So far, this has been done both in psychology and sociology. Maturana and Varela (cf. 1992) themselves applied it to epistemology by going far beyond mere biological roots of human understanding.

6. To put this in a proper perspective, it should be noted here that this quotation comes from an early study of Simmel's work by Parsons, initially conceived as a chapter in *The Structure of Social Action* though eventually not included in that book. It is certainly of extraordinary interest from the perspective of intellectual history; however, a criticism of Parsonian action theory based on one of his unpublished works would be completely inappropriate.

8

The Omicron Point
Sociological Application of the Anthropic Theory

William Sims Bainbridge

The anthropic cosmological principle is an explanation for the characteristics of the universe that has achieved some currency in cosmology and philosophy over the past twenty years. It notes that many if not all of these characteristics are constrained by the fact that the universe contains observers. That is, when we ask why the world has the attributes it does, the answer may be that only in such a world could an intelligent, living creature capable of asking such a question come into existence.

Every aspect of anthropic analysis is controversial, including a multifaceted debate over whether the idea is capable of being tested against empirical data. Yet it has proven so fruitful in discussions about the large-scale physical parameters of the universe that it is worth considering whether it has any application to the social world as well. The aim of this essay is to show that it does and that one reasonable if unusual line of argument leads to surprising predictions about the limits of sociology.

AUTHOR'S NOTE: The views expressed in this chapter do not necessarily represent the views of the National Science Foundation of the United States.

Homansian Sociology

The most logical way to link anthropic analysis, which was initially applied to questions about nature, to sociology is to approach it through a school of sociological analysis with especially close intellectual ties to the physical sciences, namely, the behavioral sociology of George Homans (1950, 1967, 1974, 1984, 1987).[1] In his influential volume, *The Human Group* (1950), Homans argued that small social groups originally came into existence as effective means for mediating between the individual and the natural environment. In many respects, cooperation in a group increases the individuals' capacity to extract rewards from the environment and to defend against external threats. Once rudimentary social life has evolved, then it may serve other purposes, and the form of social relations can become more elaborated than strictly demanded by the practical concerns of dealing with the surrounding natural environment. The human species is a product of the natural environment and has been shaped by biological evolution to possess a large, complex brain with the related capacities for language, abstract thought, and complex social behavior (cf. Homans 1987:139-141; Wilson 1975:551; Stark and Bainbridge 1987:29).

Homans stated five general propositions to explain the regularities of human behavior. The first states, "For all actions taken by persons, the more often a particular action of a person is rewarded, the more likely the person is to perform that action" (Homans 1974:16). The task of the social theorist, for Homans, was to develop logical systems that deduced from such axioms the specific propositions about behavior discovered by empirical sociologists in the course of their research. Much ink has been spilled on the issues of whether Homans actually succeeded in deducing any specific propositions from his five general ones, and he probably needed to add axioms about human cognition to his system (Turner 1991b; Stark and Bainbridge 1987). Sociologists have often lost sight, however, of the fundamental purpose of the Homansian theoretical program and the working assumptions on which it is based. The aim was to understand the regularities of human behavior in terms of fundamental facts of human nature, not merely in terms of intellectual axioms postulated by theorists. The working assumptions were that distinct laws of nature actually exist and that those immediately relevant to human behavior are few in number.

A small number of axioms does not imply that society is simple. Homans (1967:90-99) himself identified two complicating factors, historicity and divergence. Historicity is the infinitely complex set of prior events that serves as the background for even the most elementary human decision. Every human action is taken in the context of a particular, unique historical moment, and it may never be possible to learn enough about the antecedents of that moment, including the history of the individual human being, to understand or predict that action with confidence. Divergence is the principle that even a seemingly small decision could have immense consequences. Homans (1967:97) explains: "In divergence, a force weak in itself but just tipping the scales in a balance of stronger forces has big and spreading effects over time." Thus, Homans anticipated ideas of the recent intellectual movement that focuses on chaos, nonlinearity, and complexity (Mandelbrot 1983; Hao 1984; Gleick 1987; Arthur 1990; Goerner 1994).

Until very recently, sociology has been somewhat less hospitable to chaos theory than was its sister social science, economics. Indeed, among sociologists chaos arose perhaps most often in the work of exchange theorists who belong to Homans's tradition and who employ mathematical and computer tools quite similar to those of economists (e.g., Markovsky 1992). In my own computer simulations of social interaction, chaotic behavior always appears. For example, I modeled the spread of religious movements, following standard theories of influence in social networks, and discovered that success or failure was often surprisingly unpredictable (Bainbridge 1997:168-176). Neural network simulations of ethnic prejudice (Bainbridge 1995a) and religious doctrines (Bainbridge 1995b) produced chaotic subcultures that disagreed strenuously with each other about the nature of reality, even though the simulated human beings were living in the same environment.

Sociology has long believed that its unifying principles, such as societal values or class interest, were the antidote to the blooming, buzzing confusion caused by the chaotic interaction of individual human behavior. That is, from the time of Emile Durkheim ([1897] 1951), most sociologists have been convinced that distinctive "emergent" regularities exist on the level of large social groups—social facts, in Durkheim's terminology—but Homans disagreed, believing that the phenomena studied by sociology could be reduced to psychology, which in turn should be rooted firmly in biological evolution (Homans 1967:83; cf. Kontopoulos 1993). Indeed, Homans asserts, "The issue for the social sciences is not whether we should be reductionists, but rather, if we were reductionists, whether we could find any propositions to reduce" (1967:86).

Thus, the Homansian reductionist approach seeks to derive the regularities of social behavior from the complex interaction of individual behavior, rooted ultimately in the material world in which our species evolved through processes of random variation and natural selection. All the fundamental laws of this universe, including those ultimately governing social behavior, were defined at the very beginning, and (with proper obeisance to quantum uncertainties), everything that happened right up to the present moment is the logical spinning out of the principles on which the universe came into existence. This is the radical if logical conclusion of Homansian reductionism, and it carries sociology to the realm of cosmology.

The Anthropic Principle

The best starting point for a discussion of the anthropic principle is Homans's mentor, Lawrence Joseph Henderson, to whom Homans dedicated his small but pivotal book *The Nature of Social Science* (1967). A professor of biological chemistry at Harvard, Henderson also forayed into sociology and was largely responsible for Homans's philosophy of science. In the second decade of the century, Henderson published *The Fitness of the Environment* (1913) and *The Order of Nature* (1917).[2] These books offer a detailed chemical analysis to support the view that the properties of hydrogen, oxygen, carbon, and other elements are so improbably well suited for the evolution of life that no mere "mechanism" can be responsible, and the universe shows the hand of "teleology" or God.

The most comprehensive treatment appears in *The Anthropic Cosmological Principle* by John D. Barrow and Frank J. Tipler (1986). If the characteristics of certain isotopes of beryllium, carbon, and oxygen were quantitatively only slightly different than they are, the stars would not have produced sufficient carbon, on which life depends (p. 253). If the gravitational constant were slightly different from its actual value, all stars would have been red dwarves incapable of warming planets sufficiently for life, or all stars would have been blue and too short-lasting for life to evolve (p. 336). Apparently, life depends on an exceedingly improbable concatenation of coincidences in the magnitudes of various physical constants (Carr and Rees 1979; Gribbin and Rees 1989).

Improbabilities can be countered by large numbers of cases. Presumably, most planets in the universe are inhospitable to life, but we know that enough planets exist, varied sufficiently along the correct dimensions, that at least one harbors life. Physical constants appear to be uniform throughout the observed universe, but cosmologists have proposed a number of models in which the constants of nature would vary, although over larger scales than we can currently observe.

Inflationary models of the initial expansion of the universe offer one kind of solution. These postulate that the universe expanded especially fast in the first fractions of a second after the beginning, and that it is now vastly larger than we observe. In an early paper, Allan Guth (1981:23) proposed that the universe could contain fully 10^{83} "separate regions that are causally disconnected." Each region is a volume of space small enough that light could have crossed it since it came into existence, and thus a region shares a uniform set of physical constants or laws of nature. Two causally disconnected regions have always been sufficiently separated that light from one never had time to reach the other, and their physical constants are different. This large number of separate domains increases the chance that one of them will have physical constants conducive to the evolution of life.

A more elaborate version of this idea is the "self-reproducing inflationary universe" (Linde 1994). In this variant, as the domains expand, new "big bangs" occur within them, spawning daughter universes. Initially, the laws of nature in one of these daughter universes are unsettled, but the probability distribution of such laws is conditioned by the physical constants in the universe from which it sprang. In this model, the cosmos is akin to a fractal (Mandelbrot 1983), where branches proliferate within branches, perhaps having no definite number of dimensions, rather than the ordinary three-dimensional space people have always imagined. Naturally, the familiar world of human experience is contained within this exotic cosmos, but we cannot understand the cosmos by simply extrapolating from our everyday experiences of space, time, and objects.

A related line of cosmological thought concerns the ultimate origins of everything. We have come to expect that mass and energy are always conserved, and something cannot pop into being without sufficient antecedents. However, this may be a rule that applies only within a settled domain of a mature universe, rather than being a universal law. And even within an orderly domain, there may be conditions under which a daughter universe could come into existence without a cause. One such possibility is if the gravitational energy of the matter in the daughter universe (considered to be negative) exactly equals the mass of that matter. In such a case, the net total of the universe is zero, so no work is required to bring it into existence. Within that universe, the law of conservation of mass and energy may hold. Naturally, the actual speculations of physicists along these lines are somewhat more subtle and mathematical than this simple idea (Tryon 1973; Gott 1982; cf. Wheeler 1980).

The cosmos, thus, is conceived of as a chaotic ensemble of universes, varying without limit along all relevant dimensions (Leslie 1982). The fact that our universe possesses the improbable qualities required for life, therefore, is simply a selection effect. Only where those favorable conditions exist will intelligent creatures evolve and ask why the environment is so good. This is the anthropic principle.

The Pivotal Question

The anthropic principle is an answer to a question: "Why is the world capable of producing intelligent life?" Asking a question is a human, social act. Thus, the anthropic approach is grossly incomplete unless it includes an analysis of the social process by which that question comes to be asked. If all the laws of the universe lead up to the asking of the question, then we should focus on the conditions of the moment in which the question is asked for the first time. Let us call that moment in time the omicron point.

The term was chosen with deliberate symbolism in mind. Omicron, of course, is a letter of the Greek alphabet, representing short o (omicron = little o) distinguished from omega or long o (o-mega = big o). Omega, the last letter of the Greek alphabet, may signify an ultimate goal, and for theologian Pierre Teilhard de Chardin (1964) the "omega point" represented the point of convergence of God and man, possibly at a specific time in the future. In the biblical *Revelation*, the phrase "alpha and omega" refers to God, the beginning and ending of all existence. So, omega can refer to the final moment of time, toward which all history drives. But time may be open-ended, and modern cosmology can identify only one defining instant, when the expansion of the universe began from a dimensionless point. Because the "big bang" came at the beginning, it is the alpha point. Then the moment when the pivotal question is first asked, in the anthropic theory, would lie somewhere between alpha and omega. That is where we find omicron in the Greek alphabet. It is the moment when the universe acquires a fully aware consciousness.

One could argue that the pivotal question was first asked very early in the history of Homo sapiens when religion was born. Certainly, one of the standard philosophical supposed proofs of the existence of God is the argument from design, otherwise known as the teleological argument: "The order pervading the inorganic, organic, and human realm is indicative of an intended plan in an intelligent and good Purposer" (Bertocci 1945:763). However, religion is not in the first instance a philosophical system designed to answer ontological questions.

According to the sociological theory that informs this essay, religion arises as a particular kind of explanation, but a practical one not a speculative one. Because people cannot obtain some highly desired rewards in this life, they begin to postulate supernatural sources of these rewards (Stark and Bainbridge 1987:35-39). Thus, the rise of religion in human prehistory does not automatically generate the argument from design and with it the pivotal question. To be sure, Christianity believed in the sort of god suitable for the argument from design. But, as Knudson (1945:301) points out, "The existence of such a Deity was assumed in primitive Christianity. There was no need of proving it. But in the Graeco-Roman world the situation was different. There skepticism was common, and the church soon found it necessary to provide an apologetic for its faith."

In the Greek context, the argument from design predates Christianity, and it features prominently in the tenth book of *The Laws* by Plato. How do we know the Gods exist? "Why, to begin with, think of the earth, and sun, and planets, and everything! And the wonderful and beautiful order of the seasons with its

distinctions of years and months!" (Plato 1934:275). The omicron point, therefore, could well have come in classical Greece, perhaps considerably earlier than
Plato's own generation. Thales of Miletus, who may have predicted the solar
eclipse on May 28, 585 B.C., is widely regarded as the first great Greek
scientist-philosopher-mathematician, so it is conceivable that he or others of the
Ionian school first privately asked the pivotal question (Botsford and Robinson
1956:97-99).

Clearly, the Greeks came close to omicron, but we can doubt whether they
fully reached it (Longo 1993). If the teleological answer that God made the
universe is already firmly fixed in mind, then the argument from design may
touch on the orderliness of existence merely as a rhetorical point and not fully
comprehend the pivotal question. It is possible to assert that the pivotal question cannot be well and fully asked except by someone who understands its
complete import, and that requires knowledge of the anthropic answer. Apparently, some classical Greek philosophers—such as Empedocles, Anaxagoras, and
Democritus—possessed ideas that potentially could lead to the anthropic insight. Their concepts of atoms, biological evolution by competition, mechanistic
causation of physical processes, and a universe governed by the conjunction of
"nature and chance" presage modern thought but do not quite achieve it (Plato
1934:277; Botsford and Robinson 1956:256-257; cf. Marx 1841; Gomperz
1901; DeWitt 1954).

Barrow and Tipler (1986) suggest that the idea of the anthropic principle
arose from several lines of cosmological inquiry throughout the twentieth century, whereas Gale (1981:157) dates it precisely to work done in 1961 by
Princeton physicist Robert H. Dicke. The extensive literature on the anthropic
principle demonstrates that we understand it about as fully as one could short
of comprehending the precise processes that gave rise to the diversity of universes from which our fortuitous selection was made. This places the omicron
point within our own century.

To begin to understand the implications for sociology, we can distinguish
three scenarios that differ in terms of how precarious human society may be
after the omicron point. For sake of concision, I call them catastrophe, stasis,
and navigation.

Scenario I: Catastrophe

Once the pivotal question has been well and truly asked for the first time, all
the laws of existence have performed their function and can cease to operate.
This scenario is based on a view of the anthropic principle that stresses the raw
perversity of chance processes. Beyond that random sequence of events that
leads to the omicron point, the cosmos is a blooming, buzzing confusion.

Existence is like the proverbial chimpanzees banging randomly on type-writers, mentioned frequently now in essays on chaos and complexity (Casti 1995; Gell-Mann 1995; cf. Maloney [1940] 1956). If the chimps type long enough, eventually they will write all the works of human literature without having any sense what they are doing. The chimpanzee model imagines a universe in which every tiny event is independently random, and thus that order is at a tremendous disadvantage against disorder. This is not, however, the way contemporary cosmologists conceptualize things. On the contrary, they postulate that a very few laws describe the behavior of objects and that a short list of numerical parameters defines the universe we live in. The great complexity of the spatial and temporal distribution of various kinds of matter and energy might have evolved chaotically from very small and simple quantum inhomogeneities at the beginning of the inflation of the universe.

Scenario II: Stasis

Let us assume that the universe is indeed defined by a particular set of relations among a very small number of parameters. No natural laws exist beyond those required to reach the omicron point. Thus, no major functional social forms that had not already existed prior to the omicron point can exist after it. If the omicron point was in fact reached by Thales of Miletus, then all of industrial civilization is an unstable accretion on top of classical Greek forms. It is fundamentally pathological and susceptible to collapse at any moment. This deduction seems to explain the fall of the great ancient empires, a topic that once fascinated social theorists (Sorokin 1941). It is as if one of Mandelbrot's (1983) chaotic fractals produced by chance the picture of a human face in one tiny region of its graph. Any slight movement away from that region scrambles the image unrecognizably. The best that can be expected, therefore, is to conserve human society in the form existing at the omicron point.

To be sure, no complex deductive system can be shown to be complete and consistent (van Heijenoort 1967; Quine 1982), and this may apply to the natural universe itself, as well as to mathematical systems designed to describe it. This means that the conditions required to reach the omicron point may have secondary and unexpected consequences for later points in time, just as any set of axioms may lead to many theorems quite beyond those that one especially wants to derive. But the very logic of the anthropic principle suggests that these post-omicron derivations are unlikely to be favorable. They may take us away from the capacity to ask the pivotal question again, and there is no reason to expect them to be especially conducive to human life or happiness.

Ancient Greek society has been described as a contest system, in which individuals vied furiously with each other for honor and intellectual supremacy, and this quality would be especially conducive to asking the pivotal question

(Huizinga 1950; Gouldner 1971). Greece was a multicultural society, the result of all the invasions of the country and extensive trade by sea, and it was politically unstable. The same might be said of the civilization of western Europe and the United States in which twentieth-century cosmology developed. The lack of a monolithic culture dominated by an ideology that precluded questioning was required to achieve omicron. The more varied the collection of subcultures within a near-omicron society, the greater the opportunity for one of them to possess the qualities required to ask the pivotal question. Thus, whether omicron occurred twenty-five centuries ago, or in this century, the sociological description of an omicron society is that it is anomic and disorganized.

In a society that has passed the omicron point, it is impossible to solve any major social problem without burdening the functioning of that society with extraordinary costs. This is true because a clean solution of a problem that had not already been solved before omicron would require a new principle, and after omicron there are no new principles of human society. We have passed the omicron point without finding a solution to the population problem, for example. Therefore, there is no solution aside from allowing the traditional population-limiters of disease, warfare, and poverty to increase mortality and suppress fertility. Universal use of birth control technologies may produce a population collapse as dangerous in its own way as the present population explosion, and modern liberal democracies are incapable of developing rigorous population policies (Keyfitz 1986).

A challenge more closely connected with the anthropic principle is the question of whether human society can evolve into an interplanetary or even interstellar civilization (Bainbridge 1991). Colonization of Mars and several moons in the solar system is technically possible. The problem is cost, and particularly the fact that the individual people who would have to pay the bills would never receive benefits from the investment. If the Homansian paradigm is correct, then individual pursuit of rewards will never produce interplanetary colonization (Bainbridge 1984, cf. 1985).

Scenario III: Navigation

If the first scenario was extremely pessimistic, and the second one moderately so, the third scenario seeks to be optimistic. It notes that the universe is filled with an abundance of unused resources, and it suspects that the laws of nature that brought us to the omicron point have many as-yet inapplicable corollaries that wise humans of the future may selectively invoke. The human species is distinguished not only by its relatively large brain and capacity for language, but also by its ability to make and use tools, and by the tremendously effective technology that results from the combination of language and tool-making.

The problem is that after the omicron point, humanity is sailing into an uncharted sea, indeed into a possibly ever more chaotic and stormy ocean where the rules of seafaring change and darkness prevents us from distinguishing innocent foam from clashing rocks. Social science is a difficult endeavor. We are very far from having a conclusive system of analysis that will predict with certainty what the ultimate consequences of a major social innovation would be. The anthropic principle suggests a response to this quandary. In a sense it is a principle of natural selection. Given a very large number of environments, one will be suitable for intelligent beings who can ask the pivotal question. We could increase the chances for long-term human survival and for the attainment of higher forms of society by vastly increasing the number of independent human societies, each of which would constitute a different experiment in new social forms. The progressive unification of terrestrial culture means the only way to accomplish this is to colonize thousands of new worlds. Thus, the anthropic principle suggests that sociology should devote itself to research on how to navigate the right social, political, and economic course to an interstellar civilization.

Conclusion

The analysis in Homansian social theory suggests that no general laws of nature exist, except those required to bring us to the omicron point. But we should recognize that Homansian theory was only an intellectual scaffolding to convey us from conventional sociology to anthropic thinking, and the same fact would be true for any brand of sociology that derived phenomena from fundamental principles. Theories that postulate future stages in history based on new principles of organization are incompatible with the anthropic principle.

Anthropic thinking potentially contradicts Homans, however, in that it suggests sociology has a role to play in understanding the nature of the physical universe. He wanted to reduce sociology to psychology, and psychology to biology. Eventually everything reduces through Henderson's logic to the physical parameters with which the universe began. However, the anthropic principle gives a crucial role to the social situation in which human beings ask the pivotal question. It would be too much to say that at the omicron point physics reduces to sociology, completing a circle of reduction through which the universe chaotically bootstraps itself into existence. But the human-centered omicron point is comparable in significance to alpha, the spark of the big bang that excites cosmologists so greatly.

Coupled with principles from chaos theory, the anthropic principle offers a fresh approach to epistemology and ontology. The universe exists (ontology) only to the extent that someone is capable of seeking knowledge about it (epistemology). The answer depends on the questioner. As a closed reflexive system, the universe has neither meaning nor reality with respect to any objective frame of reference. An entity exists only in relation to some other entity. Our physical universe is real only in the sense that we perceive it and that our actions are constrained by it. This does not mean that physics should be subservient to sociology, or that humans can suspend the laws of nature by wishing them away. But it does mean that sociology is as fundamental an intellectual discipline as physics.

This essay harmonizes with the intellectual mood of the last years of the twentieth century, in which great social and technical accomplishments have paradoxically resulted in a widespread feeling of confusion, anxiety, and uncertainty about the future. The civil rights legislation and the moon landing of the 1960s were great advances. But neither in our social relations nor our spaceflight does any momentum seem to exist for further accomplishments. Throughout the advanced industrial nations of the world, high levels of democracy and prosperity have been achieved, but there is a pervasive sense that insoluble social, political, economic, and cultural problems have brought progress to a standstill. Perhaps the answer is simply that we have passed the omicron point, and the laws of nature will no longer sustain progress.

Notes

1. Other connections can be drawn through a deductive theory of religion based in large part on the principles of theory-construction enunciated by Homans (Stark and Bainbridge 1987, cf. 1985). The first sociological applications of anthropic theory were in a pair of publications in the sociology of religion, the first of which was given as a paper at a conference in October 1983 (Bainbridge 1987, 1993).

2. Of these two books, Homans (1984:90) says only that they "still have much to teach us," but he was unwilling to say exactly what we should learn from them.

9

The Origins of
Order and Disorder in
Physical and Social
Deterministic Systems

Alvin M. Saperstein

Physical and social scientists share an interest in the origin and dissolution of structure. Social scientists investigate, for example, the how and why of

1. Origin—individuals forming groups, groups forming nations or nation states, nations forming the "international system"; and
2. Dissolution—nations waging the modern wars that may ultimately destroy nations and their alliances. (I use the term modern here to distinguish more contemporary wars, which I view as the dissolver of the modern world system, from "old-fashioned wars," which may be viewed as part of the mechanism for creating and maintaining the system of nations in the first place and thus fall in the first category.)

Physicists have long investigated physical counterparts to these questions, for example, how do ordered crystals arise from disordered fluids, how and why do these crystals change from one form to another, and how do these structures dissolve back into the disorder of liquids and gases? The relative success of physicists over the past three centuries in dealing with these and other physical questions has been primarily based on a predictive mode of inquiry. Such a mode has been less successfully employed in the social sciences to deal with questions about the origin and dissolution of social structures. But there are other old modes of physics, which have come to prominence in the latter half of this century under the rubric of "complexity," that may be of greater use to the social sciences. In this essay, I wish to explore the possibility of their application to international relations and the problem of war.

The predictive mode is based on a deterministic mathematical theory in which all variables are uniquely and precisely defined and in which, given values for all required parameters, the values of the variables at each instant in time are uniquely related to their values at an immediately previous instant (Figure 9.1a). A rule connects successive values of any of the variables. The mathematical structure of the theory theoretically iterates the rule repeatedly, allowing the values of the theory's variables, at some future time, to be ascertained, given their values at the present or some past time. Comparison of the predicted values with those actually observed at the future time for some "simple" system allows us to reject, modify, or keep the theory. (Disagreement between observed and calculated values forces us to change the theory in some way. Agreement, however, does not "prove" the theory; it just means that, so far, the theory—or its specific representation as a model—is compatible with the real system under observation [cf., e.g., Nagel 1961].) Given successful tests of various subsets of a theory, they can then be combined (it is always assumed that their combination will not alter their individual successes) into a grand theory of some complicated system with practical purposes, for example, Newton's laws of force and motion can be combined into a theory for a working automobile. The success of the theory in making predictions about a system indicates that we "understand" that system; the theoretical model of the system is our understanding.

Prediction implies that knowledge of the future is no more uncertain than knowledge of the present—that the range of output values from the theory is of the same order as the range of input values (see Figure 9.1b). This predictive approach requires that similar inputs will lead to outputs that are also similar to each other. Otherwise, prediction would be impossible since there is always a range of inputs: the observations on a real system, required to establish the values of the input and model parameters are always accompanied by observational uncertainties, meaning that only ranges of values, not precise parameter values, can be put into the calculations. This requirement is fine for physics where one atom or one car should behave quite the same as other atoms or cars of the same type. The details of context or history in which the atom or car finds itself is usually not a major determinant of its subsequent behavior. It is not an

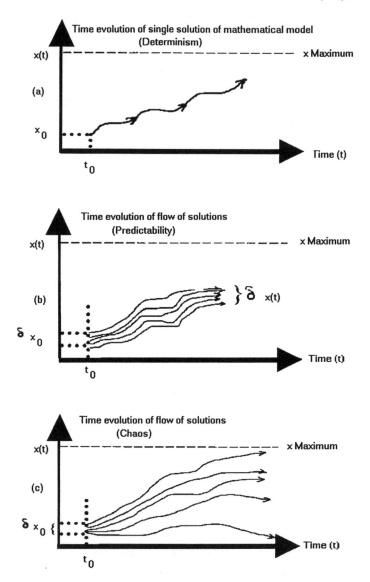

Figure 9.1. (a) A deterministic law creates a single "orbit" into the future from each starting "point." (b) Measurement of the starting configuration implies a range of starting points, each with its own associated orbit, because of unavoidable measurement errors and disturbances. If the manifold of orbits remain sufficiently close together, so that the range of end points is comparable to the range of starting points, the "law" provides as much knowledge of the future as is available as input in the present. Hence a successful prediction has been made. (c) When the range of final values, determined by the range of initial values, is much greater than the initial range, prediction is impossible. Such extreme sensitivity to initial fluctuations is termed *chaos*.

appropriate requirement for social sciences in which contextual details are a major factor: "For want of a nail . . . a kingdom is lost." In international politics, similar events or contexts can lead to very dissimilar outcomes: the 1994 shooting down of a plane in Central Africa led to the massacre of hundreds of thousands of lives beyond those of the two presidential passengers; the shooting down of the Korean airliner in the 1980s stopped with the death of its few hundred occupants; the assassination of a duke in Serbia early this century led to the downfall of many of the "high and mighty" and the loss of millions of lives throughout the world; the current assassinations in Serbia's neighborhood seem to be confined to the ordinary people of that neighborhood.

The approach called "complexity," old and familiar but newly named (cf., e.g., Waldrop 1992), brings context to the fore. It should thus be a very suitable paradigm for exploring the questions motivating this essay. Complexity may be defined as the set of deterministic theories that do not necessarily lead to long-term prediction. Such theories are still mathematical and deterministic. The numerical variables are still uniquely related to each other locally in space and time. But the structure of the mathematics is such that we cannot obtain the future values implied by the theory just as a result of the manipulation of the present values. The calculation requires the actual computational stepping through of all intermediate values of the system variables between "now" and "then." Complexity theories thus depend on the complete "path" taken by the system between its beginning and end points. As such they are sensitive to all perturbations that may affect the system as it evolves in time. Every intermediate instant of time may see the theoretical system diverted from the path it might have taken in the absence of perturbations (Figure 9.2) that are always present. Hence minute changes in the input parameters may lead to large, incalculable changes in the output. Prediction is no longer possible; the system is extremely context dependent.

Testing of such a theory depends on statistics in physical science or "plausibility" in social sciences. In physics, we would compare the statistical distribution of outcomes calculated, given a randomly distributed small set of initial conditions, with the distribution of outcomes observed with an ensemble of identical physical systems, started off in as identical manners as possible. Agreement between the two distributions means the theory "works"; we have achieved understanding. In international politics, where ensembles of identical systems are not available, understanding is obtained if the range of theoretical output possibilities are plausible—if some of them conform to the behavior of actual systems as given by historical observation or "common sense."

It is known in physics that such theories can lead to the formation of structures out of less structured constituents via a process called "bifurcation" (Figure 9.3a) (Prigogine and Stengers 1984). They can also lead to the dissolution of an

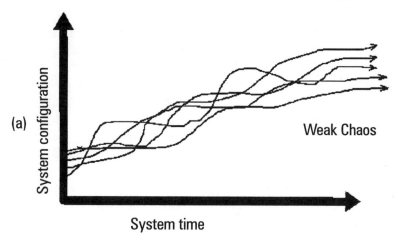

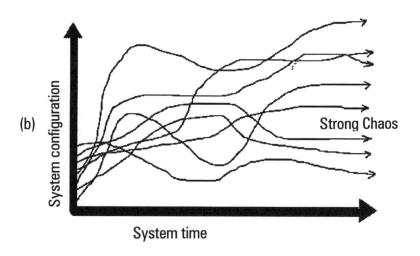

Figure 9.2. Weak versus strong chaos. Chaos implies that closely neighboring orbits, at any point in the system space, are soon quite divergent from each other. In "weak chaos," (a), the many paths are still constrained to take up only a small part of the system space. In "strong chaos," (b), the paths diverging from any point in the system space soon fill the entire available space.

ordered structure into a disordered melange of constituents via a transition to "chaos" (Figure 9.3b) (Schuster 1988; Ott 1993). The purpose of this chapter is to present and discuss some illustrative examples of the applications of these ideas to international politics.

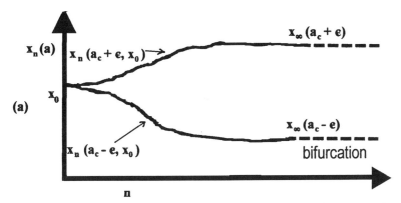

eventually know outcome of policy-making, perhaps can change

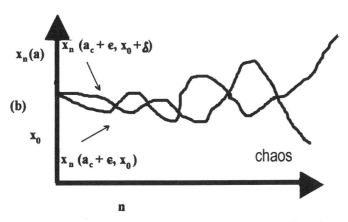

never know outcome of policy-making - can't make
rational change - war!

Figure 9.3. Bifurcation versus chaos and policy making. (a) Bifurcation: for some particular values of the model parameters, the model becomes very sensitive to small changes in the parameter or starting values. Orbits starting with closely neighboring values of system parameters or initial values soon diverge drastically. Once well away from the bifurcation point, the system follows a definite orbit even if there are small disturbances as there always are; prediction becomes possible. (b) Chaos: if orbits depart significantly from each other no matter where in their evolution they become neighboring, then each point along the orbit is a bifurcation point. A continua of bifurcations represents chaos: it is impossible to "know" which of the allowed, very different, orbits the system will follow. Prediction becomes impossible.

Structure and Its Explanations

By "structure" I mean the arrangement of a system's elements in the system's space such that the elements have definite relations to each other breaking the initial symmetry of the space. For example, the elements of ordinary matter are molecules. In the usual gas these molecules are randomly distributed throughout the three-dimensional volume occupied by the gas; any point in the space is equally likely to be momentarily occupied by a molecule (Figure 9.4a). There is no correlation between the molecules; knowing that one point in space is occupied tells you nothing about whether or not a different point is also occupied by a molecule. There is no "structure" to such a gas; the space is perfectly symmetric—every point is as "good" as every other one. Consider now a crystal lattice of molecules resulting from the condensation of this gas into a solid (Figure 9.4b). All points of space are not now equally likely to be occupied by molecules. If you know where some molecules are then you know the distances and directions to the location of others. Points not at these locations will not be occupied. The symmetry of the space is broken. You may not know where the first few molecules will locate themselves as the gas begins to condense (the initial space is still symmetric), but the location of all subsequent molecules condensing into the crystal is preordained once the initial ones are fixed.

Or consider groups of people spread uniformly ("on average") over an extensive landscape (Figure 9.4a). No location is favored; symmetry exists. But then towns spring up; people move to them. You are more likely to find people at the location of towns than at other locations (Figure 9.4c); symmetry is broken—a structure has been impressed on the space. Some of those towns amalgamate into cities; a different structure is now evident. The collections of cities may become nations, which in turn form the structure that we call the "international system"; again, new structures are evident.

Why do these structures arise?

We might be willing to accept these structures as the result of a cosmic throw of the dice but still would like to know what determines the number and shapes that the sides of the individual dice will have.

There are traditional explanations for the creation of order from disorder, of structure from chaos, of form from the void (cf., e.g., Hertz 1978; Campbell 1988). But appeals to a "god," to a formative force outside of all of the systems of which we are aware, usually lead to no further insights into the relations between the various system components, to no possibilities of effective anticipation and control. Appeals to either magic or religion, both outside of the systems, flaunts the (perhaps God- given) human need for understanding. The alternative is some logical-deterministic theory, most efficiently expressed in mathematical form.

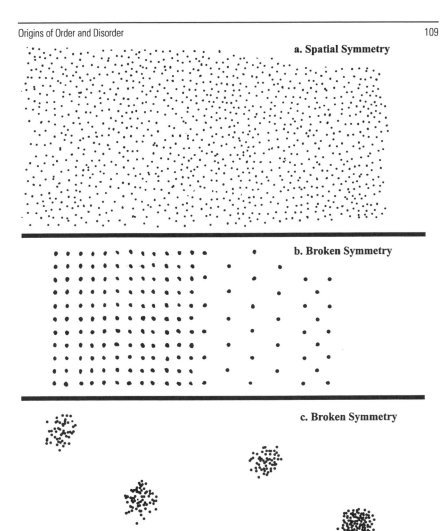

Figure 9.4. (a) In a rarefied gas, molecules are distributed randomly in space: each point is as likely to be occupied by a molecule as any other point. Since all points are thus equivalent, nothing distinguishes one from another: the space is symmetric. (b) A crystal lattice in which all occupied points are related to each other by definite rules. All points of the space are not equivalent; hence the space is less symmetric. (c) People (or molecules) in clumps. They may be randomly distributed within the clumps and the clumps may be randomly located with respect to each other. However, certain regions of the space are definitely not occupied; all points are not equivalent and so there is a lesser symmetry.

For example, consider the motion of a single planet in the given gravitational force field of a fixed sun. Newton's laws of motion completely specify the acceleration of the planet in terms of its position. Given the acceleration, the position and velocity of the planet are uniquely determined by its position and velocity at an immediately prior instant. Thus we have a logical-deterministic theory expressed as a set of second-order differential equations. The structure to be determined is the position and velocity of the planet in some future epoch, given its present position and velocity. The solution of the differential equations in closed form gives the structural variables—position and velocity—at any time, in terms of well-determined trigonometric functions. Plug in the time you want and out came the desired structural variables. There is no need to compute them at intermediate times. Modify the initial conditions slightly and the output variables come out slightly different. Thus the entire future of the system, to any specified accuracy, is completely contained in, and obtainable from, the initial parameters and the theory via finite explicitly specified numerical procedures. The closed continuous mathematical form of the solutions to the theory's equations means that output is continuously related to input—there can be no surprises, no disorder.

A biological analog of this completely predictive deterministic system is the very old idea of biological development, which held that the complete prescriptive rules for the future organism, for example, a human being, were contained in its genetic material. Everything was specified once the egg was fertilized. The future of the organism was completely determined from its center—from its "germ cell." If we could read the biological rules as well as the physicists could read their rules, there would be no surprises in the future. (A political analog of this model of biological growth, in which everything was to be specified and preordained from the center, would be the extreme Leninist state.) Of course this model of biological growth is extreme: it requires too much information to be contained in the genes; it implies that identical twin babies should grow into identical adults, contrary to observation. We know that contingency is a powerful factor in biological phenomena.

Noncontingent models have been quite prevalent in theories of international structure. I will mention two attempts to model the evolution of nations, or alliances of nations, from their constituent subnations, or nations. Lee, Muncaster, and Zinnes (1994) (LMZ) formulate the basic operating modes of groups of people (collections of nations or "subnations") in a hostile competitive world—which they take to be: the friend of my friend is my friend, the enemy of my friend is my enemy, the enemy of my enemy is my friend—as a set of nonlinear differential equations describing the time evolution of the "distances" between these groups. A large negative distance between a pair of groups represents a hostile pair: an antagonistic relation between two alliances, two nations, or two other groupings of people—the differential equations, modeling the time evolution of the relative distances between groups, do not depend on the identities of the groups. A large positive distance represents a coming together of the groups into a single entity—an alliance of nations or a nation of subnations. If the asymptotic solutions—the attractors—of the model's equations exist, for a given set of initial non-zero intergroup distances, and give a value of plus infinity for some of the final state intergroup distances, then the number of independent political entities in the system has been reduced. Alliances or nations have evolved—a structure has been created. LMZ have analyzed a very simple form of the model from a number of different starting conditions and have shown that such alliance limit-solutions do arise. The initial configurations can be put into continuous classes, all members of a given class evolving to the same final configuration. Hence knowing the initial state of the system to some reasonable accuracy, the outcome is foreordained. All information is already present in the initial information—there are no surprises, no contingency. It is true that analytic solutions to the model's equations cannot be found in general. Specific solutions must be formed numerically, by integrating over the large time interval from initial to final states; this means that the entire evolution of the system must be passed through numerically to get the final result—contrary to the simple example given above of a noncontingent physical system. However, qualitative analysis of the solutions allows them to be put into the continuous classes without knowing the specific details of the solution. Except for the few initial configurations on "basin boundaries," small changes in starting configurations do not change the outcome—the resulting structure possibilities are still preordained.

Another attempt to model the aggregation of subunits into larger units—to create structure—is that of Axelrod and Bennett (1991). Theirs is a time-independent theory in which the variables describing the "distances" between the subunits are now the independent variables. A concept called "frustration," a smooth function of the many different inter-subunit distances, is introduced and stability of the system is defined to occur at the minima of the frustration function. (Nothing is said about how the system gets from its initial given configuration—given in terms of a specified set of values for the distances—to one of the minimum frustration configurations.) Since the frustration function is given by the model, its discrete, smooth minima can be analytically determined at any time. Thus all information about the possible future outcome structures is explicitly contained in the theory at the beginning. Again, there is no contingency. (One could say that there is a contingency in that one doesn't know which of the minima, if there are several, the system will finally sink into. However, this contingency is not part of the theory—which does not contain any mechanism for moving from one value of the frustration function to another—and hence is no different than the theological contingency briefly alluded to earlier.)

I turn now to theories of structure formation that do exhibit contingency. Instead of introducing them via a physical example—such as the Ising model

(Wu 1981) for the origin of magnetic domains through the interaction between neighboring atomic magnets—which are too difficult to describe briefly in an essay such as this, I will start with a very simple model of the contingency breaking of a special symmetry, that of a circular dining table, formally set.

There are dinner plates symmetrically placed around the circumference of the table, and midway between each pair of plates is a wine glass (Figure 9.5). Nothing is specified as to whether the glass to the left or right of a given plate belongs to that plate. The initial symmetry is that either is possible. Once a person sits before one plate at the table and selects one of the two optional neighboring wine glasses, say, the left one, the symmetry is broken. The only way the table can be filled is if all subsequent people sitting at the table also select the left-hand glass; the table becomes "left-handed." A small initial contingency—a choice—puts the table into one or the other of the two very distinct classes. Assume now that there are many people milling around before being asked to be seated for dinner. Some of these people are indifferent as to whether the table they will sit at is either left- or right-handed. Others will only sit at a left-handed table. The remainder will only sit at a right-handed table. The three classes of people making up the banquet are randomly distributed throughout the hall; the a priori symmetry is that people of any of these classes are equally likely to be found anywhere. After the invitation to be seated, the symmetry is broken and a structure created in which people of the same class are clustered together. Suppose further that tables are waited on only if two neighboring tables are of the same handedness; the rest go hungry. The original crowd of people is now structured into two sets: one hungry, the other satiated. But one cannot know in advance who, if anyone, will go hungry; one has to go through the process, step by step, to find out. Moreover, if the process were to be repeated under identical circumstances, different sets of people would be selected to go hungry. The model could be extended and made more complex. For example, suppose that collections of three or more neighboring tables of the same handedness are served from large pots of food that are kept sanitary. The remaining people, those who are served, are served from small pots that harbor dangerous bacteria. The result is a new structure of ill and healthy people, arising from the original simple contingency. (There could, of course, be a series of contingencies, e.g., only some of the small pots, randomly distributed, are contaminated, etc.)

The point being made is that each step in the model is deterministic—it is rigidly connected to the previous step by rigorous rules. The randomness of the input—who initially sits at each table—determines the outcome, which cannot be foreseen. The process of getting from the initial unstructured state to the final structured one, in the deterministic system, is path dependent, resulting from a small random element within the model or in the interaction between the model

**Looking down on a dinner table,
wine glasses are equidistant
between place settings.
"Left-Right Symmetry"**

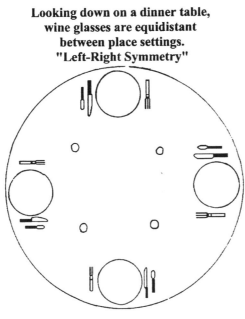

**First person to reach for wine,
breaks the symmetry.**

Figure 9.5. Dinner table with place settings; wine glasses are placed midway between the settings so that, a priori, each glass could "belong" to either of its neighboring settings.

and its environment. It is important that the system be very sensitive to the small random element, that it "bifurcates" into one of the two very different paths as a result of the small disturbance (for want of a nail . . . a kingdom is lost). This sensitive dependence, which makes contingency possible, is only possible if the mathematical model describing the system of interest is inherently nonlinear (Prigogine and Stengers 1984)—if the changes in the dependent variables are not just simply proportional to these variables.

The above paradigm is easily demonstrated in current ideas of biological growth. Instead of the whole future evolution of the entire organism being contained in each single cell, as in the predictive theory, the contingency paradigm assumes that each cell contains a complete set of rules as to how it should respond to each potential environment (internal as well as external). It will behave one way if it finds itself surrounded by liver cells, a different way if surrounded by bone cells, and so on. Which specific environment it finds itself in depends on the "path" it has taken since the "beginning." At each stage along the path there will be random small disturbances (e.g., thermal fluctuations) as well as deterministic, major rules. The sensitivity at any point, which will vary from point to point, will determine whether and what bifurcations occur. In this way biological organisms grow with the similarities and differences commonly observed.

The simple banquet game outlined above could be played by a computer rather than real people. (Random number generators take the place of individual volitions; e.g., Ekeland 1993.) The resulting path-dependent numerical structures would be isomorphic to the people-generated ones. We cannot program a computer to carry out as many complex deterministic rules as are carried out by a real biological cell, or to deal with as many interacting cells as are found in biological structures of major interest, such as mammals, but programs have been written that follow the evolutions of systems of moderate numbers of moderately complexly interacting computational cells (Flam 1994). The resultant behaviors of the computer "organisms" show many interesting parallels to the behaviors and developments of real living structures. Similar attempts have been made to model the growth of political structures, two of which are sketched below.

Robert Axelrod (1995) has produced a model of a linear array of "nations," with arbitrary initial distributions of wealth and no "commitments" to each other. At each annual cycle, random nations are chosen to make demands on their neighbors—wage war or pay ransom. A fairly simple set of rules determines the outcomes of the demands and the consequent changes in national wealth. Also, as a result of making war and transferring ransoms, "commitments" between the nations begin to develop following rules fairly similar to the LMZ rules mentioned above: losers (of war or ransom) become connected to the winners; the enemy of an enemy becomes a friend—more committed, and so forth. As a nation has more and more commitments from others, its chances of dominating in a war, or ransom demand, increase, and so on. The computer simulations are run over 1,000 cycles, each run representing one system path through time. At the end of a run, those groups of nations which are strongly tied to each other—have large resultant numerical values of mutual commitment—may be considered to be single entities: alliances or larger nations. Thus a structured international system may arise, one in which there are fewer independent "actors" than initially. Many runs, all with the same rules and parameters, produce many different paths, many different international structures. Some of these paths look strikingly similar to our "commonsense" historical images of the evolution of the real world, implying that Axelrod's model may incorporate some real understanding of important factors in world evolution.

Another model, that of Epstein and Axtell (Horgan 1994), takes place in a two-dimensional space in which there are initial local surpluses (sugar mountains) and deficits (deserts) of resources. Small "creatures" move randomly around on the surface, devouring resources, interacting with and changing each other according to simple deterministic rules. Originally one "society," they sometimes evolve into separate "nations," centered on the resource peaks. Again, complex structures arise from following simple rules in a path-dependent way.

Dissolution of Structure—Chaos

A good physical illustration of the breakdown of structure is the behavior of a river as it flows from a wide, deep, unobstructed channel into a narrow, constrained, boulder-strewn gorge. The initially slowly and smoothly flowing water—"laminar flow"—is completely predictable. Knowing the behavior of the fluid at one point and one time allows one to know the detailed behavior of the water at neighboring points at the same time, or at the same point at later times. This coherence of behavior—in space and time—is a structure determined by the physical properties of the fluid as expressed in the Newtonian laws of motion. When the water flows into the twisty, uneven, channels of the gorge, it becomes "turbulent"—no longer predictable. Knowledge of its motion at one place tells you nothing about its simultaneous behavior at neighboring places or its later motion at the same place. There is no "connectivity" of behavior, no structure. The same body of water has passed from structured to unstructured behavior—from predictability to chaos (and, of course, later downstream might transform back into structured laminar flow again). Any reasonable mathematical model of fluid behavior must be able to represent these two types of actual fluid behavior and the transitions between them.

The usual physical laws of fluid motion, obtained by applying Newton's laws of motion to conceptually isolated small sections of the fluid, are nonlinear: the effects of small changes are not necessarily proportional to the changes—the response of the system to small input changes depends not only on the system variables and the changed inputs but on the response itself. The solutions to such equations have regions in which small disturbances remain small and others in which the disturbances grow. In the latter regions, two solutions that start off very close to each other (differing only by a small "disturbance") soon bear no resemblance to each other. This makes prediction in such a region impossible since any measurement, required to specify the starting solution on which a prediction might be based, will be subject to unknown small disturbances—"experimental error." The system parameters, distinct from its starting solutions, are also subject to small disturbances—from the measurement process and because they represent the fluctuating interactions of the system with the rest of the world. This situation, in which deterministic theory precludes prediction, in which the ever-present small random disturbances lead to wildly fluctuating incoherent motions, is called "chaos" (e.g., see Fig. 9.1c). It is just what is needed to describe turbulence. Thus the same theory can represent both laminar flow and turbulence—it all depends on the input parameters (e.g., see Figure 9.6): mean fluid velocity, channel size, viscosity, and so on. Although the theory cannot predict what happens in the chaotic regime, it can predict the regimes in which turbulence is possible; it allows calculation of those parameter values that bound the chaotic region.

In practice, for example, the design and operation of an aircraft, it may be desirable to avoid turbulent fluid flow (of the air over the wings) since such turbulence may make control difficult or impossible. Control implies predictability! But the theory provides a prediction of unpredictability. Hence the theory allows the rational placing of constraints on design and maneuver behavior so as to avoid turbulence. A corresponding theory of international relations might allow the prediction of the loss of controlled behavior by nations within an international system, which we then use to represent the outbreak of war and thus allow it to be avoided, if so desired.

Many writers on war and peace in international relations have introduced the concept of crisis instability—large changes occurring in the international system as a result of small disturbances or affronts. A standard example of such a system instability is the outbreak of World War I as a consequence of an assassination in Serbia (e.g., Tuchman 1962). The disparity between disturbance and its consequence is very similar to that presumed in the definition of chaos. It is thus natural to associate the transition from predictability to chaos in a mathematical model with crisis instability and the outbreak of war in the international system being modeled. This association is particularly natural since war has long been associated with the nonmathematical concept of chaos (von Clausewitz [1832] 1968), which bears great similarity to the corresponding mathematical concept. If we wish to make this association, and thus understand the outbreak of war (or of some wars) as the transition to deterministic chaos, we must first believe in the possibility of valid deterministic models for the evolution of international behavior.

This latter possibility brings the immediate thought: how can nations—each made up of so many people, each of whom often acts in a seemingly random matter—act deterministically? A nation may be just a collection of random elements or it might be the result of small admixtures of randomness amid basically deterministic components (complexity). How get from either to an overall determinism? Again, a physical analogy is helpful. A gas is made up of many, many molecules. These individual molecules might be made up of deterministic elements, moving deterministically, as in classical physics, or they might consist of structures obeying the laws of probability, as in quantum physics. In either case, the overall motions of the myriad of molecules is completely random. And yet,

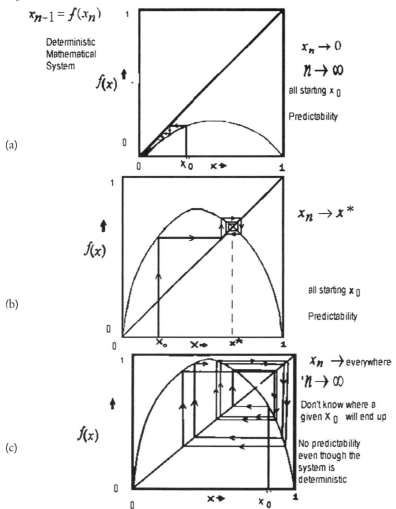

$$x_{n-1} = f(x_n)$$

Deterministic
Mathematical
System

$f(x)$

$x_n \to 0$

$n \to \infty$

all starting x_0

Predictability

(a)

$f(x)$

$x_n \to x^*$

all starting x_0

Predictability

(b)

$f(x)$

$x_n \to$ everywhere

$n \to \infty$

Don't know where a
given X_0 will end up

No predictability
even though the
system is
deterministic

(c)

Figure 9.6. An example of a "rule" that leads to predictability or chaos depending on circumstances. Here the curve $f(x)$, which gives the value of x (on the vertical axis) immediately succeeding x (on the horizontal axis), is the rule; given any value of x, its successor value is precisely determined to be the value $f(x)$. In (a), no matter what the initial value x_o is, the final value—after a long series of successors—is $x = 0$; prediction is immediate and obvious. In (b), with somewhat increased values of the parameters determining the rule $f(x)$, the final value after a long string of successions is a specific value x^* (determined by the parameters) no matter where the string starts. Again prediction is possible. After a further increase in system parameters, the rule in (c) is obtained; here there is no endpoint to the string of successions, and each given string (starting from a given specified initial value x_o) separates rapidly from each neighboring string: no matter how close together two values may be, their successors—as determined by using the rule repeatedly—are soon very far apart. Prediction is now impossible. The same rule, in going from (a) to (c), has gone from predictability to chaos.

when examined from the view of the system as a whole, the gas behaves simply and predictably. It obeys deterministic laws that result from the averaging over the many random subcomponents of the system. (Similar deterministic averages over many random variables form the basis of much common social life, e.g., mortality and other insurance tables.) On this basis, we can expect "laws" to govern the interactions of states. Certainly, much of formal history and political science is devoted to the expression of apparent regularities (laws) of the inter-actions between states. Thus I hope to be able to formulate laws of hostile interactions between nations that can manifest crisis instability—the transition from order to chaos. This transition will then be associated with the outbreak of war.

Lewis Fry Richardson was a Quaker imbued with the possibilities of human betterment while growing to maturity in the era of expanding technology and improving human life in Europe before World War I. He was appalled by the carnage and destruction of that war. It couldn't be the result of a human will striving toward universal health and prosperity since it led to such universal human disaster. Therefore, he sought to lay the war in the properties of the international system rather than in human volition (Richardson 1960a, 1960b; Hess 1995). It certainly seemed to many observers that The War occurred against the wishes of everybody. The lack of human will and control in the outbreak of the war meant that it was the result of the inexorable laws of the system of nations. The system he saw at that time was an arms race, and so he proceeded to mathematize the obvious characteristics of such a race: the rate of arms acquisition of each of a pair of hostile powers (he didn't explain the origin of hostility but took it as a given) depended on the size of the existing stocks of arms held by the opponents. The result was a linear set of differential equations that has generated much analysis and discussion in the political science commu-nity since its introduction (e.g., Hill 1992). One class of relations between the coefficients (of proportionality between rate of arms stocks increase and size of arms stocks) determining the differential equations led to decreasing armaments for all opponents, no matter what their initial stocks were. Richardson called such a system "stable"—it would remain peaceful, no matter how hostile the feelings of the nations for each other. Another class of coefficient relations pro-duced solutions that represented constantly increasing stocks of arms, no matter what the initial stocks were. This exponential growth of armaments was claimed to be "unstable"—it would lead to war. To avoid war, change the system so that the coefficients representing it fell into the appropriate class. The coefficients themselves represent response characteristics of the nations concerned; as rep-resentations of the behaviors of the societies, they can, and do, change with time but presumably on a time scale much longer than that of the significant variation of the Richardson equations in which they appear as constant input parameters.

The "unstable" exponentially growing solutions of these linear Richardson equations show no change of form, no structural transformations, no loss of predictability, and hence no loss of control. Slight changes in the initial values of the arms stocks or of the system parameters led to slight but predictable changes in the resultant arms supplies. There is nothing in his linear mathematical model that could be interpreted as "crisis instability," certainly nothing that could be viewed as a significant system change from cold to hot war (analogous to a physical "phase change," e.g., the sudden dramatic change of supercooled water vapor into a cloud in the presence of dust as centers of nucleation or the appearance of bubbles about such centers on the release of pressure in a bubble chamber or beer bottle).

But the Richardson approach can be nonlinearized (Saperstein 1984): the response (the acquisition of additional arms) of one nation to the arms supply of a second nation can be made to depend not only on the arms stocks of that second nation but also on the anticipated response of the second nation to the response of the first nation. ("If he does A then I will do B, but he will anticipate that I will respond with B and so be moving to C in which case I had better respond with D . . . .") The resultant equations then have solution classes that represent predictability and classes that represent chaos. Analysis of the equations can determine the critical model parameter relationships that produce solutions on the boundaries between the chaotic and predictable regions. When the model parameters reach these critical values, the model will exhibit transitions from predictability to chaos; the international system being modeled is on the brink of crisis instability. If war is to be avoided in the real system, its behavior—as presented by the model coefficients—must be changed so as to avoid the transition values. The response rates of each nation to the activities of the others must be kept less than the critical values.

Since the nonlinearized Richardson equations represent the interactions between competing states, changes in the forms of these equations represent corresponding changes in the nature or dominant characteristics of international relations. Thus questions about the outcomes of particular types of organization of the international system can be addressed via stability investigations of the corresponding sets of equations. For example, a question particularly pertinent today, after the demise of a cold war world dominated by two "superpowers," is whether a bipolar world is more or less stable than a multipolar world. Aside from academic interest, the question has great practical impact: do we have to be more or less careful in making policies for peace in today's successor to a bipolar world? A simple approach to this question (Saperstein 1991), leading to an unambiguous answer, is to take a nonlinear Richardson model of a two-nation arms race and bring in a third nation, arms-racing with the first two, via a coupling parameter that can vary from zero to one. A zero value means that there is no coupling of the third nation to the first two; the system is a bipolar arms race. When the parameter reaches a value of unity, the model represents three equivalent nations, each arms-racing with the other two: a fully tripolar world. With a fixed intermediate value of the coupling parameter, the size of the region of stability of the model (as measured by the allowed ranges of values of the other model parameters that produce predictive classes of solutions to the model equations) is determined. It is found that the stability region shrinks as the coupling parameter is increased. This implies that the system becomes more and more unstable as it departs further and further from pure bipolarity. Other, more traditional political science analyses (e.g., Midlarsky 1989) have led to the same conclusion, which is thus not novel. However, any science grows and thrives via the confirmation of its results by many different procedures. Science is not a simple thread connecting premise and result but a fabric of many diverse crossing and mutually strengthening threads. Hence this simple mathematical model, invoking chaos as a representation of crisis instability, is a valuable adjunct to conventional political science.

Similarly, the question of whether a world system of democratic states is more or less stable than a system of autocracies has been addressed (Saperstein 1992b). Here the model's rate parameters represent averages, over the decision-making populations of the nations involved, of hostile feelings toward competing outside nations. From sampling theory, the range in parameter values produced by a set of autocracies is greater than that produced by a corresponding set of democracies. Larger values of these parameters mean less stability—more chance of war—among a set of autocratic states. Again, similar results have been obtained by other, less model-oriented approaches (e.g., Russett 1990). I have also used the method to examine the relative stability of balance-of-power worlds versus systems made up of nations, each of which stands alone against the rest (Saperstein 1992a); the chaos domain analysis makes me come down on the side that those who maintain that balance of power (nations combining their "power" in shifting alliances to balance the power of the dominant nation at the moment) are the more stable regimes.

The above three examples of "chaos analysis" of the origin of war (disassociation of the usual international structure) have used military "capability" of the competing nations as the dependent variables. In the previous discussion of the LMZ model of the origin of international structures, the dependent variables are the "intents" of the nations toward one another. A more realistic model would include both types of variables and their interactions: intent incites capability and capability modifies intent. (The whole point of verification of arms agreements is to modify one's intents toward another nation on the basis of its observed military capabilities.) Furthermore, military capability depends on overall economic strength, which in turn is strongly dependent on inter-nation intents. The resultant combined model (Saperstein 1994), including military and economic capability as well as inter-nation "relations," is much more complex—it contains many more parameters, all of which are difficult to obtain from real-world data. Thus specific conclusions are harder to obtain. However, again, some familiar qualitative results can be simply obtained: war will not occur if "military-industrial-governmental complexes" have no significant influence on the evolution of overall economic-political power, nor will it occur if changes in military capabilities do not lead to changes in national intent toward other nations.

A chaos stability analysis can also be used to examine the effects of specific military strategies on international stability. Now that the possibilities of national missile defense regimes are again being raised (e.g., Saperstein 1996a), it is useful to recall the previous Strategic Defense Initiative (SDI)—the so-called Star Wars strategy. Using stability analysis of recursion equations relating the antiballistic missile (ABM) response of each side to the offensive ballistic missiles deployed by the other (Saperstein 1988), it was possible to show that SDI would probably be destabilizing to Soviet-U.S. relations.

Summary and Conclusion

The basic idea of complexity theory is that structure arises from, and decomposes into, elements because these elements interact with each other in a completely deterministic manner: given the rules, and a precise specification of the current state of the elements, the following state is uniquely determined. Also fundamental to the paradigm is the pervasive presence of small random disturbances from outside of the model in question: "small" in that the system changes they produce in any single stage are much less than those due to the deterministic rules of change; "outside" in that they arise from the experimental errors that always accompany any determination of system parameters and/or the interactions of the (necessarily) finite system with its surroundings. These disturbances prevent the "precise specification" of state called for by the fundamental assumption of the theory. The future evolution of the system is due to the repeated deterministic iterations of the interactions between its elements. If the repeated random disturbances cancel one another out, so that the net influence of these fluctuations remains small compared to the changes resulting from the deterministic laws of interaction, the model implies prediction and control of the system. If the disturbances do not cancel but grow and feed on each other so that the result is a cumulative random change comparable to, or greater than, the corresponding deterministic change, prediction is impossible—contingency rules. Whether or not the random perturbations cumulate depends on the details of the deterministic laws of interaction as well as on the specific configuration of the system's elements.

Several investigators have assumed simple competitive laws of interaction between "creatures" surviving by "feeding" on an underlying finite resource base. Computer iterations of these simple ideas, starting from either random or uniform distributions of these creatures over the resource base, have often (but not always!) led to the creation and growth of structures whose organized behavior looks remarkably like that of complex biological or social organisms—such as animals or nations. Similar ideas and techniques, applied to a structured system such as a world of competing nations, lead under some circumstances to chaos in the system, which can be interpreted as "crisis instability." Thus granting the premises, we have an explanation for the contingent origin and evolution of structure and the basis of war.

The similarity observed between the calculated behavior of complexity-dominated systems and the behavior of sociopolitical systems in the real world gives considerable credence to the idea that the real world is dominated by deterministic rules, that the observed contingency is due to the occasional sensitivity of the real system to minor but always present random perturbations. This paradigm is quite different from that which supports the observed contingencies of the world on an underlying stochastic foundation. The choice between the two approaches to sociopolitical reality is not purely academic but has profound practical consequences. Both paradigms rule out the possibility of long-term prediction, but the complexity schema does allow for short-term prediction and thus offers the possibility of control. If the ruling outlook in a population is that sociopolitical life is based on the stochastic paradigm, there is no point in political activity, in trying to form and direct collective behavior toward predetermined ends. The complexity paradigm makes it reasonable for a population to expect effective government, to believe in the possibility of a collective solution to a collective problem. Public opinion polls in contemporary America seem to indicate that we are not convinced of the complexity model these days, but the evidence is not yet all in.

Preliminary Thinking about Methods

10

Webs of Chaos
Implications for
Research Designs

William F. Stroup, II

*It is the mark of an instructed mind to rest
satisfied with the degree of precision which the nature
of the subject permits and not seek an exactness where
only an approximation of the truth is possible.*

—Aristotle

The essays in this volume raise important questions. How can dynamic models be tested experimentally, and how can one distinguish chaos from the randomness it mimics? Furthermore, what protocols should the social researcher take into account when designing research intended to investigate the operation of dynamic systems that are suspected of harboring chaos? The usual technique for testing a theory about potentially chaotic systems is to make a "long" series of measurements and compare them with theoretical predictions. Yet with dynamic systems, the "butterfly effect" of sensitivity to initial conditions can easily invalidate results, since the slightest measurement error typically leads to wide variability and poor fitting of observed data to a predicted model.

This observation leads to some important questions to be addressed in this chapter. For example, what is a dynamic system? What is chaos (or chaotic behavior), and under what conditions will it be manifest? What types of data are needed to test for chaoticity? What are some of the problems associated with acquiring such data?[1]

Dynamics: Terminology

To avoid later confusion, this section gives a brief and general introduction to dynamic systems theory. The reader is referred to the literature, particularly Nayfeh and Balachandran (1995) for an in-depth introduction to dynamic systems and nonlinear analysis.

A dynamic system is one whose state changes with time. Generally, a dynamic system consists of a set of highly interdependent variables evolving over time. Rules can be specified to describe how the system changes from one state to another with respect to time. Such rules need not be mathematical equations, although in this chapter we will be concerned primarily with those that are mathematical in nature.

By implication, the analysis of a dynamic system requires measures in time. The data accordingly must be one of the various forms of a time series (which will be examined later in this chapter). A system can be modeled as evolving in either discrete or continuous time. Discrete time evolution is modeled mathematically by using a set of algebraic maps composed of one or more difference equations. Continuous time evolution is modeled using (one or more) differential equations.

Within systems theory, there are two dominant perspectives used in describing a system's development: dynamic process and static structure. In dynamic systems theory, process refers to variables changing over time as reflected in the time series. Dynamic system structure is the qualitative pattern hidden in the data that can be "teased out" by analysis. The pattern seen is often referred to as the system's long-term behavior, or, mathematically, as the asymptotic behavior of the system as time tends to infinity. Short-term behavior, or state variable values leading up to structure, is called the transient solution, orbit, or trajectory (a path is metaphorically traced in hypothetical space).

The dynamic structures mentioned above may be obtained if three necessary conditions are met by the dynamic system: (1) iteration, (2) nonlinearity, and (3) sensitivity to initial conditions. Some possible social science indicators of these conditions are covered later in the chapter.

System process becomes structure under feedback or iteration. Feedback is found in various situations—amplifier "screeches" in speaking engagements and music concerts, biofeedback-guided meditation, maintenance of moderation in

Aristotelian ethics, or environmental homeostasis. Feedback simply refers to the fact that a portion of model, machine, or system output returns to be used again as input. Mathematically, feedback is called recursion or iteration and is the result of the repetitive application of a rule or set of rules. Whenever the system's future state (x_{t+1}) depends on the current state (x_t), we have iteration. Under iteration, dynamic systems may have either linear or nonlinear rules or both. What is meant by the terms linear and linearity? When an effect is proportional to an incremental change in the cause, and the resulting ratio is independent of any previous change, then we have linearity. Think of a regression equation with a beta coefficient $(Z_1 = \beta_1 Z_2)$. We expect the ratio of the dependent to independent variable $(Z_1/Z_2 = \beta_1)$ to be invariant or independent of what the indicated values previously were for a given analytical unit. Nonlinearity is the exact opposite; effects are not invariantly proportional to their causes.

There are two types of nonlinearity, functional and longitudinal. Longitudinal linearity is implied by iteration over time. Functional linearity refers to the relationship between variables in the model, machine, or system. Functional nonlinearity appears in many guises, for example, (1) simple interaction between two terms; (2) cubic, quadratic, or logarithmic terms; (3) or thresholding. The reader is referred to Brown (1995b) for an account of how longitudinal and functional nonlinear terms are embedded into models.

The last characteristic of chaotic systems is "sensitivity to initial conditions." Initial conditions are the values assigned with which the process of calculating a future state begin. These conditions may be simply the first value(s) observed in a time series or can be otherwise selected by a researcher for a theoretical reason. Sensitivity to initial conditions means that the system's asymptotic behavior varies when the initial conditions are changed by even a small amount (i.e., .00001). Change the initial conditions a little bit, and one obtains patterns of chaos instead of cycles of limited behavior (limit cycles are discussed in more detail in the next section).

Metaphorically, this condition is like holding a leaf and dropping it. The position of the leaf is its initial state. The path it traces in the air to the floor is its trajectory, orbit, or transient solution. Its position on the floor is its asymptotic behavior or its observed dynamic structure. Now take the same leaf, drop the leaf slightly to the left of the previous position (a few microns will do). The new path at first will be very similar to (in some cases exactly like) the old, but then will start to differ dramatically, ending in a new position on the floor—a new structure or pattern. The result is sometimes referred to as the butterfly effect.

Sensitivity to initial conditions means that we can take two dynamic systems, give them the same parameters and variables (i.e., functional form), but give them different starting values (even a small difference), and obtain a result whereby one system is predictable (limit point or cycle) while the other is not (chaotic).

Chaotics: Dynamic System Structures

Under the above conditions, process can lead to at least three types of structure: limit point, limit cycle, and chaos. Figure 10.1 depicts a typical plot of time series data for each structure. The reader is referred to Briggs and Peat (1989), Stewart (1989), or Hall (1991) for general orientation to the patterns.

Recall that structure is the system's long-term behavior. Structure is either time invariant (i.e., constant) or time varying. As can be seen in Figure 10.1, limit point structures, like steady state systems, are constant—unchanging. Limit cycle and chaotic structures are time varying: values change as the system settles into a routine, moving out of the transient solution. Limit points and cycles are often termed periodic behavior while chaos is a form of aperiodic behavior.

Briefly, a limit point structure refers to a variable value repeating in time. In a time series plot, one ought to be able to draw a line through the values (see Figure 10.1a). If a plot is made of x_{t+1} versus x_t, then, one should see a dot/point—hence the name. It has a period of 1.

A limit cycle pertains to variable values that repeat in time at intervals greater than one period (one unit of time). Like the limit point, the system repeats itself but only after several periods have gone by. In fact, in some cases more than one value may repeat itself. If graphed versus time, cyclic structures will be sinusoidal in form (see Figure 10.1b). If a plot is made of x_{t+1} versus x_t, cyclical structures will be circular, ellipsoid, or "corkscrew" in appearance.

Finally, chaos is behavior that is repeated irregularly. Chaos lacks periodicity; it is aperiodic. When graphing this behavior, it will appear random in comparison to both plot types mentioned above (see Figure 10.1c).

Of central concern to the social scientist, then, is how to distinguish these various system states. I explore how to "fingerprint" for chaos below. Obviously, particular types of data must be obtained and particular attention must be paid to the construction of reliable instruments. Measurement error or noise can, and does, sometimes lead to the erroneous conclusion that a dynamic system is exhibiting chaos (Sugihara and May 1990).

Theory and Methods: When to Look for Dynamic Behavior

Ever the since the twilight of Auguste Comte and Herbert Spencer, sociologists have been concerned with uncovering the dynamic essence of society, the general rubric of social change. With regard to dynamic social systems as described above, the analytical techniques have outrun the conceptual maps. What follows in this section is part speculation and part logical deduction. Since patterns flow from conditions, I deal with them first.

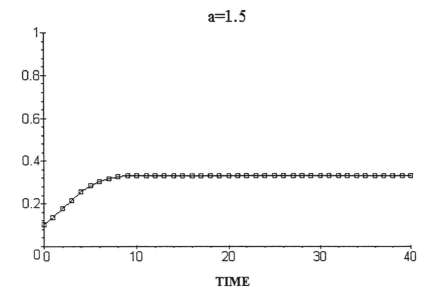

Figure 10.1a. This figure is a time series resulting from the equation $x_{t+1} = 1.5 *$ $x_t * (1 - x_t)$. It depicts limit point, equilibrium, or steady state behavior.
Note. $a = 1.5$.

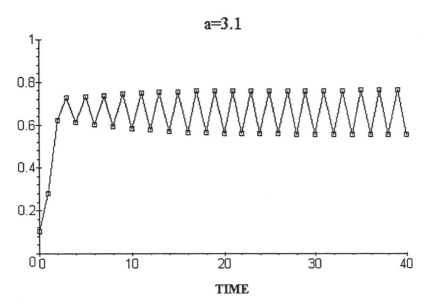

Figure 10.1b. This figure is a time series resulting from the equation $x_{t+1} = 3.1 *$ $x_t * (1 - x_t)$. It depicts limit cycle behavior of period equals two. Note the sinusoidal wave shape.
Note. $a = 3.1$.

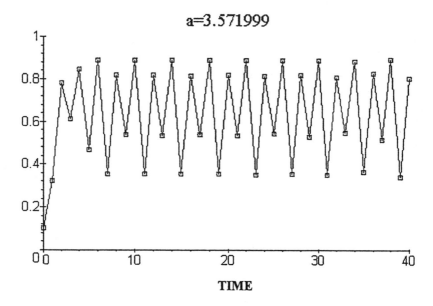

Figure 10.1c. This figure is a time series resulting from the equation $x_{t+1} =$ 3.571999 $* x_t * (1 - x_t)$. Chaos is depicted in this figure. Note a level of randomness that seems to be surrounded by a qualitative order.
Note. a = 3.571999.

The basic form of iteration is feedback. Some current aspect of society, described as its state, is dependent on the historical character of that aspect. The preexisting or historical character of social facts make them potential indicators for iteration. The persistence of institutions and groups are prima facie evidence of the reproduction of culture, norms, rules, and expectations through time. The presence of cultural artifacts and structural constraint produced by and emergent from agency are qualitative indicators of iteration. Examples of iterative social processes include socialization, adaptation, institutionalization, structuration, and reality construction. I believe it not an oversimplification to suggest that all aspects of society undergo some level of iteration.

Nonlinearity is more problematic to grasp. Social scientists have typically dealt with low levels of explained variance in our regression equations for some time. Indeed, there is a pervasive acceptance of this low standard. These low levels may actually be an indication of nonlinearity—after all, Pearson's R is a measure of linearity. Moreover, the inevitable attempt to capture more variance by adding intervening variables is an indication that one or more nonlinear relationships may be present (see below). Some conceptual cues to the presence of nonlinearity would include historical trails pointing to small changes having large effects (or vice versa), "discontinuous behavior" such as shifts in organizational policies or corporate downsizing (Gregersen and Sailer 1993), or situations involving diffusion such as the spreading of innovations, rumors, money, decision making, or cultural bestsellers.

A researcher must be creative in assessing sensitivity to initial conditions. It is very difficult to perform true experiments on large social systems as is well known. One way of getting out of this morass is to use historical data. Many social systems maintain operational records; by taking similar social systems and comparing their archived information, divergence can be assessed. Yet this type of data may not be available. In such a situation, the researcher (with variables of interest) can compare the members of a social system type (i.e., social group) that are situated in historically similar conditions, yet have also evolved differently. Although perhaps relatively homogeneous in the past, there may be characteristics that can substantively account for their divergence. Critical approaches, historiography, and knowledge genealogies are examples of orientations that can be used to uncover indicators that support assertions of sensitivity to initial conditions.

Let us now turn our attention to a brief perusal of pattern indicators. Limit points are the easiest to notice. To conceptually parallel the mathematical definition, limit points must refer to phenomena that are reproduced in the same way over time. Since there is always an element of error involved in observation, to include slight deviations during our interactions, limit points might be difficult to find. For example, most people will eat lunch around the noon hour, sometimes earlier, later, or right at noon. But, if we place bounds on how close behavior must be to qualify as repetition, then the position is tenable. In some cases, a limit point would be an adequate representation or indicator of "social structure." Other examples include instances of rationalization, goal maintenance, role enactment, and traditional work schedules.

In a like manner, we can also find instances of social limit cycles. Speculatively, in the social sciences we may find limit cycles operating when the characteristics of primary and secondary groups fluctuate or cluster around a norm or average, for example, such things as family size, matrimonial age, retirement age, national political party support (thought to be 40% apiece for each of the two dominant parties), solidarity, or value consensus. Other examples of limit cycles include grocery shopping, voting, three-meals-a-day, or, for most, people, sleep. As before, a general agreement must be reached by social scientists as to how close values must be to warrant the label of "repetition."

The last pattern is chaos—exhibited as aperiodic behavior or order mimicking randomness. Some examples of this behavior might include things such as the movement of stock market prices, the gross domestic product, macro

productivity rates, addictive disorders coupled with irregular habits, dating behavior, or social change via "incremental deviance." I believe that this latter area
of the study of chaos is, by far, the one in need of immediate attention.

A final note is in order here. Society can be examined in differing levels of
aggregation—micro, meso, macro, or institutional, national, international.
Conceptually, each level can be seen as a dynamic social system, which in turn
is coupled with levels immediately above and below it (as the case may be).
Dynamic systems theory allows for the levels to exhibit different behavioral
structures; one may be chaotic while the other two are limit cycle or steady state.
This is an area not yet addressed by chaos theory in sociology. To the degree to
which such circumstances may actually exist, our "dynamic" models will always
be less than complete.

Protocols of Data Acquisition

Variable Measurement

When constructing dynamic models, measures should be created while bearing
two things in mind. Specifically, (1) measures are to be longitudinal, and (2) the
environment or context must be measured. Context flows from the nonlinear
nature of social relations while longitudinality flows from the assumptions and
definitions of dynamic systems.

Longitudinal data for a system is called a time series: more than one measure
taken in time. Sociologists use various labels for a time series, such as longitudinal studies, panel studies, experiments, and quasi-experiments. To be time
series data, at a bare minimum the researcher must take measurements at two
points in time. There are various social science examples of a time series. For
example, measurement of public opinion on abortion prior to and after the
national political party conventions, individual perceptions of criminal justice
before and after the "dramatized" O. J. Simpson criminal trial, measures of
electoral support in two consecutive presidential elections, or the measure of
attitudes toward African Americans across consecutive years of the General Social Survey. Generally speaking, the closer together in time the measures are, the
better.

Any dynamic system is embedded within an environment that must also be
measured longitudinally. As Baburoglu (1988) indicates, not only is the system
changing but so is its environment (which ostensibly contains other "systems").
The evolution of the system is dependent in part on a dynamic environment. It
is a main staple of social theorists that a person's or group's social milieu exerts
an influence on social behavior. For example, social psychologists investigate

the role of the reference group on individual behavior and attitudes, and feminist theorists might point to the number of families where the wife does not work as indicative of a community-based normative structure serving as context for female work participation.

No matter how it is stated, some social behaviors vary across individuals or groups simply because the social or "nurture" environment has shifted. Context operates in a nonlinear manner on behavior. Of course, not all nurture variables can be accounted for by the researcher.

Because of the above specification problem (and other related issues), a common solution is for the researcher to construct a "minitheory" that explains away endogenous variables not included in a measurement model. The central idea has been that if the model was wrong or demonstrated a poor fit, then the researcher should not only rule out measurement error but also turn to the reappraisal of variables excluded. Such distinctions of exogenous versus endogenous is not useful in dynamic system analysis. It is always possible to model any given situation from a point of view where there is no exogeneity. System interdependence replaces the exogenous-endogenous distinction. Even so, I believe it can be a fruitful enterprise for the researcher to construct a miniature theory that obviates the influence of certain contextual variables. In the data analysis stage, ruling out contextual nonlinearity allows the researcher to inquire into the possible influence of excluded contextual variables before consideration of linear models and theories.

Given the above protocols, there are general considerations in the acquisition of data. Some fields will have more difficulty than others in obtaining data. History, for example, has the problem of constructing data for past nations. Historical data in the main consists mostly of information about individuals and little about institutional operations. Sociology suffers from this problem also to the degree that some researchers may be interested in constructing a theory of societal development from a particular nation's first stage. With regard to people who are standing in interaction, one possible solution is to begin by gathering data by using a panel type study. By necessity, personal time constraints, access to human participants, and economic costs limit the researcher's freedom in obtaining data. By focusing on a few key indicators and contextual variables, tied to a manageable sample size (200-500 participants), as well as by constructing the "excluded contextual variable" theory, the researcher is able to obtain sufficient data for later analysis. Another possible solution is still to construct the minitheory but use a "canned" time series. Should the time series not have contextual measurements, then archived data such as group membership rolls, census figures (not just decennial data), and local crime statistics can be tapped to provide the necessary longitudinal measures of context. The general principle is: be creative in the choice and source of dynamic variables to be investigated.

A dynamic system is modeled or simulated using differential and difference equations (see below). Their variables take in values on some portion of the real numbers. This implies that variables must be measured at the interval or ratio level and, with simplifying assumptions, at the ordinal level. However, many social science surveys and data acquisition products have nominal or categorical variables. These variables can also be used in nonlinear analysis. Categorical and nominal variables are contextual variables. Nominal variables do not change over time. For example, either a respondent voted in an election or not, or is either male or female. With few exceptions, these variables are not expected to change and do so only on rare occasions. To be of use in a theoretical approach appropriate for the study of chaos, these variable types should be aggregated and used as social context for the other dynamic variables.

Measurement levels assume a distinction between variables that are continuous versus discrete. With regard to dynamic systems, measurement implies two distinct notions of continuous and discrete variable values and measurement with respect to time. Discrete variables take on values in the integers. Choosing a discrete variable means also choosing the level of measurement as nominal, categorical, or ordinal. Continuous variables take on values in the real numbers and lead to interval- and ratio-level measurements. The point being made is that after selection of relevant concepts, the researcher must decide on whether or not the underlying variable should take on continuous or discrete values. As noted above, the choice of variables and the resulting level of measurement leads to different approaches in modeling.

A choice must also be made with regard to measurement across time. Time is taken as a measurement whose values are either real or integer. If a phenomenon, such as birthing behavior, takes place at relative equal intervals of time, then change in variable values is with respect to time, which in turn means that the variable is discrete with respect to time. Conversely, if the measurement is taking on values at every instant between two points in time (a beginning and end point), then change in the value of the variable is effected by time, which in turn means that the variable is continuous with respect to time. Concretely, if the researcher measures something at 12:00 and at 1:00, then the variable is discrete with respect to time. Should the researcher take measurements at every moment between 12:00 and 1:00, then the variable is continuous with respect to time. Discrete temporal variables are modeled by using difference equations. Continuous time variables are modeled by using differential equations.

It should be pointed out that in the real world, it is not possible to measure something at every instant in time, no matter how small the interval. In actuality, all of our measurements are discrete. Conceptually, if a variable should be changing continuously with respect to time, or can be assumed to do so, the researcher can still investigate various differential equations by approximating them with a difference equation using various numerical techniques. The algebra is well defined for converting back and forth from difference to differential equations. The important point here is that a researcher must decide whether data have been or will be measured in discrete time and leave it that way (leading to the difference equation later), or assume that an approximation to continuous time is warranted and proceed to differential equation techniques.

Establishing Reliable Measures

Thus far, we have assumed that the researcher has chosen valid measures. But whether or not a measure is reliable is a different matter. To be reliable, a measurement procedure requires a static phenomenon. Consistent scores are produced when the phenomenon is unchanging; hence we arrive at a problem because chaos theory analysis assumes that variable values are changing with respect to other variables and time.

With the assumption of validity, measures of nominal, categorical, and ordinal variables can be assumed to be reliable in a given analysis if no evidence exists to the contrary. These measures are invariant in most cases. Someone who is Catholic today is likely to be Catholic tomorrow. Similarly, a person who is a woman today will still be a woman tomorrow. In the main, these types of variables are aggregated and used as context. Reliability should not be an issue that prevents a researcher from considering tests for chaos in the data.

Interval- and ratio-level variables are an all together different problem. In a dynamic system, such variables change over time, even if measured over a consistent set of entities. In a typical reliability analysis, relatively speaking, the measurement of an object at Time 1 should have about the same score at Time 2. Obviously, measurement error is tied into this problem. Techniques have been worked out for distinguishing chaos from noise or randomness and in turn from measurement error (see below). To this author's knowledge, the problem of the reliability of measures in dynamic social system modeling has not been addressed. There are some speculative solutions, however. The first solution is to assume that the measures are reliable and stable (i.e., the literature says so), then proceed to the data acquisition phase. A second solution is to assume that the passage of time is an experiment—as in the One Group Pretest-Posttest Research design. One would create a pretest average by averaging the measures across all cases at Time 1, then do the same at Time 2. Then the researcher would proceed to the usual analysis of statistically significant change. In this analysis, though, the researcher is looking for a result of nonsignificant change. A last speculative solution is to take three measurements at two equally spaced intervals, examining their intercorrelations.

According to Heise (1969), we can partition unreliability and change. First, we calculate the reliability coefficient:

$$P_{xx}' = \frac{P_{12} P_{23}}{P_{13}}, \tag{1}$$

where the subscripts refer to the measurement period (i.e., correlation between the measurements at Time 1 and 2). Individual correlations are interpreted as test-retest correlations. The reliability coefficients have the usual interpretation of "highest is best," with one caveat: if the reliability coefficient is substantially higher than individual correlations, then a change in the underlying variables (of course, this is expected for dynamic systems) is indicated and must also be inspected. For the coefficient to positively indicate reliable measurement, one must examine change across time periods to see if they qualitatively match with what the researcher expects to observe. As always, theory guides what is to be expected. The change coefficients, with subscripts as in equation (1) above are

$$S_{12} = P_{13} / P_{23} \tag{2}$$

$$S_{23} = P_{13} / P_{12} \tag{3}$$

$$S_{13} = (P_{13})^2 / P_{12} P_{23}. \tag{4}$$

Thus, if you expect more change between one set of correlations than another, and you find it between (2)-(4), while the coefficient of reliability is also high, then the researcher could conclude that the underlying measure is stable. The reader is directed to Heise (1969) for further interpretative guidance.

Protocols of Data Analysis

Fingerprinting Chaos

Having gathered data, the researcher assumes the role of detective. A systematic approach must be taken to capture chaos. By necessity, the protocols provided here are geared toward a general overview. The reader is referred to the literature, particularly Peitgen, Jurgens, and Saupe (1992) for an excellent hands-on approach to learning to recognize and diagnosing chaos.

The graphical approach is the preferred starting point for several reasons. When the independent variable is graphed versus time, it is readily apparent if there is any periodicity present. Lack of periodicity suggests a system either whose underlying process is stochastic in nature or that is mathematically deterministic and thus productive of chaos. The vertical axis can be steadily incremented in time versus the horizontal, for example, using time $t + 2$ versus t, then $t + 3$ versus t, then $t + 4$ versus t, and so forth. In these examples, limit cycles of period two, three, and four will be revealed. These types of graphs are called return maps, specifically, a first-return map for a vertical axis of $t + 1$, a second-return map for $t + 2$, and so forth. If after this incrementalization has been performed a pattern has not been found, the researcher can tentatively conclude that the system is currently chaotic and proceed to use further tools for analysis. If pattern(s) are found, the researcher takes note of their periodicity and proceeds to confirm the graphical analysis.

The next test is to confirm the graphical findings. One method is to transform data using a Fourier power spectrum (Berge, Pomeau, and Vidal 1984). The spectrum will show peaks at the frequencies of any periodic parts of the con-verted data. A limit point will show one spike, or peak. Limit cycles will show up as multiple peaks. Last, chaos will be exhibited as a broad band of spikes. The researcher should receive relative confirmation of the graphical analysis. It is relative because the graphical analysis is inexact and subject to perceptual error. Additionally, if a limit cycle has many periods, then the potential exists that it will exhibit many peaks in the power spectrum and be confused with the broad band exhibited by potential chaos. The researcher should annotate the results and proceed to the next protocol.

The next test is called the spatial correlation test (not to be confused with linear correlation). It has been recently applied by Richards (1992) in the study of presidential popularity and the concentration of power in international set-tings. The technique is numerically intensive and requires that the researcher have a rudimentary understanding of calculus (i.e., the idea of limits) and com-puter programming expertise. Richards does provide an algorithm that can be used in a variety of different computer languages. Essentially, spatial correlation distinguishes chaos from randomness by examining two differences.

First, a chaotic process will have observations that are spatially correlated. That is, a chaotic process is constrained to a small area of the phase space-plane, cube (3-D space), or hyperspace (4-D and above). Second, a chaotic process has degrees of freedom. The iteration and nonlinearity do not allow it to range outside of the space it is contained within.

A chaotic system will have spatial correlations and low or fractional dimen-sionality. Recall that a solid object is completely three dimensional while a square on paper is planar or two dimensional. A chaotic time series, or any time series for that matter, will usually inhabit a portion of the space between two and three dimensions (or between three and four dimensions), perhaps having a dimension of 2.78, hence a fractional dimensionality.

A computer program can place a circle of given radius over the data. Then, the number of data points in the circle are counted. The goal of the test is to find to what degree the number of data points in the circle depends on its radius. The process continues with progressively smaller circles. The number of points at any given circle size is proportional to the circle's radius raised to an unknown power ($N \sim rv$). Calculus is used to find the best value for the unknown power across all the data, across all circle sizes used. Richards (1992) provides a lucid discussion on how to distinguish the type of dynamic process at work (i.e., limit point, limit cycle, chaotic, stochastic). Because this technique is rather involved, it is recommended that it only be used if the researcher has previously found the broad band phenomenon and cannot distinguish it from a multiple frequency limit cycle.

Beyond the above tests, there are many others that become progressively more tedious and mathematically intensive. Lyapunov exponents can be used to diagnose the degree to which a dynamic system is chaotic, periodic, or near stable in its behavior. This analysis indicates how much a new trajectory (produced by changing variable values) diverges from the original trajectory created with the original starting conditions and parameter values. Wolf (1986) provides details on how to calculate Lyapunov exponents from raw data.

Shaw (1981) suggests that we fit a curve to a first-return map. By averaging the slope over the curve, we are able to obtain an approximate measure of the Lyapunov exponent. For the researcher who is interested only in separating chaos from periodicity, Shaw's technique is the easiest to implement. In terms of being systematic, the researcher could start with Shaw's method and then proceed to spectral analysis for confirmation.

Other esoteric techniques include reconstructing the "chaotic attractor" using one variable's time series, lagging it, then plotting it. Attractor reconstruction is often used with the spatial correlation test. In fact, Richards (1992) deploys a combination of both. This technique will give a dimension for the attractor (limit point, limit cycle, or chaotic attractor). The dimension will be fractional such as 2.36. The dimension is then rounded to the next highest integer, giving a rule of thumb for the number of variables that will probably be needed to model the system.

Proper use of the above procedures is much like a lawyer building a case of guilt based on a preponderance of the evidence. It is my belief that a minimum of three tests must be done to confirm limit point, limit cycle, chaotic, or stochastic behavior. If for no other reason than that some of the methods can give false positives, there must be a triangulation of methods in the data analysis.

Model Selection and Fitting

Model fitting for the analysis of dynamics is more art than science. For most nonlinear systems, mathematical representations or equations cannot be fitted analytically. Generally, there are two types of models that are fitted. If the variables are changing continuously with respect to time, then one is fitting differential equations. If the variables are being measured at equal intervals of time, then one is fitting difference equations. Overall, longitudinal and functional linearity will require definite numerical integration to derive the model parameters.

Generally, computer software packages do not exist for fitting nonlinear difference or differential equations that are based on researcher-defined relationships and variables. A computer program that implements the numerical integration technique in SAS IPL language is provided by Brown (1995b). Brown (1995a) gives a general overview on strategies for fitting chaotic and catastrophe models to data. Richards (1992) also provides details on how a spatial correlation test may be used not only in developing a model but also in the evaluation of its goodness of fit. For a good overall discussion of the intricacies of dynamic modeling based on the behavior of differential equations, see Beltrami (1987).

Conclusion and Caveats

This chapter provides an orientation for the researcher who is interested in investigating dynamic systems. Dynamic systems present unique challenges and peculiarities to the researcher. Because of this, protocols have been laid out for the researcher to bear in mind when acquiring data and performing subsequent analysis for dynamic behavior patterns, particularly with regard to diagnosing chaos. Specifically, data must be longitudinal and take into account the context of the dynamic system. Choices must be made by the researcher as to whether or not measured variables change continuously or at equal intervals with respect to time. The former leads to differential equations while the latter leads to difference equations. Reliability of measurement presents a paradox to the researcher that possibly can be resolved by taking measurements at three points in time and inspecting intercorrelations. Triangulation, the process of using multiple tests, is combined with several tests so that evidence can be assembled that positively identifies chaos, randomness, limit points, or limit cycles.

At this point, I would be remiss if I did not mention further aspects of analysis not covered by this chapter. For the reader interested in applying the ideas of chaos theory metaphorically (as opposed to analytically), Wheatley (1992) applies the ideas to the study of leadership and business organizations. Hayles (1990) gives an overview of how chaos theory can be applied to literature. Dynamic systems theory is only one area of the complexity sciences. Another fruitful area that is being embraced by many of the sciences is fractal theory. Hastings and Sugihara (1993) provide a step-by-step guide to what a fractal is, what a fractal process is, how to measure fractals, and how to construct fractal models of phenomena. Pickover (1996) presents an overview of how fractals are used in art, teaching mathematics to adolescents, music, and medical practice, and Batty and Langley (1994) present an introductory text on how to model the spatial growth of communities. Finally, Peak and Frame (1994) cover the complexity sciences in "cafeteria style," having the reader dabble in exercises involving art, artificial life, neural networks, fractals, and dynamic systems theory.

Because chaos theory and the other complexity sciences are a scant thirty-five years old, there are still many obstacles to surmount in their application. However, like all new, developing theoretical and methodological innovations, creativity and determination are needed to learn how to apply and fine-tune new ideas. It is my belief that all social systems are dynamic, complex adaptive systems. Furthermore, these social systems can and do exhibit chaos. Despite our "objective observers," we must never lose sight of the point that we are part of social systems. As members of these systems, we are all caught in the webs of chaos. This point is perhaps the most important protocol to remember.

Note

1. In an attempt to address these questions, let me state from the outset that there are various research designs used in the social sciences, and this chapter eschews any specific design in favor of drawing out some general concerns and implications. Problems such as maintaining external or internal validity are not unique to dynamic systems and are, therefore, not addressed. Additionally, an extensive outline of model-fitting procedures is beyond the scope of this essay. Accordingly, the specifics of model fitting are not discussed here. Instead, readers are referred to examples of current literature in this field.

11

Chaos and
Social Reality
An Emergent Perspective

R. J. Bird

One etymology of the word "chaos" is "gap"—that which lies in the gap between heaven and earth. Between physics and God lie many sciences. Can the nature of these sciences be revealed by chaos theory?

It is the hope of many people, especially physical scientists, that a complete description of everything in the world may one day be found and that when it is found, then that description may ultimately be given in terms of just a few simple equations—the so-called Theory of Everything. Even if this turns out to be so, there will be many steps between the simplest and the most complex phenomena. Each step will be a science, and each step will create a gap to be filled. These gaps, corresponding to the boundaries between sciences, must be filled by new reformulations of the unit of description—the "atom" or most primitive thing that can be talked about within that science (Middleton 1995). And if, as seems most likely, there is no automatic ascent from the simplest to the most complex phenomena, and the transition is rather a series of sudden steps or levels, then entirely new discoveries must be made and new laws discovered at each of these levels, and those laws will have to be formulated in terms of that level's own peculiar descriptive unit.

The nature of these descriptive units is a discovery that must be made for each science itself and within each science itself. For social psychology it is the person; for biology it is the cell. In some sciences, as in physics, we are not yet sure what that unit is. One reason why it is not clear for any particular science what fundamental unit we should use is that what comes next is far from obvious from what has gone before. As we pass upward through levels of increasing scale and complexity—physics, chemistry, biology—we can get no clue from the level we are working at—from within that science—what the properties of the next lowest level are going to be. Such phenomena are truly emergent, and we cannot tell what will emerge from a combination or collection of entities exactly when they are the highest and most complex objects described by a particular science. How can one anticipate the nature of salt from that of sodium and chlorine? How can we explain consciousness in terms of what is known about neurons and glial cells? How could one foretell, knowing only the individual persons, what the nature of the social group will be if they are brought together, say, at a dinner party? These things are emergent properties, resulting from the interaction of known objects to produce something that is unknown, at least on the first occasion. We cannot in advance lay down rules about those properties that would enable them to be deduced from what is known only at the lower level. No known tautological or mathematical process will yield an emergent property of nature: that is something known only within its own science and unknown to all the others.

Chaos as Emergent Property

What is the part played by chaos theory in this process? Chaos is a mathematical theory. In this realm of mathematical chaos, processes are ergodic and divergent: they produce information. If, on two successive occasions, we choose two starting points separated by only a little, then we will end up at two completely different destinations. Even from a unique starting point in a chaotic system we never quite know where we will end up, because "new" information is continually being manufactured while "old" information is lost. As we move from the nonchaotic system to the chaotic, we may pass through regions of complete unpredictability and apparent disorder to arrive at windows of order: attractors form, strange though these may be. Again, all this is purely mathematical, but these transitions may provide us with a model of the emergent properties of nature. This raises the fascinating possibility that it might be possible to use chaos theory as a model of emergence. The attractor, for example, is implicit in, but unforecastable from, the equation that gives rise to it: to make its shape explicit we must iterate the equation and study its emergent properties. The mathematical process of iteration has emergent properties just as the natural world does: what if these two kinds of emergence correspond to one another in just the way required to enable us to talk about new sciences and their inter-relationships in a productive and consistent way? In chaos theory do we have at last a true Theory of Emergence, or only its forerunner?

All these possibilities lie in mathematics and not necessarily in the real world. Our imaginations are fired by chaos in the social sciences partly because it offers a hope of bringing the attributes of a mature science to an area that until now has seemed intractably complicated except in descriptive terms. While regulari-ties have been discovered in the social sciences, nothing has been found ap-proaching the precise functional relationships between variables, which is the goal of a mature, "mathematicized" science like physics or mechanics. It is partly for this reason—the hope of mathematical validity or perhaps, better, mathe-matical *validation*—that chaos theory is being embraced by social scientists with such enthusiasm.

But in this enthusiasm we must not lose sight of reality. Because chaos is a model that seems to promise so much, we must not be misled into thinking that the promise has already been fulfilled, or even that it can ever be fulfilled, unless we can be sure that the model applies; that chaos and social reality have some-thing in common, that we are not deluded by our optimism into overlooking the necessary methodology and verification that must be gone through in this discipline as in all other scientific enquiries. It is one thing to talk in broad, analogous terms of attractors, bifurcations, and butterfly effects; it is another to verify their existence in a given situation. It is one thing to be able to measure chaos in a chemical reaction tank or a forced pendulum, another to measure it on a city street or in an election. The chaos model has been successful in physi-cal, chemical, and to some extent biological sciences: can it succeed in social science too, or will it be yet another in a succession of mathematical theories that appear to be the key but that later turn out to be impossible to apply? Many people remember the enthusiasm with which catastrophe theory was greeted in the 1970s, and in some important ways catastrophe theory was the forerunner of chaos theory. Catastrophe theory largely failed to live up to its promise be-cause of difficulties in quantifying the parameters of its models, with a resulting failure in forecasting: in the case of chaos theory the hope is that quantities can be attached to the variables and furthermore that the variables will be seen to have meaning. Perhaps through applied chaos theory we can at last forecast and even control processes at the social level. What is the evidence so far that chaos is a model that can be applied to social science?

Chaos—Myths and Realities

Two complementary myths have developed around chaos as an explanatory model, and it would be a good idea to look at these first, to clear the ground.

The first myth, and the easiest one to dispel, is that chaos represents complete uncertainty or even complete indeterminacy. This point of view is not usually taken by those who are looking for precise mathematical explanations. On the contrary, the equation of chaos and indeterminacy is often heard from those who welcome uncertainty as the only certain thing in an uncertain world—here I am thinking especially of some postmodernist interpretations. Used in this way chaos theory is taken to be yet another in the series of twentieth-century instances of science contradicting its own aims and aspirations: relativity, Heisenberg's uncertainty principle, Goedel's theorem, and now chaos theory: the progression sounds like the death knell of certainty.

This is a very basic misconception. One of the most helpful features of chaos is that it can lead to order and indeed to a form of stability that gives us an improved ability to forecast and even control the future. The methods of Sugihara and May (1990) have been developed and work on controlling chaos by Shinbrott and colleagues (1990) has shown that it is easier not harder to control a system that is in chaos than one that is in a limit cycle: this can be done for vanishingly small energy costs by nudging it into a nearby stable orbit. Chaos is first and foremost *deterministic,* and it is this determinism that is illuminating, not indeterminacy.

The second myth is almost the reverse of the first: this is that chaos can be and has been reliably identified in very many social and psychological systems. This is not true either, but for a complex of reasons, some of which will be examined. As a preliminary observation it may be pointed out that the higher the level of a system (in the conventional scientific sense) the greater must be the degree of uncertainty attached to knowledge associated with it. Therefore, chaos may be harder to identify in the social sciences than in, say, physics or chemistry.

The Criteria of Chaos

Three conditions must be realized for a chaotic system: there must be a nonlinear operation; it must be iteratively carried out, that is, the operation is repeated with the output of one iterative cycle becoming the input of the next; and there must be sensitivity to initial conditions. Only if all three conditions are present can we say the system is chaotic: nonlinearity by itself will not guarantee sensitivity to initial conditions; a static system cannot lead to chaos.

A further constraint is that we have to be able to detect the existence of *low-dimensional* chaos if we are to arrive at any means of measuring or maybe predicting the system. Not all chaos is tractable: the higher the dimensionality of the underlying system, the more data need to be amassed to verify it, and the rate of data increase with putative dimensionality is exponential. At the higher end of complexity, chaos shades off into noise, and so far we have only penetrated the mysteries of the lower end of this spectrum.

There is very little doubt that the processes involved in behavioral and social situations are nonlinear. Human behavior is notoriously unpredictable, whether it is in the market place or the board room, and so we can certainly say that the first precondition for the existence of chaos in human affairs is fulfilled. Indeed the problem may be that the nature of the nonlinear relationship is too complex to be modeled in terms of current mathematical techniques—there is too much rather than too little complexity in social systems.

The second requirement is that the system should be iterative—in effect that it is like a fluid flow, driven by nonlinear forces in a quasi-periodic orbit. This does not seem improbable either. Crowd behavior and economic behavior, to take only two examples, both suggest fluid processes, and the linguistic use of fluid-flow analogies—"liquidity" in finance, or "river of people"—suggests this is the case. But here again there is a need to be more precise. Is the nature of the interaction more or less homogeneous, as it would have to be for the chaos model to apply? Is viscosity a constant for any given crowd of people or investors? What about the boundary conditions? Are there "marginal" traders in currencies, who move more sluggishly than those at the center of the market? One of the primary requirements of fluid dynamics is homogeneity. All the molecules in a fluid are assumed to be identical: is this true of investors, shoppers, or rioters?

This leaves us with the third requirement: sensitivity to initial conditions. Here we are on less certain ground. We have to know that a small perturbation in a system will produce very large chances in the results over time. This is not guaranteed by the nonlinear nature of the operation, since such a system may be underdriven and so not enter chaos. It does, on the other hand, presuppose the iterative nature of the system.

Practical Considerations

So far, this is theory. What happens in practice? Even when the three above conditions are satisfied, we must be able to determine that they have been satisfied, and in practice one must use observation to try to verify the existence of chaos. This means using one of the established methods of detecting the presence of low-dimensional chaos.

A number of criteria have been used. One of the first was the question of the divergence of close orbits, since this is a crucial characteristic of chaos. This can be tested by a measure of divergence such as the Liapunov exponent, the average rate at which initially close points diverge from one another. A positive Liapunov exponent is supposed to indicate the presence of chaos. However, it has been shown by Crutchfield, Farmer, and Hubermann (1982) that added noise, even in a genuinely chaotic system, produces a blurring of the iterative map and a loss of all sensitivity of the Liapunov exponent as a measure of the presence of chaos: finding a nonpositive exponent in the presence of noise would not therefore rule out chaos. Another problem is that not all orbits are piecewise smooth (consider stock market prices, which follow a completely nondifferentiable trajectory, very evident in times of crisis but always apparent on a fine enough time scale), and so there will be changes in the magnitude of the exponent from one segment of the time series to another. To smooth out these changes some mean exponent over time is taken, and this may mask big differences in divergence rate. Also, as just mentioned, the magnitude of the exponent is often unreliable as a measure of the degree of chaos. A positive Liapunov exponent is an indication that parallel or converging orbits are absent, but this can come about in other ways. In many systems the answer to the question "positive or negative?" (which is taken to be equivalent to "chaotic or nonchaotic?") gives a simple yes/no answer, which makes the crunching of millions of digits seem a waste of computer time and human effort.

Another sign of chaos is the presence of strange attractors. Again, some caveats must be observed. Not all chaos is accompanied by a strange attractor, nor is every strange attractor a sign of chaos, nor are all fractal attractors strange. But in the bulk of cases we may take a fractal attractor as good evidence for an underlying chaotic process. Here a perceptual problem arises. We can all descry the shape of the Lorenz attractor or the Roessler, but these are mathematically and not empirically derived shapes. Here we tread the verge of the familiar "patterns in the fire" syndrome; even reliably identifying a bimodal distribution presents an often difficult problem.

Yet another line of attack has been to try to measure the dimensionality of the signal and in this way demonstrate the existence of low-dimensional chaos. Given that there are enough data, a difficulty referred to just now, this may be done by means of the saturation dimension or correlation dimension technique, based on the Grassberger-Procaccia algorithm of embedding (Grassberger and Procaccia 1983). Here the method is to embed the orbit of the stepped time series in an increasingly large integral number of dimensions and see what correlation can be achieved between points. While sometimes successful, this technique depends again on a perceptual judgment: in this case of the region of the saturation curve, which can be taken as linear, for the purposes of regression. And again since this is perceptual rather than mathematical, the reliance that we can place on the seemingly numerically precise answer is reduced. It is rather like standing in the street deciding which of the passersby look to be of Russian extraction and then measuring their heights and averaging them to two decimal places.

One final problem will be referred to in this connection as an example of the kinds of difficulties that can arise. During the course of determining dimensionalities, a basis must be established for the embedding dimensions. This ought ideally to consist of orthogonal axes, on which the points of the orbit can be located. Choosing these depends on the choice of the offset interval (or tau), which is used when reconstructing the attractor by decomposing the time series into a number of segments following the method of Farmer and Sidorowich (1987). Tau can be an all-important factor in reconstructing the attractor in this artificial phase space, which is after all not the original phase space but an *imitation* of it created by courtesy of the Takens theorem. If too low a value is selected for the offset of the segments, then the axes will not be orthogonal but skewed, producing a false value for the correlation dimension. One recommendation is that the autocorrelation of the time series should be tested for increasing lags. Only when the lag has reached a value where the autocorrelation has fallen low enough (say, below 0.1) can the tau value be chosen as a value greater than or equal to this lag.

Another recommendation is that the tau value be chosen when the autocorrelation function makes its first intersection with the lag axis. This value of tau is usually much lower, since the autocorrelation function generally follows a sinuous path around the lag axis. Now if this second method is used it follows that the average value of autocorrelation of the time series is close to zero; however, this average autocorrelation is formed by taking values over the whole time series, some of which will show a positive and some a negative autocorrelation, while summating to zero. The autocorrelation value for subsections of the time series, may be very different, again leading to errors.

All this may seem to be straining at gnats: if these objections were "merely" theoretical and made little or no practical difference it would hardly be worth considering them in such detail. But the results of chaos data analysis are notoriously variable, so much so that two different attempts to determine the value of a correlation dimension or a Liapunov exponent are often not in the same ballpark. I do not cite this particular example of analytical problems because it is particularly associated with weak studies; on the contrary, it is often to be found in comparatively strong and very honestly reported ones. I cite it to question the reliability of the attempts made in general, and often on a once-only basis, to estimate such basic parameters of a supposedly chaotic system.

It is a fundamental requirement for chaos theory to be applied that we have a situation where the necessary conditions hold: as we have seen, this demands homogeneity of the system, iteration of the processes driving it, and sensitivity to initial conditions. It is necessary to examine each particular system to verify these various requirements. As an example of an attempt to verify the condition of homogeneity, I will take an experiment carried out to see whether a social act is passed on reliably from one person to another. If these conditions cannot be met there seems little point in looking for other, even less obvious, signatures of chaos.

This study was aimed at determining whether the social act of holding doors open for other people is a behavior that is passed on. The experiment was based on the observation that while at one time people simply passed through a swinging door letting it go behind them, a polite, door-holding pattern had replaced this and become established quite quickly. This led to the supposition that the situation might be a chaotic one in which a behavior becomes established in the manner of an attractor. To test this idea, the very first thing to do is to establish whether people are sensitive enough to an act received from others to pass it on consistently, and thus whether the system displays homogeneity.

The Experiment

When treated badly by others some people treat the others badly in return—this has been called a Tit for Tat (TFT) strategy and has been found among people playing the game of Prisoner's Dilemma (PD) (Rapoport and Chammah 1965), which has been explored by Axelrod (1984). In PD two prisoners can cooperate or betray one another in return for a lighter sentence. If the game is played iteratively in several rounds then various strategies emerge. Some players betray their partners either immediately or after a number of rounds. If an act of betrayal is returned on the next round this is a TFT strategy. Other strategies also appear, such as Tit for Two Tats (TFTT), where on the first occasion of betrayal the recipient shows forbearance and only retaliates on the second occasion. The implications for many phenomena of biology of strategies emerging in PD have been discussed by Hamilton and Axelrod (1984) and by Trivers (1971).

The situation becomes more complicated when, as often occurs in social situations, the Tit is directed at a different person from the one who delivered the Tat. The recipient of the Tat may then pass on another Tat to a fourth person and so on (for a discussion of the mechanisms involved in the passing-on of acts of this kind, see Hamilton 1995).

There are advantages and disadvantages in TFT, TFTT, and so on to the individual and to the population as a whole. The situation has something in common with the concept of an evolutionary stable strategy (ESS) in sociobiology (Masor, Hornstein, and Tobin 1973). An ESS is a pattern of behavior that spreads through an animal population as it evolves, for example, aggressive behavior or nonaggressive behavior ("hawks" or "doves"). Animals that behave like hawks may secure more resources, and so the hawk strategy may lead to a higher survival rate and thus spread itself through the population. Once the hawk pattern is established, however, it may not remain stable under the impact of a new strategy, and, for example, a dove strategy may pay off. Animals that behave like doves may obtain more help from others in emergencies, and so the dove strategy may make a comeback. Thus either hawk or dove or a mixture of the two may become (temporarily) an ESS. In this way we may get waves of TFT behavior spreading throughout the population.

Humans learn much of their behavior, so in TFT we are studying the spread of learned, not just genetically determined, behavior. Strategies such as TFT and No Tit for Tat (NTFT) will therefore be referred to as a (potentially) behaviorally stable strategy (BSS).

It had been observed that door-holding behavior has now become almost universal in the University of Northumbria, while at one time (about fifteen years ago) the passenger through a doorway typically released the swinging door after using it, careless of the person behind. It is interesting to speculate that door-holding has become a BSS, and the object of this experiment will be to test whether door-holding or non-door-holding is passed on, as the possible basis for the formation of a BSS.

Method

Observers noted whether door-holding or a failure to hold the door was passed on (TFT) or not passed on (NTFT). It was not possible to get enough spontaneous non-door-holding behavior out of the population, and so as an alternative to passive observation a manipulative experiment was mounted involving an observer and two agents. The agents walked one in front and one behind a person approaching a door. The first agent walked in front and either held the door open for the person behind him or her or let it go regardless (trying not to knock anyone out!). The observer then noted whether the act of minor kindness or unkindness is passed on (TFT) or not (NTFT) to the second agent walking behind.

Results

Analysis

A chi-square test was carried out and was significant ($\chi^2 = 42.02$, $df = 1$) at the .001 level. Door-holding for another is not independent of whether the door

Table 11.1 Observed Door-Holding Frequency by Behavior of Agent

	Input		
Output	Door Held by Agent 1	Door Not Held by Agent 1	Total
Door held for agent 2	226	179	445
Door not held for agent 2	88	170	258
Total	354	349	703

Table 11.2 Observed TFT and NTFT Behavior by Sex of Participant

Behavior	Female	Male	Total
TFT	163	157	320
NTFT	91	120	211
Total	254	277	531

Note. TFT = Tit for Tat; NTFT = No Tit for Tat.

is held open for you. The persons observed were nearly three times as likely to hold the door open for the next person as not when it was held open for them; when it was not held open for them they were about equally likely to hold it open for the agent as not. There was a greater tendency toward TFT than NTFT in a ratio of about 8 to 5.

TFT versus NTFT for Men versus Women

It is a question whether men have a greater tendency toward NTFT than women than vice versa. For example, if a man has a door slammed in his face is he then equally likely to hold it open for the next person, demonstrating a fixedness of purpose rather than being influenced by the last event to occur? An analysis of TFT versus NTFT for men and women was carried out.

A chi-square test was done but was not significant ($\chi^2 = 2.8$, $df = 1$) at the .05 level. TFT/NTFT behavior is not dependent on gender. However, there are gender differences. Women are almost twice as likely to return TFT as NTFT, men only slightly more likely.

Conclusion

It may be concluded that TFT is a behavior likely to be passed on to others. This opens the possibility—but does not yet establish—that the system is homogeneous and sensitive to initial conditions.

Given that we have the basis of a system that is both iterative and sensitive to initial conditions, the next step will be to progress to a further exploration in an attempt to assess the sensitivity to penetration by alternative strategies, such as TFTT. Alternative strategies may prevail for varying periods of time, and the system may also show a particular sensitivity to these when introduced. There may, for example, be critical times at which the introduction of a strategy will be possible and other times at which the system is resistant to changes of this nature. Bifurcation points (see, e.g., Schuster 1987) are a chaos model that may be worth exploring in this context; for example, at a pitchfork bifurcation the system may be diverted into one of two possible future scenarios, a feature not present at other points in the orbit in time (Abraham 1996). If these can be identified then social systems can be analyzed in terms of choice points for their penetrability by a new behavior, or fashion.

Summing Up

What is the moral of this experiment and how does it relate to the context of the applicability or otherwise of chaos theory to social science, the message I have being trying to put across? As this example has shown, much needs to be done to show how chaos explains events in a social science setting, if we are to go further than the simple use of analogies. Certainly, the complexities of human behavior seem quite sufficient to supply any degree of nonlinearity: this would fulfill the first condition for chaos. Again, social interactions are frequently iterative in nature, supplying the second requirement also. If we can further verify sensitivity to initial conditions in a given situation we may begin to get somewhere.

What has been applied here to one kind of social act could be extended to many others. Patterns of behavior—behavioral fashions almost, ranging from literal fashion in clothes to use of slang—sweep through populations in a way reminiscent of an epidemic and give rise to patterns of events deeply reminiscent of Jung's idea of synchronicity. Road rage, to take a current example, has arisen at almost the same time in many widespread places, and it is fascinating to speculate on its mode of transmission. Does it depend on the exchange of TFT and NTFT acts? Do the media play an important part with their high-profile reportage of spectacular acts of violence? Is it due to some hitherto unidentified common factor in the environment weakening psychological control?

There has been a feeling among chaologists in the social sciences that chaos theory provides an almost model-free approach to theory: analyses of time series yielding estimates of dimensionality and Liapunov exponents are examples of this. To arrive at such estimates, no model of the situation is required, and it is all too easy to forget that one may be needed. This is a dangerous tendency. In physics, chemistry, mechanics, and physiology, where chaos theory has been most successfully applied, models of the processes taking place already exist and chaos analysis serves to supplement these models and flesh out the picture with additional parameters. But in social science a very different situation prevails. In large part we still lack insight into the nature of social interactions, what the variables of social situations are, and what the functional relationships between them may be. To show that chaos theory can explain events in a social science setting, we must begin to understand the nature of those interactions, variables, and relationships. To return to the language of emergent properties once again, we must learn to know each new science and when we are using it and how to know the emergent properties of each new layer of science. We may then be in a better position to test the descriptive and explanatory power of chaos theory in a social context.

12

Chaos and Pattern in Complex Systems

Ben Goertzel

In both engineering systems theory and mathematical dynamical systems theory, one studies systems in terms of temporal changes in numerical variables. This is a powerful paradigm for modeling and data analysis, with a great deal of history behind it, and a large amount of theory backing it up. When confronted with highly complex systems, however, this numerical paradigm becomes uncharacteristically unproductive.

One possible alternative, proposed by Varela (1978) and since pursued by many others, is to found a new systems theory on the concept of autopoiesis or self-production. Another possibility, suggested in Goertzel (1993a, 1993b, 1994), is to take algorithmic pattern as the basis for the study of system dynamics. In fact these two approaches to systems theory are intricately interrelated (Goertzel 1994). Taken together, they provide a new and interesting way of thinking about complex systems.

In this chapter, inspired by this emerging nonnumerical approach to complex systems science, I will explore some of the specific ways in which algorithmic pattern manifests itself in complex system dynamics, especially chaotic complex system dynamics. I will describe the chaos language algorithm, a computational technique for inferring formal languages representing the dynamical structure of complex systems. And I will present the chaos language hypothesis, which suggests that the grammars thus derived from real-world complex social and psychological systems will tend to "cluster" into a relatively small set of categories.

Patterns in Systems

Before one can discuss algorithms to recognize patterns in systems, or principles governing patterns in systems, one must first clarify the nature of pattern itself. There are many ways to formalize the notion of "pattern." For example, algorithmic information theory (Chaitin 1986) gives us a convenient way of studying pattern using the theory of universal Turing machines. However, the concept of pattern is arguably more basic than the theory of universal computation. In previous publications (Goertzel 1993a, 1993b, 1994) I have given a very simple mathematical definition of pattern and used it to model numerous psychological and biological processes. Namely, one may define a pattern as "a representation of something simpler." In symbols, this means, roughly speaking, that a process p is a pattern in an entity e if (1) the result of p is a good approximation of e, and (2) p is simpler than e.

More rigorously, let d be a metric on the space of "entities," and let s be a "simplicity function" mapping the union of the space of entities and the space of processes into the real numbers. Let f denote the result of carrying out the process p, and suppose d is scaled so that $d(f,e) = 1 / c$ represents an unacceptably large degree of dissimilarity. Then the degree to which p is a pattern in e is reasonably defined by the formula

$$IN(p\,|\,e) = [1 - c\,d(f,e)\,/\,s(e)]\,[s(e) - s(f)]\,/\,s(e). \tag{1}$$

The set of all processes p that are patterns in e is called the structure of e; it is denoted $St(e)$ and is a fuzzy set with degrees of membership determined by equation (1).

In general, when studying a system, one is interested in patterns that are recognizable in equation (2).

$$Hist(S) = [S(t), S(t + 1), \ldots, S(r)]. \tag{2}$$

These might be called "static/dynamic patterns." They are patterns that incorporate information about both the static structure of a system at a given time and the dynamic structure of a system's temporal trajectory.

Next, to understand the complexity of systems, it pays to introduce the further concept of emergence. Let $e + f$ denote some kind of combination of the two entities e and f (such as, if x and y are two physical entities, the composite entity obtained by placing e and f next to each other). Then a process p is an emergent pattern between e and f to the extent

$$IN(p\,|\,e + f) - [IN(p \mid e) + IN(p\,|\,f)]. \tag{3}$$

So, suppose the system $S(t)$ is composed of a collection of "component parts," $\{Si(t), i = 1, \ldots, N\}$. Each component part leads to its own equation $Hist(Si)$, and hence to its own static/dynamic patterns. A complex system is one in which a great number of emergent patterns arise as a consequence of interactions between the parts. In other words, the complexity of a system should be measured in terms of the size of

$$St[Hist(S)] - \{St[Hist(S1)] + \ldots + St[Hist(S_N)]\}. \tag{4}$$

The measurement of the size of a fuzzy collection of patterns is a matter of some difficulty; one must subtract off for overlap among different patterns, and there is no entirely "fair" way to do so. This issue is discussed in Goertzel (1993a).

It is also useful to define more specific types of patterns in systems. What I call a "purely static pattern" is, quite simply, a pattern in the state $S(t)$ of a system S at some given time t. A "dynamic pattern" is, on the other hand, a pattern that is observable in the way a system changes. This pattern need have nothing to do with the actual structure of the system at any given time; it must emerge solely from observations of the way in which the system changes from one time to the next.

One way to get at purely dynamic pattern is the method of symbolic dynamics (Alekseev and Yakobson 1981). In this approach, one partitions the state space of a system into $N + 1$ regions, and assigns each region a distinct code number drawn from $\{0, \ldots, N\}$. The system's evolution over any fixed period of time may then be represented as a finite series of code numbers, the code number for time t representing the region of state space that contains the system state $S(t)$. This series of code ! numbers is called a "symbolic trajectory"; any pattern observable in the symbolic trajectory of a system will clearly be a purely dynamic pattern.

This technique for recognizing purely dynamic patterns is particularly useful where the system involved is chaotic. Chaos, which involves dynamical unpredictability, does not rule out the presence of significant purely dynamic patterns. These patterns reveal themselves as the structure of the chaotic system's strange attractor. Examples will be given in the following section.

The Chaos Language Algorithm

In this section I will describe a computational algorithm for extracting patterns from systems, developed collaboratively by the author and Gwen Goertzel, called the chaos language algorithm (CLA), and described in detail in Goertzel and Goertzel (1995). In its current implementation, the CLA is being used for the recognition of purely dynamic patterns, and it recognizes only a narrow class of patterns: context-free grammars emergent from symbolic dynamics. But this type of pattern is very common in practice; thus even this simplistic implementation is of definite use in the analysis of real systems.

The concept at the heart of the CLA is the use of formal languages to represent patterns in the trajectories of a dynamical system. In its simplest version, the CLA is a three-stage process, consisting of the following.

1. Discretization of trajectories of a dynamical system by symbolic dynamics. One divides the potential state space of the system into a finite number of disjoint regions and assigns each region a code symbol, thus mapping trajectories of the system into a series of code symbols.
2. Tagging of symbolic trajectory sequences using a self-organizing tagging algorithm. One takes the symbols derived in the first step and assigns each one to a certain "category" based on the idea that symbols that play similar roles in the trajectory should be in the same category. The "tag" of a code symbol is a number indicating the category to which it belongs. The code sequence is thus transformed into a "tag sequence."
3. Inference of a grammar from the tag sequence produced in the previous step, and iterative improvement of the tagging to maximize grammar quality.

The end result of this algorithmic process is a formal language that captures some of the statistical and algorithmic structure of the attractor of the dynamical system. Each of the three stages may be carried out in a variety of different ways; thus the CLA is as much a "meta-algorithm" as it is an algorithm in itself. A simple example of the application of the CLA is given by the "three-halves map" (Goertzel, Bowman, and Baker 1993; Goertzel and Goertzel 1995):

$$x_{n+1} = (1.5x_n) \bmod 1. \tag{5}$$

This iteration, begun from almost any x_0 in the unit interval, leads to a chaotic trajectory on the interval. But this trajectory, though chaotic, is not devoid of dynamic pattern. If one divides the unit interval into 10 equally sized nonoverlapping subintervals, a trajectory of the system is encoded as a series of integers from 0 to 9, where the tag i represents the subinterval $[i / 10, (i + 1) / 10]$. The

CLA, with appropriately chosen parameters, is able to form the optimal categories:

Category 0: 0 1 2 3 4 5 6
Category 1: 7 8 9

These categories give rise to natural grammatical rules. For instance, one finds that 00 01 10 are all grammatical constructions, but 11 is forbidden. Just as "V V" is forbidden in English (one does not have two consecutive verbs, though there are apparent exceptions, e.g., gerunds), 11 is forbidden in the language of the three-halves map. Similarly, 000 010 100 001 are all permitted, but 101 is not.

These grammatical rules are (approximate) patterns in the system. They allow one to make predictions about the system: if at time t the system is in a state that falls into Category 1, then at time $t + 1$ it will definitely not be in a state that falls into Category 1. If at time t it is in Category 0, and at time $t - 1$ it was in Category 1, then at time $t + 1$ it must remain in Category 0. Furthermore, there are statistical predictions; for example, if in Category 0 at time t, there is a two-thirds chance of remaining in Category 0 at time $t + 1$. This kind of prediction can be made despite the underlying chaos of the dynamical system. The key is in choosing a categorization that leads to a suitably restrictive grammar. This is what the CLA attempts to do. In the case of the three-halves map, the CLA can find the correct partition only if grammatical information is given enough weight in the tagging process. Purely statistical information is in this case misleading, and the most effective tactic is to explicitly search for the tagging that leads to the most informative grammar. This is a very simple example, but the CLA also works in more complex cases.

For instance, Allan Combs (1992) has collected data sets tracking the moods of four individuals, self-reported half-hourly. The data sets are two dimensional, one dimension consisting of a numerical measure of excitation, the other a numerical measure of happiness; all are on the order of 550-750 points long. These trajectories are chaotic in the sense of possessing positive Liapunov exponent (sensitivity to initial conditions). Data from one subject, using a 6×6 partition of the state space and hence an alphabet of 36 symbols, led to categorizations such as

Category 0: 5 7 8 10 11 14 22 24
Category 1: 12 13
Category 2: 0 1 2 3 6 17 18 19 20 23 28

From this categorization the following first-order probabilistic rules are derived (where, e.g., 00 # 36 indicates that the sequence 00 occurred 36 times in the data set).

    00 # 36.000000
    01 # 41.000000
    02 # 7.000000
    10 # 36.000000
    11 # 419.000000
    12 # 55.000000
    20 # 12.000000
    21 # 50.000000
    22 # 67.000000

While not as clean as the grammar for the three-halves map, this nevertheless gives some useful rules of thumb. Mood Category 1 would seem to represent a "normal mood"—it is by far the most common category. When in a normal mood this person is very likely to stay in a normal mood. On the other hand, when in Mood Category 0, the person is extremely unlikely to switch over to Mood Category 1. Instead, the two options of remaining in 0 or returning to normal are about equally likely. On the other hand, when in Mood Category 2, a switch back to Category 0 is unlikely. The most common outcome is to stay in 2, with return to normal following close behind.

The Chaos Language Hypothesis

As yet, complex systems science is peculiarly lacking in abstract principles of depth and generality. But it seems possible that the explicit study of pattern and structure may be of aid in filling this gap. In this section I will present a possible general principle of complex systems science: the chaos language hypothesis. This hypothesis is eminently falsifiable; further work on the inference of structure from complex systems will automatically put it to the test.

The chaos language hypothesis states that the CLA will tend to produce similar grammars even when applied to very different psychological or social systems. In other words, it claims that psychological and social systems demonstrate a small number of "archetypal" attractor structures and that the attractor structures observed in real psychological and social systems approximate these archetypal attractor structures. Mathematically speaking, the approximation of these archetypes should reveal itself as a clustering of inferred formal languages in formal language space. Thus one obtains the following formal hypothesis:

> *Chaos language hypothesis.* The formal languages implicit in the trajectories of psychological and social dynamical systems show a strong tendency to "cluster" in the space of formal languages.

This hypothesis suggests the following three-stage research program:

1. By computational analysis of data obtained from empirical studies and mathematical models, try to isolate the archetypal formal languages underlying complex psychological and social systems.
2. Analyze these languages to gain an intuitive and mathematical understanding of their structure.
3. Correlate these languages, as far as possible, with qualitative characterizations of the systems involved.

Space does not permit a detailed discussion of the archetypal structure s that seems likely to be found by this program.

However, if the postulated phenomenon of clustering could be shown, this would be a very useful way of using dynamical systems theory to find precise mathematical structures representing the qualitative, nonnumerical properties of complex psychological and social systems. And this would, needless to say, be an extremely significant advance.

Conceptual Models
and Applications

13

Dynamics of Children's Friendships

Lutz-Michael Alisch
Shahram Azizighanbari
Martin Bargfeldt

What are the benefits of the new sciences of chaos and complexity to the social sciences, beyond the metaphors of chaos, nonlinearity, and complexity as they apply to the dynamics of social systems? Although the dawn of catastrophe theory and its applications has broken in sociology and social psychology (Tesser and Achee 1994), the theoretical sun has yet to reach its zenith. Are implementations of the dynamical systems theory merely a reiteration of the same old social science procedures (Guckenheimer 1978; Arnold 1986) with only small perturbations of the tenor? Some researchers are likely to say that today's theory is quite different. First, we have the ability to evoke complex time series data and search for patterns, with the help of embedding techniques

AUTHORS' NOTE: The modeling is reported here without mathematical details. For further information and details, please contact Lutz-Michael Alisch at

alisch@tudurz.urz.tu-dresden.de, or at bargf@aix1.rz.uni-landau.de.

This research project is supported by the Deutsche Forschungsgemeinschaft (DFG), grants Al-368/2-1 and Wa 546/3-1.

and state space reconstruction or neural networks (Gershenfeld and Weigend 1994). Second, we can do much more than identify chaos just by inspecting pictures (Bassingthwaighte, Liebovitch, and West 1994). Third, there is a way to move from data to attractors to theory. Furthermore, why should a solution to the problem of nonlinear inverse problems (Anger 1990), or global ill-posed problems, not be true? Families of trajectories and other dynamics can be found when going back from attractor to attractor, enabling us to elaborate a theory of global inverse problems.

However, there are limitations. First, data alone cannot force a theory.[1] When we consider two alternative theories differing not in their formulas but in their expansions, on the way from data to theory we cannot decide which of the theories is the correct version (Potthoff 1981). Data can lead one only to a class of theoretical alternatives, but not to a specific theory.

Second, there is no way, from the analysis of repetitive motions alone (which are the periodic motions in some special cases), to derive the relations between properties of the repetitions and the topology of the manifold on which the dynamic is acting (Anosov and Bronshtein 1988). If one is to identify the topology (and this seems to be exactly the aim of the embedding techniques of nonlinear time series analysis), then one has to put theoretical derivations on to the results of data analysis.

Third, there is the question of whether a classification system for a minimal number of measure points in a time series can guarantee an accurate reconstruction of the phase space set and the determination of its dimensions. In the case of box-counting, the minimal number is $N = 10^D$ (cf. Bassingthwaighte et al. 1994). For the standard Grassberger-Procaccia procedure, a worst case analysis leads Smith (1988) to suggest a requirement of $N = 42^D$ data points, while Ruelle (1990) shows that in best cases $N = 10^{D/2}$ (Ellner et al. 1991). In the case of chaotic systems influenced by additional external stochastic noise, further problems in estimating dimensions are to be expected (Ramsay and Yuan 1989).

Last, because of the logical undecidability of the Julia set or the Mandelbrot set (Blum, Shub, and Smale 1989; Shub 1993; Blum and Smale 1993), it is convenient to conjecture that the basins of other strange attractors are also undecidable. That may be the reason for the nondecomposability of the dynamics of chaotic systems (Crutchfield and Young 1990). Do we go beyond the limits of the undecidability of the trajectories through the basins of chaotic attractors with the aid of data analysis? Can we derive mixed dynamics, which are not completely decomposable, from the data alone?

In view of these limitations, the question of an adequate research strategy still remains. How can we overcome these limitations? Is it possible to gain the theory directly from the data when we apply nonlinear time series analysis? Or do we have to take into consideration that theories in all cases differ from data with respect to the logical type and sort of their underlying formal language (Suppes 1969; Quine 1975)? In this case, theory needs a surplus of information that is not required to analyze attractors or to reconstruct a phase space. The options for future research appear to be limited: we can decide not to investigate such a process because of insufficient research tools; we can do a time series analysis of small observation sets (Maciejowski 1978) within traditional linear modeling; or we can further develop theoretical models that explore the various processes mathematically. Via numerical solutions or simulations, the researcher can then carefully direct empirical verification, accounting for further adaptive development of the model and tests, in a step-by-step process.

We have chosen the third option. The following pages describe the model we use and some of its flows. First, however, we need to address a further problem. If nonlinearity opens the door to a new paradigm, what are we to do with the outcomes of the old one? Are they of any use to us at all? According to Max Born (see Einstein and Born 1982:211-213), every paradigm produces important experimental results and empirical insights. The new paradigm has to account for these results and insights—termed "crass things" by Born—before moving on to new territory. Since we are proposing a model using a new paradigm contained in the data, that is, a preanalytic model that integrates the available findings and gives a platform for further theoretical derivations, we must account for crass things from the old paradigm. Are there any aspects of previous research that we have to take into consideration?

Children's friendship has spawned hundreds of studies about the characteristics of children and the things that influence them. There is, however, very little research on the process of children's friendship in terms that correspond to panel data or videography. To our knowledge, no one has investigated the thousands of values in a time series required to analyze attractors or to reconstruct a phase space.

Traditional Modeling

In the past, friendship has often been used to study microsocial relations, particularly reciprocal relationships between subject-orientated research and the development of new methodological procedures. There is, for example, the pioneering work of Lazarsfeld and Merton (1954); the Davis and Leinhardt (1972) approach; and Johnson's (1986, 1989) remarkable network studies and models that integrate Menger networks, Heider triads, Davis-Leinhardt triads, cluster clique models, the transitivity model, and macromodels for groups. In addition, some theoretical principles have been adapted from migration and population dynamics (Dendrinos and Sonis 1990), although they have not been verified empirically, for example, the principle of spatial or positional heterogeneity (no two social locations are alike) and the principle of heterochronicity (no two social time periods are alike).

Along these lines, a distinction has been made between state dynamics (change of mutual affection, also often called process dynamics) and parameter dynamics (change of friendship understanding, also called structure dynamics; see Wagner 1991), wherein global parameter dynamics incorporate the effects of the two principles. But no one has investigated the obvious problem of how to characterize the separate dynamics or tried to answer the question of how they should be coupled. Dynamical coupling often evokes nonlinearity, but research on children's friendship uses phase models, such as the ABCDE-model constructed by Levinger (1980; Levinger and Levinger 1986), originally developed to explain adult friendship or long-term dyadic relations:

A: Attraction (initial phase of process of friendship)
B: Building (elaborative phase)
C: Continuation (consolidated phase, long-term stability of personal relationship)
D: Deterioration (crumbling phase)
E: Ending (breakup of friendship; ending through death)

In the case of a life-long friendship, the ABCDE-model assumes two linear stable phases, A and B, and presupposes a discontinuous transition point between them. If the discontinuity appears, the phase entry passes into a growing linear development until it reaches the next transition. Stability of a phase is seen as the persistence in time of invariant parameters. Phase C is characterized as growing satisfying continuation, but passes a discontinuity in the neighborhood of E (i.e., misses out on phase D), which means that no further growth takes place and the friendship remains at the same level. In technical terms, phase E is not a phase at all, but rather a fixed point or stable attractor that is reached continuously from the invariant part of phase C.

Yet at the transition point from phase B to phase C, the orbit of the process of friendship can take another direction, indicating a lowering of closeness. Then phase C is identical to a placid, static continuation. Obviously, the transition point from B to C is a bifurcation point that can lead either to a "growing, satisfying continuation" (Levinger 1980:522) or weak decrease. In the latter case, another discontinuous phase change appears from C to D leading to divergence and decoupling. Thereafter the process switches into phase E, ending up with separation.

In phase C, when the process of friendship passes through the bifurcation point, yet another qualitatively different development is possible that represents an "unstable, conflictful continuation" (Levinger 1980:522, Fig. 5). The orbit fluctuates, changing continuously until phase D, where it then decreases exponentially. Finally, it moves continuously on to phase E and ends with separation. Levinger (1980) describes these transition points as switch points. He also assumed that when the friends pass the various transition points, they make the decision whether or not to initiate a friendship, to consolidate it, to let it deteriorate, or to terminate the relationship. The overall system is an open one, which means that the system interacts with its environment.

According to Baron, Amazeen, and Beek (1994:125), Levinger's model lacks specification of a measure for the observed patterns of behavior or an order parameter describing changes that occur in phase transition. Levinger suggests that involvement (referred to as "commitment" by Baron et al.) is the state parameter that indicates change in the process of friendship. Levinger holds that the value of this parameter is a result of some other varying quantities (control parameters) such as the frequency, duration, or diversity of interaction of the friends; its positivity and intensity of affect, its synchrony of behavioral accommodation, its openness of communication, its trustfulness, its commonality of plans and outcomes (Levinger 1980:537). Baron et al. (p. 126) point to intimacy, frequency of interaction, and affect intensity as being particularly good control parameters.

From this conceptual treatment, Baron et al. move on to an empirical characterization of parameters. The order parameter of commitment or mutuality of investment to the friendship can be indexed by a dynamic quantity, which changes continuously. The "empirical order parameter is the joint exclusivity of free-time investment in the other person, with complete interchangeability of time investment between target and alternative other partners anchoring one end of a continuum and nonsubstitutability anchoring the other end" (Baron et al. 1994:127). Smooth change in the control parameters is followed by change (smooth or abrupt) in the order parameter.

Levinger's ABCDE-model has not been tested empirically (Fehr 1996), but many descriptive studies of the process of children's friendship have been carried out (Gottman 1983, 1986; Gottman and Parkhurst 1980; Asher and Gottman 1981; Parker and Gottman 1989).[2] In particular, the research done by Gottman (1983) can, for example, be regarded as an indirect test of phases A and B over a series of roughly three regular observations at different points in time, the two time intervals each being of equal length (1 week). Among children who "hit it off," Gottman (1983:44) found higher frequencies of communication clarity, information exchange, conflict resolution, self-disclosure, and common-ground activities in the communications than he found among children who were strangers. Gottman recoded the data using global-level units of interaction. He coded five social processes: (1) play (including information exchange and establishing common ground), (2) self-exploration, (3) repair and maintenance of the interaction (conflict resolution), (4) amity (positive affective exchanges), and (5) conflict. Gottman (1983) tried to generate a model that explains the temporal connectedness of these five processes for children who hit it off and for strangers. Therefore, Gottman performed a sequential analysis that leads to transition frequencies from one process to another.

However, three 90-minute sessions in a 2-3 week span do not seem to constitute a sufficient number of data points and time intervals, even for children's short friendships. Furthermore, other methodological problems and shortcomings (Wagner 1991; Graziano 1983; Rizzo 1989) reduce the value of Gottman's investigation—although these shortcomings do not depreciate its value because every study has its limitations. These problems include the following:

- Measures of the social processes were only indexes of the processes and did not define them.
- The analysis was based on a static and not a dynamic model (Rizzo 1989).
- The children had been observed in asymmetric host and guest situations, which lead to unequal power relations (Abramovitch et al. 1987; Jeffers and Lore 1979).
- The choice of "hit it off" as a criterion of friendship is not sufficient, because not only friends but also strangers can get along well with each other (Staub and Noerenberg 1981).
- The initiation of the children's contact with each other was externally controlled, and therefore an active selection of a partner is inapplicable (Wagner 1991).
- Only the verbal behavior of the children was observed.

There are no other direct empirical analyses of the process of children's friendship apart from the ethnomethodological study of Rizzo (1989).[3] Following a comprehensive review of studies, Fehr (1996) has compiled only indirect evidence for the model. One has to agree with Levinger (1980:514) when he states: "How shall we conceive of the transition between casual and serious involvement, or the temporal fluctuations that occur in relationships, or the maintenance, deterioration, and breakups of established affinities?"

In the literature, static models of socially interacting persons (Kenny 1996; Zeiher and Zeiher 1994) are often discussed. There are some other linear models: Kolip (1993) puts forth a model based on structural equations using a single phase, and Olmstead and Bentler (1992) constructed a model to explain the process of becoming friends (phase A), from initial to subsequent attraction. Other research, concerning the conflictual phase D, is reviewed by von Salisch (1991). These models actually form a bridge between the important technical terms used in research on children's friendship (see below) and suitable measures.

To summarize, children's friendships have been modeled qualitatively as open, often linear, discontinuous systems by partial measurement models that are in some cases based on structural equation modeling. Several such traditional models have been criticized as follows:

1. Phase transitions are seen to be caused by explicit or implicit decisions by the friends, for or against an increased intensity of their relationship (Levinger 1980), and it is questionable whether children recognize such mental control mechanisms as transition decisions (Wagner 1991).
2. Linear systems and phase models are not coupled with parameter dynamics (as mentioned earlier).
3. Openness and discontinuity are merely postulated (but almost considered an empirical fact), and openness is not the same as it is usually taken to be within a small group: for instance, in the small group dynamics developed by Homans (1950), Simon (1952), and Casti (1979), openness consists of autonomy (which does not mean independence of the time parameter but independence of the system stability of external control parameters), self-organization, and resilience. As additional clarification on this last point, self-organization reflects context-dependent iterativity, which is not identical to linearity per se. Resilience denotes a measure of how capable the children's friendship is of absorbing external disturbances without changing its global evolvement. Resilience, to be precise, is not a property of children's friendship but depends on it and on the class of admissible perturbations, while autonomy indicates a corresponding property of the children's friendship, itself.

Parameters

Two methods are used to identify suitable state and control parameters in children's friendships: (1) comparing friends with extraneous children or strangers (Abramovitch and Strayer 1978; Foot, Chapman, and Smith 1977; Green 1933; Howes 1983; Krantz, George, and Hursh 1983; Masters and Furman 1981) and (2) comparing boys with girls (Clark, Wyon, and Richards 1969; Lever 1976; Tietjen 1982). The state parameters of children's friendship listed as follows are applied in numerous inquiries (Bukowski, Newcomb, and Hartup 1996):

Parameter	Friends	Strangers
Intimacy	+	−
Intensiveness	+	−
Exclusivity	+	−
Extensiveness	−	+
Activity	+	−
Responsiveness	+	−
Ease	+	−

Note. + = higher values of state parameters than in comparison group; − = lower values of state parameters than in comparison group.

Although all these state parameters have been used in such inquiries, not all are suitable for modeling (Wagner 1991; Wagner and Alisch 1994). Extensiveness is not logically independent of the first three properties. Activity is task dependent and situation specific. The indicators for activity are the same as those for intensiveness. Activity and feeling at ease are sometimes correlated with intimacy but then no further separation is made between intimacy and friendship. Responsiveness is mixed with intimacy. Affection is very often required as a state parameter but only verbally (Shapiro 1967). Affection has never been measured in children's friendship research, perhaps because two different scale orders are involved. While affection deals with emotions and mental states, mutuality and friendship refer to social interactions.

To sum up, there are three dynamic state parameters that are suitable for modeling the process of children's friendship: intimacy, intensiveness, and exclusivity (for details, see Wagner 1991; Wagner and Alisch 1994). They create the independent dimensions of a state (or phase) space. Thus, any point in this phase space specifies uniquely the values of the three parameters and, hence, the state of children's friendship at any instant (indicated by a vector X_t). Theoretically, the three parameters have to be measured with respect to the two principles mentioned above: the principle of spatial heterogeneity and the principle of heterochronicity. Thus, state space X is a compound of space-time-units and has the maximum norm (Döbelt 1996) $||X_t|| = \max_{i \in \{1,2,3\}} |X_{t;i}|$, where $X_{t;1}$, $X_{t;2}$, and $X_{t;3}$ denote the three state parameters.

A list of partly overlapping indicators, which can be used to develop measures, follows. However, as reported in the literature, the state parameters are not measured uniformly, so this list should not be read as implicitly including the theoretical foundations for the three measurement models.

Measures of state parameters of intimacy, intensiveness, and exclusiveness

Intimacy	Preference for the friend as a playmate in role playing games (e.g., cowboys and Indians)
	Physical proximity (short interpersonal distance)
	Readiness to respond to the friend's expressive or active behavior
	Help in case of perceived need
	Readiness to give positive emotional reactions
	Being at ease in the friend's presence
	Body contact
	To stay overnight in the friend's home
	To exchange secrets in the presence of other children
	Trust

Intensiveness	Frequency and duration of being together
	Frequency and duration of talking with each other
	Frequency and duration of body contact
	Frequency and duration of eye contact
	Frequency and duration of various reinforcements
	Strength and frequency of the feeling to miss the absent friend
	Strength and frequency of the wish to see the absent friend again
	Strength, frequency, and duration of positive emotional responses
	Frequency of speaking about the absent friend
Exclusiveness	Exclusion of third persons or failure to include third persons as friends
	Readiness to accept third persons as friends in an ongoing relationship
	Preference for dyadic over polyadic relationships

Affection lies on a lower scale than the state parameters and has an ambivalent status, on the one hand, because of a top-down dependence to children's friendship and, on the other hand, because of bottom-up effects that affection can have on the friendship. Affection seems to be a specific control parameter that plays the role of an endogenous quantity of children's friendship. The same is true with friendship understanding (Selman 1980; Staub and Noerenberg 1981) and gender preference of children (Berndt and Hoyle 1985; Feiring and Lewis 1991; Gottman 1986; Hallinan 1979; Howes 1988; Oswald and Krappmann 1984; Petillon 1993; Strätz and Schmidt, 1982). Therefore, we treat the three parameters affection, friendship understanding, and gender preference as endogenous control parameters of children's friendship.

There are other control parameters that are exogenous to children's friendship, such as parental influences (Jacobson and Wille 1986; Ladd and Golter 1988; LaFrenière and Sroufe 1985; Lieberman 1977; MacDonald and Parke 1984; Newson and Newson 1978; Parke and Bhavnagri 1989; Rubin and Sloman 1984; Schmidt-Denter 1984; Youngblade and Belsky 1992), cultural background (Fine 1980; Hofer et al. 1990; Keller and Wood 1989; Krappmann 1990; Selman 1980; Youniss 1980), and the number of potential friends in the social environment (DeVault 1957; Levinger and Levinger 1986; Schmidt-Denter 1984; Wagner 1991). Small changes in these parameters usually have no direct effects, but effects are mediated rather more by the endogenous control parameters. Normally that means that exogenous control of children's friendship is only possible if the state space runs through a contractive alternation occurring after an incident such as the daily separation of the children (when the children's friendship remains only in their minds).

Searching for a Formal Model

Under our current grant, it is our task to develop a powerful formal model incorporating the parameters mentioned above, providing a set of solutions that will fit the data that we will collect over the next two years. If the model we use is too narrow, the risk of missing data is high and cannot be compensated for methodologically (Little and Schenker 1995). In contrast, too many solutions for the formal model will bring up the problem of finding constraints, invariants, or principles to combine alternative solutions.

Another problem is the choice of a theoretical framework. For the purpose of modeling the process of children's friendship, nonlinear dynamical systems with quantitative outcomes generated by a continuous time-mixing process (e.g., deterministic and stochastic) seem particularly appropriate. Although significant stochastic influences may occur at discrete points in time (the significance given by signal amplification; cf. Peterson 1991; or by path-dependency; cf. Arthur, Ermoliev, and Kaniovski 1987), there is no smallest time unit in which changes can happen. Furthermore, discrete time models have to be constructed in explicit relationship to available data, whereas continuous time models are not dependent on the chosen observation interval. In practice, the variables will often be measured at different points in time and may not have comparable amounts of measure points. In any of these cases, continuous time models also have more advantages than discrete time approaches (Hamerle, Nagl, and Singer 1991).

Preliminaries

Our review of research on children's friendship shows that there is a discrepancy between the conceptualization of Baron et al. (1994) concerning the ABCDE-model and the usual parameter identification. Baron et al. define an order parameter called commitment or mutuality that changes when the features of the friendship change over time. Therefore, the descriptions of these features, namely, intimacy, frequency of interaction, and affectual intensiveness, are treated as control parameters.

Contrary to this interpretation, the usual starting point in the characterization of commitment is to define a state vector with three components, namely, intimacy, intensiveness, and exclusivity. The control parameters are seen as quantities that are external to the system. The values of the control parameters influence the function that describes the change of the state vector from its present to its future state. Because of the scale order of the control parameters, there was a distinction made between those that are exogenous to children's friendship and those that operate on the level of each individual child. The latter are called endogenous control parameters. Obviously, they are also external parameters with respect to the friendship as a system, because their effects are mediated through the child as an individual.

We have noted above that, theoretically, the two principles of heterogeneity and synchrony defined the properties of a state space, where the state vector takes its values, as a compound of spatio-temporal units. With respect to systems with such properties, it is convenient to model exogenous control parameters as multiplicative factors and endogenous parameters as additive factors (Hernandez-Machado 1995; Döbelt 1996). However, this is done only in case of control parameters as external sources of noise. Therefore, it is of no value for our modeling.

Baron et al. (1994) have defined commitment empirically as exclusivity. It is not yet clear what mathematical form the description of their model takes. They have reconstructed the ABCDE-model in terms of dynamical systems theory, which means in detail that they talk about a family of functions on a manifold (Willems 1989). This family can be obtained by gathering all identical functions that have the same control parameters but varying control parameter values.

What we are missing in Baron et al.'s work is an explicit specification of the function, or at least particulars about linearity and nonlinearity. Usually the control parameters can be modeled as either influencing the function or as external noise. Furthermore, some parameters may be invariant over time while others are changing, for example, cultural background can be regarded as fixed in a broader time interval while friendship understanding is evolving.

Let us assume that the control parameters influence the function. If the function describes the change of commitment over time in the sense of a causal scheme—that is, if the future state of the system is independent of the past states and is determined solely by the present—then the function adds the influence of varying control parameters to the present state. Its transition into the next state, then adds to the constant influence of the invariant control parameters. Denote commitment at the present state as X_t and the future state as X_{t+1}. The change of commitment is given by the following equation:

$$X_{t+1} = f(A, X_t) + a(t). \tag{1}$$

Here, f is a function on X_t that is influenced by a vector of control parameters A; a is an invariant control parameter. Consider a being the cultural background; then, if $a(t)$ is constant, the value of a is added constantly to commitment.

In the first paragraph of this section, we have assumed that the components of A are changing over time themselves. This parameter dynamic can be described by equations of change for each nonconstant control parameter. The resulting equation for the description of system change is a nonlinear functional (differential) equation. Although the ABCDE-model explains the process of children's friendship as a sequence of linear and nonlinear phases, the overall global dynamics is nonlinear, since control parameters change values at the phase transition and the system's behavioral dynamics are coupled with parameter dynamics.

So far, parameter dynamics have not been studied in the actual research in children's friendship, as we have already mentioned. Since we don't wish to speculate about these dynamics, we follow a proposal made by Cook et al. (1995) for a method of modeling social interactions. Cook et al. have stated that when there are problems understanding social interactions, it is convenient to propose a mechanism of change over time that has to be expressed by mathematical equations. Then one can introduce parameters that have been found to be valid. It is possible to fit an equation that describes an individual orbit of change of social interaction under a set of conditions and to simulate further interactions under different conditions. That provides a foundation for a qualitative understanding of the phenomena and for conducting experiments and empirical studies to test the validity of the simulations. This method of modeling seems to be the one that fits best with our choice of the third methodological option mentioned above.

To sum up, the process of friendship can be modeled as a change in commitment and described by a vector with three components: intensity, exclusivity, and intensiveness. Exclusivity can be regarded as a dynamical state parameter and defined in the sense of Baron et al. (1994). Intensiveness is a dynamical state parameter defined empirically as the amount of time that children spend together weighted by frequencies of verbal communication, joint play, affective utterances, body contact, and positive reinforcement. Intimacy is a dynamical state parameter defined as the spatial distance between the children when they spend time together (the three parameters are conceptualized in a slightly more complicated way, but space here does not allow details; for further explanation see other publications by the authors).

Denote commitment X_t, a vector in three-dimensional space X that describes the order parameter of the process of children's friendship with its three components of intimacy $X_{t;1}$, intensiveness $X_{t;2}$, and exclusivity $X_{t;3}$: $X_t = (X_{t;1}, X_{t;2}, X_{t;3})$. X_t is a complete state in this space. The norm of X is the maximum norm given above. Levinger (1980) assumes the process of friendship to be continuous. Therefore, we have to interpret commitment as a continuously changing quantity that represents a change in children's friendship. This leads us to a differential equation, which includes the control parameter matrix, A. Those control parameters have been set to different values to investigate the behavior of the model by means of simulations. Assuming accidental events, which occur by chance in every friendship, we must include stochastic processes in our differential equation:

$$dX_t/dt = f(A,X_t) + a(t) + bX_t \xi_t. \tag{2}$$

This differential equation models the process of children's friendship with fixed control parameters and external noise. When we consider the control parameter dynamics, a coupling of equation (2) with the parameter dynamics gives a nonlinear functional evolution equation. We have studied this via simulation, changing the values of the control parameters and looking for the behavior of the system after the change, particularly as to whether the system reaches an attractor or leaves one and passes over to another one.

To sum up, we think of children's friendship as a dynamical system under external noise. However, the precise mathematical description of the entire equation has some special features. Equations of this type are called stochastic differential equations (SDEs), whose stochastic part should include a Wiener process W_t (West 1985; Singer 1992; Hamerle et al. 1991; Benoît 1995), which nevertheless is not differentiable (no question about the derivability of its trajectories or about the density of the process can be answered; Kunita 1986; Jetschke 1989).

Our SDE is a vector SDE (VSDE) since the states of children's friendship are three-dimensional vectors. The deterministic part of the equation is called drift, and the diffusion term denotes the stochastic part. The drift describes the undisturbed process of children's friendship and the diffusion gives the changes of the process in a fluctuating environment. For simplicity and didactical reasons, but not as a matter of principle, the following section concerns linear VSDE (LVSDE), where $A(t)$, $B^1(t)$, . . , $B^m(t)$ are $d \times d$-matrix functions and $a(t)$, $b^1(t)$, . . , $b^m(t)$ are d-dimensional vector functions. We previously modeled the process of children's friendship with a nonlinear drift term, taking into account the "memory" of the system, that is, the information of past states. But we are very interested in studying the attractors of the system; unfortunately, there exists in the literature only a method to compute Lyapunov exponents for one-dimensional noisy chaotic systems (Ellner et al. 1991). If we have finished generalizing the method to three-dimensional noisy systems, we can test whether theoretically described nonlinear processes of children's friendship are chaotic:

$$dX_t = [A(t)X_t + a(t)]\,dt + \Sigma_{l=1}^{m}\,[B^l(t)X_t + b^l(t)]\,dW^l_t. \tag{3}$$

The Process of Children's Friendship

The equation describing the process of children's friendship can now be regarded as a special case of LVSDE with three-dimensional state vector. For purpose of simulation the model can be transformed into a system of scalar LSDE. Here the time-dependent components of the matrix function $A(t)$ are six of the control parameters mentioned above, two null components, and one technical interaction term. At the moment, we have no interpretation of $a(t)$; therefore, we have set each $a_i(t)$ equal to a constant $= 0$ (for $i = 1, \ldots, 3$) for our simulation. The principles of heterogeneity and heterochronicity lead to modeling the random disturbances in a differentiated form. Therefore, we postulate the existence of m Wiener processes with respect to each equation.

Stochastic Flow

The simulated numerical solutions in our model define a stochastic flow, which can be constructed using a number of independent Wiener processes (Kunita 1986). With plausible parameter changes chosen, when applying the Runge-Kutta-procedure (Singer 1992; Kloeden, Platen, and Schurz 1994), commonly used in this case, we have found five qualitatively different motions of the drift: (1) an exponential increase in the state dimensions with asymptotic behavior, (2) the same for a decrease, (3) a dampened oscillation, (4) an evolving (inversely dampened) oscillation, and (5) an undampened oscillation.

However, these differences do not depend on the change of just one of the control parameters but on change in differing parameters. Let us take the following example as an illustration: We have fixed the control parameters with a value > 0 except A_{23}, which may be interpreted as parental influence. We studied the drift while varying the value of A_{23} from -1 to -5, which means that parental influence increases with a greater intended effect on the evolution of children's friendship. Varying A_{23} from -1 to -2.9, the process of children's friendship reaches (see Figure 13.1) a fixed point (a dampened oscillation in each component of the state vector)—however, with decreasing velocity (see Figure 13.2)—the value of A_{23} increases (increasing oscillative behavior). In the figures, the dimensions are called x, y, and z, respectively.

The simulation of Figure 13.1 was done with $A_{11} = -1, A_{12} = -2, A_{13} = -1,$ $A_{21} = 0, A_{22} = -1, A_{23} = -1, A_{31} = -1, A_{32} = 0,$ and $A_{33} = -1$ as parameter settings, whereas in the following simulation (see Figure 13.2) A_{23} was changed to -2.9, keeping the other parameters constant.

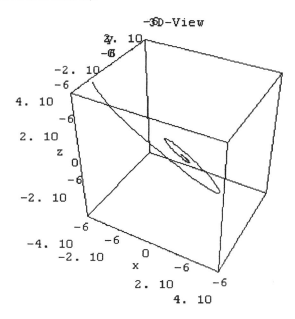

Figure 13.1. Three-dimensional view of a child friendship reaching a fixed point, with control parameter A_{23} set to −1.

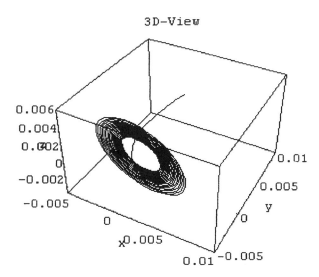

Figure 13.2. Three-dimensional view of a child friendship (with parameter setting $A_{23} = -2.9$) reaching its fixed point less quickly than in Figure 13.1.

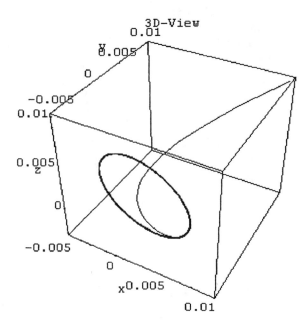

Figure 13.3. Three-dimensional view of a child friendship (with parameter setting $A_{23} = -3$) reaching a limit cycle.

If we set $A_{23} = -3$ (keeping the other parameters constant), the system passes over to a limit cycle (Figure 13.3).

After changing to $A_{23} = -5$, the system repels from a fixed point describing an evolving oscillation (Figure 13.4).

To this point, we have only presented simulations of control parameter dynamics where the stochastic parameters had been set to zero. Considering now stochastic influence, we get a friendship system whose behavior becomes less clear. As an illustration, take the case of $A_{23} = -1$. Adding a small noise term, $bi1 = 0.0001; i = 1, \ldots, 3$, we see that the system does not reach a fixed point, but fluctuates around the attractor (see Figure 13.5), which seems to be more realistic. Filtering the noise would result in Figure 13.1.

However, in addition to this kind of stochastic influence, if we change the B matrix of equation (3) we can see evolution toward a highly sensitive irregular motion. As an example, we can set $Bij1 = 1; i = 1, \ldots, 3; j = 1, \ldots, 3$ (see Figure 13.6).

With respect to the ABCDE-model, our simulations show that the sequence of phases is not expected to hold true. First, the variation of A_{23} leads to system behavior that is never a uniquely increasing development but an approach to phase-specific attractors. Second, under increasingly positive parental influence,

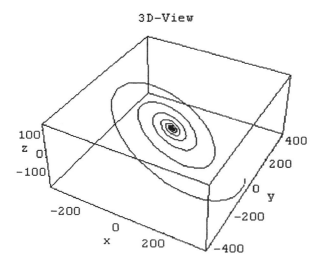

Figure 13.4. Three-dimensional view of a child friendship (with parameter setting $A_{23} = -5$) evolving from a fixed point.

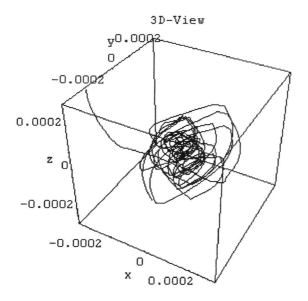

Figure 13.5. Three-dimensional view of a child friendship with a small noise added.

the process of children's friendship passes phases B (fixed point) and C (consolidation to a limit cycle). However, when the value of the parental influences gets too high, the process passes a bifurcation point resulting in system behavior such

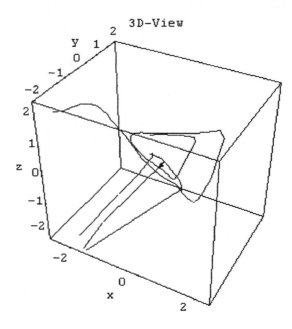

Figure 13.6. Three-dimensional view of a child friendship showing a highly sensitive irregular motion.

as increasing the distance to a fixed point. If noise is added, the system does not reach the phase attractors, but approaches them while fluctuating. Even when the system behaves in a sensitive and irregular way, this can be, for example, the effect of noise superimposed over the process as it passes through phase B. Obviously, one has to filter the noise in empirical studies before a decision can be made between the statements "friendship is passing B" or "friendship is leaving C." In the case of LSDE, the Kalman filter (Chui and Chen 1991) is appropriate.

Our simulations lead to various hypotheses (such as those in the above example) concerning the nonlinear global evolution of the process of children's friendship under different parameter values and different stochastic noise. Our future research now has to test the validity of these hypotheses empirically.

Conclusion

We argue that in nonlinear social sciences, there is a need for a method of modeling that not only analyzes, fits, and models a data series but also makes use of theoretical developments and empirical "crass things." We have reviewed the research on the process of children's friendship and identified various state and control parameters. Taking patterns from Levinger's ABCDE-model, we suggest a system of SDEs to describe the process of children's friendship. Under different values of the identified parameters incorporated into the model, we simulate numerical dynamical solutions to the model equations. The solutions describe orbits of the nonlinear, evolutionary processes of children's friendship.

Notes

1. *Force*, as used here, is a term from the theory of sets.

2. We refer only to Gottman's research on children's friendship and have to skip his illuminating mathematical modeling of marital interaction; see Cook et al. (1995), although the resulting system of equations seems to be related to our model; Azizighanbari, Bargfeldt, and Alisch (1997).

3. This corroborates parts of the ABCDE-model qualitatively but does not use any quantitative measure.

14

Short-Term Changes in the Domestic Division of Labor
Intimations of Complexity

Sara Horsfall
Elizabeth Maret

Conventional wisdom in the study of the family is that the domestic division of labor is relatively stable through time and space. Although the findings of many studies examining the effect of women's involvement on task allocation within the household are mixed, the dominant opinion is that when the structure of household labor changes, it is not so much a change in the division of labor as in the nature of the labor itself (such as time spent on particular tasks). For example, when the wife is employed there is a reduction in the amount of time spent on household tasks rather than a reallocation of responsibility for those tasks (see, e.g., Staines and Pleck 1983). The failure to confirm reallocation of tasks between men and women seems to suggest that the sexual division of labor is resistant to change.

Even the relationship between the possession of valued resources and the relative power advantage it gives to spouses in task allocation, an idea derived from exchange theory, is not consistently supported. For example, Coverman and Sheley (1986) found no convergence of men's and women's roles between 1965 and 1975 in terms of time spent on household tasks, although this was a period of rapid increase in female labor force participation. There appears to be little or no support for the hypothesis of permanent change in the sexual division of labor within the home—the so-called domestic division of household labor—either through time or among variable conditions of women's employment.

Even less support exists for the influence of other conditions on the domestic division of labor. Occupational conditions (Secombe 1986; Shamir 1986), social network effects (Rogler and Procidano 1986), and other sociological variables appear unrelated to change in the sexual division of labor within the home, as measured in previous studies. With few exceptions (see Maret and Finlay 1984), the sexual division of labor in the home appears resistant to permanent change of a unidirectional nature.[1]

However, in each of the above studies, researchers focused exclusively on an aggregate linear change from traditional to nontraditional divisions of labor. There are other types of change, including multidirectional, temporary, and nonlinear change. In the past, some social scientists have explored ideas of non-linear change, but little attention was paid to their theories, because they did not fit the popular linear scientific models of predictable, proportional cause and effect. Sorokin (1941) thought history went through cyclical, even "oscil-latory," changes. Spengler (1926) also thought of historical changes as cyclical, whereas Kondratieff (1935) suggested long waves to describe global change. Toynbee saw historical change as wheel-like or circular within an evolutionary ascent. Hegel (1977), whose thought influenced many of the first sociologists, saw social change as a dialectical development. More recently, scientists from several fields have discovered patterns of system change. What previously was thought to be system overload and breakdown of existing structures is seen by those studying chaos and complexity theories as periods of transition from one kind of organization to another. The nonlinear dynamics of chaos have led to new, nondeterministic, and nonlinear models and generalizations (Kiel 1991). It has also led to new levels of complexity, as order is sought and found in the seeming random patterns. Many of them refer to Comte, Durkheim, and Spencer as early precursors of their theories (Loye and Eisler 1987).

From the above perspective, the reason researchers failed to observe change in the domestic division of labor between 1965 and 1975 could be because they looked only for linear change. For example, a zero net change over ten years does not mean that no change took place. It is possible that the zero net change conceals a great deal of nonlinear and/or noncontinuous change. Aggregate observations of "no change" might also conceal complex changes at the individual level, including change in the opposite direction, toward an increase in traditional division of labor. This is an opposing stream of change. Consider a hypothetical illustration: the stream of change among respondents postulated by most researchers is toward a less traditional division of household tasks. In this case, respondents who have sole responsibility for cooking meals at the beginning of the time period (Time 1) are, by the end (Time 2), sharing responsibilities for meal preparation. But there could be another stream of change moving toward a more traditional division of labor. Respondents who share responsibilities at the beginning of the time period (T1) would have sole responsibility for all or some domestic tasks by the end of the time period (T2). If the two streams of change are not differentiated at the aggregate level, the summary or "net" change between the two time points would appear to be zero.

Second, there could be aggregate change in the opposite direction. Household division of labor could change from a pattern of sharing to a pattern of greater sexual division of responsibilities. The possibility of change toward a more traditional division of labor has been ignored: not expected or hypothesized. Researchers expect change in the sexual division of labor to be linear, continuous, and unidirectional toward a greater sharing of tasks based on sex.

Another change, rarely considered in the literature, is temporary or short-term change. In this case, the division of labor changes one way and then back again within a stipulated time period. The existence of short-term change over a relatively long period of time, such as ten years, would not contradict the expectation of a zero overall change at the aggregate level, or even at the individual level. But its existence would mean that we would have to reconsider the implication that a zero net change within that period is equivalent to the absence of change.

Fourth, change could exist internal to the sexual division of labor itself. That is, there could be variable change in the division of labor among the set of tasks comprising the domestic division of labor. Some tasks, like child care, for example, could change rapidly in one direction, while another task, such as washing clothes, could change in the opposite direction or not at all.

In sum, the possibilities of change in the domestic division of labor we have identified are (1) opposing streams of change, (2) aggregate change toward nontraditional division of labor, (3) short-term change, and (4) task-variable change (variable change among the different tasks). Our research examines all these types of change. In particular, we hypothesize the following.

> *Hypothesis 1.* Within a given period of time, two streams of change can be observed in the sexual division of labor: one stream of change toward a less traditional division of labor, and an opposing stream of change toward a traditional sexual division of labor.

Hypothesis 2. Within a given period of time, net change in the sexual division of labor will vary among specific domestic tasks, that is, observed changes will differ by task.

Hypothesis 3. Within a given period of time, aggregate change for one or more household tasks will be observed to change toward a traditional division of labor.

Hypothesis 4. Within the two cohorts of young and mature women, streams of change in the division of labor for a household task will be reversed.

Data and Methods

Data for this study were taken from two cohort files of the National Longitudinal Surveys of Work Experience (NLS data). Each file consists of approximately 5,000 respondents. The mature women cohort file consists of women who were 30 to 44 years of age at the time of the initial survey in 1967. The young women cohort file consists of girls who were 14 to 24 years of age at the time of their initial survey in 1968. The files are based on national probability samples drawn by the U.S. Bureau of the Census. The initial interviews were also conducted by Census personnel before the project was turned over to Ohio State University. The analysis reported here is restricted to married women subsamples of approximately 3,000 mature women and 2,230 young women.

The NLS cohort files offer a rich source of panel data on the work patterns of American women, including their patterns of domestic responsibility. For currently married women, information on responsibility for domestic tasks is available for several survey years beginning in 1974 for mature women and 1975 for young women. To study the possibility of short-term change, the research considers the period of 1974 to 1976 for mature women and 1975 to 1978 for young women. The domestic tasks included in this analysis are grocery shopping, child care, cooking, washing dishes, washing clothes, and cleaning house.

The questions on domestic work in the NLS data ask level of responsibility for each task rather than time spent. Hence this research is not in the time-use tradition. Rather, the present research considers a measure of "relative" responsibility. This measure has the advantage of controlling for variations in the amount of time devoted to a particular task among women. In other words, by asking how responsibility for a particular task is allocated among family members, a relative measure of responsibility controls for possible change in the nature of the labor itself.[2]

For purposes of this research, the response categories are dichotomized: either the respondent bears sole responsibility for the given task or she bears other than sole responsibility. The decision to use a dichotomized measure for the sexual division of household labor is based on conceptual and methodological consideration. Conceptually, according to Beer (1983), it is responsibility, rather than time spent, that distinguishes the housespouse—male or female. Methodologically, the analysis of change from "change scores" requires dichotomized variables, and dichotomization facilitates the interpretation of findings. Finally, the use of dichotomized categories allows for a more even distribution of cases.[3] Thus, dichotomizing the response categories in the data makes it easier to identify changes in the sexual division of labor. The change categories are as follows:

1. The respondent had sole responsibility in T1 and T2 (S-S) indicating the absence of change in a pattern of domestic role specialization.
2. The respondent had sole responsibility in T1 and other than sole responsibility in T2 (S-O) indicating change in the sexual division of labor from a pattern of domestic role specialization to a pattern of role sharing.
3. The respondent had other than sole responsibility in T1 and sole responsibility in T2 (O-S) indicating change in the sexual division of labor from a pattern of role sharing to a pattern of domestic role specialization. (The possibility of this pattern is virtually ignored in the sex-role literature.)
4. The respondent had other than sole responsibility in T1 and other than sole responsibility in T2 (O-O) indicating the absence of change in a pattern of domestic role sharing.

Only two of these four "change patterns," Type 2 and Type 3, actually indicate change in the sexual division of labor. The two types of change are different, but when taken together, they could yield an aggregate zero total change if the streams of change were nearly equivalent. Since they specify change in opposite directions, they would cancel each other out. The other two change patterns, Type 1 and Type 4, indicate relative stability or absence of change. However, again, the type of stability differs. Type 1 indicates a stable traditional division of labor, whereas Type 4 indicates a stable nontraditional division of labor.

Five techniques of analysis are used to assess change in the sexual division of labor within the two cohorts: (1) gross change in percentage distributions, (2) net change in percentage distributions, (3) change ratios, (4) phi, and (5) McNemar change scores. Within the cohorts, differences between the two times are assessed by the significance and strength of phi and by the McNemar test of change (Ott, Mendenhall, and Larson 1978:333-335). These test statistics also allow for a comparison of change patterns between the two age cohorts. Hypothesis 1 can be assessed by gross changes in percentage distributions among the four change categories between T1 and T2.

Six domestic tasks are taken to be the core of domestic labor. Not all the tasks are of equal importance, either in terms of time spent or in terms of their psychological importance—the extent to which they contribute to feelings of domestic well-being when they are accomplished adequately or detract when not accomplished. There is no attempt in this research to present any type of summary or cumulative value to the totality of tasks.

Tables 14.1 and 14.2 give the gross percentage distributions for each of the six tasks by each change category: the raw data for the hypotheses tests. Table 14.1 presents the findings for the mature women cohort, and Table 14.2 presents findings for the young women. The findings are limited to subsamples of married women and, for the task of child care, to subsamples of married women with children in the house, which account for the different totals (Ns). Also included in the tables are total percentage of individual change and total net aggregate change. The latter is the figure traditionally used to examine the extent of change is the domestic division of labor. The former represents the percentage of individuals who experienced change in the domestic division of labor during that time period.

Table 14.3 presents summary change scores for both cohorts of women, including "change ratios" for each task. This ratio measure of change simply compares the amount of change away from sole responsibility, identified as a positive trend, to the amount of change in the reverse direction, identified as a negative trend. In this measure, net change in trends is expressed as a change ratio. When the amount of change in one direction is equal to the amount of change in the other direction, the change ratio is equal to 1. This is the case in which no permanent or stable change would be recorded. When the amount of change toward the other category exceeds the change toward the sole category, then the change ratio is greater than 1. This is the case in which a permanent or persistent positive change would be noted. Finally, when the amount of change toward the sole category is greater than the amount of change toward the other category, then the change ratio will be less than 1. This is the case in which a persistent negative change would be observed. This measure provides important information but it is purely descriptive; there are no significance levels available.

Net change in trends is also summarized in Table 14.3 as the difference in gross percentages for the two types of change:

$$\text{Net change} = (S\text{-}O) - (O\text{-}S).$$

This measure of net change yields a positive number for a balance of change toward the other category and a negative number for a balance of change toward the sole category. This measure of net change is also heuristic and purely descriptive. It describes the extent to which the streams of change can be observed for each of the six domestic tasks, but the measure gives no information on the significance of the observations. (This is a repeat of total net aggregate change given in Tables 14.1 and 14.2.) The McNemar change scores, given in columns 5 and 6 of Table 14.3, are measures of the statistical significance of

Table 14.1 Percentage Change in Household Division of Labor among Mature Women, 1975-1978

	Child Care		Grocery		Cooking		Clothes		Cleaning		Dishes	
T1-T2	%	n^a	%	n	%	n	%	n	%	n	%	n
S-S	34.2	442	53.6	1,614	62.4	1,877	64.3	1,931	42.9	1,286	37.9	1,139
S-O	19.2	248	13.8	415	11.7	353	12.1	365	13.1	394	12.4	373
O-S	13.0	168	9.8	296	10.5	317	10.0	300	14.1	423	13.0	417
O-O	33.6	434	22.8	685	15.3	459	13.6	409	29.8	894	35.8	1,074
Total	100	1,292	100	3,010	100	3,006	100	3,006	100	2,997	100	3,003
Total % individual change	32.2		23.6		22.2		22.1		27.2		26.3	
Total net aggregate change	6.2		4		1.2		2.1		−1		−1.5	

Note. T1 = Time 1; T2 = Time 2. S-S = respondent had sole responsibility in T1 and T2; S-O = sole responsibility in T1 and other than sole responsibility in T2; O-S = other than sole responsibility in T1 and sole responsibility in T2; O-O = other than sole responsibility in T1 and T2.

a. The *n* for child care is restricted to those respondents who have dependent children living in the home.

Table 14.2 Percentage Change in Household Division of Labor among Young Women, 1974-1976

	Child Care		Grocery		Cooking		Clothes		Cleaning		Dishes	
T1-T2	%	n^a	%	n	%	n	%	n	%	n	%	n
S-S	20.1	338	48.7	1,090	60.3	1,349	69.8	1,560	47.1	1,051	44.5	993
S-O	21.3	357	12.0	269	14.8	258	11.5	258	18.8	420	20.6	460
O-S	16.0	268	15.5	347	10.9	210	9.4	210	12.3	275	11.9	265
O-O	42.6	715	23.8	532	14.0	206	9.2	206	21.8	486	22.9	511
Total	100	1,678	100	2,238	100	2,236	100	2,234	100	2,232	100	2,229
Total % individual change	37.3		27.5		25.7		20.9		31.1		32.5	
Total net aggregate change	5.3		−3.5		3.8		2.1		6.5		8.7	

Note. T1 = Time 1; T2 = Time 2. S-S = respondent had sole responsibility in T1 and T2; S-O = sole responsibility in T1 and other than sole responsibility in T2; O-S = other than sole responsibility in T1 and sole responsibility in T2; O-O = other than sole responsibility in T1 and T2.

a. The *n* for child care is restricted to those respondents who have dependent children living in the home.

Table 14.3 Change Scores for Mature and Young Women

	Change Ratios (S-O) – (O-S)		% Net Change (S-O) – (O-S)		McNemar Change Scores	
	Mature	Young	Mature	Young	Mature	Young
Child care	1.4761	1.332	6.2	5.3	15.38*	12.86*
Grocery	1.402	.775	4.0	–3.5	19.58*	9.88*
Cooking	1.114	1.362	1.2	3.9	1.93	13.49*
Clothes	1.217	1.229	2.1	2.1	6.35*	4.92*
Cleaning	.931	1.527	–1.0	6.5	1.03	30.25*
Dishes	.894	1.736	–1.5	8.7	2.45	52.45*

Note. Change ratio is the amount of change away from sole responsibility (positive number) to the amount of change in the reverse direction (negative number). A value of 1 means that opposing streams of change are equal and cancel out each other. Percent net change has a positive number for change toward other responsibility and a negative number for change toward sole responsibility; does not include significance levels. S-O = respondent had sole responsibility in T1 and other than sole responsibility in T2; O-S = other than sole responsibility in T1 and sole responsibility in T2.
*Significant at .05.

observed changes. The change scores are straightforward in interpretation, yielding the significance at which the observed change could be expected on the basis of "chance." These are the values used to assess the significance of the observed changes in the sexual division of labor. The higher the calculated change score, the less likely the observation of change can be attributed to chance. A score equal to or greater than 3.82 indicates a significant level of change at the .05 level.

It is the purpose of this research to investigate conventional wisdom regarding the absence of change in the sexual division of labor in the home. By distinguishing four different kinds of change, it is possible to assess the nature of change more accurately. By differentiating six tasks in the domestic labor set, it is also possible to look at variable patterns of change by task.

Findings

In examining the labor distributions, one can focus on either (1) the amount of stability in the sexual division of labor or on (2) the amount of change in the sexual division of labor. Traditionalists would point to the percentage of women who retain sole responsibility for domestic tasks: approximately two-thirds of the mature women retained sole responsibility for cooking and washing clothes, and approximately one-third (34.2%) retained sole responsibility for child care. Nontraditionalists would want to comment on the high proportion of mature women who share responsibilities for child care. However interesting this debate may be, the focus of this study is the amount of change in each of these tasks. While the division of labor was stable among approximately two-thirds of married respondents with children (almost equally divided between the traditional and nontraditional labor divisions), the other one-third (32%) of these respondents saw a change in their child care situation from T1 to T2. Specifically, 19.2% experienced a change from sole responsibility to an other responsibility, while 13.0% experienced a change in the *other* direction. Whereas the total percent that changed is 32.2, if one were to aggregate these two streams of change, there would appear to be a net change of only 6.2%, which is the difference between the two streams.

The same is true for the other tasks. For example, with regard to grocery shopping, approximately 14% of the mature women changed from a traditional position of sole responsibility to a position of sharing responsibility between 1974 and 1976. However, an opposing stream of approximately 10% moved in the *other* direction. Hence, while the actual magnitude of change taking place involves 23.6% of the respondents, there is only a 4-point difference between the two streams. For the other tasks, the net change is even less. The total percent of women who saw a change in the responsibility for cooking is 22.2, but the net difference between the two streams of change is only 1.2%. Similarly, for clothes washing, the total individual change is 22.1%, while the net change is 2.1. Indeed, for cleaning house and washing dishes, the opposing stream of change is greater than the change toward a traditional division of labor. If an opposing stream of change (Type 3) were not hypothesized, there would be no change observed in these two tasks. Yet the fact remains that 22.1% to 32.2% of the respondents saw a change in the responsibility for the different household tasks.

For the young women, an even higher percentage are involved in opposing streams of change. In terms of child care, whereas 42.6% have stable, nontraditional divisions of labor, and 20.1% have stable, traditional divisions of labor, a full 37.3% of the cohort changed either from traditional to nontraditional or from nontraditional to traditional divisions of labor. This is 5.1% more than changed among the mature women. More important, in child care and in two other tasks, groceries and cooking, there was more change toward a traditional division of labor among the younger cohort than among the older women. In two other tasks, clothes and dishes, the total percentage of women with sole responsibility is higher among younger cohort than among mature women.

One interpretation of these surprising findings is that the two cohorts are coming to resemble each other—that is, the younger women are moving toward a more traditional division of labor generally thought to be more characteristic of an older generation. It has generally been hypothesized that the younger cohorts are less traditional in their attitudes and divisions of labor. However, these findings suggest the opposite—that the young women are undergoing changes that will eventually give them a profile similar to the mature women, or even more traditional. Another interpretation is that the changes are short term and the effects discovered here will be reversed in the next measured time period. Although traditionalists may be heartened that more young than mature women retained sole responsibility for dish washing, cleaning house, and clothes washing—a seeming move toward traditional division of labor—the findings are reversed for the child care and grocery shopping. There is no significant difference between the cohorts in cooking.

The greatest change among the young cohort is in child care (37.2% changed), followed by washing dishes (32.5% change), and cleaning (31.1% changed), all three of which moved away from traditional patterns of labor division. The tasks that had the least change were washing clothes (20.9% changed) and cooking (25.7% changed). It is interesting to note that grocery shopping, with an overall change of 27.5%, actually had a balance of change toward a traditional division of labor.

The significance of these changes is shown in Table 14.3. Change ratios in columns 1 and 2 show a balance of change for both cohorts away from the traditional expectation of sole responsibility for domestic tasks, although there are differences between the cohorts *and* variations by task. Despite a high level of stability in child care among mature women, this task has the highest level of change toward a nontraditional sharing of responsibility. The ratio of nontraditional change to traditional change is 1.476, meaning the nontraditional change exceeds the traditional by .476. Grocery shopping, cooking, and washing clothes also show a balance of change toward the nontraditional. Cleaning and doing dishes, on the contrary, show a slight balance toward the traditional division of labor (.931 and .894, respectively).

The change ratios for the young cohort are quite different. The tasks that have the highest change ratios toward nontraditional divisions of labor are the ones that were changing toward traditional patterns in the mature women. On the other hand, the task with the lowest change ratio (grocery shopping), indicating a change toward traditional patterns of labor among the young cohort, had the second highest change ratio among mature women, indicating a change toward nontraditional patterns of labor.

Columns 3 and 4 highlight the negative trends (toward a traditional division of labor). Here a positive figure indicates change toward nontraditional patterns, and a negative figure indicates change toward traditional patterns. The magnitude of change is also reflected. A negative balance of change is observed in cleaning and washing dishes among the mature women, and in grocery shopping among the young cohort. The substantial change in grocery shopping could indicate that young men recently involved in courting are more likely to participate in the responsibilities of shared meal preparation than those who are longer married, or it could reflect the significance of changes in other factors, such as employment or career status. Clearly, more research is needed here (see, e.g., Maret and Finlay 1984).

Columns 5 and 6 in Table 14.3 give the McNemar change scores, including significance levels. For the mature women, the amount of change in the domestic division of labor is significant at the .05 level. For the young cohort, all the differences for the observed streams of change are significant. The magnitude of the differences for the young cohort varies considerably by task, from a high change score of 52.45 (dishes) to a low score of 4.92 (for clothes). There is a significant difference in the magnitude of change among the tasks, a finding that strongly supports Hypothesis 2.

The above observations appear to support our first hypothesis. We found bidirectional change in both cohorts. Some of the opposing streams of change cancel each other out, yielding an overall conclusion of no change. Our third hypothesis was also supported: the net change varied among the different tasks (and cohorts), with child care having the greatest change toward nontraditional patterns of labor, whereas cleaning and dishes (among the mature women) and grocery shopping (among the young women) have the greatest change toward traditional patterns of labor. Short-term changes were suggested by the differences between the cohorts, with the younger women having more traditional patterns in dishes, cleaning, and washing clothes, supporting our fourth hypothesis. Thus, we can say that within the household division of labor all four kinds of change were found in this sample.

Discussion

The findings of this research support the concept of opposing streams of change in the household division of labor at the aggregate level. They also support the concept of variability in the changes by task, short-term changes to and from traditional patterns, and aggregate changes toward traditional patterns. The sexual division of labor within the home is, indeed, dynamic, although not in the ways anticipated by sex-role theory or, consequently, by research.

Although long-term measures remain stable, stability, defined as the absence of change, does not describe the division of household labor. Short-term measures reveal change in almost every aspect that is examined. But these changes are not linear or unidirectional. Rather, significant streams of change appear to be going in opposite directions. One can conclude that at the individual level, there is constant negotiation and renegotiation in the divisions of domestic tasks, moving from traditional to nontraditional and then, back again to traditional. These processes of negotiation and change are not uniform for all household tasks. Indeed, child care appears to be particularly dynamic for mature women, changing predominantly from the traditional, while washing dishes and cleaning are most dynamic for young women. Changes in the household division of labor appear to belong to a complex system, and in some ways, a system approaching chaos. Responses to small disturbance, on an individual level, are not predictable, and the changes, when they occur, are not necessarily linear (they may be cyclical). Despite the outside pressures and conditions that can be hostile to family maintenance, such as lack of a paid family leave policy, and cultural values that emphasize the individual, family members appear to be struggling on a day-to-day basis to keep the family healthy and viable. This observed dynamism does not appear to be congruent with the traditional concept of a division of labor in the home that is resistant to change. The seeming unpredictability of household participants implies another dynamic at work than a gradual change from traditional patterns of household labor to nontraditional patterns.

We turn then to the newer theories of chaos and complexity for further analysis. According to most researchers using chaos and complexity, our data are not sufficient to conclusively state whether or not the household division of labor is a linear social process or nonlinear because we have only two points in time. However, using the Runge-Kutta technique, Brown (1995) has devised a way to distinguish linear social processes from nonlinear ones using two data points. In brief, he uses trajectories of differential and differenced equations from T1 to predict T2 (which he calls the end point). In linear processes, the projected end points will be the same as the real end points, whereas in nonlinear processes, they will not be. Our data have revealed four different types of change in the household division of labor, so we already know that the aggregate trajectory is unlikely to be linear because of the variation in the change ratios of responsibility for the individual household tasks that comprise the aggregate. Including more data points would increase the possibility of identifying nonlinear patterns. The next step in analyzing the household division of labor using the newer theories is to specify the system(s), because they are, most importantly, system theories. The system intimated by our data is the local household or family as an institution within the larger society. A system theory dictates that the levels are interrelated; thus changes in the household division of labor are likely to have implications for the larger society. Second, the point in the change process that describes the phenomenon of apparent chaos that we have examined should be determined, if indeed, change is indicated. There are at least six possibilities.

First, the changes we have observed are ongoing changes, at a smaller scalar level, of a larger, stable system. Cells and various other microorganisms that we cannot see with the naked eye are constantly in motion although the larger system of which they are a part, such as a body, appears at rest, or stable. The larger, or higher, system is in stasis, or balance, and is not changing, or changing very slowly. In terms of the household division of labor, the smaller, or lower, scalar level would be the individual families and households, whereas the larger system would be the gender divisions of labor and other labor organizations in the larger society. The implications of this possibility are that despite adjustment to various social, employment, and household demands, the basic division of labor in the household is not changing: all is normal—the activities and changes we observed are part of the normal activity and life of the family as an institution of society. This is in accordance with the accepted body of literature on the household division of labor.

Conversely, the changes we have observed might be a system in apparent chaos, but governed by underlying local rules. This is similar to the first possibility, except that the scalar levels at which order and chaos occur are reversed. That is, at the higher scalar level there is chaos, while at the lower scalar level there is an apparent order. A second difference is that the first possibility implies a system in stasis, whereas this possibility has no implications of stasis or nonstasis. In terms of the household division of labor, the lower scalar level, in this case, would be the decisions made by the individual men and women in the household. The higher scalar level would be the household itself. The implication is that men and women are making their decisions on consistent bases (there may be more than one) but the number of factors involved, and the number of individual cases, makes it difficult to identify the larger pattern, at least with the amount of data presented here. The challenge of this alternative would be to identify the consistent bases on which the decisions are being made. This possibility is similar to the popular conceptions of chaos theory, which was first thought to be a complete breakdown of predictability (Loye and Eisler 1987). Since then, some have come to think of chaos as a nonobvious order that is impossible to measure deterministically because the initial conditions are not known (Dooley and Guastello 1994; Kiel 1991). Only those states of apparent chaos that, on further examination, reveal identifiable patterns within the randomness, qualify as true states of chaos.

Third, the changes we observed could be part of a system that only appears to be stable, but by virtue of its unpredictability is actually nondeterministic by its very nature. A beehive, when seen from a distance, appears to be a single, coherent object. But once it is disturbed, the bees will swarm out in all directions, in an unpredictable manner, with no assurance that they will return and reform themselves in exactly the same way (they could be killed, for instance). This is similar to nonequilibrium thermodynamics, where macroscopic laws are sought to explain chaotic states (Arnopoulos 1993:240), and to conceptions of chaos as situations that are inherently unpredictable—a residual category of the nondeterministic aspects of life, another dimension that exists side by side with the deterministic phenomena (Turner 1994; Hayles 1989). If the external cause for dispersion in our example of the beehive is taken to be human agency, some would argue that this describes social actions more accurately than a completely deterministic model. In terms of household division of labor, this possibility predicts unpredictability: at any moment things could change in any direction. The challenge would be to identify the disruptive forces to the stable pattern. These could be conditions previously seen as unimportant to changes in the household division of labor: occupational conditions, social network effects, the women's movement, education, and others.

Next, a variation on the third possibility is a system that has both stable and unstable components. Similar to the first possibility, or, if taken at different scalar levels, exactly the same as the first possibility, this variation implies that movement is to be expected and does not necessarily indicate instability of the entire system. In terms of the household, this possibility would imply that the division of labor, while remaining basically stable, contains shifts back and forth—a sort of breathing motion. The challenge here, contrary to the other possibilities, would be to demonstrate that change within the household division of labor *is not* taking place, that significantly similar portions of the samples contain nonchanging segments.

Fifth, the changes that we have observed could be indicative of a normally stable system that is in the process of decay. This would be the situation where the evidence of decay has not yet reached the higher scalar levels, using the description of the relationship of the levels as in the first possibility. Theoretically, this is concurrent with the many analyses of the family in decay—leading to the further prediction that society itself has serious problems.

Last, the movement we have observed could imply a normally stable system that is developing to a phase change, and the emergence of something new. Heated water goes through a phase change to become steam. Complex systems, with multiple independent agents interacting with each other in different ways, stretch the system's ability to accommodate to the changes without collapse. This has come to be identified as complexity, a state of orderly disequilibrium found somewhere between a state of static order and a state of chaos (Waldrop 1992; Lewin 1992). The interesting thing about this state is that it seems to be more characteristic of systems per se than of life. That is, system choice is found in phenomena not classified as biologically alive, such as mathematical systems, computer automata, and elsewhere. If the household division of labor is gearing up to a phase change, the implications are that a new phenomena will emerge: a new organization of household labor, based on different "rules" than those currently acted upon. The challenges in adopting this possibility are to identify the components that are being stressed to capacity within the household and to demonstrate that the level of stress is growing to the point of a phase change.

Alternatively, the larger system (larger society) may be going through a system change, which has destabilized the situation at the household level. In this scenario, the household division of labor could be seen to be reacting somewhat ad hoc to meet the constantly changing demands from the larger society.

Which scenario is most appropriate is not clear from this limited look at the household division of labor. Further analysis, particularly the inclusion of more data points, might point to a pattern consistent with one of these six situations of change. Such analysis must be developed carefully, since a decision is likely to be based as much on methodology as on theoretical considerations (Arnopoulos 1993:237). We can nonetheless assert that chaos and complexity theories provide a larger and more fruitful framework for analyzing the domestic division of labor than the current change-limited methodologies and theories.

Notes

1. Some of the apparent "resistance to change" could be an artifact of the measures used. For example, Hood (1986) argues that inadequate measures of the "provider role" are responsible for the inconclusive findings regarding the relationship between women's employment and the domestic division of labor.

2. Relative distribution measures of household responsibility, where respondents are asked to indicate their "relative responsibility" for particular tasks, are most frequently used to assess the household division of labor. They are particularly appropriate for research that seeks to identify changes in the division of labor rather than in the nature of the labor itself, for example, how much time is devoted to a particular task or set of tasks. This source of change, stemming from change in the absolute amounts of time devoted to particular tasks, which is a contaminating variable in time-use measures of the division of labor, is thus controlled in the present research. The major criticisms of the relative distribution measures are that they are vulnerable to vagrancies of subjective reporting, in particular, respondents' tendency to overestimate their own contributions, and that equal weights are given to tasks that take varying amounts of time. Of course, the latter criticism is germane only for efforts to aggregate tasks into a cumulative index of household labor, which this research does not attempt. To the contrary, the focus of the present research is on task-specific variations.

3. The category of "other than sole responsibility" derived from the NLS data, includes the responses of (a) respondent shares responsibility for this task, and (b) someone else bears sole responsibility for this task. The responses do not include "paid help."

15

Biological Foundations of Social Interaction

Computational Explorations of Nonlinear Dynamics in Arousal-Modulation

Thomas S. Smith
Gregory T. Stevens

Even before Schachter (1959) demonstrated that raising laboratory subjects' anxiety had the effect of amplifying their "affiliative tendencies," social scientists had been aware of a pervasive connection between physiological arousal and the tendency of persons to engage in social behavior. Apart from commonsense thinking and occasional psychoanalytic speculation (Scheidlinger 1952), the connection had been rarely directly and systematically investigated (cf. Festinger, Schachter, and Back 1950; Cartwright and Zander 1960). After 1959, studies in several disciplines began to show empirically that arousal and anxiety were correlated to a wide range of social and psychological phenomena—changes in organizational structure, primary group and collective behavior, health-related patterns including emotional and mental symptoms, marital stability, occupational turnover, the sense of justice, school performance and dropout, delinquency, crime, partisanship, and a host of other dependent variables. Endless reasons for these relationships have been advanced by investigators, ranging from status inconsistency to poor parenting.

Following the trail of research, we clear a path through these explanations back to the underlying physiology of arousal. There is good reason to take this route. Many studies done after Schachter's pioneering work illustrate a simple proposition: attachment and interaction are apparently fueled by stress, anxiety, and arousal. By increasing the arousal passing through a group, we in effect create conditions under which people turn to one another for attachment and interaction. But what is behind this pattern?

In this essay, we report research designed to explore the argument that there is a physiological mechanism at work producing this pattern and that attachment and interaction are part of the mechanism. We show how this mechanism can be modeled and simulated, yielding empirical results familiar from research on arousal, including Schachter's own findings.

Comfort-Regulation and Arousal-Modulation

Why a physiological mechanism? The basis for this argument is the widespread evidence from different animal species of a connection between arousal and social behavior. Not only for humans do the most comfortable and secure social arrangements appear to involve attachments to others or interaction. Arouse any group of primates, for example, and its members band together. In recent years, an explanation for this phenomenon has been emerging from biological research (Newman, Murphy, and Harbough 1982; McGuire, Raleigh, and Brammer 1984; Reite and Field 1985; van der Kolk 1987; Wise and Rompre 1989). What the work suggests is that evolution implants in many species a powerful innate means of comfort-regulation, and this involves attachment to others. Autonomy and independence—capacities seen as markers of human adulthood—are potentials inherent in education and socialization. But according to new understandings of attachment, they are not well suited in themselves to maintain comfort, health, or feelings of security. The strongest forces behind our social nature, it appears, are shared with monkeys, guinea pigs, and puppies, and markedly constrain our capacity to stand apart from one another. Biology puts limits on the adult in all of us.

The way these limits work can be understood in relation to evidence from several places, but especially from studies of infants and their mothers. Such research shows that infant-caregiver interaction (and, by extrapolation, all other interaction as well) is the locus of an innate physiological function—the modulation of arousal and anxiety. Built into our species in the course of evolution, arousal-modulation continues, across the life span, to be served by many if not all of our interactions with others. Evidence from studies of primate "distress calls" indicates how this works: when an infant's level of arousal or anxiety passes a certain threshold of discomfort, the infant communicates distress to others using inborn signals such as fussing and crying. These signals stimulate attachment on the part of those who perceive them. Hearing a child's cries, parents and other potential caregivers feel physiological pressures that push them toward attachment—toward making use of interaction to soothe and comfort. Significantly, this is a socially mediated physiological pattern. Beyond childhood, exactly the same pattern continues: in finding relief for levels of discomfort they are unable to manage themselves, persons recapitulate the same innate patterns first seen in attachment to parents.

The Mechanism

Attachment has the effect of soothing a distressed child and producing comfort. How does it accomplish this? Empirical work supports the argument that innate brain-behavior pathways are at work. They work by causing powerful physiological forces that bolster attachment. In the bonding of babies and caregivers, such forces are so strong that they resemble those in heroin addicts. More than addicts of care, however, babies are literally addicted to their mothers. This seems a far-reaching claim, but it is an inference based on findings from careful research. First and foremost, it is derived from studies showing that attachment stimulates release of endogenous opioid peptides in the limbic structures of the brain.

Opioids are neurotransmitters whose effect is to soothe and produce feelings of calm, a matter they accomplish partly through inhibiting the release of norepinephrine (Keren, Garty, and Sarne 1994; Tanaka, Ida, and Tsuda 1988) and other arousal-related monoamines (Furst 1990). Newborns are unable on their own to cause opioid releases and depend instead on bringing about maternal attachment. One is led to recognize that what drives their attachment cravings— what moves them innately to seek attachment—are the physiological states associated with their dependence itself. Opioid releases in the brain have the same adverse effect in infants that heroin injections have in substance abusers: when the soothing effects of opioids have worn off, the brain will produce withdrawal symptoms in the form of anxiety and somatic dysphoria. Significantly, these effects arise when mothers separate from their infants. The cries of a newborn when alone are akin to the distress seen in heroin addicts who are in need of a fix. The distress amounts to a withdrawal symptom, and attachment is its anodyne.

Automatically, directly, and innately, distress communicates itself to mothers, driving them to attach themselves to their infants. This is the mainspring of the underlying sociophysiological mechanism—the connection between distress, attachment, and the modulation of distress we observe in the interaction of infants and caregivers. Tightening this mainspring is the powerful relationship between maternal separation and the onset of infants' distress calls. When a mother separates from her infant, the infant eventually exhibits opioid withdrawal, mixed (for reasons we will discuss below) with symptoms of physiological arousal—increased heart rate, elevated body temperature, and heightened levels of motor activity (Reite and Field 1985; Emde and Harmon 1982). When mother re-attaches herself, these symptoms disappear and distress abates.

What makes this mechanism significant sociologically is that it is quite general, extending beyond the relations of infants and their caregivers. Anyone in a community is susceptible to being moved by an infant's distress in the same way as a parent. Persons made uncomfortable by a child's distress are feeling the same kinds of physiological pressures parents feel, and can relieve distress by providing care for the child in need. Attachment and interaction are thus accelerated, tightened, and strengthened in proportion to the spread of such distress interpersonally.

Others' distress and discomfort move persons to attachment because it is not just in infants but in caregivers as well that attachment stimulates the release of opioids. Partly, mothers use attachment to soothe their babies and partly they use it to soothe themselves. A double-sided modulation of distress is inherent in attachment. Because both parties are beneficiaries of opioid releases in the brain, the innate mechanisms at work in this behavior have a redundancy, universality, and force that yields pervasive dynamics in all social life. Indeed, interaction serves a modulation function for anxiety, stress, or arousal quite apart from whether persons are biologically related to one another. Environmental stress—for example, the appearance of an enemy or a predator—can heighten arousal that is modulated by attachment just as can endogenous anxiety arising from opioid withdrawal. The same stress- and anxiety-driven coupling seen between mothers and babies appears wherever people are interacting. Anxiety produces distress signals, and distress signals communicate discomfort and cause attachment. Attachment elicits the release of opioids, and opioids calm. We have what engineers call a coupled system.

The Coupled System

Anxiety in the sense discussed here is a physiological effect of downward fluctuations of opioid (and other neurotransmitter) production in the brain.

Habituated to certain endogenous production levels for opioids, the brain uses somatic dysphoria of the kind we call anxiety to signal when these levels diminish below a threshold of discomfort—a point where the soothing effects of opioids begin to be exhausted. Sometimes the signaling is so subtle as to remain subliminal; at other times it grows stronger and we are conscious of it. As its strength increases, it passes into our speech, gestures, and other behavior in ways that can be communicated—quite apart from whether we want it to. Indeed, others are sometimes more aware of our anxiety than we are. Because anxiety in this sense is a product of ongoing opioid use, we think of it as a dissipation product—something given off when neurochemical processes in the brain use and, in the limit, exhaust available opioids.

This logic suggests that interaction is being fueled by dissipation products of the brain systems that are innately involved in attachment. From a certain angle, interaction might appear to be part of the brain chemistry itself—part of an arrangement whereby exogenous controls have evolved over the internal activity of the neurotransmitter systems in question. Where there is no anxiety (or exogenous stress), there is no interaction. Where there is interaction, nature has arranged matters such that it stimulates endogenous neurotransmitter release.

Also implied by this reasoning are limits on arousal-modulation that occur in relation to the finite opioid resources available to any one person. Endless demands for arousal-modulation, created by high stress levels in the environment or by extraordinary demands for comfort from anxious others, can, in effect, cause a person to "burn out." As this limit is approached, a person's own level of discomfort increases, and the person becomes less and less responsive to the needs of others for care. Stress burdens can have profound effects on the dynamic organization of social systems.

Important to understand here, moreover, is that anxiety and stress are not only to be seen as physiological "burdens" but also as critical fuels for social and psychological life. According to the way the brain systems in question work, there is always anxiety—it is what drives not only interaction but also other emergents from biological activity such as mentation. Because these higher-order "structures" function in part to regulate physiological processes, moreover, physiological equilibrium depends on fueling them from below. Indeed, they have evolved in our species on the basis of their ability to make use of the dissipation products of the brain systems in question. Functionally speaking, in other words, it is necessary not only to modulate but also to *produce* anxiety so as to support the higher-order structures involved in physiological regulation. This is why opioid levels fluctuate—why they do not remain constant. It is the fluctuations that yield the dissipation products, and it is the dissipation products that drive the controls over physiological states.

Hyperstructures

There is another, more mechanistic way to understand this: what we see here is a metabolism. The brain-behavior connections at work in attachment and inter-action actually constitute a self-organizing arrangement of linked cyclic reac-tions—a cycle, comprising subsidiary cyclic reactions, capable of fueling and feeding itself on the basis of a by-product of its own activity. We call such an embedded arrangement of cycles a hyperstructure, acknowledging that it shares causal features with the coupled cyclic systems, called hypercycles, found in naturally occurring chemical systems (Eigen and Schuster 1979). This argument can be evaluated more readily if we make use of causal representations of the brain-behavior links tied together in hyperstructures, which all have a bearing on arousal-modulation.

It has become conventional to speak of opioids as part of the brain's "opioid system" (Fox and Davidson 1984). The connection between opioid production and attachment behavior is one of the core brain-behavior relationships found in this hyperstructure. A second brain-behavior relationship also involves arousal—the connection between increases in arousal and separation behavior. Closely bound neuroanatomically to the opioid system is the arousal system, centered on the release of noradrenaline. Both the opioid system and the arousal system work cyclically, as indicated in Figure 15.1.

We show these two systems as they operate in the context of infant-caregiver attachment. Thus, maternal attachment is shown to cause the release of opioid peptides (O) in the infant, an effect that in turn diminishes infant distress ($I_w{}^o$). Infant distress is represented here as a withdrawal symptom (w^o), following our argument above. Exactly the same causal pattern appears in the arousal system, controlled by maternal separation. Here, when a mother separates (M_s) from her infant, her behavior triggers the release of noradrenaline (N). In turn, no-radrenaline diminishes withdrawal distress ($I_w{}^n$) produced by fluctuations in the production levels of the neurotransmitters controlling arousal.

By saying that these systems are neuroanatomically bound, we mean that an indefinitely large number of actual and potential pathways connect the two. Structurally coupled in this sense, the two systems produce effects that are com-plementary. Where noradrenaline excites, opioids calm. Moreover, each system is controlled interpersonally—opioids through an interpersonal channel involv-ing attachment behavior, noradrenaline through separation behavior. In the lim-iting case, these controls are available to a person through only one interaction partner, and an oscillatory pattern can develop between states of arousal and states of calm—attachment and separation cannot both occur at the same time. The production of opioids and noradrenaline vary such that where production of one is at high levels, production of the other is at low levels. Figure 15.2

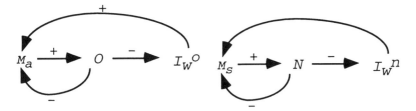

Figure 15.1. Cyclic organization of opioid and noradrenergic systems.

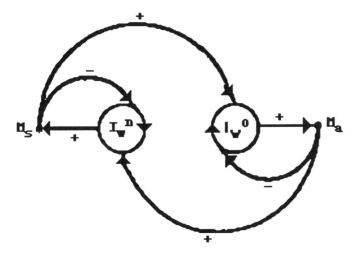

Figure 15.2. Attachment-separation hyperstructure.

shows the causal system that arises from the coupling of these two systems. In this diagram, we suppress the part played in the mechanism by brain chemistry and show only the overt or phenomenal hyperstructure—the causal system as it arises solely at the level of affect and social behavior.

Showing the coupling of the systems in this way, we ultimately derive the more complex causal structure associated with the full hyperstructure—one in which each person's attachment to (or separation from) the other has effects both on self and other, mediated by distress signals. The full logic behind this linked arrangement of brain-behavior cycles is developed elsewhere (Smith and Stevens 1995a, 1995b, forthcoming) and won't be repeated here. For current purposes, it is enough to consider a causal representation involving only the behavioral states perceptible to each interactant. This is shown in Figure 15.3.

Figure 15.3 gives some idea of the degree of complexity and nonlinearity that can appear in systems where there is an approximation to global coupling. Here we are dealing with two interactants. As argued, the only limits on the number

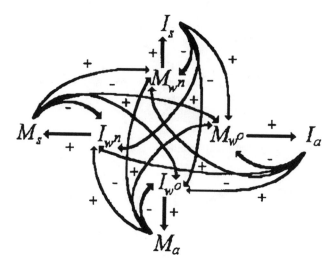

Figure 15.3. Dyadic hyperstructure.
Source. Smith and Stevens (forthcoming).

of persons who might be coupled into such a system arise in relation to finite opioid resources—a limit we have elsewhere called the "carrying capacity" of a network with respect to arousal (Smith and Stevens 1995a). Distress signals pass unimpeded into everyone able to perceive them. The communication of one person's distress into a large number of others means that, viewed in sum, a total effect can arise from such communication that is out of all proportion to the magnitude of the initial stimulus. That is, under some parameter conditions, interaction systems will be marked by the phenomenon of sensitive dependence, commonly seen in other globally coupled complex systems.

Decoupling the Hyperstructure

Sensitive dependence is amplified in an interaction system in proportion to the degree of coupling, and the degree of coupling is a function of the level of anxiety and stress passing through the system. We say passing through the system because some amount of distress will go no further than the first person who initially experiences it. Any person equipped with the strengths to modulate arousal and anxiety apart from attachment and interaction is in effect decoupled from an interaction system. Considered as a whole, an interaction system itself will become progressively decoupled as the growth of this capacity for autonomy appears among its members.

Early in the first year of life, for example, infants cease being full-fledged addicts of maternally stimulated opioid releases and begin exhibiting behavior that indicates they have started to learn how to control their own opioid levels.

As they further develop, they become in effect "controlled users" of attachment, resorting to it only when their autonomous capacity to modulate arousal has been overtaxed. We speak of persons with these more fully developed strengths as "high functioning," and persons without such strengths as "low functioning," echoing a developmental notion widely found in clinical literature on family systems (see Kerr and Bowen 1988).

Functionally speaking, what supports a child's growing independence from attachment is access to caregiver substitutes. Most persons, by virtue of emotional and intellectual strengths they develop as part of growing up, can modulate moderate amounts of anxiety and stress by themselves. In part, what equips them this way are cognitive structures such as memories and "self," along with access to cultural systems including technology and information—structures that in effect enable them to parent themselves. In general, caregiver substitutes function biologically to decouple the attachment mechanism. They are extremely important in accounting for the observed dynamics of social interaction because they relax the dependence of physiological regulation on social life. What these structures create is a biopsychological coupling whose dynamics are stronger than and able to displace the biosociological coupling in the hyperstructure—in effect, a psychological hyperstructure that can displace the social hyperstructure.

When this occurs, we find a morphogenetic principle at work in interaction interposing a strong and robust level of organization between the biological and the sociological. Cognitive activity emerges from the innate physiological link between persons. But the deeper, biologically implanted structure—the one all humans resort to on a regular basis—is the social hyperstructure.

Simulating the Hyperstructure

The links between arousal-modulation and interaction go beyond those discussed here, and they include ancillary causal loops connecting the arousal-inhibiting effects of testosterone production to dominance behavior. Although we have modeled and simulated these additional brain-behavior connections (Smith and Stevens forthcoming) as part of an expanded hyperstructure, our focus here is on the attachment mechanism alone.

Simulating the complex causal system present in the hyperstructure depends on first formalizing it mathematically. Formalization follows as a straightforward generalization of the logic we have presented so far. As we have seen, there are parameter conditions under which persons have to compete for the comfort resources inherent in attachment. When there are only two persons present in an interaction system, for example, each person during any short time interval can produce only one of the two important causal resources scavenged by the hyperstructure—either attachment or separation. Scarcity then appears in the supply of these resources. When these conditions arise, we witness the equivalent of what population biologists describe as "competitive exclusion"—in this case, competitive exclusion among the causal controls over comfort. The causal controls over calming and opioid production can then exclude the controls over arousal and noradrenaline production, and vice versa. For this reason, in two-person interaction systems we commonly observe cycles of arousal and calming, controlled by cycles of separation and attachment (Smith 1992, 1994).

This pattern of exclusion is analogous to what occurs when two species are competing in the same ecological niche. Here, the two "species" are our two neurotransmitter populations, and the resources over which they compete are the two social behaviors of attachment and separation. Exploiting this insight, we can explore the dynamics of the hyperstructure by adapting some of the modified Lotka-Voltera models population biologists use to study interspecies competition. (The interested reader will find these models developed briefly here in an appendix and described more fully elsewhere [Smith and Stevens 1995a, 1995b, forthcoming].)

Exploring Attachment Landscapes

The simulation procedures used here are those widely employed in neural network research and are also detailed elsewhere (Smith and Stevens 1995a, 1995b). For example, when we generalize the model from dyads to triads and larger networks, we make use of a gradient descent algorithm that explores the space of all possible pairwise interactions in a network. Because the hyperstructure leads us to define a person's comfort in terms of minimizing the amplitude of fluctuations in the production of opioids and noradrenaline in the brain, the algorithm works in this case to discover where and under what conditions local minima (low-frequency fluctuations) appear in all possible pairwise interactions in a network (see Rumelhart, Hinton, and Williams 1986; Hopfield 1982). We can thus tell in which pairings people will feel best, to whom they are likely to turn for care, where they will find the attachment resources enabling them to improve how they feel, who is likely to prove responsive to distress and the need for care, and where they are likely to be repudiated.

Following our theory, the model explores not only individual but also global comfort, examining the way the comfort criterion leads to configuring persons into specific patterns and networks of attachment. Thus, when and where responsiveness appears among social actors—where there are strong interactions, where there aren't—is addressed on a dyadic level as well as on a network level.

In networks, this becomes an interesting way to see how burdens of arousal sometimes lead to partitioning of interaction systems into subsystems and levels.

To see such effects, we have conducted various simulation experiments—running simulations under different initial conditions, observing where the gradient descent algorithm locates the local minima in which interactions are likely to stabilize. We have explored a wide variety of initial conditions, but those most interesting to us have to do with varying the relative psychological and emotional maturity of our hypothetical actors. Again, we speak of mature actors as "high functioning" and immature actors as "low functioning," implying that only high-functioning persons are developmentally prepared to be decoupled from the hyperstructure. The simulations thus vary two elements: the number persons in a network and whether they are high or low functioning.

These simulations address a number of general theoretical matters: reciprocity, dyadic and triadic balance, network structure and dynamics, domination, hierarchy, and so forth. Accordingly, the mechanism is able to simulate a wide range of dynamic phenomena: pairings and coalition, assortative mating, diffusion of information, fashion processes, neighborhood integration and segregation, ordered segmentation, and other familiar matters. Space limitations permit us to report only two of these here: biological constraints on reciprocity and network structure.

Biological Constraints on Reciprocity

Among the most interesting issues addressed in the simulations is reciprocity—for many social scientists, the cornerstone of social organization. Reciprocity becomes an issue in a special sense addressed by our models but not elsewhere. Given the biological function of interaction, our simulations show that some conditions better accomplish arousal-modulation than others. For example, interactants are best suited to mutual modulation of arousal only when they are in opposite states, physiologically speaking. Two persons, both of whom are either aroused or calm, damp one another's arousal poorly compared to two persons in opposite states of arousal. A calm parent and an aroused child are better suited to arousal-modulation than an anxious parent and an aroused child.

Similarly, two high-functioning persons are better able to damp arousal than two low-functioning persons. Indeed, the relationship between the functional level of interactants and their stability is itself telling: as functional levels of interactants are decreased in our simulation, their interaction comes successively under the control of different attractors. In terms of the hyperstructure's dynamics, cognitive development does not itself affect the interactants' optimal physiological state (maximization of both opioid and noradrenergic activity

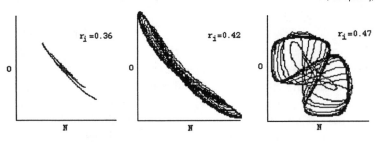

Figure 15.4. Trajectories in mood space for different values of G.
Source. Smith and Stevens (1995b).

within the constraints of their reciprocal action), but rather affects the dyad's ability to stabilize at that optimal point. Within a two-dimensional state space of psychobiological "mood," where mood is considered a joint function of opioid and noradrenergic activity, the "optimal state" can be seen as an attractor (see Figure 15.4). As cognitive development decreases, the dynamics of the system around that attractor site change from a stable fixed-point attractor to an attractor cycle and finally to a chaotic attractor. (In Figure 15.4, cognitive development G is inversely proportional to the parameter there called r_i.) These attractors manifest themselves at first in increasing oscillations of mood, then in increasing overall psychological and behavioral disorganization of the individual (Smith and Stevens 1995b).

Related to this pattern is an observation bearing directly on understanding the biological underpinnings of reciprocity. In some of our simulations, we considered a parameter (ρ_{ij}) defined as the coefficient of responsiveness. This coefficient scales the effect on a person of the difference between their partner's arousal levels and their own, representing the dyad's degree of "psychobiological attunement" (Field 1985). Apart from effects of other considerations also operating in interaction, simulations show that the most stable region for interaction occurs close to the point where $\rho_{12} = \rho_{21}$. This is an underlying physiological condition of reciprocity—the place where responsiveness of i to j is approximately the same as responsiveness of j to i. Violate this symmetry of responsiveness too much, and interaction loses its capacity to serve its physiological function of arousal-modulation. Persons leave interaction feeling no better (and often worse) than when they entered it.

Significantly, this biological constraint on the stability of interaction—the condition of reciprocal responsiveness—is relaxed in proportion to increases in interactants' functional levels. Raise their functional level, and interactants tolerate larger and larger asymmetries of responsiveness. The model reproduces not only this pattern found among peers but the biologically more critical situation found in child care, where the stabilizing function of interaction between a parent and an infant is much less conditional on the infant's responsiveness to the parent than the parent's to the infant.

These results ought to affect how we think more generally about matters such as reciprocity. If reciprocity is understood solely as an effect of normative controls or of self-interested calculations, for example, we miss how feelings constrain it. We have seen that any person can be moved to care for another by being steered toward optimizing comfort—their own comfort as well as the comfort of a person in need. This is how the hyperstructure works—as an innate steering mechanism, coupling persons in need, and using their feelings to constrain mutual responsiveness. But even if interactants' initial motivations were not to comfort each other but, say, to exchange one possession for another, it follows from the way the hyperstructure communicates feelings back and forth that they would be constrained physiologically to approximate reciprocity. Violations of objective reciprocity that increased the discomfort of one party to an exchange would increase the discomfort of the other as well. They would begin to feel steered by their feelings back to the place where the contribution of each was "equal enough" to optimize their comfort.

Such discomforts do not guarantee reciprocity, but make its violation unlikely in proportion to the scarcity of attachment—that is, in proportion to how valuable attachment to an other is relative to maximizing material benefits in exchange. It is thus crucial in economic markets that rationality supports itself with norms that seek to move decision making outside of contexts dominated by attachments, as Max Weber (1968) argued. Where denials of reciprocity result physiologically in discomfort and where attachments are important, there are biological pressures undermining rational maximizing behavior among the parties to exchange.

Network Structure

Some of the most dramatic results of our simulations arise when we consider networks. Increasing the number of persons coupled into an interaction system, we observe how the hyperstructure produces stable dynamic patterns of attachment and separation. Because the model tells us where "strong interactions" will appear in a network, it serves as a tool to study how interaction systems are naturally organized into subsystems. That is, it tells us how a naturally occurring partitioning principle, based on segregating into subsystems persons among whom there are strong interactions, creates what Herbert Simon (1969) once described as a system's "architecture."

Subsystems in this sense are collections of persons, among whom appear high-frequency dynamics: strong couplings driven by the function of arousal-modulation. When we simulate networks along these lines, natural dynamic principles found in family systems emerge from the operation of the mechanism. Assortative mating, for example, appears as a "local rule" operating in interaction. That is, we can both derive and show, "bottom up," that there is a tendency for persons of comparable levels of maturity to stabilize as interaction partners. Between persons of unmatched maturity there appear separations—weak interactions and even negative ties.

Ramify this rule through a network, and we find patterns that are the equivalent of age grading. Increase the level of arousal in an age-graded system, and we find the collapse of subsystem boundaries: de-differentiation. Considered together, these two local matters yield both the neighborhood dynamics of "ordered segmentation" (Suttles 1968) and the appearance of "local bridges" connecting ordinarily separated subsystems (Granovetter 1973).

In sum, many of the macroscopic features of networks appear as global properties arising from the local dynamics of interaction. When this is the case, the micro-macro problem in social theory reduces to a matter of showing how global patterns emerge in interaction systems from local dynamics (see Chapter 5 of this text).

Conclusions

In hindsight, of course, Schachter's principal finding—that "affiliative tendency" among social actors was dramatically amplified by anxiety—now appears as part of the innate biology of attachment and interaction. Schachter reasoned that arousal-induced affiliation might be understood in view of "needs for self-evaluation" (1959:132-133). Feelings stirred up by his experiments, he thought, created pressures in subjects to define what was happening to them and to form appropriate responses. As in conditions eliciting social comparisons, subjects thus turned to one another.

Subsequent research on the role of cognitive factors in defining the subjective states associated with physiological arousal—states induced, for example, by injecting subjects with epinephrine (see Schachter 1971)—has produced ongoing controversy among psychologists and others (see Kemper 1978; Zajonc 1980; Lazarus 1980). Much of this controversy has centered on whether cognitions defined emotions or whether emotions were independent of how they were defined cognitively. Sidestepping the finer points of this controversy, the theory presented here suggests that each of these viewpoints is consistent with yet a different interpretation of the underlying pathways between behavior and feeling, since both cognition and affiliation appear to be driven by anxiety. Affiliation modulates anxiety directly by eliciting opioid releases in the brain, using the brain-behavior connections innate in attachment. But within limits, cognition can apparently accomplish the same thing—that is, entrain opioid responses in the service of arousal-modulation.

While attachment and interaction involve innate anxiety-modulation pathways, cognitive activity provides a secondary pathway, available only among high-functioning persons, to supplement (and, in some cases, to override) attachment. A conditional hierarchical relationship between mental activity and arousal-modulation is entailed by such cognitive embedding of arousal. Under conditions where cognitive activity can be effective in arousal-modulation, it competes with and sometimes functionally displaces attachment and interaction. But as soon as this functional capacity is exceeded, anxiety and arousal spill back into attachment and interaction. Interpersonal dynamics then become strong relative to intrapersonal dynamics, and the innate attachment hyperstructure displaces its psychological substitute. Understood in this way, the hyperstructure concept provides a formal theoretical model of brain-behavior mechanisms that Schachter's research unknowingly addressed, and the simulations reported here show how his findings can be computed.

Computational explorations of the dynamics of the hyperstructure have begun to show many such remarkable results. Conceptualizing social interaction as a self-organizing dissipative system, the hyperstructure provides a model of how interaction metabolizes anxiety and arousal and in the course of its work produces orderly features of interaction, many of which are familiar from empirical research. Among these patterns are those that arise as part of reciprocity—chiefly through the operation of comfort constraints on interacting parties. In addition, we have discussed patterns that appear as naturally occurring links and partitions in social networks. These and other subjects in sociology appear to be freshly opened-up by research on dynamic mechanisms, providing us with new ways to make sense of old observations. Other work (Smith and Stevens forthcoming) not reported here leads into other traditional subjects of sociology such as the study of dominance and hierarchy, using these same theoretical tools in ways that point empirical research toward potentially novel observations and new interpretations.

Because the concept of the hyperstructure highlights many robust features of interaction that could only arise through nonlinear dynamics, it also helps to underline the potential of theoretical research making use of computational strategies. Further work along these lines should increasingly align structural and developmental concepts in sociology with those emerging elsewhere in the study of complex systems.

Appendix

We present here a brief summary of the equations of the simulation model, stated in terms of opioid and noradrenergic activity. The presentation is brief since full details of this model require more space than is available here. We refer the interested reader to Smith and Stevens (1995b).

First, some definitions:

N = noradrenergic activity   (= "population" to be regulated, N_a)
O = opioid activity   (= "population" to be regulated, N_b)
S = separation behavior   (= production regulation mechanism, r_a)
A = attachment behavior   (= production regulation mechanism, r_b)
W_n = noradrenergic withdrawal   (= ratio of equilibrium to actual production levels, E_a/N_a)
W_o = opioid withdrawal   (= ratio of equilibrium to actual production levels, E_b/N_b)

The simple attachment hyperstructure shown in Figure 15.2 then translates into the following equations:

$$N_t = N_{t-1} + S_{t-1}N_{t-1} \tag{1}$$

$$O_t = O_{t-1} + A_{t-1}O_{t-1} \tag{2}$$

$$S_t = r_i\left(1 - \frac{N_{t-\theta}}{E_{t-\theta}^n}\right) \tag{3}$$

$$A_t = r_i\left(1 - \frac{O_{t-\theta}}{E_{t-\theta}^o}\right) \tag{4}$$

$$E_{t-\theta}^n = K^n - K^n\left(\frac{O_t^2}{C_o^2}\right) \tag{5}$$

$$E_{t-\theta}^o = K^o - K^o\left(\frac{N_t^2}{C_n^2}\right). \tag{6}$$

In these equations, r_i is the intrinsic rate of production for each neurotransmitter system; K^n and K^o are carrying capacities or maximum receptor response rates for noradrenergic and opioid neurotransmitters, respectively; C_n and C_o are critical densities for noradrenergic and opioid activity, the levels of production of each at which the other's production stops; and θ is the time delay. For the simulation experiments, the constants K^n and K^o were set to 1000, and C_n

and C_o were set to 1500. We chose the constants only to fulfill the requirement that $C > K$. The dynamics of the model do not change significantly when the constants are given other values. So long as $C > K$, a stable attractor appears where $N = O = 750$. In line with other simulation experiments, the time delay θ was set to 4 to reproduce complementary action from inhibition. The dynamics were examined as r_i was allowed to vary.

When the full dyadic hyperstructure is considered, some of the equations of the model change. Figure 15.3 shows a reduced form of the graph corresponding to the full set of pathways operating in the model. In this revised model, we add a regulatory mechanism involving negative feedback that is based on each interactant's own physiological state compared to the other's:

$$S_t^i = r_i \left(1 - \frac{N_{t-\theta}^2}{E_{t-\theta}^{n_2}} \right) + \rho_{12} \, (N^1 - N^2) \tag{7}$$

$$A_t^1 = r_i \left(1 - \frac{O_{t-\theta}^2}{E_{t-\theta}^{o_2}} \right) + \rho_{12} \, (O^1 - O^2) \tag{8}$$

$$S_t^2 = r_i \left(1 - \frac{N_{t-\theta}^1}{E_{t-\theta}^{o_1}} \right) + \rho_{21} \, (N^2 - N^1) \tag{9}$$

$$A_t^2 = r_i \left(1 - \frac{O_{t-\theta}^1}{E_{t-\theta}^{o_1}} \right) + \rho_{21} \, (O^2 - O^1). \tag{10}$$

Here we make use of numerical subscripts and superscripts to designate each partner to interaction. Just as in the original hyperstructure equations, the left-hand side of each equation includes a behavioral variable, either A or S, shown to depend in part on the interaction partner's neurotransmitter values. This causal pathway connecting one partner's physiological state to the other partner's behavior represents a demand or solicitation of the caregiver by the dependent. When one partner's opioid withdrawal ($E_{t-\theta}^{o_2}/O_{t-\theta}^1$) increases, the solicitation of the other's attachment increases. See equation (10). Yet the actual degree to which the caregiver partner is able to respond with attachment is now scaled by an additional term representing the difference ($O^2 - O^1$) between the partner's own opioid level and the opioid level of the soliciting partner. The scaling results in a pathway that connects the physiological state of a person to his or her own behavior, representing the person's capacity for attachment or separation—his or her ability to respond with caregiving to a dependent partner.

Similarly, when one partner perceives withdrawal symptoms in the other ($E^{o_2}_{t-\theta}/O^2_{t-\theta}$), and accordingly feels both external and internal pressures to increase attachment, A^1, such increases in attachment are scaled by the differences in their relative opioid levels. See equation (8).

To highlight how this kind of response to a partner's state varies according to the partner's own psychobiological condition, each equation also includes a "coefficient of responsiveness," ρ_{ij}, indicating the degree to which partner i is sensitive to opioid and noradrenergic differences between persons i and j. The ρ parameter indicates relative degrees of responsiveness.

When these equations are adapted to treat networks of interactants, some of the equations change still again:

$$S^i_t = r_i \left(1 - \frac{N_{t-\theta}}{I^n_w} \right) + \sum_j \rho_{ij} (N^j - N^i), \text{ where } i \neq j \tag{11}$$

$$A^i_t = r_i \left(1 - \frac{O_{t-\theta}}{I^o_w} \right) + \sum_j \rho_{ij} (O^j - O^i), \text{ where } i \neq j \tag{12}$$

$$W^n_i = K^n \left(1 - \frac{O^2}{C^2_o} \right) \tag{13}$$

$$W^o_i = K^o \left(1 - \frac{N^2}{C^2_n} \right). \tag{14}$$

These network models have been further adapted to treat dominance in relation to arousal-modulation, as discussed by Smith and Stevens (forthcoming).

16

Collective Behavior Following Disasters
A Cellular Automaton Model

Eve Passerini
David Bahr

Two often-quoted bodies of research, Friesema et al. (1979) and Rossi et al. (1978; Wright et al. 1979), conclude that across a broad array of disasters and for a limited number of variables (primarily economic), disasters have no long-term effects on communities. Similarly, others have noted that for most of recorded history communities have experienced very little social change after disasters, returning to normal as soon as possible (Walters 1978; Aysan and Oliver 1987; Mileti and Passerini 1996). On the other hand, many case studies of specific disasters, looking at other variables, have found that disasters often spark long-term social change by triggering increased interaction and the process of issue formation, blaming, framing, and collective action (Cobb and Elder 1983; O'Brien 1991; Mileti and Darlington 1997; for a summary of other case studies, see Drabek 1986:293-298). For example, major federal legislation addressing disasters usually follows on the heels of especially devastating disasters (Berkland 1996). Individual politicians' responses to major snowstorms and floods have made and broken many political careers (O'Brien 1991). The disaster at Three Mile Island nuclear reactor sparked new regulatory mandates and helped mobilize an antinuclear movement and numerous "not in my backyard" movements, resulting in a nation quite skeptical about the use and safety of commercial nuclear power. And finally, entire towns (e.g., Soldiers Grove, WI; Valmeyer, IL; Pattonsburg, MO) have moved to safer ground after experiencing decades of severe flooding, or after one catastrophic earthquake (Valdez, AK). Whatever the methodological shortcomings of the research that argues either of these points (see Drabek 1986:293-298), it seems clear that in some cases disasters produce significant grievance leading to social change and that in other cases they do not. Sometimes disasters become grievances, but other times communities get back to normal with little call for change or new perspective. Our model will allow prediction of such differences in community response to disasters. While suddenly imposed grievances (Walsh 1981; McAdam, McCarthy, and Zald 1988) and disasters have been studied in terms of how they encourage individuals to join movements, change opinions, or act on their opinions, no one has yet tried to predict how substantial or frequent an external event must be, given certain community factors, for it to spark grievances and collective action. This essay offers a model for predicting social change after a disaster, given particular community contextual factors and the magnitude (severity) and frequency of the disaster.

In this chapter we model the process by which large ensembles of individuals (a city council, community, city, or state) act as a group under the influence of a disaster, although we do not propose to understand the details of how each individual will decide to act on specific issues. Just as a physicist can describe the large-scale flow dynamics of a river without knowing the details of every water molecule, we suggest a method for understanding the collective action (i.e., voting, activism, opinion changes) of large groups of individuals. In fact, the type of model we will use to understand fluctuations in opinion and sudden collective action is fundamentally the same as the model used by physicists to understand fluctuations in the density of a fluid and sudden phase changes from liquid to solid (Ma 1985).

We use a cellular automaton model (a primary research tool of complexity sciences; Wolfram 1994) to illustrate the process by which an external event (a disaster) drives social interactions that may lead to grievance and collective action. Cellular automaton computer simulations have been largely accepted in physics as a technique for understanding the complex interactions of systems with many components (such as a group with many members). This type of simulation is new to social sciences (Lewenstein, Nowak, and Latane 1992; Nowak, Szamrej, and Latane 1990) but offers a unique and ideally suited approach to analyzing the response and interactions of many individuals to a sudden external event. Our model is similar to the cellular automaton used by Nowak et al. (1990) to examine the self-organizing emergent behavior of large numbers of individuals who each make decisions based on their "neighbor's" opinions. In both models, members of a group or community are influenced, to varying degrees, by the other people with whom they interact and by their community in general. As people interact, group opinions will fluctuate, sometimes randomly, as individuals alter their opinions in response to the decisions of others (Lewenstein et al. 1992). Pockets of majority and minority opinions continually evolve in shape and size, and a large enough random fluctuation in opinions can influence large groups of other people also to change their minds. If a fluctuation is large enough, then there will be a sudden avalanche of changing opinions; a legislative body will move from a split vote to a majority opinion, or an entrenched public opinion will radically change.

In our model, opinions (and fluctuations in opinion) may be influenced by an external event (such as a disaster). By adding this external bias, a smaller fluctuation may be sufficient to alter opinions in favor of the bias, but larger fluctuations are necessary to alter opinions counter to the bias. Contrary to intuition, large external events may not always lead to significant changes in group behavior. For example, in some cases the presence of strong leaders who actively try to frame the situation as a nongrievance may encourage a lack of grievance or change, even if the disaster damage is large. Likewise, under many conditions, the size of an external event may be quite small but can still trigger complex group behaviors and seemingly unpredictable collective actions. In these cases, there is an emergent and sometimes intricate and complicated collective action created by no more than simple interactions between individuals. Such emergent group behavior formed from the interaction of individuals is the distinguishing characteristic of complex systems (Wolfram 1994; Weisbuch 1991). With a cellular automaton model, for the first time, specific predictions can be made regarding the magnitude and frequency of an event likely to cause collective action.

The Cellular Automaton Model

A cellular automaton model is used to examine the magnitude and frequency of the disaster necessary to influence a group with an established social structure or voting pattern. Will multiple small floods change the minds of a community that, in the past, has refused to vote for taxes aimed at purchasing hazardous land and relocating flood-prone homes and businesses? Or, how devastating must a single flood be to change the minds of a community? Similarly, in a community where debate regarding the importance of strict building regulations is split evenly, how large a hurricane is necessary to swing opinion in favor of more regulations? Our cellular automaton model of social reaction to disasters begins with a community of people, represented by a grid of squares, each square representing an individual (Figure 16.1). Each individual begins with an opinion regarding the appropriateness of his or her town being located in a floodplain. Those who think the town should move to a less hazardous location are colored white, while those who think the town is fine where it is are colored black. An individual interacts with friends, family, and co-workers, represented by the eight squares surrounding each individual square. A "social geometry" is specified for the community that represents the individual's physical location in the group (for example, an office building), or more generally, indicates the individual's social position in the group, so that "location" merely reflects proximity to a subset of the group with whom the individual interacts. Members of the subset with whom the individual interacts are called "neighbors." In our model neighbors are represented by the physically adjoining eight squares; however, neighbors could also be specified as being randomly (or deliberately) located at different points on the grid (as in the case of members of a family distributed across different parts of a community).

Each person (or square) has varying degrees of investment in his or her personal opinion and varying degrees of influence with people with whom he or she interacts (the neighbors). So, each black or white square is assigned a "strength of opinion," which indicates the ability of that person to persuade (or support) another individual. The probability of one person choosing one opinion will depend, in part, on the sum of the strengths of opinions of his or her neighbors. For example, if a person with a low strength of opinion interacts with people with opposite opinions with high strengths, the person is likely to change his or her mind.

There is always some probability (generated by the model with a random number) that the individual will take the opposite stance to the strongest opinions of neighbors (Bahr and Passerini 1996). Including such a probability incorporates the possibility of irrationality to the model. Most similar previous models have assumed some form of rationality; those models have, for example, assumed that each person will logically choose an opinion that matches the majority opinion of neighbors. This choice would hold even if there were 100 neighbors with one opinion and 99 neighbors with the opposite stance. In reality, though, people cannot make distinctions between such close splits in opinion. Furthermore, even if they could make such fine distinctions, people do not always make clear-cut, rational decisions; in fact, other computer simulations have shown that irrational choices can significantly change the collective behav-

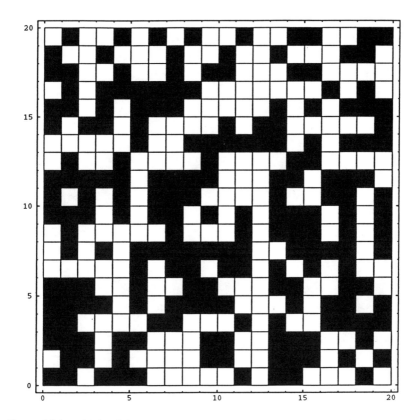

Figure 16.1. Initial opinions.

ior of groups (Macy 1990, 1991). Our model, therefore, allows for the possibility of irrationality.

In addition to individual interactions, people's opinions are influenced by the general mood of the community, the media, the state of the economy, and so on. This general mood has been identified as "social temperature" (Bahr and Passerini 1996), and unlike individual opinion strength, it is measured as a property of the group, not of individuals. Social temperature (T_s) indicates the volatility of every individual's decision, or the tendency for each member of a group to "jump on the bandwagon." For example, when the social temperature of a community is high, an individual with a low strength of opinion will quickly change opinions if interacting with many others with high strengths of opinion. However, under community conditions of low social temperature, the same person will take longer to change opinions, even though he or she is still interacting with the same people (who still have the same high opinion strengths). Interestingly, there is a precise correspondence between social temperature and

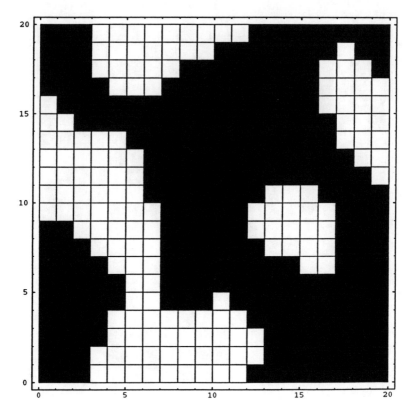

Figure 16.2. Opinions at equilibrium.

irrational behavior (Bahr and Passerini 1996). As the temperature rises, decisions become increasingly irrational. Miscommunication, mistakes, and misunderstandings are also included in the model as "noise," which is a random perturbation of the probabilities of having a given opinion. Noise, for example, allows for an individual's apparently inexplicable change to a dissenting opinion, even when the entire group has previously settled on another opinion. Unlike social temperature, in which people may irrationally choose an opinion, the likelihood of noise is not quantifiable. Noise accounts for the unknown, the individual personality quirks, or otherwise unquantifiable perturbations to the system.

In this modeled community, flooding, in the beginning, is not high on most people's list of community concerns (Figure 16.1). People (squares) in the community (grid) begin with a randomly assigned opinion and strength of opinion. As they interact with each other over time, they reach a fairly stable equilibrium of opinions (Figure 16.2). People go about their daily interactions until, one day,

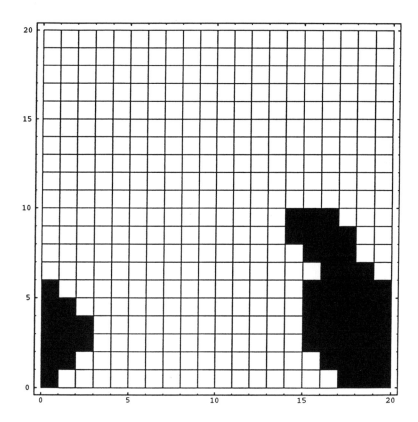

Figure 16.3. Opinions at Time 150.

a moderate-sized flood inundates the town. As the community's vulnerability is revealed and framed by various social actors, and as people interact and discuss this new information and experience, public opinion may be swayed toward increased disaster mitigation (Figure 16.3). The flood is parameterized by a number (h_s) that indicates the magnitude (or persuasiveness) of its influence on the community. For example, a small flood will make everyone only slightly more likely to change their minds in favor of moving out of the floodplain, and is represented in the model as an external event with a small number, or small persuasiveness.

We hypothesize that the magnitude and frequency of the flood will have an effect on people's willingness to move out of the floodplain. Oliver (1989:11) notes that major events (such as disasters) create opportunities for people to talk to each other about the possibility of collective action. The likelihood of change, she says, is positively related to "the size and drama of the action . . . [and] . . . to the number of prior actions that have occurred recently." While Oliver was primarily referring to prior collective actions (by other people), the same could be said for external events such as disasters. The "size and drama" of the flood, and the frequency with which it is experienced (every 2 years vs. every 100 years) will, in some cases, create interactions that create suddenly imposed grievances and influence collective action. The eventual action taken by the community may depend on whether the moderate flood is followed by 60 years of fairly small floods every 5 years, or 60 years of a large flood every 10 years, or other mixtures of flooding possibilities.

At every time step (every year, in this model) each individual has an opportunity to change opinions (think of it as an opinion poll done every year in the community). Whether or not an individual changes opinion depends on the strength of the opinion, the strength of neighbors' opinions, the social temperature, the noise, and the magnitude and frequency of the disaster.

Keeping in mind the general description outlined above, the model is more precisely described with the following mathematics. Each individual i has one of two opinions, $s_i = 1$ or $s_i = -1$. (These correspond, for example, to the opinions that the town should or should not move out of the floodplain.) For a given social geometry, each individual also has some total number of neighbors, N. Individuals interact with each of the neighbors, all of whom have some varying degree of influence on the individual's opinion formation process. In particular, the influence of each neighbor j is controlled by the strength of that neighbor's opinions, p_{ij}; that is, p_{ij} is the ability of individual j to persuade (or support) individual i. A high value of p_{ij} indicates a highly persuasive and influential neighbor, while a low value of p_{ij} indicates an unconvincing and uninfluential neighbor. Therefore, the total influence of all of i's neighbors is

$$I_1(i) = \sum_1 p_{ij} / \sum_{j=1}^{N} p_{ij}, \tag{1}$$

$$I_2(i) = \sum_2 p_{ij} / \sum_{j=1}^{N} p_{ij}, \tag{2}$$

where the summations in the numerator are over only those neighbors with opinions one or two, respectively. The denominator calculates the total opinion strength of all the neighbors. Therefore, the ratios in equations (1) and (2) represent the fraction of the total opinion strength that is due to individuals with opinion one or two, respectively. For example, if all individuals were equally persuasive, then equations (1) and (2) would reduce to the percentage of the neighbors that have each opinion. In other words, if n_1 is the number of neighbors with opinion one, and n_2 is the number of neighbors with opinion two, then, for equal opinion strengths,

$$I_1(i) = n_1 / N \tag{3}$$

$$I_2(i) = n_2 / N. \tag{4}$$

In this case, it is now clear that if more neighbors have opinion one ($n_1 > n_2$), then their influence is greater than those neighbors with opinion two (i.e., $I_1 > I_2$). This agrees with micro-sociological experiments on small groups (Bahr and Passerini 1996; Latane 1981).

Now let the strength of the external social event (disaster) be represented by h_s, and let the social temperature be T_s. Then, as detailed in Bahr and Passerini (1996), the probability that individual i will have opinion one ($s_i = 1$) or two ($s_i = -1$) is

$$P_1 = \frac{1}{z} e^{h_s/T_s} [I_1(i)]^{1/T_s} \tag{5}$$

$$P_2 = \frac{1}{z} e^{-h_s/T_s} [I_2(i)]^{1/T_s}, \tag{6}$$

where z is a constant determined by

$$z = e^{h_s/T_s} [I_1(i)]^{1/T_s} + e^{-h_s/T_s} [I_2(i)]^{1/T_s}. \tag{7}$$

(For those unfamiliar with statistical mechanics, z is called the "partition function" and is nothing more than a normalizing constant that ensures probabilities between 0 and 1.) Notice that if neighbors with opinion one are highly influential (high I_1), then the probability of having opinion one goes up (high P_1). Likewise, if neighbors with opinion two are more influential than neighbors with opinion one ($I_2 > I_1$), then the probability of choosing opinion two is greater than the probability of choosing opinion one ($P_2 > P_1$). Similarly, if the social event (disaster) grows larger, then e^{h_s/T_s} in equation (5) gets larger, and the probability of having opinion one gets larger. On the other hand, small social events (or small disasters) will have little influence on either of the probabilities of choosing an opinion, because e^{h_s/T_s} will approach 1. As expected, large negative social events will have the opposite effect and will make the probability of choosing opinion two much higher.

The cellular automaton model operates by calculating the probabilities (equations 5 and 6) that each individual in a group will have a particular opinion, one or two. For each person, a random number θ is generated and if it is greater than the probability of choosing the opposite opinion, the individual changes opinion. For example, suppose individual i has opinion $s_i = 1$. Then if $\theta > P_2$, the individual changes to opinion $s_i = -1$, but if $\theta < P_2$, the individual keeps the original opinion. At every time step (in this case a year) each individual's opinion is updated. The potential for an individual to change opinions is always present at every time step, because neighbors are constantly reevaluating their opinions as well, and as neighbors change opinions, the influence functions I_1 and I_2 will change. Noise (miscommunications, etc.) is also added to the model by adding a small random number to P_1 and P_2 at each time step. More details of the model and its derivation can be found in Bahr and Passerini (1996).

Analysis

What effect does the magnitude and frequency of disasters have on a community's opinion of what to do about disasters? To answer this question we first ran the cellular automaton model assuming a community of 400 people, holding social temperature constant, distributing strength of opinion and noise randomly, and assuming a 50-50 initial split between opinions. In the case of a large or moderate disaster occurring constantly (i.e., all the time; an impossible occurrence, but a useful ideal type), people will almost always come to a consensus to do something about the disaster. Only in the case of an extremely small continuous disaster will consensus not be reached. However, even in a case of small continuous disasters, a group that has an initial 50-50 opinion split will always end up with a majority that believes something should be done about the disaster. If the group is initially split less equally in opinion, say 25% for mitigation and 75% for doing nothing, then a slightly greater magnitude disaster is needed to change minds in favor of doing something. If the opinions are switched, 75% for mitigation and 25% for doing nothing, then a slightly smaller disaster is needed to change minds in favor of doing something about the disaster. In summary, there is always a "threshold" value for the magnitude of a constant disaster, beyond which a consensus will always occur, and the threshold is typically very small. These simulation results agree with the analytical results found elsewhere (Bahr and Passerini 1996).

Next we ran a number of models in which one (noncontinuous) disaster occurs every 100 time steps (which can be thought of as every 100 years). To begin with, social temperature was held constant, strength of opinion and noise were distributed randomly, and opinions began with a 50-50 split. Initially, before the disaster, the people in the community interact, changing or retaining opinions, until opinions reach some kind of equilibrium (see A, Figure 16.4). When a disaster occurs, there is a sudden jump in the number of people who believe that some kind of mitigative action should be taken to deal with the disaster (see B, Figure 16.4). We first ran the model assuming that everyone acts completely rationally, defined as adding up the opinions and strengths of opin-

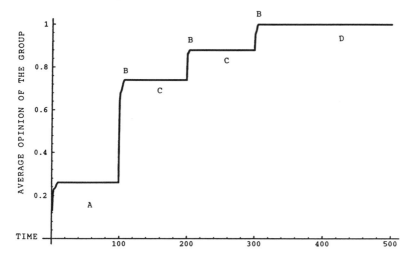

Figure 16.4. Cumulative effects of disasters.

ions of those around him or her and choosing to take the opinion of the strongest force (Johnson and Feinberg 1977; Collins 1988). This, of course, is also an ideal type. In the case of complete rationality, where social temperature (T_s) is zero (see Bahr and Passerini 1996 for analytical justification of the correspondence between social temperature and rationality): (1) a disaster occurs, (2) most people change opinions in favor of increased mitigation, (3) no one changes opinions during the interval in which there are no disasters (see C, Figure 16.4), (4) more people change their minds after the next disaster, until (5) there is consensus among everyone in the community that something must be done about the disaster (see D, Figure 16.4). Note that after each disaster, the community does not return to its original equilibrium but is stuck at a new ("higher") equilibrium. When everyone is completely rational, the effect of each disaster is cumulative.

Under these conditions of complete rationality, we then varied the magnitude of the disasters that occurred. When a very large magnitude disaster occurs, consensus in the community is usually reached that "something must be done." For smaller magnitude disasters the group does not reach consensus; however, small pockets of minority opinions (who believe that nothing needs to be done) are converted. Many small disasters can slowly "eat away" at the number of people in a community who believe that nothing needs to be done about disasters. However, in most cases small disasters do not have the power to convert everyone. When the disaster is especially small there are very few converts to the opinion that something should be done, and the disaster makes very little difference to the overall opinion of the community.

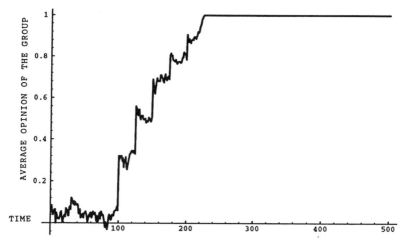

Figure 16.5. Frequent disasters: every 25 time steps.

Next we modeled the more realistic conditions in which not everyone makes decisions rationally, $T_s \neq 0$. In other words, the number of neighbors with a particular opinion does not necessarily dictate the opinion of each individual (although it might). As irrationality increases, people who initially changed their opinions after the disaster in favor of mitigation are more likely, over time, to change their opinions back to the view that nothing needs to be done. In other words, as people become less rational, they forget the lessons of past disasters, and their opinions slip back toward the old equilibrium. As the social tempera-ture (T_s) gets larger (i.e., as irrational behavior increases), the effect of a disaster on opinion change becomes less and less cumulative (compare Figure 16.4 to Figure 16.5).

After a disaster it takes a while for opinions to drop back to the old equilib-rium. Thus, the frequency of disasters plays a large role in their cumulative nature when people are not completely rational. Compare Figure 16.5, where disasters occurred often (every 25 years), to Figure 16.6, where disasters oc-curred infrequently (every 100 years). As the frequency of disasters increases, the likelihood of the community reaching a consensus, or at least reaching a majority in favor of mitigation, increases.

We also found that the presence of noise (miscommunication, misinforma-tion, etc.) tends to make groups within a community more stable in opinion. This is because noise will occasionally change the opinion of some individuals in a group. When this happens to an influential individual, the change in opin-ion will cause many others also to change opinion. After a while, therefore, the only groups left unaffected by noise are the ones that are mutually supportive; for those groups, when noise changes one person's opinion, the support of the

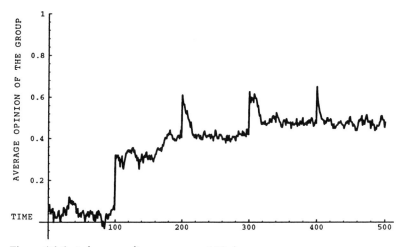

Figure 16.6. Infrequent disasters: every 100 time steps.

other members will change it back. In other words, noise encourages groups of opinion to form around mutually supportive people; these groups are not easily perturbed by miscommunications or misinformation, and will appear more "stubborn" or stable in opinion. Empirically, we know that people do miscommunicate and make mistakes—noise does exist. Therefore, as shown in the cellular automaton simulations, noise is an important element of social behavior and should be included in any model of collective action.

Conclusions

The analysis shows that a simple model, with very few initial assumptions about social behavior, can accurately reproduce well-accepted empirical knowledge about social behavior after disasters. For example, Berkland (1996:221) expresses a widely held opinion among disaster researchers when he writes that "after disasters, public and policy makers' interest in disaster preparation, mitigation and relief rapidly but briefly increases, driven either by the need to respond or by dramatic news media accounts of disasters in neighboring states or communities. The interest in disasters and possible responses to disaster then fades rather quickly. The next disaster rekindles interest, and the cycle repeats." Our model agrees with this assessment and, like the quote, illustrates the inaccuracy of social models that assume rational behavior.

The cellular automaton model also shows that the higher the magnitude and frequency of the disaster, the more likely there is to be consensus regarding what to do about it. The model also shows that the more rational people's behavior after a disaster, the more likely they are to "learn" from past disasters. In addition, noise plays an important part in modeling collective action and should not be overlooked in formal models.

One of the most important implications of this model is that one's likelihood of supporting mitigation after a disaster, and to continue to support mitigation long after the disaster has been experienced, depends on the social temperature of the community. Given this information, empirical studies could be designed that poll a community for social temperature, and then make predictions regarding which communities are more likely to support mitigation after a disaster. This information, for example, could be useful to government agencies trying to allocate resources which encourage communities to move out of floodplains (FEMA, for example). Such a study could identify communities that would be especially easy to sway, and those unlikely to be swayed.

The success of the model in explaining simple, commonsense social behavior, as well as less obvious social behavior (for example, the dependence of learning on social temperature), suggests that cellular automaton simulations can be used for more complex simulations in the future. These simulations might be designed, for example, to say exactly how frequent and how large a disaster must be to stimulate social action. It should be noted that in our simulations we have, at times, held some variables constant to better explain other variables (primarily, magnitude and frequency of disasters). However, the model is certainly capable of explaining much more than the focus of this essay. For example, simulations could also examine the impact of different percentages of the community being affected by each disaster or examine the impact of state and federal incentives for particular opinions or actions. Simulations could also incorporate "disaster cultures" in disaster-prone areas, changes in news coverage of the disaster, variations in people's access to media information, the presence or absence of social movement organizations addressing disasters, and the difference between urban and rural disaster sites.

The fact that the cellular automaton model, by itself, discovered specific patterns that match general assumptions about behavior after disasters (and that, if one doubts them, can easily be tested with empirical studies) is promising. Such findings contribute to the robustness of the model and suggest that in the future the model can be used with confidence to predict/simulate more complicated large-scale social behavior.

17

Organizations and Constraint-Based Adaptation

Kathleen M. Carley

Organizations can and do adapt to their environment; however, this adaptation is subject to various institutional constraints. Laws, institutional norms, and so forth set the parameters in which the organization can adapt. A question that arises in this context is whether organizations can locate optimal forms if they are subject to such constraints. That is, does constrained but strategic adaptation admit optimization? Further complications arise for organizations because they are composed of intelligent agents who themselves are learning as they pass through a multitude of experiences. Organizations alter their forms and adapt to their environments (Stinchcombe 1965a; DiMaggio and Powell 1983; Romanelli 1991) both through strategic reorganization (Kilmann and Covin 1988; Butler 1993) and through accumulative experience on the part of the organizational members (March 1981). Thus, a second question is

AUTHOR'S NOTE: This work was supported in part by the Office of Naval Research (ONR), United States Navy Grant No. N00014-93-1-0793 (UConn FRS 521676). The views and conclusions contained in this document are those of the author and should not be interpreted as representing the official policies, either expressed or implied, of the Office of Naval Research or the U.S. government.

whether the institutional constraints on strategic adaptation interact with the ability of the organization to take advantage of the experience gained by the individual members of the organization, who themselves are continuously adapting.

Organizational change dynamics result from simple, but nonlinear, processes. An example of such a nonlinearity is the decreasing ability of a new piece of information to alter an agent's opinion as the agent gains experience. Such nonlinearities make it nontrivial to think through the implications of the combined experiential and strategic adaptation processes. Computational analysis enables the theorist to think through the possible ramifications of such nonlinear processes and to develop a series of consistent predictions. Consequently, computational models can be, and have been, used in a normative fashion to generate a series of hypotheses by running virtual experiments. The resultant hypotheses can then be tested in other empirical settings.

This is the approach taken herein. Specifically, the potential impact of constrained adaptation will be examined from a computational theoretic perspective. Organizations are modeled as complex adaptive agents composed of complex adaptive agents. As in any complexity model, stable structures and patterns of behavior emerge from the application of simple rules on the part of the agents and agents coevolve. Rate of learning influences what patterns emerge. The process of strategic organizational adaptation is modeled as a simulated annealing process in which the organization seeks to locate its optimal form but is subject to constraints on its ability to change. The process of experiential learning is modeled using a stochastic learning model with limits on attention, memory, and information processing that effectively bound the agent's rationality. Both of these models are combined into a single computational framework called ORGAHEAD. To use ORGAHEAD, a virtual experiment is run in which the types of constraint on adaptive mechanisms are altered. At the strategic level, the adaptive mechanisms examined include adding personnel, dropping (or firing) personnel, altering the reporting structure (who reports to whom), or altering the task structure (who is doing what).

ORGAHEAD

ORGAHEAD is a dual-level information processing model of organizational adaptation. The two levels are the strategic and the operational. At the strategic level, organizational performance is affected by the CEO's ability to take the appropriate strategic actions, to alter the organization in response to environmental cues, and to anticipate the future. Institutional constraints affect this process by limiting or defining the set of options for change that the CEO can choose among. A computational analog of this process is simulated annealing (Carley and Svoboda 1996). At the operational level, organizational performance is affected by the actions of the organizational members (or agents) as they work on specific tasks, communicate to others, and learn. At this level, constraints take the form of bounding rationality both by socially limiting who has access to what information and by cognitively limiting the individual's ability to process acquired information (Simon 1955, 1956; March and Simon 1958). A computational analog of this process is the CORP model (Carley 1992; Carley and Lin forthcoming).

ORGAHEAD is used to estimate the performance of an organization as it adapts in response to cues from its environment. The cues take the form of the question, is performance higher or lower than it was previously? Performance is measured as accuracy in classifying objects. In other words, the organization is facing a sequence of classification choice tasks and must determine for each time (or equivalently, task) whether the object it is seeing is of type A or type B. The specific task used is a binary choice task, also referred to as a pattern matching and classification task. Classification tasks such as this have been widely studied in the organizational literature, both in a binary version (Carley 1992; Ouksel and Mihavics 1995) and in a trinary version often described as a stylized radar task (Ilgen and Hollenbeck 1993; Carley and Lin 1994, 1995; Tang, Pattipati, and Kleinman 1992), and in a dynamic version (Lin and Carley forthcoming; Carley and Lin forthcoming).

Each time period, the organization receives a new choice task and makes a decision as to how to classify that task. The specific task used is a binary choice in which the organization sees a binary string of length 9 and must determine on the basis of the pattern whether that overall pattern indicates an A (1) or a B (0) choice. There is, unbeknownst to the organization, a correct classification. The correct value is defined to be A (1) if the majority of bits in the string are 1, else B (0). Again, performance within a given period is measured as the fraction of the tasks seen during that period that were correctly classified.

Strategic Adaptation and Simulated Annealing

Strategic adaptation refers to the changes the organization (due to its CEO or executive committee) makes to its structure. Strategic adaptation is modeled as a simulated annealing process (Kirkpatrick, Gelatt, and Vecchi 1983; Rutenbar 1989), such that the organization's strategies are the move set. Simulated annealing is a reasonable computational analog of the way in which organizations, over extended periods of time, alter their structures (Eccles and Crane

1988). The set of potential moves includes augment $\overline{N}$ add n personnel, downsize $\overline{N}$ drop n personnel, retask $\overline{N}$ move agent i from task s to task j, reassign $\overline{N}$ have agent i stop reporting to j and start reporting to agent k.

At any one time, all personnel changes made are of the same type; however, the number of personnel changes made that time is given by a Poisson distribution. Each type of allowable move is initially equally likely. However, over time, the CEO will learn which moves are more likely to improve performance and so will change which adaptive strategies are employed. Institutional constraints can be modeled in this framework by fixing the probability of a particular move at a particular level and not allowing it to change. For example, tenure could be modeled by setting the probability of downsizing to 0 for all time.

The organization continuously cycles through a series of stages: general operation, evaluate performance, suggest form, evaluate form, select form, and alter form. Each time period, the organization observes the environment (sees a new task). After a sequence of 500 tasks (general operation) performance is calculated (evaluate performance), then the CEO proposes a strategy from the move set for altering the organization's structure (suggest form), then the CEO "looks ahead" and tries to imagine how the proposed new organizational structure will affect performance (evaluate form), then the CEO determines whether or not to implement the new structure (select form), and then the organization's structure may be changed (alter form). The limited lookahead is simulated by creating a hypothetical organization with the proposed new structure and simulating its performance on a sequence of 100 tasks. After the lookahead, the CEO decides whether or not to accept the new design. The probability of accepting the new form is based on the Boltzman probability criteria.

According to this criteria the CEO always accepts the change if the resulting hypothetical organization exhibits better performance during the 100-task lookahead than the current organization has recently (past 500 trials). Otherwise, the risky change is accepted with a probability given by $e^{-\delta \, \text{cost}(t)/T}$ such that $\text{cost}(t) = 1/\text{performance}(t)$. If the structural change is accepted the CEO puts the change in place and then proceeds to process another sequence of tasks, at which point another alteration to the organizational form is considered. If a proposed change is not accepted the organization continues with its current structure for another sequence of 100 tasks. The rate of organizational change is set by the temperature cooling schedule.

Temperature (T) will drop each time period (such that one time period equals 100 tasks) as $T(t + 1) = a * T(t)$, where a is the rate at which the organization becomes risk averse and t is time. In other words, over time the CEO and the organization become increasingly risk averse, increasingly conservative. The initial high-risk-taking behavior can be thought of in terms of the liability of newness (Stinchcombe 1965b; Bruderl and Schussler 1990).

Experiential Learning and Bounded Rationality

Experiential learning refers to the ability of the agents within the organization to garner experience and improve their ability to perform the task. At this operational level the CORP model of organizational performance is used. Within CORP an organization is composed of a set of complex adaptive agents who are responsible for doing the task and who are situated within an organization with a particular structure. Each time period each agents sees a set of information (a certain number of bits). These bits may be information from the task or they may be the "recommendations" of other agents as to the classification of the string. Each agent is limited to being able to handle a maximum of seven bits of information at a time (thus a maximum of $2^7 = 128$ patterns). Which agent sees which bits of information, and which agent reports what to whom, depends on the organizational structure.

Agents are thus boundedly rational both from a cognitive or information processing standpoint (can only handle seven bits) and from a social standpoint (what information they have access to is determined by their position in the organizational structure) (March and Simon 1958). Given these bounds on rationality, no agent in the organization has the capability or sufficient information to make the decision completely unassisted.

Training

If the agents follow standard operating procedures (SOPs) then they always act as majority classifiers and return a 1 if they see more 1s than 0s and a 0 otherwise. If there is no majority they guess (basically, flip a fair coin). If the agents followed their experience then they keep track of the frequency with which each pattern they see is associated with a correct answer of either a 1 or 0. For each task, the agents return a 1 if the correct answer most frequently observed for this pattern was a 1, and a 0 if that was historically the most frequently observed answer. If neither answer historically dominates then the experiential agents simply guess (flip a coin). This experiential procedure is similar to a stochastic learning model (Busch and Mosteller 1955). With sufficient experience for binary tasks, experiential agents come to resemble those following a SOP of majority classification. Specifically, they can only remember the first 100 and most recent 250 tasks that they have done. This gives a forgetting, a recency, and a primacy effect. Experiential agents, however, have an additional cognitive constraint. CORP, specific elements of CORP, and predictions from the CORP model have been extensively described in previous studies (e.g., Carley 1992; Carley and Lin 1995, forthcoming). CORP has been shown to be a reasonable model of organizational performance both against experimental lab studies (Carley 1996, forthcoming) and archival data on actual organizations (Lin 1994; Carley and Lin 1995), particularly for more complex organizational structures. Models like CORP, or extensions of CORP, have received extensive attention (Ouksel and Mihavics 1995; Mihavics 1996; Mihavics and Ouksel 1996) as has the binary and trinary choice tasks underlying CORP (see, e.g., Tang et al. 1992; Pete, Pattipati, and Kleinman 1993, 1994; Pete 1994; Carley 1992; Lin and Carley forthcoming; Hollenbeck, Ilgen, Sego, Hedlund, Major, and Phillips 1995; Hollenbeck, Ilgen, Tuttle, and Sego 1995).

Initial Conditions

The organization begins with a particular organizational structure chosen at random from the possible set. These organizations have from one to three levels below the CEO, with a maximum of fifteen personnel per level, from one to forty-five personnel (not counting the CEO), and nine distinct subtasks. The initial determination of size, the organizational structure (who reports to whom), the resource access structure (who has access to information on what subtasks), and how many individuals occupy each organizational level is determined randomly from the set of possibilities.

The CEO always acts as a majority classifier and is not cognitively limited. All other agents are either trained as experiential learners or follow SOPs. If they are experiential learners then they begin by knowing nothing and build up their patterns over time. Agents, when they have no information to go on, make their decisions by guessing. Individual learning occurs using a stochastic experiential learning process (Carley 1992). Over time, agents build up their experience and begin to act as majority classifiers if they experience a random sample of tasks with an equal expectancy for the true answer to be an A (1) or a B (0). If the agents follow SOPs then they always act as majority classifiers.

Performance Criteria

Performance is calculated over a sequence of 500 tasks (evaluate performance) as the percentage of tasks that were correctly classified. The level of performance expected by chance is 50.00%. Performance is also looked at categorically, by dividing up the organizations into the following categories based on their final performance: $x \leq 70$ (0), $70 < x \leq 75$ (1), $75 < x \leq 80$ (2), $80 < x \leq 85$ (3), $85 < x \leq 90$ (4), $90 < x$ (5). In addition to performance the level of redundancy in access to resources (average number of personnel accessing the same bit of information on the task), average span of control (measured as the average number of subordinates per manager below the CEO), average density (ties between personnel), isolation (measured as the number of agents who neither report to others nor have others report to them), and overlooks (measured as the number of decision-making factors that are not attended to by any agent) are considered. These measures are calculated both at the beginning of the simulation for each organization and after it reaches quiescence.

Virtual Experiment

Using ORGAHEAD, the computational model just described, a virtual experiment was run. In this virtual experiment the following factors were systematically varied: training, a tenure-based dismissal constraint, and a redesign-based constraint. Agents could be trained either to follow SOPs (Carley and Lin forthcoming) or to follow their experience (Carley 1992). Organizations either had a tenure system (in which cases agents could not be dismissed or fired from the organization), or did not. Organizations either used a redesign strategy, simply altering the connections between existing agents (or agents and tasks), or used a flexible strategy, in which they either could redesign or could alter their personnel base by hiring (or firing if they were not in a tenure situation). This is a $2 \times 2 \times 2$ design. For each cell in this design, a total of 1,000 different organizations were simulated, for each condition, such that the organization's initial design was randomly generated from the set of all possible organizational designs.

The specific task used was a nine-bit binary string resulting in a population of 512 distinct tasks. The correct answer is defined to be a 1 if there are more 1s than 0s in the string and a 0 otherwise. Each organization was simulated for 20,000 tasks (time periods) or until it reached quiescence, whichever came first. Organizations were defined as reaching quiescence when the approximate probability of accepting a new design dropped to 55% (which corresponded to a "freezing" temperature of 0.0345). The initial temperature was 0.433; consequently, approximately 90% of the proposed changes were initially accepted. The organization became increasingly risk averse at a rate of $\alpha = .975$. The timing of the organization's life cycle is controlled by multiple windows defined in terms of the number of tasks. The 20,000 tasks are divided into a sequence of 200 cooling windows each of length 100. Temperature is dropped after each cooling window. The proposed hypothetical design is simulated for 100 tasks (the length of the lookahead window). The expected performance of the proposed design is calculated in just this lookahead window and contrasted against actual performance of the organization during the previous 500 tasks. Initial analyses indicated that there were no significant differences in the long-term behaviors due to the training condition. Essentially, even though the organization's structure can be changed every 100 time periods, the structures that emerged were such that very few bits of information were assigned to any one agent. Thus, experiential learners developed their repertoire of rules sufficiently quickly that most of the agents were acting as majority classifiers regardless of whether they were trained to act on experience or SOPs. Consequently, in the ensuing analysis these cases will be combined, and the analyses will be run using a basis of 2,000 organizations. The reduced 2 × 2 design then simply looks at the type of constraints—tenure or strategic. This final design is displayed in Table 17.1. As can be seen, the two types of constraints combine to create relatively severely and unconstrained institutional contexts.

Results

Institutional constraints are expected to have important effects on organizational behavior. For example, we might expect that severe constraints on the organization's ability to restructure itself might limit its performance and might decrease the variance in the types of forms observed. In the first case, the idea is that organizations are trying to optimize their form for a specific task environment; however, the optimal form might require the organization to take a nonallowable action. For example, if the organization cannot fire personnel, then getting rid of personnel who have learned the wrong behavior and simply are making wrong decisions—thereby lowering overall performance—would not be an option. As to the second point, constraints are expected to lower variance because there will be fewer organizational forms to choose among, and so organizations that are trying to locate the best form are more likely to end up in the same place and so are more likely to have the same performance.

In Table 17.2, the results from the virtual experiment that speak to this issue are displayed. As can be seen, the prediction with respect to performance did not hold out. That is, while severely constrained organizations are more similar in their performance, their performance is higher (and significantly so) than the relative unconstrained organizations. Why are we seeing higher performance in the severely constrained case? The answer has to do with averaging. Severe constraints by restricting the number of forms are restricting not only what good forms are possible but what bad ones are possible as well. In this particular case, the specific set of constraints, tenure and only redesign, serves to eliminate those organizational forms where performance is very bad, thus, on average, resulting in better performance. If, rather than looking at average performance, we look at the number of organizations that make more than 90% of their decisions correctly, we see that there are fewer (in fact no) top performers in the case of severe constraint (see Table 17.3). However, being unconstrained does not

Table 17.1 Design of Virtual Experiment

Constraint	Tenure	No Tenure
Redesign strategy	Severe	Moderate
Flexible strategy	Moderate	Unconstrained

Table 17.2 Mean Effect of Constraint on Performance

Constraint	Tenure	No Tenure
Redesign strategy	82.30	79.00
	(2.83)	(5.18)
Flexible strategy	75.51	76.03
	(5.84)	(5.53)

Note. N = 2,000 per cell. Standard deviations are in parentheses.

Table 17.3 Mean Number of Top Performers by Type of Constraint

Constraint	Tenure	No Tenure
Redesign strategy	0	3
Flexible strategy	27	13

Note. N = 2,000 per cell.

maximize the number of top performers (note there are only 13 organizations in this case). No constraints on organizational adaptation may actually overly facilitate experimentation and decrease the likelihood of finding the optimal form.

Another assumption that we might make about institutional constraints is that severe constraints will decrease organizational efficiency and decrease the variance in efficiency across organizations. That is, severe constraints may cause the organization to retain certain pockets of inefficiency. We can measure inefficiency as the number of agents that are isolated or the number of decision factors that are overlooked.

The results of testing these assumptions are shown in Table 17.4 for isolates and Table 17.5 for factors overlooked. For both isolates and factors overlooked, we see that there is greater efficiency (significantly lower values) and lower variance in the severely constrained than the unconstrained situation. In this case, the default assumption is seen to hold.

We might expect that high-performance organizations are high performance because they start out as highly efficient and remain so. This question is addressed in Table 17.6 where the percentage change over time in various factors

Table 17.4 Mean Effect of Constraint on Number of Isolates

Constraint	Tenure	No Tenure
Redesign strategy	2.06	1.90
	(0.85)	(1.10)
Flexible strategy	2.74	2.75
	(1.22)	(1.24)

Note. N = 2,000 per cell. Standard deviations are in parentheses.

Table 17.5 Mean Effect of Constraint on Number of Factors Overlooked

Constraint	Tenure	No Tenure
Redesign strategy	0.05	0.29
	(0.21)	(0.52)
Flexible strategy	0.39	0.39
	(0.66)	(0.65)

Note. N = 2,000 per cell. Standard deviations are in parentheses.

Table 17.6 Percentage Change by Level of Final Performance

	Final Performance Level					
Variable	0	1	2	3	4	5
No tenure						
Redundancy						
Redesign strategy	−0.13	−0.59	0.00	−0.45	−0.22	0.00
Flexible strategy	−25.64	−12.92	−2.73	14.24	19.36	20.21
Isolates						
Redesign strategy	0.79	−1.35	0.77	1.73	1.56	0.00
Flexible strategy	−4.87	−19.08	−29.54	−36.19	−47.84	−37.40
Factors overlooked						
Redesign strategy	−0.86	−7.94	0.00	−36.36	−66.67	0.00
Flexible strategy	147.92	0.00	−52.54	−85.37	−84.21	−100.00
Tenure						
Redundancy						
Redesign strategy	−1.01	0.47	−0.34	−0.22	−0.11	N/A
Flexible strategy	65.15	47.38	44.45	36.25	30.59	23.19
Isolates						
Redesign strategy	−0.26	1.40	1.19	−0.46	0.00	N/A
Flexible strategy	−14.03	−26.43	−33.03	−24.81	−21.93	−15.14
Factors overlooked						
Redesign strategy	−6.78	8.33	−12.50	−25.00	−100.00	N/A
Flexible strategy	−43.82	−88.46	−85.97	−92.11	−100.00	−100.00

indicating inefficiency is shown. This percentage change is measured as 100 times the average value for all organizations at that level of performance at the end of the simulation minus the average value that those same organizations had at the beginning of the simulation divided by their value at the beginning. Since for each of these measures a higher value indicates lower efficiency, and since the contrast is new minus old, a negative value indicates an increase in efficiency.

In general, regardless of their final performance level, all organizations tend to overlook fewer factors in making their decisions. However, organizations that do not have flexible strategies often end up with more isolates, and those that do have flexible strategies often end up with a more redundant workforce. Second, the organizations that manage to locate the high-performing, more optimized forms are not those that started out more efficiently.

Within organizational theory it is generally recognized that there is no one right form. Indeed, the dominant claim is that the optimal form depends on, or is contingent on, the task environment that the organization is facing and the specific task being pursued (Lawrence and Lorsch 1967). For a particular task environment, however, there should generally be a simple pattern relating the various aspects of form, such as size and span of control, to performance. Institutional constraints, in other words, should not matter.

However, the results from the virtual experiment suggest that institutional constraints can alter the perception of the relation between organizational form and performance even when holding constant the task environment. For example, in Figure 17.1 we see the relationship between performance and size and span of control for the organizations where there was little institutional constraint (flexible strategy and no tenure). In Figure 17.2, the same relationship is shown for severely constrained organizations (redesign strategy and tenure). There is quite a contrast between the two figures. Under these different types of institutional constraints, the relationship between organizational form and performance appears to vary.

It is important to stress that this is a perceptual and not a real difference. That is, if two organizations had exactly the same form, but one was in a severely constrained environment and one was in an unconstrained environment, they would exhibit the same performance if given the same set of tasks. Different institutional constraints lead to different organizational forms emerging over time. Thus, in the long run, the field of organizations that emerges under one set of constraints may tend to exhibit a different relationship between form and performance than will a set of organizations that emerges under a different set of constraints. Thus, one would expect that individuals working under different sets of institutional constraints will perceive, and so learn, different lessons about the relationships between form and performance.

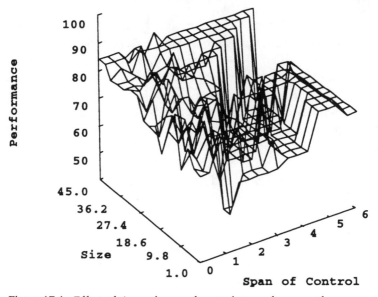

Figure 17.1. Effect of size and span of control on performance for unconstrained organizations.

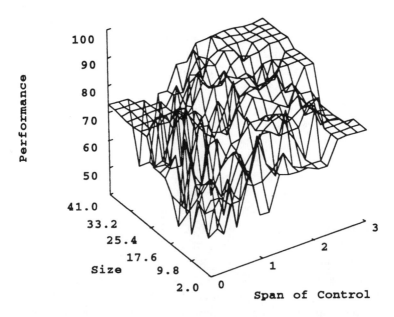

Figure 17.2. Effect of size and span of control on performance for severely constrained organizations.

Discussion

In the foregoing analysis the organizations were attempting to optimize their performance defined simply as accuracy. As such, no cost was attached to size or connections among individuals. A consequence was that since additional personnel added resolution on problem solution, the organizations grew arbitrarily large. Alternative cost functions, such as simultaneously optimizing performance and minimizing personnel, could be considered. Work on computational models suggests that changing the cost function can affect the particularities of the results. In this case, it would affect the number of decision factors overlooked, the level of redundancy, and the tradeoff between accuracy and organizational form.

Future studies should investigate alternate cost functions to locate the relation between form and performance. However, changing the cost function is unlikely to change the following results: there are few high performers, there are equi-performance plateaus, small changes in the organization's architecture can result in dramatic changes in performance, the way in which the organization alters its structure and its initial form combine to affect ultimate performance, institutional constraints affect what forms emerge and the apparent relation between form and performance.

Despite altering their structure, organizations are typically trapped in equi-performance plateaus. This equi-performance result suggests that CEOs can, within reason, reorganize their organization with relative impunity. Moreover, the mere act of reorganization, while it may not generate improvements in performance, is likely to be advantageous to the organization from an efficiency standpoint (that is, such reorganization may minimize isolates or the number of decision factors that are overlooked).

The model examined in this chapter is not a classic chaos model; that is, it is not a set of difference or differential equations, but rather has a few stochastic elements. Behavior, even that which is process driven such as in this simulation, often appears chaotic without a simple relation between input/independent and output/dependent variables. Indeed, the results reported here, and others from this same model (Carley and Svoboda 1996), are consistent with the behavior one would expect from a chaotic system. For example, small changes in organizational form can result in dramatically different performance level. Organizations with almost equivalent organizational forms can exhibit very different performance profiles. Organizations, as complex systems, have the characteristic that the organizational design features are not systematically related to performance; rather, small differences in the initial design for a set of organizations, particularly when coupled with their response to the environment can result in dramatically different emergent structures and final performance.

Furthermore, although organizations can locate good designs regardless of the intelligence of the agents within them, they may not locate the optimal design, and what designs emerge depends on the specific institutional, cognitive, and social constraints that influence individual and organizational behavior. In a constrained environment, organizations can rarely locate the optimum form simply through heuristic-based search procedures like that embodied in a simulated annealing process. Indeed, in such an environment, standard procedures for optimizing performance may not be sufficient. Alternative mechanisms for optimizing performance, such as mimicry, should be examined.

The model used herein is highly nonlinear. The resultant performance surfaces, such as those relating performance to size and span of control, can be seen as highly nonlinear. What are the implications of this for organizational theory? In most organizational studies, the R^2 for models exploring performance tends to be quite small. Such low R^2s are often attributed to measurement error or missing variables. An alternate explanation suggested by the foregoing results is that organizations and their performance are essentially chaotic. Organizations as complex systems composed of adaptive agents may engage in relatively simple rules of operation; however, the coadaptation of the agents and the organization may result in complex patterns of behavior. In such systems, linear models cannot capture the complexities, and the use of such models enables only low levels of prediction.

In this essay, these results have specific implications for institutional constraints. The results from the virtual experiment demonstrate that naive intuition about organizations and the impact of constraints can be wrong, particularly when there are complex interactions. For example, it was demonstrated that while the naive expectation might be that severe institutional constraints will lower performance, in actuality, severe constraints may result in performance improvements by keeping organizations from going down erroneous paths. Institutional constraints may improve performance if they happen to take advantage of individuals' cognitive capabilities. Institutional constraints can actually create a supportive environment. Finally, fields of organizations faced with different sets of institutional constraints may "learn" or perceive different relationships among organizational form and performance even when faced with the same task.

18

Chaotic Behavior in Society
Adolescent Childbearing in Texas, 1964-1990

Kevin Dooley
Patti Hamilton
Mona Cherri
Bruce West
Paul Fisher

The United States leads other developed nations in adolescent pregnancies and births (Norr 1991). Estimates are that 43% of all female adolescents and 63% of black female adolescents will experience at least one birth before their 20th birthday (Jones et al. 1985). The effect of this is not trivial, nor does it have only "moral" implications. Adolescent mothers are likely to be economically poor, and they and their children are more likely to face health risk (Furstenburg 1987). Adolescent mothers are less likely to acquire adequate

AUTHORS' NOTE: This research has been partially supported by a grant from the National Institute for Nursing Research (R15 NR03733-01). Development of Rosenstein's software was supported by a grant from the Rehabilitation Research and Development Service of Veterans Affairs.

prenatal care, leading to health complications and increased societal costs (U.S. Department of Health and Human Services, Public Health Service [DHHS] 1990). Public health agencies at the local, state, and national levels, such as Medicaid, are burdened with the cost of this phenomenon; some hypothesize that adolescent mothers are more likely to become welfare dependent. While there have been a number of policy responses to the problem, their effect has been minimal at best, and costly (Stafford 1987).

Many government officials have called for studies on the patterns and reasons behind this phenomena; as public agencies can better forecast behavior, they can "better identify children and adolescents at greater risk for early parenthood . . . [and] provide early interventions which might positively impact adolescent decision-making" (Schlitt 1992:1). Changing state and federal policy is seen as a means to influence behavior (Lerberg and Lee 1995). Previous studies have shown that about one-fourth the variation in pregnancy rates and one-half the variation in birth and abortion rates can be explained by demographic characteristics of the region (Singh 1986). This implies that attempting to invoke a change in sexual behavior alone will not be adequate; instead, solutions must also be socioeconomic in nature.

The United States appears to have a larger problem with adolescent births than other nations because of lack of openness about sex, a paucity of sex education and limited distribution of contraception, and unequal distribution of income (Jones et al. 1985). Norr (1991) asserts that within the United States there are three demographic patterns visible. First, in many southern and western states (except California), adolescent pregnancy reflects "a continuation of a preindustrial pattern of early family formation. Higher rates of adolescent childbearing are associated with higher levels of religiosity, especially fundamentalism, social and sexual conservatism, and a pattern of early marriage and low education" (p. 180). A second pattern, seen in the midwest and northeast and in California, is more European—liberal attitudes toward sexual activity lead to more pregnancies, and also more use of abortion. A third pattern "may be a response to community disorganization and the inability to control youth activities plus a lack of perceived opportunities that would reward delayed childbearing" (Norr 1991:180). This latter pattern manifests itself in economic rather than geographic ways.

The state of Texas is acutely affected by this issue. Texas ranked second behind California in the number of births to mothers between 14 and 20 years of age (DHHS 1990). During FY 1991, over $215 million was spent in Texas on 131,804 Medicaid-paid deliveries, of which approximately 29% were to teenage mothers, costing $96 million on newborn care (Texas Department of Human Services 1992).

Predicting the number of births in a given time period has proved elusive, in part because of the nature of the data (Catalano and Serxner 1987; Heckman and Walker 1989; Joyce 1989; Schaffer and Kot 1985); indeed, only one formal time series study has been done, showing teen births following a "seasonal" pattern of cyclical fluctuations, with "noise" added in (Izenman and Zabell 1981).

The data analyzed here were obtained from birth certificates at the Texas Department of Health. Data included dates and frequencies of births to women 10 to 19 years old on each day from 1/1/64 to 12/31/90. Summary statistics show that the average number of births to adolescents in Texas each month over the 27 years was 3,984. The average daily incidence was 126 with a standard deviation of 17.2; over 1.2 million births were incorporated in the data set (Hamilton et al. 1994).

Hamilton et al. (1994) have performed the initial study of this data set. They report:

- Power spectrum analysis shows strong periodicities in the daily counts, of length 7, 182, and 372 days.
- Singular value decomposition seems to indicate a dimension of 4 in the weekly tallies—namely, four variables appear to be driving the behavior of the system (of course, this method of analysis does not indicate which four variables are key).

The purpose of this essay is to extend the analysis of this data set to determine

A. What are the (linear) periodicities present in the data?
B. Is the system better modeled by functions that are stochastic and linear, deterministic and linear, or stochastic and nonlinear?
C. Is there evidence of chaotic behavior in the data?
D. Are the dynamics of the data different at different time scales (weekly, monthly, and annually)?
E. Are the data stationary?
F. Are changes in complexity related to health policy or legal changes over the period?

The methods used to determine answers to questions A, B, and C are described in the next section. The subsequent section attempts to answer questions A-C via analysis of the data, applied across different time scales (to answer questions D and E). A final section includes implications and directions for future study, including potential hypotheses regarding question F.

Methods

A standard data analysis protocol was developed to ensure fair treatment of the data and subsequent testing of hypotheses; each step was separately applied to the data aggregated by year, month (actually four weeks), and week:

1. Plot the data on a run chart. Visually analyze for patterns. Split the data into separate epochs if it appears appropriate.
2. Standardize the data by subtracting the sample average and dividing through by the sample standard deviation.
3. Construct and visually examine return maps (a scatter diagram that plots $x[t]$ vs. $x[t - t]$). Look for patterns that might indicate interesting dynamical behavior.
4. Calculate the sample autocorrelation function, and examine how much "memory" is in the system, whether there are strong or weak patterns of association, and whether these patterns are "statistically significant."
5. Calculate the sample periodogram, and estimate the (linear) frequencies (periodicities) present in the data.
6. Fit three time series models to the data—one representing a linear, stochastic system (an autoregressive model of order one, or AR[1]), one representing a linear deterministic system with added noise (a sine wave defined by the parameters of magnitude, frequency, and phase), and one representing a stochastic, nonlinear system (an exponential time series model). Model adequacy is checked in standard ways via residual analysis (Pandit and Wu 1983), and models are compared via the r^2 measure.

These steps were carried out using the SYSTAT statistical package (Systat 1992). In step six, the models being fit are in the basic form:

$$\text{linear:} x(t) = a * x(t - 1) \tag{1}$$

$$\text{periodic:} x(t) = a * \sin(b * t + c) \tag{2}$$

$$\text{exponential:} x(t) = a * \exp[b * x(t - 1)], \tag{3}$$

where a, b, and c are empirically determined parameters. Model complexity can be enhanced by adding on additional lag and periodic terms.

If the best fit model is (1), it confirms the hypothesis that the system is stochastic and linear; likewise, model (2) is deterministic and linear and (3) is stochastic and nonlinear. One might argue that a more conventional nonlinear time series model, such as one that adds quadratic autoregressive terms, may be more general (Pandit and Wu 1983). While that is true, we have chosen this particular nonlinear time series model because it has direct correspondence to chaotic dynamics (Guastello 1995), a phenomenon we are particularly interested in studying here.

After this analysis is done, exploration for chaotic dynamics begins. This essay shall not review the "basics" of nonlinear dynamical systems; instead, the reader is referred to other authors (Bassingthwaighte, Liebovitch, and West 1994; Guastello 1995; Kaplan and Glass 1995; West and Deering 1995).

There are many reasons why the discovery of chaotic dynamics might be interesting in this case:

A. It estimates the number of "essential" variables that are driving the system.
B. A change in dimension between two epochs of time may signal a significant system change.
C. It quantifies the implicit randomness, or consequently, orderliness of the system.
D. It may indicate something about how the attributes of the system are interacting in a nonlinear way.

To determine whether the system is chaotic or not, a Lyapunov exponent is first calculated; this estimated parameter quantifies the divergence (if positive) or convergence (if negative) of closely spaced trajectories in the system. Divergence is indicative of chaos; a special algorithm for small data sets is used here (see Rosenstein, Collins, and De Luca 1993). Second, the fractal (Grassberger-Procaccia correlation) of the attractor is calculated, using Guastello's method as well as one implemented by Rosenstein et al. (1993).

The equations for Lyapunov exponent and fractal dimension are well defined in numerous texts (e.g., Kaplan and Glass 1995; West and Deering 1995). Guastello's (1995) general exponential method is less well known and shall be described here. From equation (3), let b be an estimate of the Lyapunov exponent and let D be dimension where

$$D = \exp(b). \tag{4}$$

If $D < 1$, the process converges to a fixed point; if $D > 1$, chaotic dynamics may be present. Note that for a linear process, b will tend toward zero and D tends toward one. Note that this is a different interpretation than usual. Typically a random sequence would be considered to have infinite dimension. Because this method works underneath the noise, it finds a single-point attractor (the statistical mean), and thus dimension, of one.

In practice, the model

$$x(t) = a * \exp[b * x(t - K)] \tag{5}$$

is fit with different values of lag K. The dimension estimate as a function of K, $D(K)$, is $\exp(b)$. $D(k)$ is plotted and when $D(K)$ is observed to undergo "catastrophic" change at lag K^*, $D(K^* - 1)$ is used as the estimate of dimension (Johnson and Dooley 1996); this is roughly equivalent to setting lag for a correlation dimension estimate equal to the lag where the sample autocorrelation function goes to zero (Skinner 1994). For an example of how this is done, see the results section of the weekly data, Figures 18.19 and 18.20.

The next section presents the results of our analysis. The first three subsections provide results on the "protocol" analysis for annual, monthly, and weekly data; the fourth subsection provides results for the nonlinear dynamical analysis; the fifth subsection summarizes the results.

Results

The raw data (birth counts) exist in daily increments; they have been previously analyzed by Hamilton et al. (1994) in that context and so that analysis will not be repeated here. Instead, we have aggregated the data into weekly, monthly, and yearly increments. These increments are not only "natural" from a calendar perspective, but they also correspond to previously discovered period lengths of fluctuation. If indeed teenage birth is the outcome of a complex system, then one would expect dynamics to be self-similar across different scales of analyses.

Annual Data

Figure 18.1 shows a time plot of the original data aggregated by year ($n = 27$), from 1964 to 1990. Note the apparent step increase in the mean after point five or six (starting in 1969 or 1970), and the subsequent periodicity. It also appears that there is a 9- or 10-year cycle. The return maps (Figure 18.2) indicate nothing dynamically interesting.

Eliminating the first six cases, with years 1970-1990 remaining, a plot of the sample autocorrelation function demonstrates periodicity (Figure 18.3). The parentheses in Figure 18.3 indicate that only the first lag autocorrelation is considered statistically significant; nevertheless, periodicity remains evident. A periodogram (power spectrum) indicates two dominant frequencies at approximately 8 years and 16 years. Similarly, wavelet analysis (Morlet et al. 1982) shows the data set could be decomposed into three 8-year periods. Fitting models (1), (2), and (3) to the data we find the periodic model has two frequencies, at 19.33 and 9.39 years; the second (lower) frequency is dominant. One con-

Figure 18.1. Annual adolescent births in Texas.

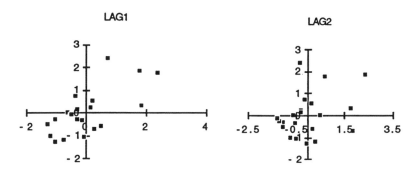

Figure 18.2. Return maps, annual data.

cludes that the best model is linear periodic, with a primary frequency of 9-10 years (Table 18.1).

Monthly

The monthly aggregation of the data (Figure 18.4, $n = 352$) actually represents 28 days' worth of daily tallies (i.e., 13 "months" per year). Note the apparent step increase in the mean after 84 months (starting in 1971), and the

```
LAG   CORR    SE -1.0  -.8  -.6  -.4  -.2   .0   .2   .4   .6   .8  1.0

                   |----|----|----|----|----|----|----|----|----|----|

1   0.683  0.218                    (          |·········)········

2   0.314  0.303                 (             |········      )

3  -0.087  0.319                 (               ··|           )

4  -0.407  0.320                 (        ···········|          )

5  -0.571  0.343              (     ···············|              )

6  -0.487  0.386            (      ············|                )

7  -0.276  0.414          (           ·······|                  )

8  -0.114  0.423        (              ··|                    )

9   0.091  0.424        (                |··                   )

10 0.121  0.425        (                |···                  )
```

Figure 18.3. Autocorrelation plot, annual data.

Table 18.1 Model Results, Annual Data

Model	r^2	Hypothesis
Exponential autoregressive	0.248	Chaotic
Linear autoregressive	0.481	Linear stochastic
Unimodal	0.572	Linear periodic
Bimodal	0.846	Linear periodic

subsequent periodicity. It appears that there are 1- and 10-year cycles. The data will be analyzed in two separate epochs: months 1-84 and months 85-352.

Epoch One

The return maps do hint at an attractor, cyclical in nature (Figure 18.5). The return map at lag 4 also demonstrates some orderliness in the trajectory (Figure 18.6). A plot of the autocorrelation function also shows strong periodicity (Figure 18.7). The power spectrum shows strong periodicities at one-half and 1 year; the fit of model (2) (the best fit model) also shows a strong 1-year periodicity.

Monthly Adolescent Pregnancies

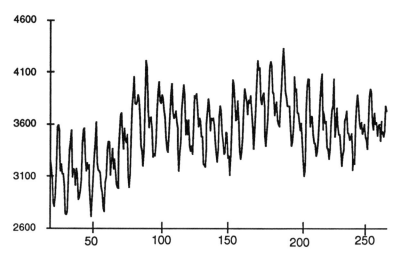

Figure 18.4. Time series, monthly data.

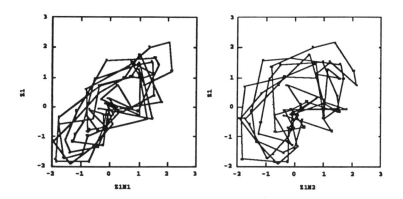

Figure 18.5. Return maps, monthly data, epoch one.

Epoch Two

The return maps demonstrate dynamic similarity between epoch one and epoch two (Figure 18.8). The autocorrelation function shows periodicity and long memory (Figure 18.9). The power spectrum shows a strong period at 128 months, or 9.85 years cycle; model (2) shows a strong 1-year periodicity. The linear model fits the data best.

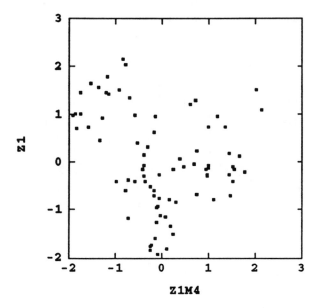

Figure 18.6. Return map, Lag 4, monthly data, epoch one.

Weekly

The weekly data ($n = 1,409$) are broken into two epochs: 1964-1971 (Figure 18.10, $n = 285$) and 1971-1990 (Figure 18.13, $n = 1,124$).

Epoch One

The return maps do not show any particular patterns, although there is an obvious elliptical bounding of trajectory (Figure 18.11). The sample autocorrelations show periodicity and long memory (Figure 18.12). The sample periodogram reveals frequencies at 51.2 weeks and 25.6 weeks; these are also found in fitting model (2) (the best fit model).

Epoch Two

The sample autocorrelations hint at a low-frequency process (Figure 18.14). The periodogram shows frequencies at 1,020 weeks (19.6 years), 512 weeks (9.85 years), 255 weeks (4.90 years), 102 weeks (1.96 years), and 85 weeks (1.62 years); fitting of model (2) shows half-year and year periodicities. The linear model is superior (Table 18.5).

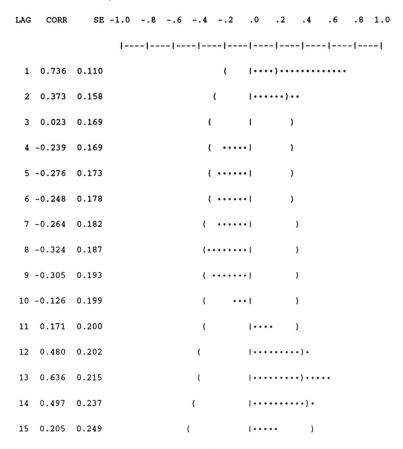

Figure 18.7. Autocorrelation plot, monthly data, epoch one.

Table 18.2 Model Results, Monthly Data

Model	r^2	Hypothesis
Exponential autoregressive	0.218	Chaotic
Linear autoregressive	0.537	Linear stochastic
Unimodal	0.575	Linear periodic

Nonlinear Dynamical Analysis

The first step in testing the data for chaos is to find the (first) Lyapunov exponent (West and Deering 1995); this exponent, if positive, indicates that nearby "orbits" in the system's trajectory diverge exponentially over time. This

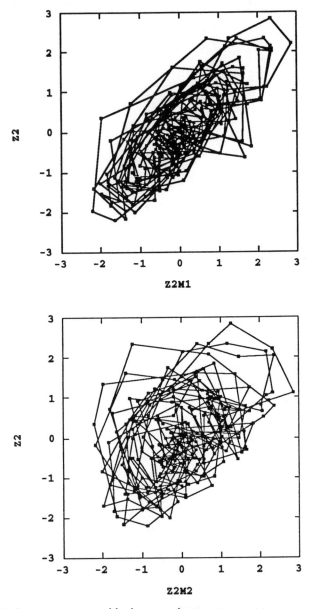

Figure 18.8. Return maps, monthly data, epoch two.

sensitivity to initial conditions in indicative of chaos (West and Deering 1995). Two methods were used to estimate the Lyapunov exponent: Rosenstein's algorithm (Rosenstein et al. 1993) and Guastello's algorithm (Guastello 1995). The

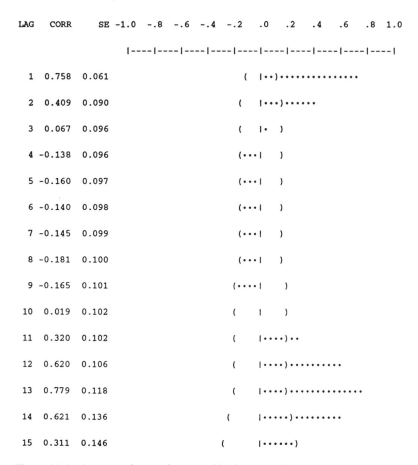

LAG	CORR	SE	-1.0	-.8	-.6	-.4	-.2	.0	.2	.4	.6	.8	1.0

```
 1  0.758  0.061                    (  |..)................
 2  0.409  0.090                    (  |...).......
 3  0.067  0.096                    (  |.  )
 4 -0.138  0.096                    (...|  )
 5 -0.160  0.097                    (...|  )
 6 -0.140  0.098                    (...|  )
 7 -0.145  0.099                    (...|  )
 8 -0.181  0.100                    (...|  )
 9 -0.165  0.101                   (....|   )
10  0.019  0.102                   (    |   )
11  0.320  0.102                   (    |....)..
12  0.620  0.106                   (    |....)..........
13  0.779  0.118                   (    |....)...............
14  0.621  0.136                   (       |.....)..........
15  0.311  0.146                   (       |.......)
```

Figure 18.9. Autocorrelation plot, monthly data, epoch two.

Table 18.3 Model Results, Monthly Data, Epoch Two

Model	r^2	Hypothesis
Exponential autoregressive	0.238	Chaotic
Linear autoregressive	0.576	Linear stochastic
Unimodal	0.405	Linear periodic

exponent was found to be positive for the monthly and weekly data, for both epochs.

Next, Rosenstein's algorithm (Rosenstein et al. 1993), an implementation of the Grassberger-Procaccia algorithm (Grassberger and Procaccia, 1983), is used to find fractal dimension. The delay time was set at 3 months for the monthly

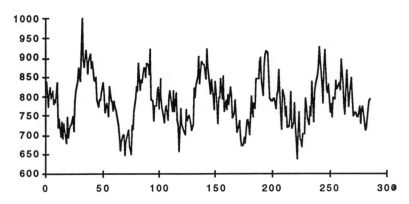

Figure 18.10. Time series, weekly data, epoch one.

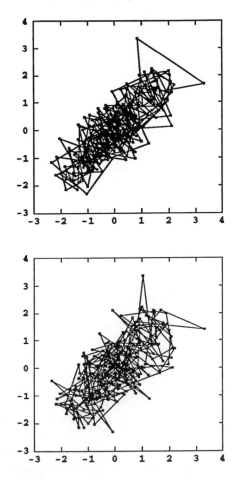

Figure 18.11. Return maps, weekly data, epoch one.

```
LAG   CORR     SE -1.0  -.8  -.6  -.4  -.2   .0   .2   .4   .6   .8  1.0

                      |----|----|----|----|----|----|----|----|----|----|

  1  0.752  0.059                          (  |•)················

  2  0.665  0.086                        (    |•••)·············

  3  0.616  0.103                      (      |••••)···········

  4  0.582  0.115                      (      |••••)··········

  5  0.474  0.125                     (       |•••••)·····

  6  0.415  0.131                     (       |•••••)····

  7  0.332  0.136                     (       |••••••)··

  8  0.234  0.138                     (       |••••••)

  9  0.166  0.140                     (       |•••• )

 10  0.091  0.141                     (       |•• )
```

Figure 18.12. Autocorrelation plot, weekly data, epoch one.

Table 18.4 Model Results, Weekly Data, Epoch One

Model	r^2	Hypothesis
Exponential autoregressive	0.200	Chaotic
Linear autoregressive	0.580	Linear stochastic
Unimodal	0.673	Linear periodic

data and 11 weeks for the weekly data and was determined from examination of the sample autocorrelations (Skinner 1994); the mean response time was set equal to one year, and the divergence time was set equal to the sample size corresponding to epoch one. Care was taken during examination of the correlation plots; dimension is determined by selecting the "linear region" of the plot, so endpoints were tracked and kept relatively constant. Figures 18.15-18.18 show dimension estimate as a function of embedding dimension.

The leveling off of these plots indicate dimension is low. The monthly data for epoch one show a dimension around two, whereas epoch two appears more complex, with a dimension of around three. The weekly data show a dimension of 3.5 during epoch one and are slightly larger in epoch two. Next, Guastello's method is used to determine dimension. Dimension estimates were obtained

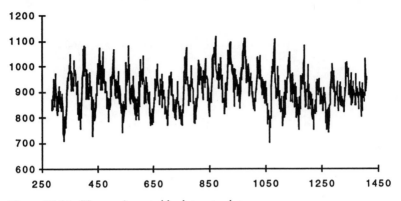

Figure 18.13. Time series, weekly data, epoch two.

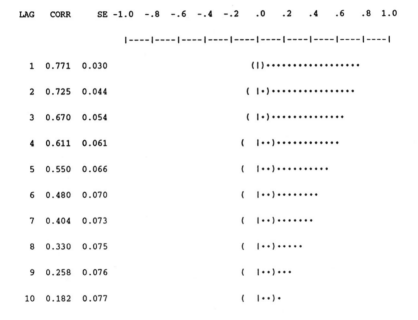

Figure 18.14. Autocorrelation plot, weekly data, epoch two.

using increasing time delays. The "correct" estimate will be taken as the estimate occurring directly before a significant change in the correlation dimension versus embedding dimension plot occurs. In the monthly data, epoch one yields a dimension estimate of 3.98, and 3.29 is estimated for epoch two. In the weekly data, the estimate is taken at embedding lag 10 as 3.23 for epoch one (Figure 18.19), whereas an estimate of 3.55 is obtained for epoch two (Figure 18.20).

Table 18.5 Model Results, Weekly Data, Epoch Two

Model	r^2	Hypothesis
Exponential autoregressive	0.232	Chaotic
Linear autoregressive	0.595	Linear stochastic
Unimodal	0.411	Linear periodic

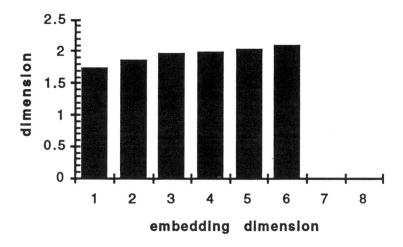

Figure 18.15. Dimension, monthly data, epoch one.

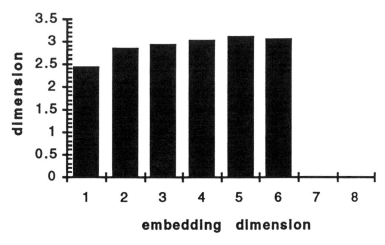

Figure 18.16. Dimension, monthly data, epoch two.

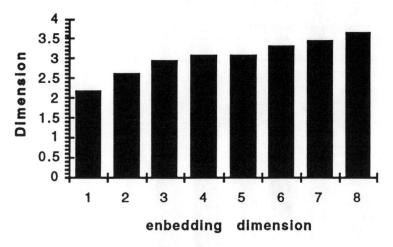

Figure 18.17. Dimension, weekly data, epoch one.

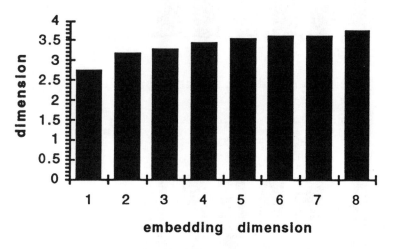

Figure 18.18. Dimension, weekly data, epoch two.

As a visual confirmation, with knowledge of a possible dimension of three or four, and an appropriate delay time of 3 months (in the monthly data), a different return map is generated. The three-dimensional plot is generated by plotting the triplet $[x(t), x(t-3), x(t-6)]$. The orderliness of this (possibly "strange") attractor is a strong visual clue pointing toward a chaos model (Figures 18.21-18.22).

To further test the validity of the results indicating chaos, a series of surrogate tests (Theiler et al. 1992; Theiler 1994) was performed. Data were sequentially shuffled and dimension estimates found. A sample of nine was used, for the

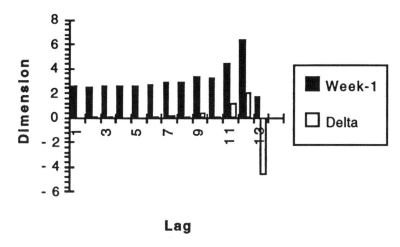

Figure 18.19. Guastello dimension, weekly data, epoch one.

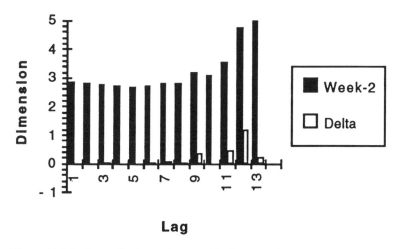

Figure 18.20. Guastello dimension, weekly data, epoch two.

monthly and weekly data, for both epochs. A statistical significance level can be assigned to the dimension result by finding out how many times a dimension randomly is low or lower than the said estimate. For example, if the actual estimate is the lowest among the pool of ten estimates (the nine surrogates and itself), then a significance level of .10 can be assigned. Surrogate testing showed a significance level of .10 for the monthly data and .20 for the weekly data.

Sequentially shuffled surrogates test the null hypothesis of independence and randomness; it has been found that by phase-shuffling the data, one can directly test the null hypothesis of a linear, periodic system (Kaplan and Glass 1995).

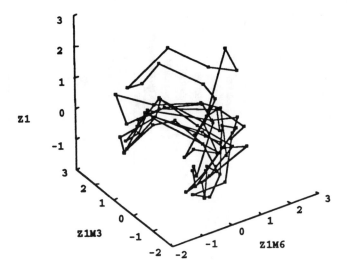

Figure 18.21. Three-dimensional return map, monthly data, epoch one.

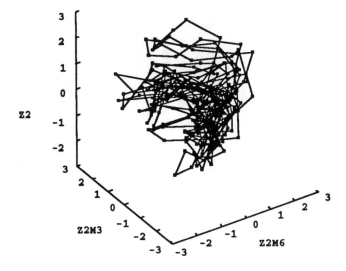

Figure 18.22. Three-dimensional return map, monthly data, epoch two.

Thus, if phase-shuffled surrogates allow rejection of the null, then one can conclude that the system is not linear periodic. In our case this is especially important because it is unclear whether dimensional estimates are low because the
system is linear periodic, or chaotic dynamics are truly present. While Rosen-

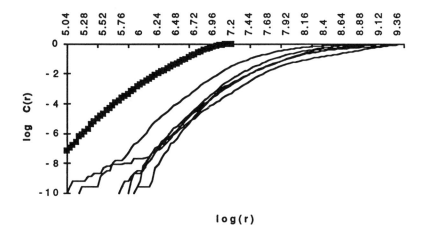

Figure 18.23. Correlation integral, monthly data, epoch two, with surrogates.

stein's method yielded a 3.05 fractal dimension for monthly data in epoch two, the phase surrogates yielded dimensions of {3.74, 4.06, 3.49, 3.95, 4.46, 3.49, 3.61, 4.15, 5.49}, therefore we can reject the null with $p = .10$.

Figure 18.23 shows the log of the correlation integral (log [C(r)] vs. the log of the "radius" [log(r)]); it is from this plot that a slope is estimated, and that slope becomes the dimensional estimate (Kaplan and Glass 1995). This plot shows the actual data (monthly, epoch two) in dark, and the nine phase-randomized surrogates. Chaotic data will tend to have a relatively flatter shape. One can readily see that the dark line retains far more height than any of the other curves, a good indicator of chaos.

Finally, a Hurst exponent was calculated. The Hurst exponent is a measure of long-term memory in the system (West and Deering 1995). If the exponent is around 0.5, a random series is indicated. Exponents lower than 0.5 represent an antipersistence, or infinite variance system; exponents greater than 0.5 represent persistence, or long-term positive correlation (Peters 1991). Using the monthly epoch two data, we found a Hurst exponent of 0.26, indicating anti-persistence or mean-reversion. The nine phase-randomized surrogates had exponents of {.45, .48, .47, .47, .48, .46, .47, .52, .45}, indicative of a random series and showing the 0.26 result to likely be relevant. This result shows that the birth counts tend to revert back to the mean after undergoing a fluctuation away from the mean; this may have to do with the fact that we are dealing with (an essentially) fixed population size.

Thus, one may conclude that the data sets are indicative of chaotic behavior. Table 18.6 summarizes the dimensional results.

Table 18.6 Dimension Results

	Epoch One		Epoch Two	
	Rosenstein	*Guastello*	*Rosenstein*	*Guastello*
Monthly	2.10	3.98	3.05	3.29
Weekly	3.11	3.23	3.62	3.10

Summary and Discussion

The following results can be drawn from the analysis.

First, the data have periodicities of 7 days, 28 days, 1 year, and 10 years.

A plausible reason for a 7-day periodicity may be that "problem" pregnancies are scheduled for inducement on Monday, so if complications arise the patient is discharged by the weekend; other inducements may occur before the weekend, on Friday. Some plausible reasons for the 1-year periodicity might include the school year calendar, and its milestones (e.g., starting the school year), and other seasonal differences. It is not clear now why there are 28-day and 10-year cycles, although the answer to such would undoubtedly shed more understanding on the system. If the "10-year" cycle is actually an 8-year cycle, this may correspond to behavior being coupled to the 4-year high school cycle or the 8-year grade school cycle, or it may indicate coupling with the state's political and/or budgetary cycle.

Second, the best model fit was an AR(1) model, a linear stochastic model.

Even though the periodicities are quite strong, the simple AR(1) model consistently outpredicted others. From a practical standpoint this means that policymakers may be best off making short-term predictions with a simple random walk model.

Third, there is a step increase in the mean number of births, in 1971.

There is no definitive explanation for this, although this could represent a baby-boom wave, or it could represent reaction to a number of "favorable-to-conception" policy actions that took place in the 1970s: Title X (1970; contraceptives become available at federally funded clinics); *Roe v. Wade* (1973; legalizes abortion); and *Planned Parenthood of Central Missouri v. Danforth* (1976; parental consent for abortion unnecessary) (see Figure 18.24 for more detail).

Fourth, the data may be chaotic.

Chaotic behavior indicates the system may be sensitive to initial conditions. In practical terms this means any small change in the system could have profound effects in the dynamical outcome. While previous policy changes have not seemed to have any effect, let alone a "sensitive" effect, this does not preclude it from happening in the future. The low fractal dimension indicates the system has a high degree of orderliness to it, with just three or four state variables (constructs) interacting together in a nonlinear fashion, determining behavior. While it may not be possible to identify the exact state variables, it may be possible to identify observable measures of such.

One must also recognize, though, that other explanations are possible. For example, a sine wave with noise will tend to show a fractal dimension of around 3.0. While this was somewhat tested for via the phase-randomized surrogates, one can never reach a definitive conclusion. Other behavior may induce the "look of chaos," including nonstationarity, non-Gaussian inputs, nonlinearity in the measurement process, and nonlinearities that do not involve chaos (Kaplan and Glass 1995).

Fifth, the fractal dimension of the data may change over time.

Current tests are inconclusive as to whether fractal dimension differed between the two epochs, although it appears they might. Calculations of the "point dimension" (Skinner 1994), which gives a dimensional estimate every fourth point in the series, seems to indicate a drifting of dimension over time, with dimensions of 4, 5, and 6 being most prevalent. This could have serious implications regarding systemic interventions. Specifically it is hypothesized that interventions (policy and otherwise) may be more effective when dimension is low than higher. Fractal dimension is an indicator of the degree of coupling taking place in an agent-based system. If dimension is high the agents (in this case, teenagers, their families, and peers) are relatively uncoupled and interventions will have difficulty catching on; if dimension is low, agents tend to be coupled tightly, so that an effect to one agent could trigger an effect to yet another, and so on—that is, interventions are more likely to be effective during low-dimensional chaos than during high-dimensional chaos, or random behavior.

Sixth, the data are nonstationary and may be linked to significant policy and legal changes.

A recurrence plot (Mayer-Kress 1994a) is a way of graphically showing the data's autocorrelation structure over time. The two axes represent time, and the (x,y) pixel represents the correlation between two points in time. The darker the pixel, the more correlation present. If the patterns are consistent from left to right, the data can be taken as stationary. Figure 18.24 clearly shows, though, that the data are not stationary. At least three sections of behavior can be seen: 1964-1970, representing the "base case"; 1970-1980, representing a period when a number of favorable-to-conception policy actions took place; and 1980-1990, when a number of "unfavorable-to-conception" policy actions took place. Figure 18.24 shows the different events that occurred (Spitz et al. 1987; Spitz et al. 1996).

Timeline of U.S. Legislation Affecting Teen Births

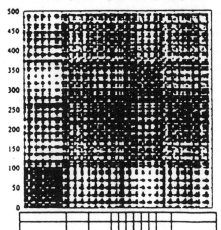

a. 1964
b. 1970
    1. Title X passes (contraceptives become available at federally funded clinics).
c. 1973
    1. *Roe v. Wade, Doe v. Bolton* (legalizes abortion).
d. 1976
    1. *Planned Parenthood of Central Missouri v. Danforth* (parental consent for teen abortion unnecessary).
e. 1977
    1. Hyde Amendment (restricts Medicaid funding used to pay for abortion).
    2. *Carey v. Population Services International* (legalizes display, advertisement, and sale of over-the-counter contraceptives to minors).
    3. Health Assistance Program Extension Act of 1977 (specifically targets adolescent group as an intended recipient of Title X benefits).
f. 1978
    1. Adolescent Health Services and Pregnancy Prevention and Care Act of 1978 and the creation of the Office of Adolescent Pregnancy Programs (emphasizes teens age 17 and under, attempts to integrate existing pregnancy care and prevention legislation into an accessible and cohesive unit).
    2. Title X amended (requires family planning services to offer a "broad range of acceptable and effective family planning methods and services").
    3. Department of Health discontinues involuntary sterilization of minors and the mentally incompetent; it also disallows use of Medicaid funds to pay for abortions.
g. 1979
    1. Department of Health and Human Services considers minors on basis of their own financial resources (not parents') to evaluate payments.
    2. Bellotti II (adolescents denied abortion by parents may appeal to the courts, which judge if teen is mature enough to make the decision or if the abortion would be in her best interests).

Figure 18.24. Recurrence plot

h. 1980
   1. *Harris v. McRae and Williams v. Zharaz* (declares that state and federal governments are not legally bound to provide women with funds for abortions).
   2. *Doe v. Irwin* (providers of contraceptives to teens are not legally bound to inform parents of such).
i. 1981
   1. The Adolescent Family Life Act "Chastity Bill" (repeals the Adolescent Health Services and Pregnancy Prevention and Care Act of 1978; ceases funding to clinics providing abortions or abortion counseling; encourages parent participation in teen birth consent; participation in program requires parental consent; funds are provided by parents).
j. 1982
   1. DHHS proposes Title X amendment (requires parental notification of contraceptives given to teens. This never passes, however, clinic attendance is grossly affected).
k. 1984
   1. Title X passes without amendment.
l. 1990

Figure 18.24. Continued

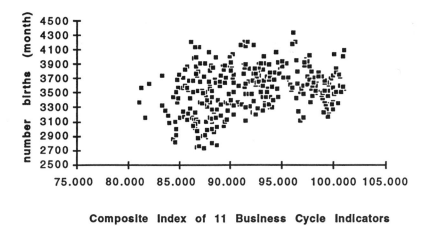

Composite Index of 11 Business Cycle Indicators

Figure 18.25. Monthly births and the business cycle.

One may hazard that these fluctuations were due to the natural "business cycle" that exists in the economy. While by no means exhaustive, Figure 18.25 does not support such a claim. The figure shows the monthly birth counts plotted against a composite index of business indicators (Media Logic Enterprises 1996), and there appears to be no correlation; clearly more investigation is warranted.

Conclusions and Future Work

Our data analysis of teenage pregnancies in the state of Texas from 1964 to 1990 indicated strong periodicities of 7 days, 28 days, 1 year, and 10 years. The best predictive model fit was an AR(1) model, a linear stochastic model, showing that from a practical standpoint policymakers may be best off making short-term predictions with a simple random walk model. There is a step increase in the mean number of births, in 1971, which could represent a baby-boom wave or a reaction to a number of favorable-to-conception policy actions that took place in the 1970s.

Further analysis shows the data may be chaotic. The low fractal dimension indicates the system has a high degree of orderliness to it, with just three or four state variables (constructs) interacting together in a nonlinear fashion, determining behavior. The fractal dimension of the data may change over time. This could be significant from a practical perspective: interventions are more likely to be effective during low-dimensional chaos than during high-dimensional chaos, or random behavior. Finally, the data are nonstationary, and this may be linked to significant policy and legal changes.

The analysis of this data set (and subsequently, this problem) is far from complete. Work is ongoing to generate a more complete data set, working from the original birth certificates. This will allow separate data analysis on various stratifications of the original data (e.g., by age, county, economic strata). Additionally, the "Easterlin effect" must be explored as an explanatory hypothesis (Pampel 1993). The Easterlin effect states that fertility rates and relative cohort size track one another. Relative cohort size is defined by the number of persons ages 30 to 64 to the number of persons ages 15 to 29. If there are, for example, far fewer (relatively) younger than older people, then younger people will face a relatively better job market and expect relatively higher wages and standards of living, thus leading to higher fertility.

A pure time series model allows for prediction and explanation; by combining this perspective with other exogenous (demographic, economic, and sociologic) variables more specific propositions and recommendations are expected to be generated.

Afterword
So Where Are We Now?
A Final Word

Raymond A. Eve

The task of parsimoniously summarizing the many excellent points made by contributors to this book makes one feel a bit like a sociological Icarus. The great number of astonishing and important concepts presented in this volume makes the offering of closing remarks an exercise in both risk tolerance and misplaced vanity for any writer. Nonetheless, having no one else at hand unwise enough to undertake the severing of this particular Gordian knot, some attempt will be made here to bring order out of, ahem, chaos.

First, we'll consider what we have learned about misunderstandings that commonly seem to surround the study of chaos, complexity, and self-organizing systems. Thereafter, we offer some rather more unusual remarks. Unusual in the sense that much has been written about the gain in mastering these concepts, but what is less often discussed is what might be lost if one acknowledges a rightful place for them in science, social or otherwise. Since it is generally thought best to end discourse on an optimistic note, we will have the happy opportunity to argue in closing that more is gained than is lost.

What Chaos, Complexity, and Self-Organizing Are Not

At the outset, it is devoutly hoped that by this point in the volume the reader recognizes that the use of the term chaos to describe many of the systems we have been investigating is an unfortunate choice. Systems and behavior called chaotic have often been assumed by casual readers to be completely random. In fact, as can be readily seen throughout this book, there is much order in chaotic systems. No one can look at a Mandelbrot set or a Julia set (the graphic representation of the work of strange attractors) and not immediately comprehend with the naked eye that there are overwhelmingly obvious patterns here. The term chaotic, therefore, cannot be assumed to accurately describe such geometric arrays. What then is "chaotic" about chaos mathematics? The answer is, of course, that in some sets of simultaneous equations (but not all), feedback operates in such a way that any one iteration of a given set of equations may not have a specific predictable solution. The effect of this state of affairs can be easily seen. If we assign color to a point in a volume of space, representing the coordinates of any given solution to a single iteration of our set of interdependent equations, and we then iterate the set millions of times, the graphic that will emerge is said to be a "strange attractor." (Properly, we should understand that the amazing and aesthetically pleasing pattern we actually see by applying such mathematical operations is actually the end result of the operation of chaotic dynamics.) If by chaos, one means that one cannot say in advance where the next point will appear on the strange attractor, perhaps such liberty of language can be tolerated. However, what is abundantly obvious, even at a glance, is that any given point does not appear in a truly random fashion, instead it appears somewhere on the strange attractor! (Why the attractor operates in such a way to produce the pattern is beyond the reach of nearly all of us, hence the term "strange." Isn't it strange that the multiplicity of such points form the magnificent symmetry our eye beholds, even if we are unable to state with precision from whence came the magnificent symmetry?)

Perhaps this very mysteriousness of a chaos that isn't and of strange attractors that have occluded origins invites many to treat the whole business as the latest cocktail party methaphysics for the well-heeled intellectual. Whatever the reason, chaos theory has generated more than its fair share of misunderstandings, convenient myths, and gross misunderstandings. It has frequently been expropriated to provide alleged legitimacy for a host of special agendas within academe. It seems useful at this point to examine the veracity of some of the more common myths that have grown up around chaos theory. By doing so, we can hope to find a few conclusions whose validity appears to stem more from the application of rigorous science than from a mere debate of competing intuitions or politically inspired rhetorical truth-claims.

Myth: Chaos = "Complete Randomness"

If one turns on the tap just so, it is possible to view a stream of water headed for the bottom of the kitchen sink in such manner as to manifest a primarily smooth, laminar flow (or "linear" flow, if you prefer). However, part way down, you may on occasion see a turbulent region—below which the water returns to laminar flow. If you could inspect the individual water molecules in that region of turbulence, you'd find that these molecules are momentarily caught up in a "chaotic" system. The interaction of the molecules of water in the turbulent region involves so much feedback (bumping each other repeatedly) that our most powerful computers could not hope to predict the path of any given molecule through this turbulent region. But what *can* be said is that the molecules will remain within the blob, no one molecule will suddenly hit the ceiling all by itself, none will suddenly appear on the opposite side of the observer's body. It is readily seen that much order is displayed by the system—even within the region of turbulence. Did you say that you want an analogy in the social sciences? How about the disappearance of the former Soviet Union? First, it was nonlinear. No one, apparently, predicted the immediacy of the impending event or the speed of transformation with which the process unfolded. To try to make sense of this, let's suppose that there is a strange attractor for the collapse of late-stage socialist societies (as there probably is, but how one would investigate the shape of the attractor with a series of experiments is supremely unclear). Where on the attractor will the next "solution" to the equations locate the new political entity? No one can say. However, if the results are doomed to always land *somewhere* on the attractor, it might be possible to say where it will *not* fall. If social system organizations are taken as individual points on the relevant attractor, it is most unlikely that the former Soviet Union would suddenly end up as a hunting-and-gathering society, or as an exact duplicate of any existing capitalist society. Metaphorically speaking, it will not hit the ceiling. Where will it land? Who can say! But in spite of our confusion, the problem is not one of chaos in the sense of no pattern at all; it is merely a lack of predictable, specific solutions *within* certain mathematical limits.

It is largely for the reasons we have just examined that many whose studies of dynamics comprise the heart of this book began to prefer to use the term complexity instead of chaos. Nonetheless, many extremists of the postmodern deconstruction camp (of which Price's article told us) and many among the orthodox Marxists have expropriated the term chaos from mathematics, proceeding to exercise their own revisionist streak in an attempt to redefine the term as "complete randomness." In both the cases, this expropriation is intended to accomplish the same goal: the delegitimation of science as a useful and admirable enterprise. It may well be possible to delegitimate science on some grounds, but the new study of nonlinear dynamics will not be the tool that brings the house of science crashing to the ground.

Myth: Systems Are Either Chaotic or Not

Axiomatically, the above illustration allows us to dispel another myth: that systems are either chaotic or not. Just as we saw in the kitchen tap example above, chaotic or complex dynamics may appear in cycles alternating with linear dynamics. It is important to grasp from earlier chapters a lucid understanding of "bifurcation points." Frozen ice is about as linear a system as one can hope to find. It is remarkably stable as long as the temperature is below freezing. However, if one introduces energy in the form of heat slowly but continuously, the ice doesn't slowly go from 20 degrees to 25 degrees to 32 degrees and then to water. It remains at 32 degrees until it undergoes a phase transition into water, without first gradually increasing its temperature. First it was in one phase, we introduced energy, and it is suddenly found in another state. Perhaps this allows another analogy with the former Soviet Union. It is often heard in the press and everyday language that the former Soviet Union "collapsed." On the contrary, it is easy to see that it is, in a sense, still there. None of the population was destroyed, the same towns are still there, people still go to the same jobs, and so on. It might be more appropriate to suggest that "energy" was at last being poured into the Soviet Union in the form of information (as a result of the globalization of telecommunications, industry, and markets). Perhaps the Soviet Union did not collapse, perhaps instead it simply underwent a bifurcation into a more complex phase state of the same system (just as ice may become water, which looks nothing like ice but is still H_2O). The new phase state may now need a new categorical noun to describe it, but elements of the former system remain. Perhaps they are now undergoing a dynamical trial and error in which the process seeks an evolutionary best fit to an environment that would have been beyond imagination at the time of the 1917 revolution.

Returning to our main point, that a system can be both chaotic and stable depending on when one observes it, the exchange rate of the ruble can ordinarily be predicted with reasonable accuracy for some weeks or months ahead of a given point in time. Certainly this was the case before the phase transition of the Soviet system. It appears that same price stability has also largely returned to the prediction of the exchange rate of the ruble in the present. However, during the bifurcation the economic dynamics (as with all the other dynamics) of Russia were of such an order of nonlinearity that prediction of the exchange rate for even a few days ahead of time would have been an exercise in absurd overconfidence. Thus, one can see the dynamics of Russia, or the whole of the

Soviet system, as typically "laminar" (continuous), but at moments it is also subject to chaos. Thus, it is readily seen that even a single complex system can be both stable and chaotic depending on the moment in time when one is looking at it.

Myth: Chaos Theory Proves That Empirical Social Science Is Impossible

As Price pointed out in his article, one principle espoused by the more extreme camp of postmodern deconstructionists is that there is no such thing as reality other than that in which thinking makes it so. Specifically, it is maintained that since one's worldview is made of symbols, and that the meaning of those symbols varies according to the power relationships within any given society, all worldviews are social-psychological "constructions." Therefore, it is argued, there are an infinite number of realities, each as valid (or as false) as any other. Therefore, it is concluded by deconstructionism that scientists' "truth claims" are just as constructed as any other type of truth claim. As such, they are often depicted as mere convenience intended to justify privilege for middle-class, white, Western males. Chaos theory seems on the surface to some postmodernists (partly due to an unfortunate and somewhat inaccurate name for itself) as proving that empirical science is an illusion rooted in self-deception. However, there are two dire difficulties with such a claim. For one thing, there is the "double-reflexivity" problem. Reflexity is the postmodern term for the idea that no truth claim can be understood as other than grounded in the power relations experienced by those making the claim. Thus, it is said that scientists' truth claims are no better than anyone else's. However, if we follow the logic on further, it is easy to see the evolution of the double-reflexivity problem. If all truth claims are equally subjective, why should the postmodernists' truth claim that scientists' truth claims are useless be anything but a radically subjective, self-interested statement in its own right? The supreme nihilism of this doubly reflexive position demonstrates the problem with deconstructionism in general: it is an excellent technique for deconstructing existing worldviews, but offers nothing to replace the worldviews that are annihilated. If we seek a worldview that empowers us to manipulate the physical world and perhaps even the future, the problem with deconstructionism is the same as the problem with so-called scientific creationism: both attempt to pick holes in the mainstream consensus of modern science, but neither offers a viable alternative. It is difficult to see how we can get spacecraft to other planets using creation science or deconstructionism.

The second problem with the assertion that chaos theory disproves an empirical science (including social science) can be seen in the discussion of the previous myth. Specifically, many systems are typically only episodically chaotic. On "either side" of the chaotic phase states, such systems are readily amenable to analysis using ordinary mathematical techniques familiar to the social sciences. Indeed, as we shall see below, even systems undergoing the dynamics of chaos are not completely unanalyzable with mathematics. The graphical representation of strange attractors *is* a type of statistics.

Myth: Chaos Theory Is Applicable Only in the Natural Sciences

While it is true that, to date, chaos, complexity, and emergence as concepts have been best applied in the natural sciences, such as in the study of fractals in geology or the study of chaos as an equilibrating system regulating the human heart beat, this state of affairs is likely due to the fact that the problems faced in those disciplines are in some sense much simpler than those faced in the social sciences. It is precisely because social life is so fraught with interactions among a multitude of variables, and so self-evidently a sphere involving many interdependencies that are exquisitely sensitive to small changes in initial conditions, that the easy application of the new perspectives described here will be difficult to apply. However, some of the essays in this volume have already demonstrated early if sometimes halting steps suggesting that, eventually, sociological analyses that use the core concepts of this new science will be commonplace.

Perhaps structuralism is not so well slain by chaos theory as we often hear. Most systems in the physical sciences that exhibit chaos are obviously composed of elements that are not sentient elements. However, in the case of humans there is some evidence for sentience, and perhaps this changes things.

When I drive my car to work each day, many chaotic dynamics occur within the inner workings of the vehicle. However, contrary to the postmodernist position that chaos means nothing is predictable, I seem to arrive each day at the same office. How is this miracle possible? It seems the likely explanation that the designers of cars intuitively understand that the car, even lacking some control mechanism over chaos among nonsentient parts, could indeed convey me to the same place each day after 20 minutes of driving activity (assuming the unlikely outcome that there was no crash first). Intuitively, they provided for an inelegant situation by installing in the vehicle a steering mechanism that could be attached to a sentient system (the driver). Could it be that, likewise, most of the structure in society represents human attempts to monitor deviations and to minimize chaotic outcomes? Perhaps this is indeed exactly why humans found it prudent to develop institutions and complex organizations as "steering mechanisms" that would limit both individual and collective deviation—thus, it is hoped, keeping society on the straight and narrow "road." If this is so, however, it presents us with an interesting question derived from the nonsentient world. In the action of continental drift theory, when two tectonic plates are rubbing against each other in different directions, they sometimes "hang" because ragged edges catch and hold the plates temporarily. The result is stored potential energy such that, when they finally do move, they do so much more explosively and energetically than had they not hung in the first place. Could it be that the institutions of society function in the same way? In other words, if we use these same institutions to prevent the onset of chaos and self-emergence, will it be the case that when movement finally comes it will be that much more intense? What implications might such a view have for the study of social movements and revolutions? In any event, it is readily apparent from both this discussion and from the earlier chapters that chaos theory's usefulness will not be limited only to the study of physical events.

Myth: Chaos and Complexity Theory Will Completely Replace Existing Paradigms in the Social Sciences

It is a widely misunderstood myth about scientific revolutions that a major "paradigm shift" (such as from a geocentric view of the solar system to a heliocentric one) means that all the scientific knowledge that went before is immediately null-and-void as a result of the new paradigm shift. In reality, the case is much less dire in its effects. Typically, the new paradigm demonstrates that knowledge gained under the old paradigm is true *under specific boundary conditions*. Thus, the rules of motion put forth by Newton are not demolished by Einsteinian physics, but are shown to be a special case of a larger, more inclusive physics. Similarly, the rise of chaos theory does not, as some would claim, mean that all our past social science findings and statistical methods are useless. Instead, complexity and chaotic dynamics should be thought of as elucidating whole classes of phenomena that traditional methods and theories have been inadequate to describe. Chaos and complexity do not "overthrow" former conceptions and scientific knowledge, but merely supplement them. As we have seen above, it is possible even for a specific system to be stable at times (and therefore well understood and modeled by traditional techniques) and chaotic at other times (requiring special modeling techniques, such as those described by Stroup elsewhere in this book).

What Is Lost?

The emergence of chaos, complexity, criticality, and self-organization does, however, cost us something. It is possible to argue that most of human intellectual activity has been largely stimulated by the desire to avoid two existential dreads: first, that things are meaningless and random and, second, that even if they have meaning, we as humans have no control over things as they are. Every major thought system seems to have been largely developed to try to refute or overcome these anxieties. Both magic and religion, for example, can be thought of as (among other things) attempts at "metaphysical technologies." They were intended to explain why things happen as they do (or did) and to provide a set of tools such as incantations, prayers, and so on for effecting outcomes that seemed beyond the reach of available material technology. It can be argued that the rise of science was but another example of an attempt to meet these existential anxieties. And science was more successful, by and large, at allaying our fears. At least this was true for the physical world, where science seemed often to predict ahead of time better than did other thought systems. With the rise of Newtonian science, the belief emerged and was widely accepted that there was a definite and unique mathematical solution (usually a number) that could describe the state of any system at a given moment. Sir Francis Bacon's view of science reinforced this comforting view. Bacon promoted inductivism in the firm belief that if one only collected enough discrete "facts" (which were taken as self-evident, and not understood to be subject to the nuances of individual selective perception and psychological accommodation), then the true nature of reality would readily be discerned at some point.

These were very comforting ideas. We only had to keep our noses to the empirical grindstone and collect an ample sufficiency of data and we would understand everything and, more important, be able to control all within our ken. However, as with most anticipations of Utopia close at hand, we would shortly discover that escape from the lair of our existential demons would not come so easily after all. Quantum mechanics was the spear that first pierced our smugly tidy faith that science could explain all. Even concepts as simple as whether a thing was energy or matter suddenly became problematic. Then there was the problem of the Uncertainly Principle that said that the act of measuring things so interfered with phenomena (under certain conditions) that some aspects of phenomena might never be fully understood. It seems, sometimes, that humankind's dreams of reason and control through science have been all downhill from that point.

One of the places where things seem to have been going downhill is in the utility of mathematical modeling for social phenomena. In spite of the fact that we developed ever more sophisticated mathematical ways of modeling social processes, typically the amount of variance we were able to explain by examination of empirical data remained quite low. Worse yet, if one tries to apply the models ahead of time to create practical change in the real world, the results more often than not have been ineffectual, and sometimes outright disastrous. Why have we gotten such gloomy results so often?

In part it may well be that in our search to create elegant and parsimonious models, typically in the form of path diagrams and the sets of simultaneous equations that describe them, we found it necessary to make simplifying assumptions. If we didn't, the coefficients that resulted from "solving" these sets of equations were of a very small magnitude. So we tended to try to impose linearity on the universe (or at least nonlinearity that was easily mimicked by log transformations and similar data tweakings). Perhaps worst of all, we tenaciously clung to the belief that a stable coefficient was the natural outcome of our computations. This tenacity is all the more curious because of the evidence in our own lives that many social processes around us are supremely interactive, nonlinear, and exquisitely sensitive to initial conditions. Indeed, it should be obvious that there is a sampling distribution of replications of any given experiment. Why did we ignore this obvious truth at our peril? Presumably because it was beyond imagination that anyone would have the time and the funding to perform a multitude of replications of the same experiment. And somewhere deep inside, we knew the magnitude of the parameter estimates would change anyway in the time it took to perform the needed multitude of replications. Nonetheless, we went about in public places in the emperor's new clothes, pursuing the respectability that was certain to come to us from producing larger coefficients in our causal models (even if the model had to look very little like what we actually saw in the world around us to make it mathematically soluble). What chaos theory implies, of course, and what makes it anathema to many of us, is that the whole business of trying to describe the world with summary digits is likely to often be quite impossible. And then where are we? Just when it appeared that social scientists might be able to hold their heads up in public as "real scientists" because we had elaborate mathematical models on hand, it seems that our cultural capital and practical legitimacy has been torn from our hands. Why? Because the elaborate path models seen in the top journals in the social sciences could be frequently evidenced by chaos theory to be nothing more than crass pseudoscience, as rank as any alchemy. If this be so, might we lose not only professional face but even our jobs? No wonder the new concepts considered in this book seem so objectionable to many of us.

A depressing picture indeed! Is there no balm in Gilead for our pain? Fortunately, the answer seems to be that, on closer inspection, many of these first reactions are excessive. It may well be that more is gained than is lost by the rise of chaos and complexity as paradigms for the social sciences.

What Is Gained?

If you have ever been through any type of psychotherapy, you will probably have heard (with mixed emotions) the platitude that "there is no growth without pain." Unlike many platitudes, there is often much truth in this particular dogma. What is really being said, of course, is that until one is willing to give up old ways of seeing things and doing things, one cannot move on to a more effective way. So while there is pain that comes with the need to deal with the implications of chaos and complexity, there is also the very real hope that once they are fully incorporated into our discipline, we will be more effective and useful than ever before. For one thing, there is the good news that the old causal modeling techniques are probably useful *much* of the time. (The real reason that most explained variance coefficients are quite low is typically either inadequate theorizing or operationalization of methods, or—and even more common— that even simple behaviors have a vast number of causal elements, many of them operating in unique ways for different cases in the sample, but this need not be due to chaotic dynamics.) Of course, all the news is not so reassuring. For example, even very simple sets of equations *may* be chaotic if changes in the variable to be predicted are a function of one or more variables on the other side of the equal sign (and in the real world, they typically are). So all we need to do is determine ahead of time whether our set of equations represents a chaotic model. "Aye, there's the rub!" in Hamlet's terms. As Stroup shows in his chapter, the determination *in advance* of whether a set of equations represents a chaotic system is no easy matter. And there's an even more intractable problem, not addressed in that chapter. Specifically, how do we know when an apparently stable system is about to undergo a phase transition into an at least temporary chaotic phase? This is the equivalent of saying, for example, why was it that apparently no one in the social sciences was predicting the "collapse" of the Soviet Union just before it happened? So we are faced with an uphill task for awhile consisting of trying to find ways to predict the onset of chaotic dynamics.

On the other hand, we now may be able to at least *describe* many of the actions of complex systems that we see around us, those that hitherto remained mysterious. The signature of chaos is no longer written in invisible ink. We may not be able to predict the result of the next iteration of a set of equations that describes a chaotic system, or when a system will be in chaos and when not. However, we can at least now understand what a chaotic system is doing, and how it is doing it, when we see it. It is often said by those who know just enough to be dangerous that chaos theory shows that the use of statistics in the social sciences is a useless endeavor. Far from this gloomy view, what chaos theory actually does is to give us a new kind of statistics, albeit one that is graphical rather than digital. The polychromatic images of the operation of strange attractors so often seen in books on the new science *are* probability statements. While one cannot say where the next point will appear on a strange attractor, it *will* appear somewhere on the strange attractor! Areas where the number of points are dense are areas of higher probability of the appearance of the next point than are areas where preexisting points are rare. How is this different from a Pearson's product-moment coefficient of, say, $r = .20$? The two digits in that coefficient tell us very little about the strength of the relationship between any given data point for the independent variable and any given data point for the dependent variable. All that is discernible is that there is some type of pattern, even if a weak one, that suggests that the two phenomena are not wholly unrelated. So too, does a strange attractor say something about probability, albeit the message can be interpreted with one's aesthetic rather than numeric sense. No one who has ever seen an image of a strange attractor can fail to be struck by the fact that there is *not* randomness present, but instead there is a startling and easily perceived graphical statement about repetition and density. When one is viewing a strange attractor, one is looking at a probability diagram, neither more nor less "statistical" in nature than the more familiar digital measures of association. Because of this, one of the gifts that chaos brings to contemporary knowledge is a degree of reunification of art with science.

Another important implication of chaos and complexity for the promotion of our better understanding of the world and the people in it is the idea of emergence. We have traditionally assumed that macro-level social structure created individual attitudes, opinions, and even personalities. At least most of us have made this assumption. However, interactionists have argued all along that society could only be understood as the outcome of a nearly infinite myriad of individual interactions. Perhaps the interactionists, who often have eschewed statistics, were nearer the empiricist mark than they ever suspected. One lesson from this book should be that very simple rules for interaction among even inanimate objects (if they involve the right kind of feedback), once put into motion, can produce hugely complex and apparently living structures. Here we may at least have an answer for how micro-level forces are wed to macro-level forces, and indeed how the latter may even have emerged from the former.

Just as chaos theory seems poised to reunite art and science to a degree, so too does it appear to offer a reuniting of the so-called physical sciences with the so-called social sciences. If chaos theory is right, a myriad of interactions in the nonhuman world is required to support and sustain the human world. Furthermore, it may be possible to use chaos, complexity, self-organization, and emergence to begin to see better how dynamics at the nonhuman level shape and sustain interactions at the human and societal levels. Perhaps the Gaia hypothesis is undergirded by the mathematics of chaos to a degree even its originator might be surprised to learn of.

While celebrating the good side of the rise of chaos, it is well to consider its positive warnings also. We have been tempted to argue in the past that our previous mathematics gave us the wisdom, perhaps even the "right," to engage in social and physical engineering. While these are worthy goals and indubitably worth pursuing, chaos reminds us that we cannot always be sure that the feedback effects of such changes will be predictable in a specific sort of way. If we stumble into a set of dynamics unknowingly that is chaotic, we cannot anticipate emergent properties and phenomenon that are not deducible by extrapolations from earlier data or conditions. We are once again reminded of Icarus, who dared too much through vanity. I will probably be accused of being reactionary by making these statements, but examples of the backfire of good intentions due to the unanticipated effects of chaotic dynamics are not hard to find. One example can be seen in the case of the water distribution system in Bali, based in the temples of that nation. Complex adaptive systems often exist on the edge of chaos. In Bali, an ancient system of water rights surrounding temple life supported a precariously balanced but intensive rice-growing economy. Western "experts" assumed that indigenous methods of water allocation were primitive and in need of replacement. When the Western ideas were implemented, the results were disastrous for the rice harvests (Pherigo, Nehman, and Eve 1996). The point being made here is that a complex adaptive system had developed, over many generations of feedback, very simple rules for allocation of water. The effect of the system was the containment of chaotic dynamics—until the system was disrupted by outside influences. This message from chaos theory is clear—the Bali story will be only one of many similar outcomes if social scientists fail to understand the operation of chaos and complexity.

As with all great breakthroughs in science, the incorporation into science of the ideas of chaos, complexity, emergence, and complex adaptive systems brings with it increased power to understand and manipulate the world. As with all other major scientific breakthroughs, both good news and bad news are inherent in the new conceptual advances. And, as with all other scientific breakthroughs, whether the new knowledge is considered a heavenly blessing or an evil incarnate depends entirely on the wisdom and the motivations of those who wield it.

References

Abraham, F. D. 1996. Science Dialog Mailbase discussion group (URL http://www.mailbase. ac.uk/lists-p-t/science-structure/1996-04/0187.html).

Abramovitch, R., C. Corter, D. J. Peple, and L. Stanhope. 1987. Sitting and peer interaction: A final follow-up and comparison. *Child Development* 57:217-229.

Abramovitch, R., and F. Strayer. 1978. Preschool social organization: Agonistic, spacing, and attentional behaviors. In *Aggression, dominance, and individual spacing*, edited by L. Krames, P. Pepliner, and T. Alloway. New York: Plenum.

Alekseev, V. M., and M. V. Yakobson. 1981. Symbolic dynamics and hyperbolic dynamical systems. *Physics Reports* 75:287-325.

Allen, P. M. 1982. Evolution, modelling and design in a complex world. *Environment and Planning A* 9:95-111.

Anderson, P. W., K. J. Arrow, and D. Pines, eds. 1988. *The economy as an evolving complex system.* Redwood City, CA: Addison-Wesley.

Ando, A., F. Fisher, and H. Simon. 1963. *Essays on the structure of social science models.* Cambridge: MIT Press.

Angelides, C., and G. Caiden. 1994. Adjusting policy thinking to global programmatics and future problematics. *Public Administration and Development* 14:233-239.

Anger, G. 1990. *Inverse problems in differential equations.* Berlin: Akademie-Verlag.

Anosov, D. V., and I. U. Bronshtein. 1988. Topological dynamics. In *Dynamical systems,* edited by D. V. Anosov and V. I. Arnold, 197-219. Berlin: Springer.

Arnold, V. I. 1986. *Catastrophe theory.* 2d ed. Berlin: Springer.

Arnopoulos, P. 1993. *Sociophysics: Chaos and cosmos in nature and culture.* Commack, NY: Nova Science Publishers.

Arthur, B. 1990. Positive feedback in the economy. *Scientific American* 263:92-99.

Arthur, W. B., M. Ermoliev, and M. Kaniovski. 1987. Path-dependent processes and the emergence of macro-structure. *European Journal of Operational Research* 30:294-303.

Artigiani, R. 1987. Revolution and evolution: Applying Prigogine's dissipative structures model. *Journal of Social and Biological Structures* 10:249-264.

Ash, M. 1995. *Gestalt psychology in German culture 1890-1967: Holism and the quest for objectivity.* Cambridge, UK: Cambridge University Press.

Asher, S. R., and J. M. Gottman. 1981. *The development of children's friendships.* New York: Cambridge University Press.

Axelrod, R. A. 1984. *The evolution of cooperation.* New York: Basic Books.

————. 1995. A model of the emergence of new political actors. In *Artificial societies: The computer simulation of social life,* edited by N. Gilbert and R. Conte. London and Bristol, PA: UCL Press.

Axelrod, R., and S. Bennett. 1991. *A landscape theory of aggregation.* University of Michigan preprint.

Aysan, Y., and P. Oliver. 1987. *Housing and culture after earthquakes.* Oxford: Oxford Polytechnic.

Azizighanbari, S., M. Bargfeldt, and L. M. Alisch. Forthcoming. *A comment on the mathematics of marital conflict.*

Baburoglu, O. N. 1988. The vortical environment: The fifth in the Emory-Trist levels of organizational environments. *Human Relations* 41(3): 181-210.

Back, K. W. 1992. This business of topology. *Journal of Social Issues* 48:51-66.

————. 1997. Super-paradigms in art and science: Romanticism and birth of social science. *European Legacy* 2(4).

————. 1998. Field theory in physics, psychology and art. In *Einstein meets Magritte,* edited by D. Aerts. New York: Kluwer.

Baecker, D. 1993. Die Metamorphosen des Geldes. In *Georg Simmel's Philosophie des Geldes,* edited by J. Kintzel and P. Schneider, 277-300. Frankfurt: Anton Hain.

Bahr, D., and E. Passerini. 1996. Statistical mechanics of opinion formation, collective behavior and rational vs irrational choice. Unpublished paper (submitted).

Baier, G., and M. Klein, eds. 1991. *A chaotic hierarchy.* London: World Scientific.

Bailey, K. D. 1990a. *Social entropy theory.* Albany: SUNY Press.

————. 1990b. Why H does not measure information. *Quality and Quantity* 24:159-171.

————. 1994. *Sociology and the new systems theory: Toward a theoretical synthesis.* Albany: SUNY Press.

Bainbridge, W. S. 1984. Computer simulation of cultural drift: Limitations on interstellar colonization. *Journal of the British Interplanetary Society* 37:420-429.

————. 1985. Beyond bureaucratic policy: The spaceflight movement. In *People in space,* edited by James Everett Katz, 153-163. New Brunswick, NJ: Transaction.

————. 1987. Science and religion: The case of Scientology. In *The future of new religious movements,* edited by D. G. Bromley and P. E. Hammond, 59-79. Macon, GA: Mercer University Press.

————. 1991. *Goals in space: American values and the future of technology.* Albany: SUNY Press.

————. 1993. New religions, science and secularization. In *The handbook of cults and sects in America,* edited by D. G. Bromley and J. K. Hadden, 277-292. Greenwich, CT: JAI.

————. 1995a. Minimum intelligent neural device: A tool for social simulation. *Journal of Mathematical Sociology* 20:179-192.

————. 1995b. Neural network models of religious belief. *Sociological Perspectives* 38:483-495.

————. 1997. *The sociology of religious movements.* New York: Routledge.

Bak, P., and K. Chen. 1991. Self-organized criticality. *Scientific American* 264(1): 46-53.

Bak, P., K. Chen, and M. Creutz. 1989. Self-organized criticality in the game of life. *Nature* 342:780.

Barnett, W. A., J. Geweke, and K. Shell, eds. 1989. *Economic complexity: Chaos, sunspots, bubbles and nonlinearity.* Cambridge, UK: Cambridge University Press.

Baron, R. M., P. G. Amazeen, and P. J. Beek. 1994. Local and global dynamics of social relations. In *Dynamical systems in social psychology,* edited by R. R. Vallacher and A. Nowak, 111-138. San Diego, CA: Academic Press.

Barrow, J. D. 1991. *Theories of everything.* Oxford: Oxford University Press.

Barrow, J. D., and F. J. Tipler. 1986. *The anthropic cosmological principle.* New York: Oxford University Press.

Bassingthwaighte, J. B., L. S. Liebovitch, and B. J. West. 1994. *Fractal physiology.* New York: Oxford University Press.

Batty, M., and P. Langley. 1994. *Fractal cities.* New York: Academic Press.

Baudelaire, C. 1965. *Art in Paris 1845-1862.* London: Phaidon.

Baudrillard, J. 1983. *Simulations.* New York: Semiotext(s).

Bechtel, W., and R. C. Richardson. 1992. Emergent phenomena and complex systems. In *Emergence or reduction? Essays on the prospects of nonreductive physicalism,* edited by A. Beckermann, H. Flohr, and J. Kim, 257-288. Berlin: Walter de Gruyter.

Becker, E. 1968. *The structure of evil: An essay on the unification of the science of man.* New York: Free Press.

Beckermann, A., H. Flohr, and J. Kim, eds. 1992. *Essays on the prospects of nonreductive physicalism.* Berlin: Walter de Gruyter.

Beer, W. R. 1983. *Househusbands.* South Hadley, MA: J. F. Bergin.

Bell, D. A. 1976. *The cultural contradictions of capitalism.* New York: Basic Books.

Beltrami, E. 1987. *Mathematics for dynamic modeling.* New York: Academic Press.

Benoît, E. 1995. Random walks and stochastic differential equations. In *Nonstandard analysis in practice,* edited by F. Diener and M. Diener, 71-90. Berlin: Springer.

Benzon, W. L., and David G. Hays. 1990. Why natural science leads to complexity. *Journal of Social and Biological Structures* 13(1): 33-40.

Berge, P., Y. Pomeau, and C. Vidal. 1984. *Order within chaos.* Translated by L. Tuckerman. Paris: Wiley.

Berkland, T. 1996. Natural disasters as focusing events: Policy communities and political response. *International Journal of Mass Emergencies and Disasters* 14(2): 221-243.

Berndt, T. J., and S. G. Hoyle. 1985. Stability and change in childhood and adolescent friendships. *Developmental Psychology* 21:1007-1015.

Berry, B. J. L., and H. Kim. 1996. Intermittency, chaos and control. In *Chaos theory in the social sciences: Foundations and applications,* edited by L. Douglas Kiel and Euel Elliott, 215-236. Ann Arbor: University of Michigan Press.

Bertocci, P. A. 1945. Teleological argument for God. In *An encyclopedia of religion,* edited by Vergilius Ferm, 763. New York: Philosophical Library.

Best, S., and D. Kellner. 1991. *Postmodern theory: Critical investigations.* New York: Guilford.

Blau, P. M. 1964. *Exchange and power in social life.* New York: John Wiley.

Blum, L., M. Shub, and S. Smale. 1989. On a theory of computation and complexity over the real numbers: NP-completeness, recursive functions and universal machines. *Bulletin (New Series) of the American Mathematical Society* 21:1-46.

Blum, L., and S. Smale. 1993. The Gödel incompleteness theorem and decidability over a ring. In *From topology to computation: Proceedings of the Smalefest,* edited by M. W. Hirsch, J. E. Marsden, and M. Shub, 321-339. New York: Springer.

Botsford, G. W., and C. A. Robinson. 1956. *Hellenic history.* New York: Macmillan.

Briggs, J., and F. D. Peat. 1989. *Turbulent mirror.* New York: Harper and Row.

Brock, W., D. Hsieh, and B. LeBaron. 1991. *Nonlinear dynamics, chaos and instability: Statistical theory and economic evidence.* Cambridge: MIT Press.

Brooks, R. A., and P. Maes, eds. 1994. *Artificial life IV: Proceedings of the Fourth International Workshop on the Synthesis and Simulation of Living Systems.* Cambridge: MIT Press.

Brown, C. 1994. Politics and the environment: Nonlinear instabilities dominate. *American Political Science Review* 37:292-303.

———. 1995a. *Chaos and catastrophe theories.* London: Sage.

———. 1995b. *Serpents in the sand: Essays on the nonlinear nature of politics and human destiny.* Ann Arbor: University of Michigan Press.

Bruderl, J., and R. Schussler. 1990. Organizational mortality: The liabilities of newness and adolescence. *Administrative Science Quarterly* 35(3): 530-547.

Bukowski, W. M., A. F. Newcomb, and W. W Hartup, eds. 1996. *The company they keep: Friend-ship in childhood and adolescence.* Cambridge, MA: Cambridge University Press.

Bush, R. R., and F. Mosteller. 1955. *Stochastic models for learning.* New York: John Wiley.

Butler, R. 1993. The evolution of the civil service: A progress report. *Public Administration* 71(3): 395-406.

Campbell, J. 1988. *The power of myth.* New York: Doubleday.

Carley, K. M. 1992. Organizational learning and personnel turnover. *Organization Science* 3(1): 20-46.

———. 1996. A comparison of artificial and human organizations. *Journal of Economic Behavior and Organization* 896:1-17.

———. Forthcoming. A theoretical study of organizational performance under information dis-tortion. *Management Science.*

Carley, K. M., and Z. Lin. 1994. Relating shifts in C2 structure to performance. In *Proceedings of the 1994 Symposium on Command and Control Research.*

———. 1995. Organizational designs suited to high performance under stress. *IEEE Transactions on Systems, Man and Cybernetics* 25(1): 221-230.

———. Forthcoming. Organizational decision making and error in a dynamic task environment. *Journal of Mathematical Sociology.*

Carley, K. M., and D. Svoboda. 1996. Modeling organizational adaptation as a simulated anneal-ing process. *Sociological Methods and Research* 25(1): 138-168.

Carr, B. J., and M. J. Rees. 1979. The anthropic principle and the structure of the physical world. *Nature* 278:605-612.

Cartwright, D., and A. Zander. 1960. *Group dynamics.* Evanston, IL: Row, Peterson.

Casti, J. 1979. *Connectivity, complexity, and catastrophe in large-scale systems.* Chichester: Wiley.

Casti, J. L. 1990. *Searching for certainty: What scientists can know about the future.* New York: William Morrow.

———. 1994. *Complexification.* New York: HarperCollins.

———. 1995. Bell curves and monkey languages. *Complexity* 1(1): 12-15.

Catalano, R., and S. Serxner. 1987. Time series designs of potential interest to epidemiologists. *American Journal of Epidemiology* 126:724-731.

Chaitin, G. 1986. *Algorithmic information theory.* New York: Addison-Wesley.

Chui, C. K., and G. Chen. 1991. *Kalman filtering with real-time applications* (2d ed.). Berlin: Springer.

Clark, A. H., S. M. Wyon, and M. P. M. Richards. 1969. Free play in nursery school children. *Journal of Child Psychology and Psychiatry* 10:205-216.

Cobb, R. W., and C. D. Elder. 1983. *Participation in American politics: The dynamics of agenda building.* 2d ed. Baltimore: Johns Hopkins University Press.

Cohen, J., and I. Stewart. 1994. *The collapse of chaos.* New York: Penguin.

Coleman, J. S. 1964. *Introduction to mathematical sociology.* New York: Free Press of Glencoe.

———. 1986. Social theory, social research and a theory of action. *American Journal of Sociology* 91:1309-1335.

———. 1990. *Foundations of social theory.* Cambridge, MA: Harvard University Press.

Collins, R. 1988. *Theoretical sociology.* San Diego, CA: Harcourt Brace Jovanovich.

Combs, A. 1992. Chaotic dynamics in mood and nostril cycles. Poster presentation at the Second Annual Conference of the Society for Chaos Theory in Psychology, Washington, D.C.

Cook, J., R. Tyson, J. White, R. Rushe, J. Gottman, and J. Murray. 1995. Mathematics of marital conflict: Qualitative dynamic mathematical modeling of marital interaction. *Journal of Fam-ily Interaction* 9:110-130.

Cooper, B. 1981. *Michel Foucault: An introduction to the study of his thought.* New York: Edwin Mellen.

Coser, L. 1975. Presidential address: Two methods in search of substance. *American Journal of Sociology* 40:691-700.

Cousins, M., and A. Hussain. 1984. *Michel Foucault.* New York: St. Martin's.

Coveney, P., and R. Highfield. 1990. *The arrow of time.* New York: Fawcett Columbine.

———. 1995. *Frontiers of complexity: The search for order in a chaotic world*. New York: Fawcett Columbine.

Coverman, S., and J. F. Sheley. 1986. Change in men's housework and child-care time, 1965-1975. *Journal of Marriage and the Family* 48 (May): 413-422.

Cowan, G. A., D. Pines, and D. Meltzer, eds. 1994. *Complexity: Metaphors, models and reality*. Vol. 19 of *Proceedings, Santa Fe Institute Studies in the Sciences of Complexity*. Reading, MA: Addison-Wesley.

Crutchfield, J. P. 1994. Is anything ever new? Considering emergence. In *Complexity: Metaphors, models and reality*, edited by G. A. Cowan, D. Pines, and D. Meltzer, 515-533. Vol. 19 of *Proceedings, Santa Fe Institute Studies in the Sciences of Complexity*. Reading, MA: Addison-Wesley.

Crutchfield, J. P., J. D. Farmer, and B. A. Hubermann. 1982. Fluctuations and simple chaotic dynamics. *Physics Reports* 92:45.

Crutchfield, J. P., and K. Young. 1990. Computation at the onset of chaos. In *Complexity, entropy and the physics of information*, edited by W. H. Zurek, 223-269. Redwood City, CA: Addison-Wesley.

Cunningham, A., and N. Jardine, eds. 1990. *Romanticism and the sciences*. Cambridge, UK: Cambridge University Press.

Darley, V. 1994. Emergent phenomena and complexity. In *Artificial life IV: Proceedings of the Fourth International Workshop on the Synthesis and Simulation of Living Systems*. Vol. 4, edited by R. A. Brooks and P. Maes, 411-416. Cambridge: MIT Press.

Daston, L. J. 1990. Rational individuals versus laws of society: From probability to statistics. In *The probability revolution*, edited by L. Krüger, L. J. Daston, and M. Heidelberger, 295-304. Cambridge: MIT Press.

Davis, J. A., and S. Leinhardt. 1972. The structure of positive interpersonal relations in small groups. In *Sociological theories in progress*. Vol. 2, edited by J. Berger et al., 218-251. Boston: Houghton Mifflin.

Dendrinos, D. S., and M. Sonis. 1990. *Chaos and socio-spatial dynamics*. New York: Springer.

Denhardt, R. 1993. *Theories of public organization*. 2d ed. Belmont, CA: Wadsworth.

DeVault, M. V. 1957. Classroom sociometric mutual pairs and residential proximity. *Journal of Educational Research* 50:605-610.

DeWitt, N. W. 1954. *St. Paul and Epicurus*. Minneapolis: University of Minnesota Press.

DiMaggio, P. J., and W. W. Powell. 1983. The iron cage revisited: Institutional isomorphism and collective rationality in organizational fields. *American Sociological Review* 48:147-160.

Ditto, W., and L. Pecaro. 1993. Mastering chaos. *Scientific American*, August, 78-84.

Döbelt, G. 1996. Zu den Verlaufsprozessen bei Kinderfreundschaften. Unpublished paper, Technical University of Dresden.

Dobuzinskis, L. 1992. Modernist and post-modernist metaphors of the policy process: Control and stability vs. chaos and reflexive understanding. *Policy Sciences* 25:355-380.

Dooley, K., and S. Guastello. 1994. Research methods for chaos and complexity. Paper presented at Evolving Complexity: Challenges to Society, Economy and Individual, Dallas, Texas.

Drabek, T. E. 1986. *Human system response to disaster: An inventory of sociological findings*. New York: Springer-Verlag.

Duhem, P. [1908] 1969. *To save the phenomena*. Chicago: University of Chicago Press.

Durkheim, E. [1897] 1951. *Suicide*. New York: Free Press.

Dyke, C. 1992. From entropy to economy: A thorny path. In *Advances in human ecology*. Vol. 1, edited by Lee Freese, 149-176. Greenwich, CT: JAI.

Eccles, R. G., and D. B. Crane. 1988. *Doing deals: Investment banks at work*. Boston: Harvard Business School Press.

Eigen, M., and P. Schuster, 1979. The hypercycle: A principle of natural self-organization, part C: The realistic hypercycle. *Naturwissenschaften* 65:341-369.

Einstein, A., and M. Born. 1982. *Briefwechsel 1916-1955*. Frankfurt: Edition Erbrich.

Ekeland, I. 1993. *The broken dice*. Chicago: University of Chicago Press.

Elliott, E., and L. D. Kiel. 1996. Introduction. In *Chaos theory in the social sciences: Foundations and applications*, edited by L. D. Kiel and E. Elliott, 1-15. Ann Arbor: University of Michigan Press.

Ellner, S., A. R. Gallant, D. McCaffrey, and D. Nychka. 1991. Convergence rates and data requirements for Jacobian-based estimates of Lyapunov exponents from data. *Physics Letters A* 153:357-363.

Emde, R. N., and R. J. Harmon, eds. 1982. *The development of attachment and affiliative systems.* New York: Plenum.

Etzioni, A. 1985. Making policy for complex systems: A medical model for economics. *Journal of Policy Analysis and Management* 4:383-395.

Farmer, J. D., and J. J. Sidorowich. 1987. Predicting chaotic time series. *Physical Review Letters* 62:845-848.

Farr, R. M., and S. Moscovici, eds. 1984. *Social representations.* Cambridge, UK: Cambridge University Press.

Featherstone, M. 1988. In pursuit of the postmodern: An introduction. *Theory, Culture and Society* 5:195-215.

———. 1989. Towards a sociology of postmodern culture. In *Social structure and culture*, edited by H. Haferkamp, 147-174. Berlin: Walter de Gruyter.

Fehr, B. 1996. *Friendship processes.* Thousand Oaks, CA: Sage.

Feiring, C., and M. Lewis. 1991. The development of social networks from early to middle childhood: Gender differences and the relation to school competence. *Sex Roles* 25:237-253.

Festinger, L. 1949. The analysis of sociograms using matrix algebra. *Human Relations* 2:153-158.

Festinger, L., S. Schachter, and K. Back. 1950. *Social pressures in informal groups.* New York: Harper.

Field, T. 1985. Attachment as psychobiological attunement: Being on the same wavelength. In *The psychobiology of attachment and separation*, edited by M. Reite and T. Field, 415-454. New York: Academic Press.

Fine, G. A. 1980. The natural history of preadolescent male friendship groups. In *Friendship and social relations in children*, edited by H. C. Foot, A. J. Chapman, and J. R. Smith. New York: John Wiley.

Flam, F. 1994. Artificial-life researchers try to create social reality. *Science* 265:868-869.

Foot, H. C., A. Chapman, and J. R. Smith. 1977. Friendship and social responsiveness in boys and girls. *Journal of Personality and Social Psychology* 35:401-411.

Forrester, J. W. 1987. Nonlinearity in high-order social systems. *European Journal of Operational Research* 30:104-109.

Foucault, M. 1970. *The order of things: An archaeology of the human sciences.* New York: Vintage.

———. 1972. *The archaeology of knowledge and the discourse on language.* New York: Pantheon.

———. 1980. *Power/knowledge.* New York: Pantheon.

Fox, M. F., and S. Hesse-Biber. 1984. *Women at work.* Palo Alto, CA: Mayfield.

Fox, N. A., and R. J. Davidson. 1984. *The psychobiology of affective development.* Hillsdale, NJ: Lawrence Erlbaum.

Freese, L. 1988. Evolution and sociogenesis, parts I and II. In *Advances in group process.* Vol. 5, edited by E. J. Lawler and B. Markovsky, 53-118. Greenwich, CT: JAI.

Friesema, P., J. Caporaso, G. Goldstein, R. Lineberry, and R. McCleary. 1979. *Aftermath: Communities after natural disasters.* Beverly Hills, CA: Sage.

Furst, S. 1990. Brain monamines are involved in the sedative effects of opiates and neuroleptics. *Progress in Clinical and Biological Research* 328:311-314.

Furstenburg, F. 1987. Race differences in teenage sexuality, pregnancy and adolescent childbearing. *Millbank Quarterly* 65(2): 381-403.

Gale, G. 1981. The anthropic principle. *Scientific American* 245(6): 154-171.

Geertz, C. 1973. *The interpretation of cultures.* New York: Basic Books.

Gell-Mann, M. 1995. What is complexity? *Complexity* 1(1): 16-19.

———. 1994. *The quark and the jaguar: Adventures in the simple and the complex.* New York: W. H. Freeman

George, M. S., T. A. Ketter, P. I. Papekh, B. Horowitz, P. Herscovitch, and R. M. Post. 1995. Brain activity during transient sadness and happiness in healthy women. *American Journal of Psychiatry* 152:341-351.

Gershenfeld, N. A., and A. S. Weigend. 1994. The future of time series: Learning and understanding. In *Time series prediction: Forecasting the future and understanding the past,* edited by A. S. Weigend and N. A. Gershenfeld, 1-70. Reading, MA: Addison-Wesley.

Giarini, O. 1985. Notes on the limits to certainty: Risk, uncertainty and economic value. In *Laws of nature and human conduct,* edited by I. Prigogine and I. Stengers, 285-296. Brussels: Task Force of Research Information and Study of Science.

Gleick, J. 1987. *Chaos: Making a new science.* New York: Penguin.

Goerner, S. J. 1994. *Chaos and the evolving ecological universe.* Luxembourg: Gordon and Breach.

Goertzel, B. 1993a. *The evolving mind.* New York: Gordon and Breach.

———. 1993b. *The structure of intelligence.* New York: Springer-Verlag.

———. 1994. *Chaotic logic.* New York: Plenum.

Goertzel, B., H. Bowman, and R. Baker. 1993. Dynamics of the radix expansion map. *Journal of Mathematics and Mathematical Sciences,* January.

Goertzel, B., and G. Goertzel 1995. *The chaos language algorithm: A technique for inferring the grammatical structure overlying chaotic dynamics, applied to the generalized Baker map.* (Submitted for publication).

Gomperz, T. 1901. *Greek thinkers.* Vol. 1. London: Murray.

Gordon, T. J. 1991. Notes on forecasting a chaotic series using regression. *Technological Forecasting and Social Change* 39:337-348.

Gott, J. R. 1982. Creation of open universes from de Sitter space. *Nature* 295:304-307.

Gottman, J. M. 1983. How children become friends. *Monographs of the Society for Research in Child Development* 48(3) (Serial No. 201).

———. 1986. The world of coordinated play: Same- and cross-sex friendship in young children. In *Conversations of friends: Speculations on affective development,* edited by J. M. Gottman and J. G. Parker, 139-191. Cambridge, UK: Cambridge University Press.

Gottman, J. M., and T. J. Parkhurst. 1980. A developmental theory of friendship and acquaintanceship processes. *Minnesota Symposium on Child Psychology.* Vol. 13, edited by W. A. Collins. Hillsdale, NJ: Lawrence Erlbaum.

Gouldner, A. W. 1971. *Enter Plato.* New York: Harper and Row.

Granovetter, M. 1973. The strength of weak ties. *American Journal of Sociology* 78:1360-1380.

Grassberger, P., and S. Procaccia. 1983. Characterization of strange attractors. *Physics Review Letter* 50:189-208.

Graumann, C. F. 1992. Lewin 1990. In *Kurt Lewin—Person, Werk, Umfeld,* edited by W. Schönpflug. Frankfurt: Peter Lang.

Graziano, W. G. 1983. Commentary. *Monographs of the Society for Research in Child Development* 48(3) (Serial No. 201): 83-85.

Green, E. 1933. Friendships and quarrels among preschool children. *Child Development* 4:237-252.

Gregersen, H., and L. Sailer. 1993. Chaos theory and its implications for social science research. *Human Relations* 46:778-802.

Gribbin, J., and M. Rees. 1989. *Cosmic coincidences: Dark matter, mankind and anthropic cosmology.* New York: Bantam.

Grobstein, C. 1973. Hierarchical order and neogenesis. In *Hierarchy theory: The challenge of complex systems,* edited by H. H. Pattee, 29-48. New York: George Braziller.

Guastello, S. 1995. *Chaos, catastrophe and human affairs.* Mahwah, NJ: Lawrence Erlbaum.

Guckenheimer, J. 1978. The catastrophe controversy. *The Mathematical Intelligencer* 1(1): 15-20.

Guth, A. H. 1981. Inflationary universe: A possible solution to the horizon and flatness problems. *Physical Review D* 23:347-356.

Gutting, G. 1989. *Michel Foucault's archaeology of scientific reason.* New York: Cambridge University Press.

Habermas, J. 1975. *Legitimation crises.* Boston: Beacon.

Hall, N., ed. 1991. *Exploring chaos: A guide to the new science of disorder.* New York: Norton.

Hallinan, M. T. 1979. Structural effects on children's friendships and cliques. *Social Psychology Quarterly* 42:43-54.

Hamerle, A., W. Nagl, and H. Singer. 1991. Problems with the estimation of stochastic differential equations using structural equations models. *Journal of Mathematical Sociology* 16(3): 201-220.

Hamilton, P., B. West, M. Cherri, J. Mackey, and P. Fisher. 1994. Preliminary evidence of nonlinear dynamics in births to adolescents in Texas, 1964 to 1990. *Theoretical and Applied Chaos in Nursing* 1(1): 15-22.

Hamilton, W. D. 1995. *The narrow road to geneland: The evolution of social behaviour.* London: Freeman.

Hamilton, W. D., and R. A. Axelrod. 1984. The evolution of cooperation. *Science* 211:1390-1396.

Hannan, M. T., and G. R. Carroll. 1992. *Dynamics of organizational populations: Density, competition and legitimation.* New York: Oxford University Press.

Hanneman, R. A. 1987. *Computer-assisted theory-building: Modeling dynamic social systems.* Beverly Hills, CA: Sage.

———. 1995. Simulation modeling and theoretical analysis in sociology. *Sociological Perspectives* 38:457-462.

Hanneman, R. A., R. Collins, and G. Mordt. 1995. Discovering theory dynamics by computer simulation: Experiments on state legitimacy and imperialist capitalism. *Sociological Methodology* 25:1-46.

Hansson, P. A. 1991. Chaos: Implications for forecasting. *Futures* 23(1): 50-58.

Hao, B., ed. 1984. *Chaos.* Singapore: World Scientific.

Harré, R. 1965. *Matter and method.* New York: St. Martin's.

Harrington, A. 1996. *Reenchanted science: Holism in German culture from Wilhelm II to Hitler.* Princeton, NJ: Princeton University Press.

Harvey, D. 1989. *The condition of postmodernity: An inquiry into the origins of cultural change.* Oxford: Basil Blackwell.

Hastings, H., and G. Sugihara. 1993. *Fractals: A user's guide for the natural sciences.* New York: Oxford University Press.

Hayles, N. K. 1989. *Chaos and order: Complex dynamics in literature and science.* Chicago: University of Chicago Press.

———. 1990. *Chaos bound: Orderly disorder in contemporary literature and science.* Ithaca, NY: Cornell University Press.

Heckman, J., and J. Walker. 1989. Forecasting aggregate period-specific birth rates: The time series properties of a microdynamic, neoclassical model of fertility. *Journal of American Statistical Association* 84(408): 958-965.

Hegel, G. W. F. 1977. *The phenomenology of spirit.* Oxford: Clarendon.

Heise, D. R. 1969. Separating reliability and stability in test-retest correlations. *American Sociological Review* 34:93-101.

Henderson, L. J. 1913. *The fitness of the environment.* New York: Macmillan.

———. 1917. *The order of nature.* Cambridge, MA: Harvard University Press.

Hernandez-Machado, A. 1995. The effect of noise on spatio-temporal patterns. In *Spatio-temporal patterns in nonequilibrium complex systems,* edited by P. E. Cladis and P. Palffy-Muhoray, 521-528. Reading, MA: Addison-Wesley.

Hertz, J. H., ed. 1978. Genesis. In *The Pentateuch and Haftorahs.* London: Soncino.

Hess, G. D. 1995. An introduction to Lewis Fry Richardson and his mathematical theory of war and peace. *Conflict Management and Peace Science* 14:77-113.

Hill, W. A. 1992. Several sequential augmentations of Richardson's arms race model. *Mathematical and Computer Modelling* 16 (8/9): 201-212.

Hofer, M., U. Becker, B. Schmid, and P. Noack. 1990. Die Altersabhängigkeit von Vorstellungen über Freundschaft bei 6- bis 14-jährigen (Age dependency of friendship understanding of 6- to 14-year-old children). In *Entwicklung. Allgemeine Verläufe—individuelle Unterschiede—*

pädagogische Konsequenzen. Festschrift zum 60. Geburtstag von Franz Emanuel Weinert, edited by M. Knopf and W. Schneider, 65-82. Göttingen: Hogrefe.

Hollenbeck, J. R., D. R. Ilgen, D. J. Sego, J. Hedlund, D. A. Major, and J. Phillips. 1995. The multi-level theory of team decision making: Decision performance in teams incorporating distributed expertise. *Journal of Applied Psychology* 80:292-316.

Hollenbeck, J. R., D. R. Ilgen, D. Tuttle, and D. J. Sego. 1995. Team performance on monitoring tasks: An examination of decision errors in contexts requiring sustained attention. *Journal of Applied Psychology* 80:685-696.

Homans, G. C. 1950. *The human group.* New York: Harcourt, Brace and World.

———. 1967. *The nature of social science.* New York: Harcourt, Brace and World.

———. 1974. *Social behavior: Its elementary forms.* New York: Harcourt Brace Jovanovich.

———. 1984. *Coming to my senses: The autobiography of a sociologist.* New Brunswick, NJ: Transaction.

———. 1987. *Certainties and doubts.* New Brunswick, NJ: Transaction.

Hood, J. C. 1986. The provider role: Its meaning and measurement. *Journal of Marriage and the Family* 48 (May): 349-359.

Hopfield, J. 1982. Neural networks and physical systems with emergent collective computational abilities. *Proceedings of the National Academy of Sciences USA* 81:3088-3092.

Horgan, J. 1994. Sex, death, and sugar. *Scientific American* (November): 20-24.

———. 1995. From complexity to perplexity. *Scientific American* 272(6): 104-109.

Howes, C. 1983. Patterns of friendship. *Child Development* 54:1041-1053.

———. 1988. Same- and cross-sex friends: Implications for interaction and social skills. *Early Childhood Research Quarterly* 3:21-27.

Huizinga, J. 1950. *Homo Ludens.* Boston: Beach.

Hutter, M. 1994. Communication in economic evolution: The case of money. In *Evolutionary concepts in contemporary economics,* edited by R. W. England, 111-136. Ann Arbor: University of Michigan Press.

Ilgen, D. R., and J. R. Hollenbeck. 1993. *Effective team performance under stress and normal conditions: An experimental paradigm, theory and data for studying team decision making in hierarchical teams with distributed expertise.* Final report, NR 93-2. East Lansing: Michigan State University.

Isnard, C. A., and E. C. Zeeman. 1976. Some models from catastrophe theory in social science. In *The use of models in the social sciences,* edited by L. Collins, 44-100. London: Tavistock.

Izenman, A. J., and S. L. Zabell. 1981. Babies and blackout: The genesis of a misconception. *Social Science Research* 10:282-299.

Jacobson, J., and D. E. Wille. 1986. The influence of attachment pattern on developmental changes in peer interaction from the toddler to the preschool period. *Child Development* 57:338-347.

Jantsch, E., ed. 1981. *The evolutionary vision: Toward a unifying paradigm of physical, biological and sociocultural evolution.* Boulder, CO: Westview.

Jeffers, V., and R. Lore. 1979. Let's play at my house: Effects of the home environment on the social behavior of children. *Child Development* 50:837-841.

Jetschke, G. 1989. *Mathematik der Selbstorganisation* (Mathematics of self-organization). Braunschweig: Vieweg.

Johnson, E. C. 1986. Structure and process: Agreement models for friendship formation. *Social Networks* 8:257-306.

———. 1989. The micro-macro connection: Exact structure and process. In *Applications of combinatorics and graph theory to the biological and social sciences,* edited by F. Roberts, 169-202. New York: Springer.

Johnson, N., and W. Feinberg. 1977. A computer simulation of the emergence of consensus in crowds. *American Sociological Review* 42:505-521.

Johnson, T., and K. Dooley. 1996. Looking for chaos in time series. In *Nonlinear dynamics in human behavior,* edited by W. Sulis and A. Combs, 44-76. Singapore: World Scientific.

Jones, E., J. Forest, N. Goldman, S. Henshaw, R. Lincoln, J. Rosoff, C. Westhoff, and D. Wulf. 1985. Teenage pregnancy in developed countries: Determinants and policy implications. *Family Planning Perspectives,* 53-63.

Joyce, T. A. 1989. Time series analysis of unemployment and health: The case of birth outcomes in NY City. *Journal of Health Economics* 8:419-436.

Kaern, M. 1990. The world as human construction. In *Georg Simmel and contemporary sociology,* edited by M. Kaern, B. S. Philips, and R. S. Cohen, 75-98. Dordrecht: Kluwer.

Kampis, G., and V. Csanyi. 1990. Coevolution and the units of evolution. In *Organizational constraints on the dynamics of evolution,* edited by J. M. Smith and G. Vida, 385-398. Manchester: Manchester University.

Kaneko, K. 1991. Climbing up [the] dynamical hierarchy. In *A chaotic hierarchy,* edited by G. Baier and M. Klein, 235-250. London: World.

———. 1994. Chaos as a source of complexity and diversity in evolution. *Artificial Life* 1:163-177.

Kaplan, D., and L. Glass. 1995. *Understanding nonlinear dynamics.* New York: Springer-Verlag.

Kauffman, S. 1993. *The origins of order: Self-organization and selection in evolution.* New York: Oxford University Press.

Kaufmann, A. 1975. *Introduction to the theory of fuzzy subsets.* New York: Academic Press.

Keller, M., and P. Wood. 1989. Development of friendship reasoning: A study on interindividual differences in intraindividual change. *Developmental Psychology* 25:820-826.

Kemper, T. 1978. *A social interactional theory of emotions.* New York: John Wiley.

Kenny, D. A. 1996. The design and analysis of social-interaction research. *Annual Review of Psychology* 47:59-86.

Keren, O., M. Garty, and Y. Sarne. 1994. Dual regulation by opioids of 3H-norepinephrine release in the human neuroblastoma cell-line SK-N-SH. *Brain Research* 646(2): 319-323.

Kerr, M., and M. Bowen. 1988. *Family evaluation.* New York: Basic Books.

Keyfitz, N. 1968. *Introduction to the mathematics of population.* Reading, MA: Addison-Wesley.

———. 1986. The family that does not reproduce itself. Supplement to *Population and Development Review* 12:139-154, *Below-replacement fertility in industrial societies*

Kiel, L. D. 1991. Lessons from the nonlinear paradigm: Applications of the theory of dissipative structures in the social sciences. *Social Science Quarterly* 72(3): 431-442.

———. 1992. The nonlinear paradigm: Advancing paradigmatic progress in the policy sciences. *Systems Research* 9(2): 27-42.

Kiel, L. D., and E. Elliott. 1992. Budgets as dynamic systems: Change, variation, time and budgetary heuristics. *Journal of Public Administration Research and Theory* 2:139-156.

Kilmann, R. H., and T. J. Covin, eds. 1988. *Corporate transformation: Revitalizing organizations for a competitive world.* San Francisco: Jossey-Bass.

Kirkpatrick, S., C. D. Gelatt, and M. P. Vecchi. 1983. Optimization by simulated annealing. *Science* 220(4598): 671-680.

Kloeden, P. E., E. Platen, and H. Schurz. 1994. *Numerical solution of SDE through computer experiments.* Berlin: Springer.

Knudson, A. C. 1945. God. In *An encyclopedia of religion,* edited by V. Ferm, 301-302. New York: Philosophical Library.

Köhler, W. 1920. *Die Physischen Gestalten in Ruhe und im Stationären Zustand.* Braunschweig: Vieweg.

Kolip, P. 1993. *Freundschaften im Jugendalter* (Friendship in adolescence). Weinheim: Juventa.

Kondratieff, N. 1935. The long waves in economic life. *Review of Economic Statistics* 17(6): 105-115.

Kontopoulos, K. M. 1993. *The logics of social structure.* New York: Cambridge University Press.

Kosko, B. 1993. *Fuzzy thinking: The new science of fuzzy logic.* New York: Hyperion.

Krantz, M., S. George, and K. Hursh. 1983. Gaze and mutual gaze of preschool children in conversation. *Journal of Psychology* 113:9-15.

Krappmann, L. 1990. Friendship conception and friendship performance of six- through fifteen-year-old children. Paper presented at the Fourth European Conference on Developmental Psychology, Stirling, Scotland, August.

Krüger, L., L. J. Daston, and M. Heidelberger. 1990. *The probabilistic revolution.* Cambridge: MIT Press.

Kuhn, T. S. 1962. *The structure of scientific revolutions.* Chicago: University of Chicago Press.

Kunita, H. 1986. *Lectures on stochastic flows and applications.* Berlin: Springer.

Ladd, G. W., and B. S. Golter. 1988. Parents' management of preschoolers' peer relations: Is it related to children's social competence? *Developmental Psychology* 24:109-117.

LaFreniere, P. J., and L. A. Sroufe. 1985. Profiles of peer competence in the preschool: Intercorrelations between measures, influence of social ecology, and relation to attachment history. *Developmental Psychology* 21:56-69.

Lal, B. B. 1995. Symbolic interaction theories. *American Behavioral Scientist* 38:421-441.

Langton, C. G., ed. 1989. Artificial life. In *Artificial life,* edited by Christopher G. Langton, 1-47. Vol. 6 of *Proceedings, Santa Fe Institute Studies in the Sciences of Complexity.* Redwood City, CA: Addison-Wesley.

Langton, C. G. 1995. *Artificial life: An overview.* Cambridge: MIT Press.

Lansing, J. S., and J. N. Kremer. 1995. The goddess and the Green revolution. In *Yearbook of science and the future 1996,* 198-219. Chicago: Encyclopedia Britannica.

Laslett, P. 1989. *A fresh map of life.* London: Weidenfeld and Nicholson.

Latane, B. 1981. The psychology of social impact. *American Psychologist* 36(4): 343-356.

Latour, B. 1991. The impact of science studies on political philosophy. *Science, Technology, & Human Values* 16(1): 3-19.

Lawrence, P. R., and J. W. Lorsch. 1967. *Organization and environment: Managing differentiation and integration.* Boston: Harvard University.

Lazarsfeld, P. F., and R. K. Merton. 1954. Friendship as social process: A substantive and methodological analysis. In *Freedom and control in modern society,* edited by M. Berger, T. Abel, and C. H. Page, 18-66. New York: Van Nostrand.

Lazarus, R. 1980. Thoughts on the relations between emotion and cognition. *American Psychologist* 37:1019-1024.

Lee, M. E. 1994. The evolution of technology: A model of socioecological self-organization. In *New directions in technology studies: Evolutionary economics and chaos,* edited by L. Leydesdorf and P. van den Besselar, 167-179. London: Pinter.

Lee, S. C., R. G. Muncaster, and D. A. Zinnes. 1994. The friend of my enemy is my enemy: Modeling triadic international relationships. *Syntheses* 100:333-358.

Lemert, C. 1994. Social theory at the end of a short century. *Sociological Theory* 12(2): 140-152.

Lerberg, J., and Y. S. Lee. 1995. Teenage pregnancy and public policy: What do the pregnant teens say about prevention? Presented at the 1995 National Association for Welfare Research and Statistics Conference, Jackson Hole, Wyoming.

Leslie, J. 1982. Anthropic principle, world ensemble, design. *American Philosophical Quarterly* 19:141-151.

Lever, J. 1976. Sex differences in the games children play. *Social Problems* 23:479-487.

Lévi-Strauss, C. 1958. *Anthropologie structurale.* Paris: Plon.

Levinger, G. 1980. Toward the analysis of close relationship. *Journal of Experimental and Social Psychology* 16:510-544.

Levinger, G., and A. C. Levinger. 1986. The temporal course of close relationships: Some thoughts about the development of children's ties. In *Relationships and development,* edited by W. W. Hartup and Z. Rubin, 111-133. Hillsdale, NJ: Lawrence Erlbaum.

Lewenstein, M., A. Nowak, and B. Latane. 1992. Statistical mechanics of social impact. *Physical Review A* 45(2): 763-776.

Lewin, K. 1936. *Principles of topological psychology.* New York: McGraw-Hill.

———. 1951. *Field theory in social sciences.* New York: Harper and Row.

Lewin, R. 1992. *Complexity: Life at the edge of chaos.* New York: Macmillan.

Lieberman, A. 1977. Preschoolers' competence with a peer: Relation with attachment and peer experience. *Child Development* 48:1490-1497.

Lin, Z. 1994. Organizational performance Ñ theory and reality. Ph.D. diss., H. J. Heinz III School of Public Policy and Management, Carnegie Mellon University.

Lin, Z., and K. M. Carley. Forthcoming. Organizational response: The cost performance tradeoff. *Management Science* 43(2).

Linde, A. 1994. The self-reproducing inflationary universe. *Scientific American* 271(5): 48-55.

Little, R. J. A., and N. Schenker. 1995. Missing data. In *Handbook of statistical modeling for the social and behavioral sciences,* edited by G. Arminger, C. C. Clogg, and M. E. Sobel, 39-75. New York: Plenum.

Longo, O. 1993. Anthropic principle and ancient science. In *The anthropic principle: Proceedings of the second Venice Conference on Cosmology and Philosophy,* edited by F. Bertola and U. Curi, 17-25. Cambridge, UK: Cambridge University Press.

Loye, D., and R. Eisler. 1987. Chaos and transformation: Implications of nonequilibrium theory for social science and society. *Behavioral Science* 32:53-65.

Luce, D. R., and A. D. Perry. 1949. A method of matrix analysis of group structure. *Psychometrika* 2:95-116.

Luhmann, N. 1976. Generalized media and the problem of contingency. In *Explorations in general theory in social sciences: Essays in honor of Talcott Parsons,* edited by J. J. Loubser, R. C. Baum, A. Effrat, and V. M. Lidz, 507-532. New York: Free Press.

———. 1982. *The differentiation of society.* New York: Columbia University Press.

———. 1988. *Die Wirtschaft der Gesellschaft.* Frankfurt: Suhrkamp.

———. 1990a. The cognitive program of constructivism and a reality that remains unknown. In *Selforganization: Portrait of a scientific revolution,* edited by W. Krohn, G. Kuppers, and H. Nowotny. Dordrecht, The Netherlands: Kluwer.

———. 1990b. *Essays on self-reference.* New York: Columbia University Press.

———. 1994. "What is the case?" and "What lies behind it?": The two sociologies and the theory of society. *Sociological Theory* 12(2): 126-139.

———. 1995. *Social systems.* Stanford, CA: Stanford University Press.

Ma, S. K. 1985. *Statistical mechanics.* Philadelphia: World Scientific.

MacDonald, K., and R. D. Parke. 1984. Bridging the gap: Parent-child play intersection and peer interactive competence. *Child Development* 55:1265-1277.

Maciejowski, J. M. 1978. *The modelling of systems with small observation sets.* Berlin: Springer.

Macy, M. 1990. Learning theory and the logic of critical mass. *American Sociological Review* 55(6): 809-826.

———. 1991. Chains of cooperation: Threshold effects in collective action. *American Sociological Review* 56(6): 730-747.

Maes, P. 1995. Modeling adaptive autonomous agents. In *Artificial life: An overview,* edited by Christopher G. Langton, 135-162. Cambridge: MIT Press.

Maloney, R. [1940] 1956. Inflexible logic. In *The world of mathematics,* edited by James R. Newman, 2262-2267. New York: Simon & Schuster.

Mandelbrot, B. B. 1983. *The fractal geometry of nature.* San Francisco: Freeman.

March, J. G. 1981. Footnotes to organizational change. *Administrative Science Quarterly* 26:563-577.

March, J. G., and Herbert Simon. 1958. *Organizations.* New York: John Wiley.

Maret, E., and B. Finlay. 1984. The distribution of household labor among women in dual-earner families. *Journal of Marriage and the Family* 46 (May): 357-364.

Markovsky, B. 1992. Network exchange outcomes: Limits of predictability. *Social Networks* 14:267-286.

Marx, K. 1841. *Differenz der Demokritischen und Epikureischen Naturphilosophie.* Jena, Germany: Friedrich-Schiller Universität.

Masor, H. N., H. A. Hornstein, and T. A. Tobin. 1973. Modeling, motivational interdependence and helping. *Journal of Personality and Social Psychology* 28:236-248.

Masters, J. C., and W. Furman. 1981. Popularity, individual friendship selection, and specific peer interaction among children. *Developmental Psychology* 3:344-350.

Maturana, H. R., and F. J. Varela. 1980. *Autopoiesis and cognition, the realization of the living.* Boston: D. Reidel.

———. 1992. *The tree of knowledge, the biological roots of human understanding* (rev. ed.). Boston: Shambhala Publications.

Mayer-Kress, G. 1994a. Localized measures for non-stationary time series of physiological data. *Integrative Physiological and Behavioral Science* 29(3): 205-210.

———. 1994b. Speech presented at Chaos and Complexity: Their Meaning for Business, Economics and Society Conference at the University of Texas at Dallas.

McAdam, D., J. McCarthy, and M. Zald. 1988. Social movements. In *Handbook of sociology,* edited by Neil Smelser, 695-737. Beverly Hills, CA: Sage.

McGuire, M. T., M. J. Raleigh, and G. T. Brammer. 1984. Adaptation, selection and benefit-cost balances. *Ethology and Social Biology* 5:269-277.

McNeill, D., and P. Freiberger. 1993. *Fuzzy logic.* New York: Simon & Schuster.

Mead, G. H. 1932. *The philosophy of the present,* edited by Arthur E. Murphy. Chicago: Open Court.

———. 1938. *The philosophy of the act,* edited by Charles W. Morris. Chicago: University of Chicago Press.

Media Logic Enterprises. 1995. Business Cycle Indicators software and data (WWW site address: http://www.cris.com/ netlink/bci /1BCIlst.html). Los Angeles: NetLink Limited in cooperation with Media Logic Enterprises.

Middleton, E. 1995. Science Structure Mailbase discussion group (URL http://www.mailbase.ac.uk/lists-p-t/science-structure/1995-12/0040.html).

Midlarsky, M. I. 1989. Hierarchical equilibria and the long-run instability of multipolar systems. In *Handbook of war studies,* edited by M. I. Midlarsky, 55-81. Boston: Unwin Hyman.

Mihavics, K. 1996. A model for the study of the effects of organizational structure on organizational learning. Ph.D. diss., University of Illinois at Chicago.

Mihavics, K., and A. Ouksel. 1996. Learning to align organizational design and data. *Computational and Mathematical Organization Theory* 1(2): 143-155.

Mileti, D., and J. Darlington. 1997. The role of searching in shaping reactions to earthquake risk information. *Social Problems* 44(1): 401-415.

Mileti, D., and E. Passerini. 1996. A social explanation of urban relocation after earthquakes. *International Journal of Mass Emergencies and Disasters* 14(1): 97-110.

Mirowski, P. 1990. From Mandelbrot to chaos in economic theory. *Southern Economic Journal* 57:289-307.

Moles, A. 1966. *Information theory and esthetic perception.* Urbana: University of Illinois Press.

Moreno, J. 1934. *Who shall survive?* Boston: Beacon.

———. 1941. *The words of the father.* Boston: Beacon.

Morlet, J., G. Arehs, I. Fourgeau, and G. Haubs. 1982. Wave propagation and sampling theory. *Geophysics* 47:203-236.

Morrison, F. 1991. *The art of modeling dynamic systems.* New York: John Wiley.

Nagel, E. 1961. *The structure of science.* New York: Harcourt, Brace and World.

———. 1979. *The structure of science: Problems in the logic of scientific explanation.* 2d ed. Indianapolis, IN: Hackett.

Nayfeh, A. H., and B. Balachandran. 1995. Applied nonlinear dynamics: Analytical, computational, and experimental methods. New York: John Wiley.

Newman, J. D., M. R. Murphy, and C. R. Harbough. 1982. Naloxone-reversible suppression of isolation call production after morphine injections in squirrel monkeys. *Social Neuroscience Abstracts* 8:490.

Newson, J., and E. Newson. 1978. *Seven year olds in the home environment.* Harmondsworth: Penguin.

Nicolis, G., and I. Prigogine. 1977. *Self-organization in non-equilibrium systems.* New York: John Wiley.

———. 1989. *Exploring complexity: An introduction.* New York: Freeman.

Nicolis, J. S. 1986. Dynamics of hierarchical systems: An evolutionary approach. New York: Springer-Verlag.

Norr, K. 1991. Community-based primary prevention of adolescent pregnancy. In *Adolescent pregnancy: Nursing perspectives on prevention,* edited by S. Humenick and N. Wilkerson. White Plains, NY: March of Dimes.

Nowak, A., J. Szamrej, and B. Latane. 1990. From private attitude to public opinion: A dynamic theory of social impact. *Psychological Review* 97:362-367.

O'Brien, S. 1991. Disasters and the making of political careers. In *Risky business: Communicating issues of science, risk and public policy,* edited by Lee Wilkins and Philip Patterson, 177-196. New York: Greenwood.

Oliver, P. E. 1989. Bringing the crowd back in: The nonorganizational elements of social movements. *Research in Social Movements, Conflict and Change* 11:1-30.

Olmstead, R. E., and P. M. Bentler. 1992. Structural equations modeling: A *new friend?* In *Methodological issues in applied social psychology,* edited by F. B. Bryant et al., 135-158. New York: Plenum.

Oswald, H., and L. Krappmann. 1984. Konstanz und Veränderung in den sozialen Beziehungen von Schulkindern (Invariance and change in the social relations of school children). *Zeitschrift für Sozialisationsforschung und Erziehungssoziologie* 4:271-286.

Ott, E. 1993. *Chaos in dynamical systems.* Cambridge, UK: Cambridge University Press.

Ott, E., C. Grebogi, and J. Yorke. 1990. Controlling chaos. *Physical Review Letters* 64(11): 1196-1199.

Ott, L., W. Mendenhall, and R. F. Larson. 1978. *Statistics: A tool for the social sciences.* 2d ed. Belmont, CA: Duxbury.

Ouksel, A., and K. Mihavics. 1995. *Organizational structure and information processing costs.* Technical Report IDS-95-1, University of Illinois at Chicago, College of Business Administration.

Pagel, H. 1988. *The dreams of reason.* New York: Simon & Schuster.

Pampel, F. C. 1993. Relative cohort size and fertility: The socio-political context of the Easterlin effect. *American Sociological Review* 58:496-514.

Pandit, S. M., and S. M. Wu. 1983. *Time series and system analysis with application.* New York: John Wiley.

Parke, R. D., and N. P. Bhavnagri. 1989. Parents as managers of children's peer relationships. In *Children's social networks and social supports,* edited by D. Belle, 241-259. New York: John Wiley.

Parker, J. G., and J. M. Gottman. 1989. Social and emotional development in a relational context: Friendship interaction from early childhood to adolescence. In *Peer relationships in child development,* edited by T. J. Berndt and G. W. Ladd, 95-132. New York: John Wiley.

Parsons, T. A. 1937. *The structure of social action.* Glencoe, IL: Free Press.

———. 1951. *The social system.* Glencoe, IL: Free Press.

———. 1977. Social structure and the symbolic media of interchange. In *Social systems and the evolution of action theory,* edited by T. Parsons, 204-228. New York: Free Press.

———. 1994. Georg Simmel and Ferdinand Tonnies: Social relationships and the elements of action. *Simmel Newsletter* 4:63-78.

Parsons, T., and N. J. Smelser. 1956. *Economy and society: A study in the integration of economic and social theory.* London: Routledge and Kegan.

Pattee, H. H. 1973. Postscript: Unsolved problems and potential applications of hierarchy theories. In *Hierarchy theory: The challenge of complex systems,* edited by H. H. Pattee, 129-156. New York: George Braziller.

Peak, D., and M. Frame. 1994. *Chaos under control: The art and science of complexity.* New York: Freeman.

Peat, F. D. 1991. *The philosopher's stone: Chaos, synchronicity and the hidden order of the world.* New York: Bantam.

Peitgen, H. O., H. Jurgens, and D. Saupe. 1992. *Chaos and fractals: New frontiers of science.* New York: Freeman.

Pete, A. 1994. Optimization of detection networks with multiple event structures. *IEEE Transactions on Automatic Control* 39:1702-1707.

Pete, A., K. R. Pattipati, and D. L. Kleinman. 1993. Distributed detection in teams with partial information: A normative descriptive model. *IEEE Transactions on Systems, Man and Cybernetics* 23:1626-1648.

———. 1994. Optimization of detection networks with multiple event structures. *IEEE Transactions on Automatic Control* 39:1702-1707.

Peters, E. 1991. *Chaos and order in the capital markets.* New York: John Wiley.

Peterson, I. 1991. The signal value of noise. Adding the right kind can amplify a weak signal. *Science News* 139(8): 127.

Petillon, H. 1993. *Das Sozialleben des Schulanfängers. Die Schule aus der Sicht des Kindes* (The social life of children who just started school). Weinheim: Psychologie Verlags Union.

Pherigo, R., J. Nehman, and R. A. Eve. 1996. Utilizing complex adaptive systems theory to develop regional cooperative strategies for environmental policy making. Paper presented at the American Sociological Association annual meetings, New York.

Pickover, C., ed. 1996. *Fractal horizons: The future use of fractals.* New York: St. Martin's.

Plato. 1934. *The laws of Plato.* Translated and edited by A. E. Taylor. London: Dent.

Popper, K. R., and J. C. Eccles. 1977. *The self and its brain.* New York: Springer International.

Poster, M. 1989. *Critical theory and poststructuralism.* Ithaca, NY: Cornell University Press.

Poston, T., and I. Stewart. 1978. *Catastrophe theory and its applications.* London: Pittman.

Potthof, K. 1981. *Einführung in die Modelltheorie und ihre Anwendungen* (Introduction to model theory and its applications). Darmstadt: Wissenschaftliche Buchgesellschaft.

Prigogine, I., and P. M. Allen. 1982. The challenge of complexity. In *Self-organization and dissipative structures,* edited by W. C. Schieve and P. M. Allen, 3-39. Austin: University of Texas Press.

Prigogine, I., and I. Stengers 1984. *Order out of chaos.* New York: Bantam.

Quine, W. V. 1975. On empirically equivalent systems of the world. *Erkenntnis* 9:313-328.

———. 1982. *Methods of logic.* Cambridge, MA: Harvard University Press.

Rabinow, P., ed. 1984. *The Foucault reader.* New York: Pantheon.

Ramsey, J. B., and H. J. Yuan. 1989. Bias and error bars in dimension calculation and their evaluation in some simple models. *Physics Letters A* 134:287-297.

Rapoport, A., and A. M. Chammah. 1965. *Prisoner's dilemma.* Ann Arbor: University of Michigan Press.

Rasch, W. 1991. Theories of complexity, complexities of theory: Habermas, Luhmann and the study of social systems. *German Studies Review* 14:65-83.

Raskin, M. G. 1987. Reconstruction and its knowledge method. In *New ways of knowing: the sciences, society and reconstructive knowledge,* edited by M. G. Raskin and H. J. Bernstein, 8-36. Totowa, NJ: Rowman & Littlefield.

Reite, N., and T. Field, 1985. *The psychobiology of attachment and separation.* Orlando, FL: Academic Press.

Renfrew, C., and T. Poston. 1979. Discontinuities in the endogenous change of settlement patterns. In *Transformations: Mathematical approaches to culture change,* edited by C. Renfrew and K. L. Cooke, 437-462. New York: Academic Press.

Reynolds, C. W. 1987. Flocks, herds and schools: A distributed behavioral model (Proceedings of SIGGRAPH '87). *Computer Graphics* 21:25-34.

Richards, D. 1992. Spatial correlation test for chaotic dynamics in political science. *American Journal of Political Science* 36(4): 1047-1069.

Richardson, L. F. 1960a. *Arms and insecurity.* Pittsburgh, PA: Boxwood.

———. 1960b. *Statistics of deadly quarrels.* Pittsburgh, PA: Boxwood.

Rickert, H. 1921. Psychologie der Weltanschauungen und Philosophie der Werte. *Logos, Internationale Zeitschrift fur Philosophie der Kultur* 9:1.

Rizzo, T. A. 1989. *Friendship development among children in school.* Norwood, NJ: Ablex.

Rogler, L. H., and M. E. Procidano. 1986. The effect of social networks on marital roles. *Journal of Marriage and the Family* 48 (November): 693-701.

Romanelli, E. 1991. The evolution of new organizational forms. *Annual Review of Sociology* 17:79-103.

Rosenstein, M., J. Collins, and C. De Luca. 1993. A practical method for calculating largest Lyapunov exponents from small data sets. *Physica D* 65:117-134.

Rosser, J. B., Jr. 1991. *From catastrophe to chaos: A general theory of economic discontinuities.* Boston: Kluwer.

Rossi, P., J. Wright, S. Wright, and E. Weber-Burdin. 1978. Are there long term effects of American natural disasters? *Mass Emergencies* 3:117-132.

Rubin, Z., and J. Sloman. 1984. How parents influence their children's friendships. In *Beyond the dyad,* edited by M. Lewis, 223-250. New York: Plenum.

Rumelhart, D. E., G. E. Hinton, and R. J. Williams. 1986. Learning internal representations by error propagation. In *Parallel distributed processing,* edited by D. E. Rumelhart and J. McClelland, 318-362. Cambridge: MIT Press.

Russett, B. 1990. *Controlling the sword.* Cambridge, MA: Harvard University Press.

Rutenbar, R. A. 1989. Simulated annealing algorithms: An overview. *IEEE Circuits and Devices Magazine* 5:12-26.

Salisch, M. V. 1991. *Kinderfreundschaften* (Children's friendships). Göttingen: Hogrefe.

Salmon, W. 1971. *Statistical explanation and statistical relevance.* Pittsburgh: University of Pittsburgh Press.

Saperstein, A. M. 1984. Chaos—A model for the outbreak of war. *Nature* 309:303-305.

———. 1988. A non-linear dynamical model of the impact of SDI on the arms race. *Journal of Conflict Resolution* 32:636-670.

———. 1991. The long peace—Result of a bi-polar competitive world? *Journal of Conflict Resolution* 35:68-79.

———. 1992a. Alliance building vs. independent action: A non-linear modeling approach to comparative international stability. *Journal of Conflict Resolution* 36:518-545.

———. 1992b. Are democracies more or less prone to war? A dynamical model approach. *Mathematical and Computer Modelling* 16(8/9): 213-221.

———. 1994. Mathematical modelling of the effects of "capability" and "intent" on the stability of a competitive international system. *Synthese* 100:359-378.

———. 1995. War and chaos. *American Scientist* 83:548-557.

———. 1996a. Demarcation between theater missile defense and strategic missile defense. *Security Dialogue* 27(1): 110-112.

———. 1996b. The predictability of unpredictability: Applications of the new paradigm of chaos and dynamical systems to the old problem of the stability of a system of hostile nations. In *Chaos theory in the social sciences: Foundations and applications,* edited by L. Douglas Kiel and Euel Elliott, 139-164. Ann Arbor: University of Michigan Press.

Schachter, S. 1959. *The psychology of affiliation.* Stanford, CA: Stanford University Press.

———. 1971. *Emotion, obesity and crime.* New York and London: Academic Press.

Schaffer, W., and M. Kot. 1985. Do strange attractors govern ecological systems? *BioScience* 35(6): 342-350.

Scheidlinger, S. 1952. *Psychoanalysis and group behavior.* New York: Norton.

Schlitt, J. 1992. *Primary prevention of adolescent pregnancy among high-risk youth.* Washington, DC: Southern Governor's Conference.

Schmidt-Denter, U. 1984. *Die soziale Umwelt des Kindes. Eine ökopsychologische Analyse* (The social environment of the child). Berlin: Springer.

Schuster, H. G. 1987. *Deterministic chaos.* Weinheim: VCH Verlagsgesellschaft.

———. 1988. *Deterministic chaos—An introduction.* 2d rev. ed. Weinheim, Germany: VCH Verlagsgesellschaft.

Secombe, K. 1986. The effects of occupational conditions upon the division of household labor. *Journal of Marriage and the Family* 48 (November): 839-848.

Seidman, S. 1994. The end of sociological theory. *Sociological Theory* 9(2): 131-146.

Selik, R., S. Chu, and J. Buehler. 1993. HIV infection as leading cause of death among young adults in U.S. cities and states. *Journal of the American Medical Association* 269(23): 2991-2994.

Selman, R. L. 1980. *The growth of interpersonal understanding: Developmental and clinical analysis.* New York: Academic Press.

Serres, M. 1993. *Les origines de la géometrie.* Paris: Flammarion.

Shamir, B. 1986. Unemployment and household division of labor. *Journal of Marriage and the Family* 48 (February): 195-206.

Shannon, C., and W. Weaver. 1949. *The mathematical theory of communication.* Urbana: University of Illinois Press.

Shapiro, B. Z. 1967. Dissolution of ties in group of children. *Dissertation Abstracts* 27(10-11): 3517-3518.

Shaw, R. 1981. Modeling chaotic systems. In *Chaos and order in nature,* edited by H. Haken. New York: Springer-Verlag.

Shinbrott, T., E. Ott, C. Grebogi, and J. A. Yorke. 1990. Using chaos to direct trajectories to targets. *Physical Review Letters* 65:3215-3218.

Shub, M. 1993. On the work of Steve Smale on the theory of computation. In *From topology to computation: Proceedings of the Smalefest,* edited by M. W. Hirsch, J. E. Marsden, and M. Shub, 281-301. New York: Springer.

Simmel, G. 1922. *Zur Philosophie der Kunst.* Potsdam: Gustav Kiepenheuer Verlag.

———. 1989. *Philosophie des Geldes.* Frankfurt: Suhrkamp.

———. 1990. *The philosophy of money,* edited by D. Frisby. London: Routledge.

———. 1991. *Parerga zur Socialphilosophie.* In *Einleitung in die Moralwissenschaft.* Vol. 2, 391-402. Frankfurt: Suhrkamp.

———. 1992. *Soziologische Ästhetik.* In *Aufsätze und Abhandlungen (1894-1900),* 197-214. Frankfurt: Suhrkamp.

———. 1994. *Lebensanschauung, Vier metaphysische Kapitel.* Berlin: Duncker & Humblot.

———. 1995. *Schopenhauer und Nietzsche.* In *Gesamtausgabe.* Vol. 10, 167-408. Frankfurt: Suhrkamp.

Simon, H. A. 1952. A formal theory of interaction in social groups. *American Sociological Review* 17(1): 202-211.

———. 1955. A behavioral model of rational choice. *Quarterly Journal of Economics* 69:99-118.

———. 1956. Rational choice and the structure of the environment. *Psychological Review* 63:129-138.

———. 1969. *The sciences of the artificial.* Cambridge: MIT Press.

———. 1973. The organization of complex systems. In *Hierarchy theory: The challenge of complex systems,* edited by H. H. Pattee, 1-27. New York: George Braziller.

Singer, H. 1992. *Zeitkontinuierliche Dynamische Systeme* (Continuous time dynamical systems). Frankfurt: Campus.

Singh, S. 1986. Adolescent pregnancy in the U.S.: An interstate analysis. *Family Planning Perspectives* 18(5): 210-219.

Skinner, J. E. 1994. The point correlation dimension: Performance with nonstationary surrogate data and noise. *Integrative Physiological and Behavioral Science* 29(3): 217-234.

Slater, P. 1963. On social regression. *American Sociological Review* 28:339-363.

Smith, L. A. 1988. Intrinsic limits on dimension calculations. *Physics Letters A* 133:283-288.

Smith, T. S. 1992. *Strong interaction.* Chicago: University of Chicago Press.

———. 1994. Catastrophes in interaction. *Social Psychology Quarterly* 57(3): 274-282.

Smith, T. S., and G. T. Stevens. 1995a. The architecture of small networks: Strong interaction and dynamic organization in small social systems. Unpublished manuscript, University of Rochester.

———. 1995b. Hyperstructures and the biology of interpersonal dependency. Unpublished manuscript, University of Rochester.

———. 1996. Emergence, self-organization and social interaction: Arousal-dependent structure in social systems. *Sociological Theory* 14(2): 131-153. (Also appears as Santa Fe Institute Publication Series, Paper No. 94-08-046.)

———. Forthcoming. Comfort-regulation as a morphogenetic principle: Local dynamics of dominance, competition and attachment. In *Advances in group processes,* edited by B. Markovsky.

Sorokin, P. A. 1941. *Social and cultural dynamics.* New York: American Book.

Spengler, O. 1926. *The decline of the West.* New York: Knopf.

Spitz, A. M., L. T. Strauss, B. J. Maciak, and L. Morris. 1987. Teenage pregnancy and fertility in the United States, 1970, 1974, and 1980. *Morbidity and Mortality Weekly Report* 36(1): 1-10.

Spitz, A. M., P. Velebil, L. M. Koonin, L. T. Strauss, K. A. Goodman, P. Wingo, J. B. Wilson, L. Morris, and J. Marks. 1996. Pregnancy, abortion, and birth rates among U.S. adolescents, 1980, 1985, and 1990. *Journal of the American Medical Association* 275:989-994.

Stafford, J. 1987. Accounting for the persistence of teenage pregnancy. *Social Casework: The Journal of Contemporary Social Work,* 471-476.

Staines, G. L., and J. H. Pleck. 1983. *The impact of work schedules on the family.* Ann Arbor: University of Michigan, Institute for Social Research.

Stanley, E. A. 1989. Mathematical models of the AIDS epidemic: An historical perspective. In *Lectures in the sciences of complexity,* edited by D. L. Stein, 827-840. Reading, MA: Addison-Wesley.

Stark, R., and W. S. Bainbridge. 1985. *The future of religion.* Berkeley: University of California Press.

———. 1987. *A theory of religion.* New York: Toronto/Lang. (Reprinted by Rutgers University Press, 1996.)

Staub, E., and H. Noerenberg. 1981. Property rights, deservingness, reciprocity, friendship: The transactional character of children's sharing behavior. *Journal of Personality and Social Psychology* 40:271-289.

Stephan, A. 1992. Emergence—A systematic view on its historical facets. In *Emergence or reduction? Essays on the prospects of nonreductive physicalism,* edited by A. Beckermann, H. Flohr, and J. Kim, 25-48. Berlin: Walter de Gruyter.

Stewart, Ian. 1989. *Does God play dice? The mathematics of chaos.* Cambridge, MA: Blackwell.

Stigler, S. M. 1986. *The history of statistics.* Cambridge, MA: Harvard University Press.

Stinchcombe, A. 1965a. Organization-creating organizations. *Transactions* 2:34-35.

———. 1965b. Social structure and organizations. In *Handbook of organizations,* edited by J. G. March, 153-193. Chicago: Rand McNally.

Strätz, R., and E. A. F. Schmidt with M. v. W. Hospelt. 1982. *Die Wahrnehmung sozialer Beziehungen von Kindergartenkinder* (The perception of the social relations of kindergarten children). Köln: Kohlhammer.

Sugihara, G., and R. M. May. 1990. Nonlinear forecasting as a way of distinguishing chaos from measurement error in time series. *Nature* 344:734-741.

Suppes, P. 1969. Models of data. In *Studies in the methodology and foundations of science,* edited by P. Suppes, 24-35. Dordrecht: Reidel.

Sussman, H. J., and R. S. Zahler. 1978. Catastrophe theory as applied to the social and biological sciences. *Synthese* 37:117-216.

Suttles, G. 1968. *The social order of the slum.* Chicago: University of Chicago Press.

Systat. 1992. *SYSTAT version 5.2 edition.* Evanston, IL: Systat.

Tainter, J. A. 1988. *The collapse of complex societies.* New York: Cambridge University Press.

Tanaka, M., Y. Ida, and A. Tsuda. 1988. Nalaxone, given before but not after stress exposure, enhances stress-induced increases in regional brain noradrenaline release. *Pharmacology, Biochemistry, and Behavior* 32(3): 791-795.

Tang, Z., K. R. Pattipati, and D. L. Kleinman. 1992. A distributed M-ary hypothesis testing problem with correlated observations. *IEEE Transactions on Automatic Control* 37:1042-1046.

Teilhard de Chardin, P. 1964. *The future of man.* New York: Harper.

Terr, L. 1990. *Too scared to cry.* New York: HarperCollins.

Tesser, A., and J. Achee. 1994. Aggression, love, conformity, and other social psychological catastrophes. In *Dynamical systems in social psychology*, edited by R. R. Vallacher and A. Nowak, 96-109. San Diego, CA: Academic Press.

Texas Department of Human Services. 1992. *Adolescent pregnancy prevention: A progress report.*

Theiler, J. 1994. Two tools to test time series data for evidence of chaos and/or nonlinearity. *Integrative Physiological and Behavioral Science* 29(3): 211-216.

Theiler, J., S. Eubank, A. Longtin, B. Galdrikian, and J. Farmer. 1992. Testing for nonlinearity in time series: The method of surrogate data. *Physica D* 58:77-94.

Thom, R. 1975. *Structural stability and morphogenesis.* New York: Addison-Wesley.

———. 1983. *Paraboles et catastrophes.* Paris: Flammarion.

Thomas, D. 1979. *Naturalism and social science.* Cambridge, UK: Cambridge University Press.

Thompson, M. 1979. *Rubbish theory.* New York: Oxford University Press.

Tietjen, A. M. 1982. The social methods of preadolescent children in Sweden. *International Journal of Behavioral Development* 5:111-130.

Trivers, R. L. 1971. The evolution of reciprocal altruism. *Quarterly Review of Biology* 46:35-57.

Tryon, E. P. 1973. Is the universe a vacuum fluctuation? *Nature* 246:396-397.

Tuchman, B. 1962. *The guns of August.* New York: Dell.

Turner, F. 1994. Values and strange attractors. Paper presented at the conference Evolving Complexity: Challenges to Society, Economy and Individuals, Dallas, Texas.

Turner, J. C., P. J. Oakes, S. A. Haslam, and C. McGarty. 1994. Self and collective: Cognition and social context. *Personality and Social Psychology Bulletin* 20:454-463.

Turner, J. H. 1986. *The structure of sociological theory.* Chicago: Dorsey.

———. 1991a. Simmel and Weber on money, exchange and structural differentiation. *Simmel Newsletter* 1:80-89.

———. 1991b. *The structure of sociological theory.* Belmont, CA: Wadsworth.

U.S. Department of Health and Human Services, Public Health Service. 1990. *Healthy people 2000.* PHS Publication No. 91-50213. Washington, DC: Government Printing Office.

Udry, J. R. 1995. Sociology and biology: What biology do sociologists need to know? *Social Forces* 73:1267-1278.

van der Kolk, B. 1987. *Psychological trauma.* Washington, DC: American Psychiatric Press.

van Heijenoort, J., ed. 1967. *From Frege to Gödel: A source book in mathematical logic, 1879-1931.* Cambridge, MA: Harvard University Press.

Varela, F. 1978. *Principles of biological autonomy.* New York: North-Holland.

von Clausewitz, C. [1832] 1968. *On war.* English translation, edited by A. Rapoport. New York: Penguin.

von Neumann, J., and O. Morgenstern. 1947. *The theory of games and economic behavior.* Princeton, NJ: Princeton University Press.

Wagner, J. W. L. 1991. *Freundschaften und Freundschaftsverständnis bei drei- bis zwölfjährigen Kindern* (Friendship and friendship understanding of children aged 3 to 12 years). Berlin: Springer.

Wagner, J. W. L., and L.-M. Alisch. 1994. Verlaufsprozesse bei Kinderfreundschaften (The processes of children's friendships). *Antrag an die Deutsche Forschungsgemeinschaft auf Gewährung einer Sachbeihilfe* 15(11).

Waldrop, M. M. 1992. *Complexity: The emerging science at the edge of order and chaos.* New York: Simon & Schuster.

Wallerstein, I. 1992. The challenge of maturity: Whither social science? *Fernand Braudel Center Review* 15(1): 1-7.

Walsh, E. J. 1981. Resource mobilization and citizen protest in communities around Three Mile Island. *Social Problems* 29:1-21.

Walters, K. J. 1978. The reconstruction of Darwin after Cyclone Tracy. *Disasters* 2(1): 59-68.

Weber, B. H., D. L. Depew, and James D. Smith, eds. 1988. *Entropy, information and evolution.* Cambridge: MIT Press.

Weber, M. 1968. *Economy and society,* edited by G. Roth and C. Wittich. New York: Bedminster.

Weintraub, E. R., ed. 1992. *Toward a history of game theory.* Durham, NC: Duke University Press.

Weisbuch, G. 1991. *Complex systems dynamics, lecture notes.* Vol. 2 of *Proceedings, Santa Fe Institute Studies in the Sciences of Complexity.* Reading, MA: Addison-Wesley.

West, B., and W. Deering. 1995. *The lure of modern science.* River Edge, NJ: World Scientific.

West, B. J. 1985. *An essay on the importance of being nonlinear.* Berlin: Springer.

West, C., and S. Fenstermaker. 1995. Doing difference. *Gender & Society* 9:8-37.

West, C., and D. H. Zimmerman. 1987. Doing gender. *Gender & Society* 1:125-151.

Wheatley, M. J. 1992. *Leadership and the new science: Learning about organizations from an orderly universe.* San Francisco: Berrett-Koehler.

Wheeler, J. A. 1980. Beyond the black hole. In *Some strangeness in the proportion: A centennial symposium to celebrate the achievements of Albert Einstein,* 341-375. Reading, MA: Addison-Wesley.

Willems, J. C. 1989. Some thoughts on modeling. In *Newton to Aristotle: Toward a theory of models for living systems,* edited by J. Casti and A. Karlquist, 91-119. Boston: Birkhäuser.

Wilson, E. O. 1975. *Sociobiology: The new synthesis.* Cambridge, MA: Harvard University Press.

Wimsatt, W. C. Forthcoming. Emergence as non-aggregativity. *Natural contradictions: Perspectives on ecology and change. Festschrift for Richard Levins,* edited by P. J. Taylor and Jrlo Haila. Chicago: University of Chicago.

Wise, R. A., and P. Rompre. 1989. Brain dopamine and reward. *Annual Review of Psychology* 40:191-225.

Wolf, A. 1986. Quantifying chaos with Lyapunov exponent. In *Chaos,* edited by A. V. Holden, 273-290. Princeton, NJ: Princeton University Press.

Wolfram, S. 1994. *Cellular automata and complexity.* Reading, MA: Addison-Wesley.

Woodbury, M. A., and K. G. Manton. 1982. A new procedure for the analysis of medical classification. *Methods of Information in Medicine* 21:210-220.

Wright, J., P. Rossi, S. Wright, and E. Weber-Burdin. 1979. *After the cleanup: Long-range effects of natural disasters.* Beverly Hills, CA: Sage.

Wu, F. 1981. Ising model. In *Encyclopedia of physics,* edited by R. G. Lerner and G. L. Trigg, 455-456. Reading, MA: Addison-Wesley.

Young, T. R. 1991. Chaos theory and symbolic interaction theory: Poetics for the postmodern sociologist. *Symbolic Interaction* 14(3): 321-334.

Youngblade, L. M., and J. Belsky. 1992. Parent-child antecedents of 5-year-olds' close friendships: A longitudinal analysis. *Developmental Psychology* 28:700-713.

Youniss, J. 1980. *Parents and peers in social development.* Chicago: University of Chicago Press.

Zadeh, L. 1975. The concept of a linguistic variable and its application to linguistic reasoning. *Information Sciences* 8:199-249, 301-357, 9:43-80.

Zajonc, R. B. 1980. Feeling and thinking. *American Psychologist* 35:361-369.

Zeeman, E. C. 1977. *Selected papers: 1972-77.* Reading, MA: Addison-Wesley.

———. 1979. A geometrical model of ideologies. In *Transformations: Mathematical approaches to culture change,* edited by R. Colin and K. L. Cooke, 463-480. New York: Academic Press.

Zeeman, E. C., C. S. Hall, P. J. Harrison, G. H. Marriage, and P. H. Shapland. 1976. A model for institutional disturbances. *British Journal of Mathematical and Statistical Psychology* 29:66-80.

Zeiher, H. J., and H. Zeiher. 1994. *Orte und Zeiten der Kinder* (Children's space and time). Weinheim: Juventa.

Zukier, H. 1989. Introduction. In *Extending psychological frontiers: Selected works of Leon Festinger,* edited by S. Schachter and M. S. Gazzaniga, xi-xxiv. New York: Russell Sage.

Name Index

Subject Index

ABCDE-model, 166, 167, 172, 173, 174, 178-179
Accumulation, paradox of, 43, 44
Action:
    collective, following disasters, 215-228
    conditions of, at local levels, 23
    money and, 87-88
    rewarded, 92
    success of, 87-88
    teleological, 87-88
Actors, affiliative tendencies, 210
Adaptation:
    complex, 24-25, 31-32
    complex, self-organized, 22-29
    emergence through, 22-29, 55-57
    organizational constraint-based, 229-242
    self-organized, 24-25
    social systems, 75
Adolescent childbearing, in Texas, 243-268
Advertising, fuzzy logic and, 49
Aggregation, 50, 52, 56, 59
    adolescent childbearing in Texas, 248-252
    changes in domestic division of labor, 183-184, 185, 186, 187, 192
    nations, 111
    neighborhood, 60
    positive feedback reinforcing, 25
    technology and, 27
Aggregation levels, society studies in, 132
AIDS, forecasting spread of, 70

Algorithmic complexity, 66, 153-159
Alpha point, 96
Amplifying effects, of positive feedback, 66
Analytic-synthetic model, 41
Anthropic theory, sociological application of, 91-101
Anti-antireductionism, 57
Anxiety:
    attachment and interaction fueled by, 197, 198, 199-200, 201, 210-211
    scavenged by interaction, 61
Aperiodic behavior, 128, 131
Archaeological approach, Foucault's, 5
Archaeology, discursive rules, 5-6, 10
Archetypal attractor structures, 158-159
Arms races, 118-121
Arousal-modulation, attachment behaviors and, 57-58, 197-214
Artificial life, 35
Asymmetrical dependencies, 26-27
Asymptotic behavior, 127
Attachment behavior, biologically innate, 57-59, 61, 197-214
Attraction, basins of, 22
Attractors:
    adolescent childbearing in Texas, 247, 250
    arousal-modulation, 207-208
    phase-specific, 178
    reconstruction, 138, 147
Attractor structures, archetypal, 158-159

About the Contributors

Lutz-Michael Alisch studied educational sciences, psychology, sociology, and philosophy in Braunschweig, Germany. Now a professor of the philosophy of human sciences and research methods in educational sciences at the Technical University in Dresden, he is especially interested in nonlinear dynamics, currently researching children's friendships.

Shahram Azizighanbari, Technical University in Dresden, is a doctor of medicine—having studied medicine in Teheran, Iran. He also studied computer science in Hildesheim, Germany, where he performed special work in nonlinear optics. He now works in Dresden as a computer scientist.

Kurt W. Back is James B. Duke Professor Emeritus at Duke University. He obtained his Ph.D. in group psychology at MIT and has worked on the history and theory of social psychology and sociology and the application of these sciences to sociophysiology, population control, housing, the life course, and social movements. Among his books are *Beyond Words: The Story of Sensitivity Training and the Encounter Movement*, and *Family Planning and Population Control: The Challenge of a Successful Movement*.

David Bahr is a research associate at the Cooperative Institute for Research in Environmental Sciences, at the University of Colorado. His research interests include glacier/climate interactions and collective behavior in both sociology and the Earth sciences. He has been a guest of the Sante Fe Institute, and he recently completed a Visiting Fellowship in complex systems research at the University of Colorado where he has been an active and founding member of the Colorado Center for Chaos and Complexity. His doctoral dissertation in geophysics at the University of Colorado focused on chaotic growth of calculation errors in glacier dynamics, and his undergraduate thesis in mathematics at Harvard University studied the cyclic behavior of finite cellular automata.

William Sims Bainbridge directs the Sociology Program of the National Science Foundation and serves on a number of NSF's committees concerned with advanced computing. He is the author of 13 books and more than 100 articles, reviews, and software packages. He has written extensively on the sociology of religion, general theory, and the space program. His latest books are *The Sociology of Religious Movements* and *Religion, Deviance and Social Control*.

Martin Bargfeldt, University Koblenz-Landau in Landau, Germany, studied computer science in Hildesheim and has done special work in computer science applied to ecology. He now works as a computer scientist performing research into children's friendships and also in the field of linguistics.

R. J. (Dick) Bird graduated with a degree in mathematics from the University of Durham and first worked as Assistant Lecturer in Maths and Computing at the University of Sunderland. He completed two postgraduate degrees in psychology, a master's and a doctorate, and is the author of two books and several papers on subjects including psychology, anthropology, sociology, mathematics, and biology.

Kathleen M. Carley *(contributor and peer review panel member)* is Associate Professor of Sociology and Organizations in the Department of Social and Decision Sciences at Carnegie Mellon University. She received her Ph.D. in sociology at Harvard University. She has developed methodological techniques for analyzing mental models and changes in social networks over time. Her research is in the areas of computational organization theory, social and organizational adaptation and evolution, statistical models for network analysis, computational text analysis, and the effect of telecommunication technologies on communication and information diffusion.

Mona Cherri is currently Associate Professor in the Department of Mathematics and Computer Science at Texas Woman's University, Denton, Texas. She earned her B.S. degree in mathematics from Lebanese University, Lebanon and her M.S. and Ph.D. degrees in mathematics from Oklahoma State University. She holds a second Ph.D. in computer science from the University of North Texas. Her research interests include linear and nonlinear modeling, data compression, and automatic speech recognition. She is a member of the American Mathematical Society and was recently nominated for membership in *Who's Who Among America's Teachers*.

Kevin Dooley *(contributor and peer review panel member)* is Associate Professor of Mechanical Engineering at the University of Minnesota, Twin Cities, and is currently Director of the university's Industrial Engineering Program. He has research interests in quality management, quality engineering, organizational behavior, and complex systems and has published in a number of engineering and management journals. He is currently on the editorial boards of the *Journal of Operations Management* and the Society for Nonlinear Dynamics, Psychology, and Life Science. He is a board member of the Chaos Network and formerly of the Deming Management Forum. He is helping to implement quality improvement at the University of Minnesota. His Ph.D. in mechanical engineering is from the University of Illinois at Urbana-Champaign.

Euel Elliott is Associate Professor of Government, Politics and Political Economy at the University of Texas at Dallas and Director of the Master of Public Affairs Program. His research interests include the application of nonlinear dynamics to political and social phenomena, public opinion, and public policy. He has published in numerous journals and is the coauthor with Douglas Kiel of *Chaos Theory in the Social Sciences*. He is now beginning work on a project that explores the relationship between technological innovation and political change.

Raymond A. Eve *(contributor and coeditor)* is Professor of Sociology at the University of Texas at Arlington. He has published in the area of sociology of science (with special attention to conflicts between science, religion, and postmodernism) and in the areas of socialization and delinquency, child development, geographic literacy, and sociology of education. He is the author of *The Creationist Movement in Modern America* and coeditor of *Cult Archaeology and Creationism*. He has authored a multimedia CD-ROM version of *Introduction to Sociology* for Harcourt Brace Publishers (with parts that present chaos/complexity ideas). He received his Ph.D. from the University of North Carolina at Chapel Hill.

Paul Fisher is currently Professor at the University of North Texas, Computer Science Department, Denton, Texas. He received his Ph.D. in computer science from Arizona State University. He also serves as Chief Scientist at Computer and Information Science, Inc., Denton, Texas. Previously, he served on the faculty at Kansas State University, Manhattan and as adjunct faculty at North Carolina State University, Raleigh. His present research interests include pattern recognition systems, compression, neural computing, and multimedia systems. He has written over 100 proposals, resulting in numerous funded projects, and is an active consultant, working with entities such as General Electric, the U.S. Army Engineering Topographic Laboratory, EDS, and the U.S. Department of Justice.

Ben Goertzel obtained his Ph.D. in mathematics from Temple University. He has held faculty positions in the Mathematics Department of the University of Nevada, Las Vegas, and the Computer Science Department of Waikato University in Hamilton, New Zealand. Currently, he is a Research and Teaching Fellow in the Psychology Department at the University of Western Australia, Perth. He has published numerous articles in mathematics, computing, philosophy, psychology, and related disciplines and has authored four books developing an original complex-systems-based model of the mind (*The Structure of Intelligence*, *The Evolving Mind*, *Chaotic Logic*, and *From Complexity to Creativity*). He is coauthor of a recent biography, *Linus Pauling: A Life in Science and Politics*, and chief editor of the electronic journal *Dynamical Psychology*.

Patti Hamilton is currently Professor and Director of Research at Texas Woman's University, College of Nursing, Denton, Texas. She earned her B.S., M.S., and Ph.D. degrees in nursing from Texas Woman's University. Previously, she was Assistant Professor at the University of Texas at Arlington, School of Nursing, and a Public Health Nurse for the county of Dallas and the city of Fort Worth. She has been nominated for membership in *Who's Who in American Nursing* and is currently Principal Investigator for an NINR AREA grant, examining patterns in teen birth data from 1964 to 1990. She has numerous publications and presentations both within and outside of nursing and was an Invited Convener of sessions on chaos theory applied to social science research at the Fourth Annual International ISA Conference on Social Science Methodology, UK.

Sara Horsfall (*contributor and coeditor*) worked as an international correspondent for a number of years before returning to the academic world to get her Ph.D. in sociology at Texas A&M University (1996). Her interests are in social psychology, sociology of religion and knowledge, and sociology of the family. Her dissertation, "Identifying the Spiritual Experience," broke new ground, substantively in terms of understanding the subject matter, as well as in developing new methodology. She organized sessions on non-linear sociology for the Southwest Sociological Association (1995, 1996) and co-organized a similar session for ASA (1996), all while still a graduate student. Research prospects include a proposal under review with Fetzer Institute on the effect of individual levels of responsibility on rehabilitation.

L. Douglas Kiel is Associate Professor of Public Administration and Political Economy in the School of Social Sciences, University of Texas at Dallas. In his work, he has applied nonlinear dynamics to subjects as diverse as management, public policy studies, and general social science. He is the author of *Managing Chaos and Complexity in Government: A New Paradigm for Managing Change, Innovation, and Organizational Renewal.* He is the coeditor, with Euel Elliott, of *Chaos Theory in the Social Sciences: Foundations and Applications.*

Mary E. Lee *(contributor and coeditor)* holds a doctoral degree in sociology from Texas A&M University. She is currently Fund Administrator with the State of Texas Office of State-Federal Relations and writes and conducts social research as an independent scholar. She previously held the position of Associate Research Sociologist with Texas A&M University System's Texas Engineering Experiment Station. She has interests in social theory and the interdisciplinary area of science and technology studies. Her previous work in complexity and self-organization includes "The Evolution of Technology: A Socioecological Model of Self-Organization," published in *Chaos Theory and Evolutionary Economics: New Directions in Technology Studies* (Loet Leydesdorff and Peter van den Besselaar, eds.).

Elizabeth Maret is Associate Professor of Sociology at Texas A&M University. Her work focuses on social stratification, women and work, and gender. She is author of two books, *Women's Career Patterns* and *Women of the Texas Range,* and numerous articles published in journals such as *ASR, AJS,* and *SMR.* She was Director for the Women in Development Projects Office at Texas A&M from 1984 to 1986, President of the Southwest Sociological Association in 1984, and associate editor of *Sociological Inquiry* from 1986 to 1993. She is a member of the New York Academy of Sciences, Phi Delta Gamma, and Phi Gamma Phi. She is listed in the *Who's Who of American Women, Who's Who in the South and Southwest,* and *American Men and Women of Science.* Her Ph.D. is from the University of Texas at Austin.

Kevin Mihata is a Ph.D. student in sociology at the University of Washington. His current research interests include social theory and methodology, social psychology, and the sociology of science.

Eve Passerini is a Ph.D. student in sociology at the University of Colorado, Boulder. Her research interests include environmental sociology, collective action, disaster research, and non-linear dynamics.

Bob Price is a Ph.D. student in sociology at the University of Texas at Austin. His primary research interests are the nature of knowledge and the long-term prospects for democracy. He is currently exploring the effects of specialization and technology on civic engagement.

Alvin M. Saperstein is Professor of Physics and a Fellow of the Center for Peace and Conflict Studies at Wayne State University. He has published many articles in physics and in physics pedogogy and also has many publications in the area of mathematical modeling of international relations and conflict. He has been a Fellow of several policy organizations, physics institutes, and universities in this country and in Europe. He has been elected to fellowship in the American Association for the Advancement of Science and the American Physics Society (APS), serving as a member of the Executive Committee and Chair of the APS Forum on Physics and Society and editor for their quarterly journal *Physics and Society.*

Thomas S. Smith is Professor of Sociology at the University of Rochester. His present research makes use of computer simulation to explore the dynamics of social interaction. Based on new understandings of the neurophysiology of attachment, this work extends and deepens the approach to general theory in sociology developed in his book *Strong Interaction.*

Helmut Michael Staubmann holds an M.A. and a Ph.D. in sociology from the University of Vienna and has been a postgraduate researcher at the Institute for Advanced Studies, Vienna. He is currently Associate Professor in the Department of Sociology at the University of Innsbruck and Visiting Scholar at the University of Pennsylvania, Philadelphia, focusing on sociological theory and the sociology of culture. He has been a Visiting Scholar at the University of California, Los Angeles, and the University of Maryland at College Park, and has been awarded an Erwin Schrödinger grant from the Austrian Science Foundation and an APART (Austrian Program for Advanced Research and Technology) grant from the Austrian Academy of Science.

Gregory T. Stevens is a second-year graduate student in the Cognition and Perception Program, Department of Psychology, at the University of Michigan. He is currently further exploring the theory developed in his forthcoming collaborative book *Hyperstructures* (with Thomas S. Smith), using computational techniques to model the dynamics of attachment behavior.

William F. Stroup, II is a Ph.D. candidate in sociology at Purdue University and an Army National Guard Captain. His interest are chaos methodology, the use of metaphor in theory, and deconstructionism as an explanatory tool. He believes that sociology suffers from an unhealthy bias toward structure, linearity, and order. He presented papers on nonlinear dynamics at the Midwestern States Anthropological Society and the Southwestern Sociological Association. A paper with Glenna Simons, Purdue University, titled "Law and Social Change: Some Implications of Chaos Theory in Understanding the Role of the American Legal System," is forthcoming in *Chaos, Criminology, and Social Justice*, edited by Dragon Milovanovic. He holds a B.S. in political science, an M.S. in sociology, and a M.P.A. from Indiana State University in Terre Haute.

Frederick Turner *(contributor and editorial adviser)*, Founders Professor of Arts and Humanities at the University of Texas at Dallas, is a poet, an interdisciplinary scholar, an aesthetician, an essayist, and a translator. Born in England to anthropologist Victor W. and Edith L.B. Turner, he grew up in Central Africa, and read English language and literature at Oxford University. His dissertation, "Shakespeare and the Nature of Time," was published by Clarendon Press. He taught at the University of California, Santa Barbara, and at Kenyon College and was editor of the *Kenyon Review*. A winner of the Levinson Poetry Prize and the Milan Fust Prize, Hungary's highest literary honor, he is the author of 17 books, including *Natural Classicism: Essays on Literature and Science* and *The Culture of Hope*.

Bruce West *(contributor and peer review panel member)* received his Ph.D. in physics from the University of Rochester. He has worked in industry and was a founding member of the not-for-profit La Jolla Institute, serving as Associate Director and Director of a division that emphasized nonlinear dynamics. He has collaborated with Jonas Salk of the Salk Institute and with scientists at the University of California, San Diego, and the UCSD Medical School on the application of nonlinear dynamics. Previously, he was Professor of Physics and Chair of the department at the University of North Texas. He is currently Director of the UNT Center for Nonlinear Science. He has over 240 publications and is an editor of various scientific journals as well as a book series, Studies of Nonlinear Phenomena in the Life Sciences. He has received the Decker Scholar Award and the UNT President's Award, and he is a Fellow of the American Physical Society.